BETWEEN VENICE AND ISTANBUL

Hesperia Supplements

The *Hesperia* Supplement series (ISSN 1064-1173) presents book-length studies in the fields of Greek archaeology, art, language, and history. Founded in 1937, the series was originally designed to accommodate extended essays too long for inclusion in the journal *Hesperia*. Since that date the Supplements have established a strong identity of their own, featuring single author monographs, excavation reports, and edited collections on topics of interest to researchers in classics, archaeology, art history, and Hellenic studies.

Hesperia Supplements are electronically archived in JSTOR (www.jstor.org), where all but the most recent titles may be found. For order information and a complete list of titles, see the ASCSA website (www.ascsa.edu.gr).

Hesperia Supplement 40

BETWEEN VENICE AND ISTANBUL: COLONIAL LANDSCAPES IN EARLY MODERN GREECE

EDITED BY
SIRIOL DAVIES AND JACK L. DAVIS

The American School of Classical Studies at Athens
2007

Cover illustration: Map of Kythera (Cerigo). T. Porcacchi, *L'isole piu famose del mondo . . . intagliate da Girolamo Porro . . .* (Venice 1572), p. 106

Library of Congress Cataloging-in-Publication Data

Between Venice and Istanbul : colonial landscapes in early modern Greece / edited by Siriol Davies and Jack L. Davis.

p. cm. — (Hesperia supplement ; 40)

Includes bibliographical references and index.

ISBN 978-0-87661-540-9 (alk. paper)

1. Greece—History—1453–1821. 2. Greece—Antiquities. 3. Landscape archaeology—Greece. 4. Excavations (Archaeology)—Greece. I. Davies, Siriol. II. Davis, Jack L. III. Title: Colonial landscapes in early modern Greece.

DF801.B48 2007

949.5′05—dc22 2007019714

CONTENTS

ILLUSTRATIONS

TABLES

INTRODUCTION

by Jack L. Davis and Siriol Davies

Most of the chapters in this volume were composed in preliminary form for the April 2003 workshop "Between Venice and Istanbul: Colonial Landscapes in Early Modern Greece ca. 1500–1800 A.D.," sponsored by the Department of Classics of the University of Cincinnati.[1] The publication of these papers in a supplement to *Hesperia* now seems particularly appropriate, inasmuch as the American School of Classical Studies has been a leader in the study of medieval and early modern Greece. Notable have been its sponsorship of the Gennadius Library and its monograph series.[2] Also deserving mention are the many studies of later Greek monuments and artifacts that have been conducted by its members, in particular, examinations of finds from excavations at Corinth and in the Athenian Agora.[3] The many references to this work by contributors to this volume attest its significance.

Nonetheless, the archaeology of the so-called post-Byzantine era in Greece remains a poor stepchild of classical archaeology, particularly with regard to the period during which most of the area of the current nation-state of Greece was incorporated within the Ottoman empire. To some extent, the rarity of research programs explicitly designed to investigate the material culture of these times reflects a general scholarly neglect of this subject.[4]

1. The term "colonial" used in the title of this volume is slippery and can be defined in a variety of ways, none of which seem entirely satisfactory, but usually include elements of settlement, economic exploitation, and cultural domination. See discussions in, e.g., van Dommelen 1998, pp. 16, 121–129, 141–142; Cohn 1996; McKee 2000, pp. 1–7 (on ethnicity as a tool of domination on Venetian Crete). For an argument that Venetian Greece was not "colonial," see Finley 1976, pp. 176–177.

Terms that might be unfamiliar to the reader are glossed at first use. Ottoman Turkish is transliterated according to the general practice employed in Zarinebaf, Bennet, and Davis 2005, p. xxii.

2. E.g., Paton 1940; Andrews 1953, 2006; Eliot 1992.

3. E.g., *Corinth* III.1; *Corinth* III.3; *Corinth* XI; *Agora* IX; *Agora* XX; Sanders 1987; MacKay 2003; Williams 2003.

4. A review of the state of historical archaeology in areas once embraced by the Ottoman empire has appeared recently, however; see Yenişehirlioğlou 2005.

LATER GREEK STUDIES AND ARCHAEOLOGY

In their introduction to the only volume of collected essays from a symposium on Ottoman archaeology yet to be published, the editors, Uzi Baram and Lynda Carroll, noted:

> Throughout the 1990s, mostly implicitly and without any sustaining scholarly organization, archaeologists began to face the challenge of an archaeology of the Ottoman Empire, and a wealth of new archaeological materials recovered from excavations were retained for analysis. It became clear to us that the archaeological literature on the Ottoman period was growing, as an increasing number of scholars from a variety of different disciplines, such as history, art history, classics, and geography, expanded their examination of the Ottoman period in terms of its material culture.[5]

Essays in that volume range widely in their focus. Kuniholm, for example, emphasizes the enormous potential in employing evidence from dendrochronological dating in conjunction with Ottoman records to reconstruct complete histories of construction and repair for specific Ottoman buildings (e.g., the Octagonal Tower in Thessaloniki). In addition, he presents evidence from his own studies for dating Ottoman monuments on Acrocorinth, at Didymoteichon, in Thessaloniki, and in Trikala.[6]

Other contributors consider the social role that various types of artifacts played in Ottoman society. Baram, for example, suggests that the study of tobacco pipes can "shed light on the active histories of peoples who did not enter the documentary record."[7] Carroll considers the potential that the examination of archaeologically observable distribution patterns in ceramics has for shedding light on the consumption of various styles and varieties of pottery by different socioeconomic groups within the Ottoman empire.[8]

This otherwise praiseworthy book neglects research that addresses the interface between text and material culture, however. Only one chapter, that by Ziadeh-Seely, observes that a dialectic can exist between written and nonwritten sources, and that more is to be gained from examining areas of conflict and disagreement than by trying to use one category of documentation to confirm the other. In this regard, she notes that evidence from excavations at the site of Tiʿinnik in Palestine appears to contradict the picture of prosperity in the 16th century that has been drawn on the basis of information recorded in Ottoman *defters* (tax registers).[9]

Similarly, within the field of Greek archaeology itself, there have as yet been few attempts to combine textual and artifactual evidence to produce a genuinely integrated archaeology for the centuries following the fall of Constantinople in 1453. The use of Ottoman documents for writing the history of modern Greece is still uncommon, and when they have been mined for the study of material culture, the purpose has more often been art historical than archaeological. Such efforts have been spearheaded by Machiel Kiel, whose many studies have clarified the architectural histories of individual monuments in Greece and elsewhere in the Balkans (although he also has devoted much attention to studying settlement patterns and population trends, a point to which we return later).[10]

5. Baram and Carroll 2000, p. ix.
6. Kuniholm 2000, p. 113.
7. Baram 2000, p. 155.
8. Carroll 2000.
9. Ziadeh-Seely 2000. For the conversion of Islamic dates to Christian dates in this volume, see below, p. 35, n. 3.
10. E.g., Kiel 1970, 1971, 1981, 1983.

Kiel's study of the date of construction of the most famous building in Thessaloniki, the White Tower, or Lefkos Pyrgos, is characteristic of this genre.[11] Various scholars had previously assigned this event to a time anywhere from the early 13th century, under the Latin Empire of Thessaloniki, to the first half of the 15th century, when the city was under Venetian occupation. In the 17th century, however, Evliya Çelebi described the tower as an Ottoman work of the time of Süleyman the Magnificent, basing his conclusion on a dedicatory inscription that once could be read over the entrance to the tower. Evliya's conclusion was verified by Kiel's transcription and reading of the dedicatory inscription from a photograph preserved in the archives of the Deutsches Archäologisches Institut in Athens. He concludes that the Lefkos Pyrgos is "a remarkable piece of Ottoman military architecture of the first half of the 16th century."[12] In a similar vein, Kiel has more recently recovered documents pertaining to the planning and execution of the building of the fortress of New Navarino.[13] Significantly, these texts also clarify the political context in which it was deemed necessary to embark on this project in the wake of the Ottoman defeat at Lepanto in 1571.

At the same time, other research projects have attempted to document and date later medieval and early modern architectural remains in Greece, but largely without recourse to Ottoman documentary evidence or even to any detailed site-specific Western written accounts. Fred Cooper and Joseph Algaze's ambitious Morea Project, for example, had as its goal the examination of Frankish and Ottoman architectural styles in the western Peloponnese. The project mapped standing remains of buildings that were constructed prior to the introduction of reinforced concrete in a selection of villages and citadels in the western Peloponnese, principally in Elis and Arcadia, but also in northern Messenia. In some instances the ubiquitous fragments of tiles found in abandoned settlements were demonstrated to derive from specific types of roofing systems that appear to be temporally diagnostic.[14]

Although they too have not yet received the attention they deserve, manifestations of Venetian and Frankish material culture in Greece, in contrast to Ottoman, have been greatly favored by scholars. Such a prejudice is not unique to archaeology, but reflects the prejudices of Greek historians and of allied Western scholars who, for the most, part have fully embraced an ideology of Hellenism. Such a preference for things Venetian as opposed to Ottoman reflects, in Michael Herzfeld's words, "how well the nationalist ideology of the Greek state, embodied in a more or less continuous condition of hostility with Turkey and embedded in larger, neo-Classical claims to European status, has done its work . . . and the current rehabilitation of the [Venetian] indicates the force of a cultural economy that ranks the European stereotype over the Oriental."[15] In this context it is worth noting that three decades after the publication of Kiel's decisive study of the Lefkos Pyrgos in Thessaloniki, the internet site of the Ministry of Culture of Greece continues to refer to this tower as a construction of the 15th century, built to replace a Byzantine tower on the same spot.[16]

If archaeologists have neglected the study of later Greece, a similar attitude often has characterized the research programs of historians of

11. Kiel 1973.
12. Kiel 1973, p. 357.
13. Kiel 2005.
14. Cooper 2002.
15. Herzfeld 1991, p. 57.
16. "Hellenic Ministry of Culture: The White Tower," posted at http://odysseus.culture.gr/h/2/eh251.jsp?obj_id=859.

both the Venetian Republic and the Ottoman Empire. Between 1500 and 1800, most of present-day Greece was either a distant colony of Venice or an outlying province of the Ottoman empire. This fact consigned Greece to a marginal place in the history of both empires as scholars have focused on their mainland territories and have been more interested in the earlier years of their imperial expansion than the later centuries of their decline. Greek scholars, however, for more than a century have been mining Venetian archives for the history of Greece in the medieval and early modern periods. In the past 25 years there have appeared a number of significant studies of those parts of Greece that were still under Venetian control in the 16th and 17th centuries: for example, Crete, Corfu, Kythera, Cyprus, and the Peloponnese.[17] At the same time, scholars have begun to investigate more intensively the resources of Ottoman archives for Greek history.[18] They also have restudied documents in Greek archives, extracting new types of information from them.[19]

Interest in investigating the Venetian monuments of Greece is longstanding. In the first decades of the 20th century, for example, Giuseppe Gerola documented significant buildings on Crete, in the Aegean islands, and in the Morea.[20] Because many of the structures he photographed have since fallen victim to programs of urban renewal, the archive of images that he assembled constitutes an irreplaceable scholarly resource today.[21] His work has been supplemented by studies by Johannes Koder of the important Venetian possession of Negroponte (Euboia), by Kevin Andrews's analysis of plans of fortresses in the Peloponnese that were executed by engineers in the employ of Venice during its occupation of the Morea (1686–1715), and, above all, by Antoine Bon's monumental study of the physical remains of Frankish domination of the Peloponnese.[22]

The work of this older generation of scholars continues to serve as a solid foundation for contemporary scholarship. Maria Georgopoulou's monographic examination of Crete and Euboia offers case studies of built environments in colonial settings that expressed close cultural ties both to the Byzantine past and to the Venetian present.[23] Patrice Foutakis's research sheds light on the history of the fortress at Methoni.[24] Peter Lock and Guy Sanders, on the other hand, have published a varied collection of essays concerning Frankish Greece;[25] these include relatively traditional studies of medieval churches,[26] fortifications and fortified settlements,[27] grave monuments,[28] and pottery.[29]

17. E.g., Arbel 2000; Aristeidou 1990; Dokos and Panagopoulos 1993; Liata 1998, 2003; Maltezou 1997, 2002; Greene 2000; Nikiforou 1999; Maltezou and Papakosta 2006.

18. E.g., Alexander 1999; Balta 1989, 1992, 1997, 1999; Greene 2000; Kiel 1992, 1997; Kiel and Sauerwein 1994; Parveva 2003; Zarinebaf, Bennet, and Davis 2005. Regarding Ottoman documents preserved in Greek archives, see Balta 2003.

19. E.g., Kasdagli 1999; Koukkou 1989; Liata 1987.

20. Gerola 1916–1920, 1921–1922, 1923–1924, 1930–1931.

21. Curuni and Donati 1988.

22. Koder 1973; Andrews 1953; Bon 1969. The drawings published by Andrews had come into the possession of the Gennadius Library of the American School just prior to World War II. They are reprinted in color in Andrews 2006.

23. Georgopoulou 2001.

24. E.g., Foutakis 2005.

25. Lock and Sanders 1996.

26. Cooper 1996; Coulson 1996.

27. Gregory 1996; Hodgetts and Lock 1996; Lock 1996; Sanders 1996.

28. Ivison 1996.

29. MacKay 1996.

THE IMPACT OF REGIONAL STUDIES

In the volume edited by Lock and Sanders, two essays, taking a different perspective, explicitly consider the impact that regional archaeological investigations have had on the study of later Greece. John Bintliff's essay addresses the contribution that the Boiotia Project has made to our understanding of the nature of the countryside of central Greece under Frankish domination, and the one by Nancy Stedman looks at published accounts of early travelers to the area examined by the Boiotia Project as well as traditional village and domestic architectural forms.[30] Bintliff's analysis of archaeological data collected from intensive surface survey draws on information gleaned from Western historical sources and inferred from Ottoman documents pertinent to the period immediately preceding the Ottoman conquest of this area.[31]

The contributions by Bintliff and Stedman are exceptional in their regional focus, and they stand out from other essays in that volume in the same manner in which Allaire Brumfield's chapter in the volume edited by Baram and Carroll does. There Brumfield considers Ottoman and Venetian administrative documents and local Greek records pertaining to monastic holdings and disputes over them; she adds to these sources her own thorough ethnographic inventory of Ottoman-period architectural remains in a region in eastern Crete that had been the target of systematic archaeological survey.[32]

In fact, in the past decade in Greece and on Cyprus, modern history has become a subject of great interest to archaeologists who are involved in regional studies, as are Bintliff and Brumfield. It has arguably been the popularity of diachronic surface surveys that has led to a growing interest in the medieval and post-medieval countryside.[33] The use of travelers' reports as sources for the history of the rural landscape has been complemented by investigations into Venetian and Ottoman archival records.

In conjunction with the Boeotia Project, Kiel, for example, systematically gathered data in Istanbul and Ankara in order to define local and regional trends in population growth and decline, and to reconstruct the agricultural economy of the areas investigated by that project.[34] A special concern has been spatial variation in the locations of populations of various ethnicities (Albanian, Slavic, Greek, Turkish, and Jewish). Explicit comparisons between the results of survey and Ottoman documentary information note, among other things, the much greater chronological resolution currently possible from the written evidence.[35]

Other regional studies have followed the lead of the Boeotia Project. Gerstel and her colleagues, with assistance from Kiel, have attempted to

30. Bintliff 1996; Stedman 1996.

31. Bintliff 1996.

32. Brumfield 2000; Stallsmith (2004) treats the same topics in much greater detail.

33. The conference held in Corfu in 1998 titled "New Approaches to Medieval and Post-Medieval Greece" was specifically designed to examine interfaces between text and material culture at the regional level. Elsewhere in territories of the former Ottoman Empire, interest in designing research programs that draw on both archival documentation and archaeological evidence also has grown in recent years; see, e.g., Robinson 2002; Wilkinson 2004.

34. Kiel 1997, 2000.

35. Bintliff 1999; Sbonias 2000, pp. 223–225.

reconstruct Ottoman-period patterns of settlement and abandonment in a small region on the border of Attica and Boiotia. In this instance, evidence from excavation and an absence of reference in the earliest Ottoman sources to the significant village of Panakton suggest that it already had been abandoned by the time of the Ottoman conquest.[36]

In Arcadia, Björn Forsén has integrated information from surface survey with Ottoman data supplied at the village level by John Alexander and Machiel Kiel.[37] Finally, in Messenia, a partnership involving Siriol Davies and Jack L. Davis (the editors of this volume), John Bennet, and Fariba Zarinebaf, an Ottomanist, has used archaeological, topographical, and Venetian and Ottoman archival evidence to compose a social and economic geography for the area of Pylos in the late 17th and early 18th centuries.[38]

The difficulty shared by all these projects in closely dating local pottery of the modern period has encouraged more intensive efforts to understand local ceramic sequences.[39] The work of Joanita Vroom, one of the contributors to this volume, has significantly improved the ability of archaeologists involved in regional studies to date surface finds of the modern period. Vroom has shown that it is possible to relate a detailed study of the distribution of surface ceramics of various dates not only to cycles of population increase in a region, but also to the life-histories of sites in Boiotia.[40]

At the same time, her warnings should be heeded that in parts of Greece, such as Aitolia, few ceramics are likely to have been used until recently. Therefore, only a negligible ceramic trace of human presence may remain in the landscape, particularly on sites located at higher altitudes at a greater distance from the sea.[41] Nonetheless, Vroom's own Ph.D. dissertation is a successful attempt to consider Ottoman-period pottery from surface survey in the context of the particular locations where it was identified, and to relate such observations to documentary evidence extracted from Ottoman sources.[42]

Based on results of the Laconia Survey of the British School at Athens, Pamela Armstrong's research in the area of Sparta evinces a similarly impressive command of local ceramic sequences, although documents examined are principally those of Venice, composed during the period of its brief control of the Morea (1686–1715), and of the French Expédition scientifique de Morée, based on censuses and surveys conducted following the Greek Revolution of 1821–1829 and the establishment of independence from the Ottomans.[43]

Certain categories of portable and durable artifacts other than pottery—clay tobacco pipes, for example—also have been studied in some detail and have facilitated the dating of archaeological surface finds.[44]

Despite such encouraging results, it unfortunately remains a fact that, even though regional diachronic archaeological investigations have now been a feature of archaeology in Greece for nearly three decades, there is still woefully little communication between historians and those archaeologists engaged in such activities. There is little concern to integrate the evidence of text and material culture on a regional scale. This fact is all the more surprising when one considers the concerns that the two disciplines have in common.

36. Gerstel et al. 2003.

37. Forsén 2003.

38. Zarinebaf, Bennet, and Davis 2005.

39. Regarding the difficulties, see, e.g., Shelton 2003.

40. Similarly impressive results are now evinced by archaeological investigations of medieval and post-medieval remains in several of the Cycladic islands (Vionis 2005).

41. Vroom 1998.

42. Vroom 2003.

43. Armstrong 1996.

44. E.g., Robinson 1985.

HISTORICAL ARCHAEOLOGY AND THE EASTERN MEDITERRANEAN

Where does this relatively new field, the study of the archaeology of the Greek world in the 16th–18th centuries, fit in terms of theoretical developments in the archaeology of this period as conducted in other parts of the world? The term "historical archaeology" in its broadest definition is the study of the material remains of literate societies, which implies different starting dates in different places around the globe. In Europe, naturally, the classical world is included according to this definition, but in North America it has quite a different significance. There, literacy is deemed to commence with the arrival of Europeans, that is to say, post-1492, and the earlier history of the continent is considered "prehistoric." An acceptance of the late 15th century as a start date has put an emphasis on themes such as the impact of European colonialism on native peoples, the development of capitalism and, ultimately, "modernity." Orser settles on a rationale for historical archaeology as seeking "to understand the global nature of modern life."[45] Implicit in this approach, in which the discovery of the "New World" is seen as the beginning of the modern world, is the assumption of a clean break with the past, a lack of continuity with medieval Europe.[46] This appears to exclude, as a subject of inquiry, the archaeology of Europe from the 16th century onward, although Matthew Johnson has argued that an "archaeology of capitalism" must include study of the "Old World": "If we are serious about writing an archaeology of capitalism, the preconditions of its emergence must be addressed. In the first place we need to discuss core as well as periphery, 16th- and 17th-century Europe as well as its colonies."[47]

Although this is a welcome recommendation, it still leaves the emphasis on Western Europe. What of the southern and eastern Mediterranean, which developed in quite a different manner? Baram and Carroll, concerned with the Ottoman world, have dealt with this question by suggesting that "there are many paths toward an archaeology of the Ottoman empire." An examination of Western influence and the rise of capitalism may be valuable, but these factors counsel against placing the Ottomans in a passive position vis-à-vis the West and promote alternative approaches, such as examining the empire from the perspective of Middle Eastern studies or an archaeology of Islam.[48]

In this call for a pluralistic approach, Baram and Carroll are joined by others. Funari, Hall, and Jones remark that "the archaeology of post-1492 America is only one of many possible historical archaeologies, including classical and medieval archaeology, and that there is much to be gained from a reunification of these fields within the wider discipline of archaeology."[49] As Funari points out, an emphasis on the growth of capitalism is problematic, different societies having experienced its advent at different times. He argues instead for a world perspective that defines historical archaeology as the study of the "material culture of literate societies" with special attention given to the relationship between artifacts and documents.[50]

American historical archaeology, having evolved largely in anthropology departments, has not had a close link with history; therefore, the treatment of historical sources has generated considerable debate. Eager

45. Orser 1996, p. 23.

46. Funari, Hall, and Jones 1999, pp. 6–7.

47. Johnson 1999a, p. 224.

48. Baram and Carroll 2000, pp. 16–18.

49. Funari, Hall, and Jones 1999, pp. 1–17. Davis (1998, p. 297) writes of "the struggle to create a polyvocal archaeology," that is, one that incorporates a diversity of sources that offer perspectives from various segments of the populations of past societies.

50. Funari 1999, pp. 55–57.

that material evidence should not be seen as subservient to documents, historical archaeologists have claimed that the contribution of archaeology is to tell the story from the subaltern point of view, on the assumption that material remains are exempt from the elitist bias of documentary sources. This view implies that the two types of evidence, having been produced independently, can act as a check against each other. Such a view has been somewhat refined by Johnson, who argues that if material culture is treated as text (i.e., designed for communication), then the two classes of evidence (material and documentary), rather than being produced independently, could be generated by the same underlying processes, and thus material culture can also be an elitist creation. Neither does he regard documents as unproblematic, advocating an "archaeology of documents."[51] Clearly, the relationship between textual evidence and material remains is complex and subject to ongoing debate.

Another potential divide between the disciplines may be the particularist/generalist one. The historical archaeologist looking for underlying social processes may be dismissive of detailed local studies. As Robert Paynter, in a review of developments in the field, puts it, the dilemma of the historical archaeologist lies in "trying to understand local history with perspectives that tend to trivialize such an endeavor."[52]

One possible solution to the problem of linking the particularities of time and place with broader social processes may be, as suggested by Baram and Carroll for the Ottoman world, taking a geopolitical perspective and thinking in terms of an "archaeology of empire": "An archaeology of empire provides crucial information about the local histories and social developments of the empire, in what Sinopoli (1994:169) calls the material consequences of an empire. . . . We can examine social action on the local level as a part of the development of the empire, to be compared and contrasted with other regions. An archaeology of the Ottoman empire links local and imperial histories in dynamic relationships."[53]

Although neither the Venetian nor the Ottoman Empire fits the paradigm common to historical archaeology of the dominion of Western Europeans over non-Western peoples, taking an imperial view may facilitate comparison with the colonialism of the New World.

Historians too have called for an approach that views Greek history in this period as part of wider imperial histories. Historians of Crete, for example, have drawn our attention to the importance of the Venetian colonial model in the context of the history of European colonialism, and to the usefulness of comparative studies of the Venetian and Ottoman regimes.[54] The landscapes of Greece and Cyprus were "imperial" in a number of senses. Their political subjection to either Venice or Istanbul determines the fact that much of the documentation available was created by imperial administrators. It was designed to classify and order the property and persons of foreign subjects and weighted to describe those matters that most interested the rulers, namely, revenues and defense. The increasing sophistication of such endeavors is naturally connected to the development of the state and its needs for centralization and rationalization. The immense complexity of customary systems of land tenure, and the difficulty of reducing them to a system comprehensible to outsiders, has been well

51. Johnson 1999b, pp. 30–32. For a detailed examination of the "conjoint" use of documentary and archaeological evidence, see Wylie 1999.

52. Paynter 2000, p. 22. This article usefully surveys recent thinking in the field.

53. Baram and Carroll 2000, p. 12.

54. Greene 2000; McKee 2000.

documented in many areas and should make us wary of taking too literally the record of a state of affairs "frozen" in official data.[55]

Local economies and therefore landscapes were inevitably shaped by imperial policies on matters such as grain export, vine or olive cultivation, and immigration. The defensive requirements of empire determined much of the building that is still standing, and ideologies concerning urban space influenced the street plans of major towns. The particularities of time and place must be borne in mind, however; imperial policies of the 15th century were not the same as those of the 18th.

Another reason for taking an imperial view is the difficulty of categorizing this period of Greek history, for which there is no satisfactory term: "post-Byzantine," "post-medieval," "premodern"? The investigation of this period's social, economic, and material history lies uneasily among many disciplines (Byzantine studies, Ottoman studies, Venetian studies, Middle Eastern studies, and modern Greek studies, to name but a few). Readers will notice the employment of a variety of chronological designations in this volume, particularly by archaeologists, which reflects the lack of common terms of reference. "Early modern," when understood by historians of Western Europe to be bounded by the Renaissance at one end and the agricultural and industrial revolutions at the other, may seem inappropriate when applied to the eastern Mediterranean.[56] Instead, it is a period most easily defined by the struggle for dominion between the Venetian and Ottoman empires.

In the framework of such studies of empire, there are many questions of interest to both historians and archaeologists: What was the significance for the Orthodox community of the transition from Venetian to Ottoman rule in Cyprus, Crete, the Peloponnese, and the Cyclades? To what extent did each regime adapt to the preceding one? How is this transition reflected in architecture, urban plans, settlement patterns, forms of land tenure, and administrative, fiscal, and judicial structures? What effect did it have on intercultural contacts, definitions of community, economic development, and population movement?

Collaboration between historians and archaeologists may raise specific issues about the use of evidence. How were Venetian and Ottoman cadastral surveys used to exert control, and how useful are they now as sources for historical geography and the study of power relations? How much can archival material tell us about material culture of the period? Is it correct to say that archival sources are useful only for studying the history of the city, and that we must rely on archaeology to reveal the life of the countryside?

There is a natural fit between Ottoman and Venetian documentary records of population and economic resources that can be exploited to address such questions in instances where these empires succeeded each other chronologically and occupied the same territory. In the case of archaeological projects, information has been collected at the regional level because such studies were explicitly designed to investigate entire landscapes. It is equally obvious that archival documentation also holds promise of providing potentially complete regional statistics concerning patterns of settlement and land use that may be spatially continuous. Faroqhi, for example, has

55. On "state projects of legibility and simplification," see Scott 1998, pp. 1–52; on the British acquisition of knowledge in India, see Cohn 1996.

56. The term has been retained in the title of this volume in the interests of communicating with a wider audience that will immediately recognize the chronological period intended. The reader will note, however, that in several of the archaeological contributions to this volume, it is used in a very different way—namely, to refer to the 19th and early 20th centuries; see, e.g., Chap. 4.

discussed the regional nature of Ottoman sources, particularly the potential of the *tapu tahrir defters*.[57] These tax registers, regularly prepared in the 15th and 16th centuries as a basis for assignment of revenue to Ottoman administrators, officials, members of the military, or to the sultan and his family, offer the possibility of reconstructing regional settlement and land-use patterns over continuous landscapes. In areas of the Aegean that were conquered or reconquered later, detailed tax registers continued to be composed at the beginning of the 18th century.[58]

It is therefore unfortunate that detailed analysis of Ottoman tax registers has fallen out of favor among a younger generation of Ottomanists in the West. Faroqhi has commented:

> During the last few years it seems that *tahrirs* occupy a less central place on the agenda of Ottomanist historians. This may partly be due to the fact that today we understand the limitations of this source better than we did 30 years ago. But the main reason is that in the historiography of the 1990s, qualitative analysis happens to be in favor. Concomitantly "hard data" are no longer regarded as the sole desirable result of historical study. Ottomanists have tended to move away to sources in which the subjective intentions of the author are more obvious. An analysis of the mind and world view of the compilers of *tahrir* registers remains a desideratum.[59]

There is, we think, a serious risk of indiscriminately discarding good sources of information when the focus of scholarship tips too far in the direction of interpretation, and analysis of the texts of the registers is slighted. Ottoman studies might well profit from the application of methods of textual editing and criticism that have long been familiar tools of the classical philologist and literary critic. Systematic transcriptions and transliterations of Ottoman *defters* (those that reflect ambiguities in textual readings) would facilitate interdisciplinary cooperation.

The availability of such texts permits scholars who have a solid knowledge of historical geography and archaeological evidence to make a contribution to understanding the worldview of the Ottoman scribes.[60] Archaeology can enter into debates over the emptiness of the landscape at the time of the Ottoman conquest, so-called transition studies.[61] Anthropology may also be added to the mix. Faroqhi proposes combining village sociological studies with deeper historical investigations of the same places, but notes that modern "anthropologists are quite rightfully concerned with present-day problems, such as the social consequences of mechanized agriculture and the growing integration of villagers into the national or world market. Viewed from the historian's standpoint, the anthropologist works within a 'short' time horizon, often limited to the 1950s."[62] Fortunately, this generalization is not entirely accurate for Greece, where some cultural anthropologists have adopted a long-term historical perspective and have shown considerable interest in material culture.[63]

Faroqhi bemoans the lack of archaeological evidence concerning the rural population of the Ottoman empire. To be sure, this is a deficiency that archaeology has the potential to address. But regional archaeological data also would seem to provide a means by which the completeness of documentary data can be evaluated. At the same time, researchers can

57. Faroqhi 1999, esp. pp. 86–109.

58. E.g., Greene 2000; Parveva 2003; Zarinebaf, Bennet, and Davis 2005.

59. Faroqhi 1999, p. 95.

60. E.g., see Zarinebaf, Bennet, and Davis 2005, pp. 116–117, regarding scribal "routes."

61. Faroqhi 1999, p. 101.

62. Faroqhi 1999, p. 107.

63. E.g., Sutton 1990.

approach well-known problems in evaluating the appropriateness of the use of Ottoman *defter*s for population estimation by comparing their contents with similar Venetian records for the same areas. In this regard, special opportunities await in places—such as the Morea and Crete—that belonged successively to the Venetian and the Ottoman empires, but these as yet have been little exploited.[64]

Heath Lowry, the historian who coined the term "defterology," has discussed the limitations of Ottoman taxation registers at length.[65] He defines four schools of approach among Ottomanists, admittedly caricatures of much more complex traditions: (1) a "Hungarian School," which emphasizes the use of such registers for local history and includes transliterations and translations, but little interpretation; (2) a "Barkan-Braudelian School," which treats *defter*s as though they are genuine censuses and not taxation documents; (3) a "Turkish School," which stresses the analysis of a series of registers for the same region; and (4) a "French School," which puts a premium on a microscopic word-by-word examination of a single entry, or focuses on the meaning of a single term (e.g., "taxable crop").

Common to all of these approaches are spatial and temporal constraints that make it difficult to recognize inconsistencies in the registers that may "limit their value for many of the purposes [for] which scholars have attempted to use them."[66] In addition, they often exclude sources of income outside the *timar* (military fief) system that consisted of tax-free income from private property or religious endowments, or revenue intended to go directly to the central treasury.

In his own work, Lowry has tried to control for such difficulties by using Byzantine monastic documents, by examining complementary Ottoman documents (*icmal* [summary] and *vakıf* [pious foundation] registers), and by comparing earlier and later *tapu tahrir* registers. Data from regional studies projects would offer an alternative solution to such problems that would be of special importance in the greater part of the Ottoman empire where earlier Byzantine documentation is nonexistent, and in those places where Ottoman documentation is temporally discontinuous or lacking altogether in later centuries.

THE CINCINNATI WORKSHOP

It was the enormous potential for cooperation between historians and archaeologists that encouraged us to organize the workshop in Cincinnati in 2003. That meeting followed a profitable, but much more informal, gathering in Cincinnati the previous year.[67] We believed that the general lack of communication between the disciplines was largely the result of disciplinary compartmentalization rather than any intentional disregard for one another's work. Our particular goal was to assemble archaeologists and historians who, in the context of their own research, had been concerned with patterns of settlement and land use in regions. The University of Cincinnati was a suitable place for a workshop in light of Peter Topping's pioneering research conducted there in collaboration with the Minnesota Messenia Expedition and the enviable strength of its library's holdings in modern Greek studies.

64. See, however, Davies 2004.
65. Lowry 1992, pp. 3–18.
66. Lowry 1992, p. 6.
67. Participants included the editors of this volume and several contributors to it (namely, Bennet, Forsén, and Kiel).

We hoped that an awareness of one another's research would in itself stimulate discussion, and would encourage participants to think about how in the future they might draw on the fruits of studies in other disciplines to the benefit of their own research. It needed to be demonstrated that both history and archaeology have much to gain from collaboration, or we risked opening up yet another divide, such as has existed between classical archaeologists and philologists for so long. We believed it was important for both groups of scholars to recognize that the flow of benefits from cooperation is not in one direction.

The collection of papers published here addresses many of the issues discussed in the preceding section of this introduction by bringing to bear on them the differing perspectives of archaeologists, historians, and anthropologists. Archaeological data are drawn from the results of regional studies projects as well as excavations. Documentary evidence and historical texts in Italian, Greek, and Ottoman Turkish are considered. Scholars with expertise in Venetian and Ottoman studies are included. The result is a book that is, we hope, genuinely interdisciplinary and that assembles contributions by scholars who do not normally communicate easily with one another.

Our choice of geographical areas addressed in this volume (Map 1, and Fig. 1.1 below) needs comment. First, to take advantage of the complementary nature of Venetian and Ottoman sources, it was deemed valuable to focus on areas that had experienced dominion by both powers: the Peloponnese, Crete, Cyprus, the Cyclades, and Kythera. Second, we invited archaeologists who were known to be working on survey projects with a declared interest in the early modern period and keen to use documentary evidence (Bennet in Messenia and on Kythera, Gregory in the Corinthia and on Kythera, Bintliff in Boiotia, Given on Cyprus, Vroom in Boiotia and on Kythera, Stallsmith on Crete). Next we thought of historians and ethnographers specializing in Venetian, Ottoman, or Greek documents whose work demonstrates the value of these sources for illustrating issues pertaining to landholding, cultivation, and mobility patterns, important themes for the student of the history of the landscape and material culture (Kiel on the Sporades, the Cyclades, and Kythera; Kasdagli on the Cyclades; Malliaris and Forbes on the Peloponnese). Naturally, in geographical terms we have excluded large parts of the Greek mainland (Thessaly, Macedonia, Thrace) that did not undergo periods of Venetian dominion; this is not to say that there is not enormous potential for combining Ottoman sources with the results of survey in these areas. Nor have we included every Aegean region that experienced the dominion of both empires, such as Chios and Euboia, or those Ionian islands that knew only Venetian dominion. In any future attempt to evaluate the imprint on the landscape of one empire or the other, these areas would, of course, provide very interesting comparisons.

Chapter 1 offers a brief survey of the historical background to the period, for the benefit of any reader new to it. The chapters by the three historians (Kiel, Kasdagli, and Malliaris) discuss the potential of very different sources of documentation for reconstructing rural and agrarian histories of early modern Greece. It should be obvious, although the authors have not always chosen to emphasize this point explicitly, that the economic

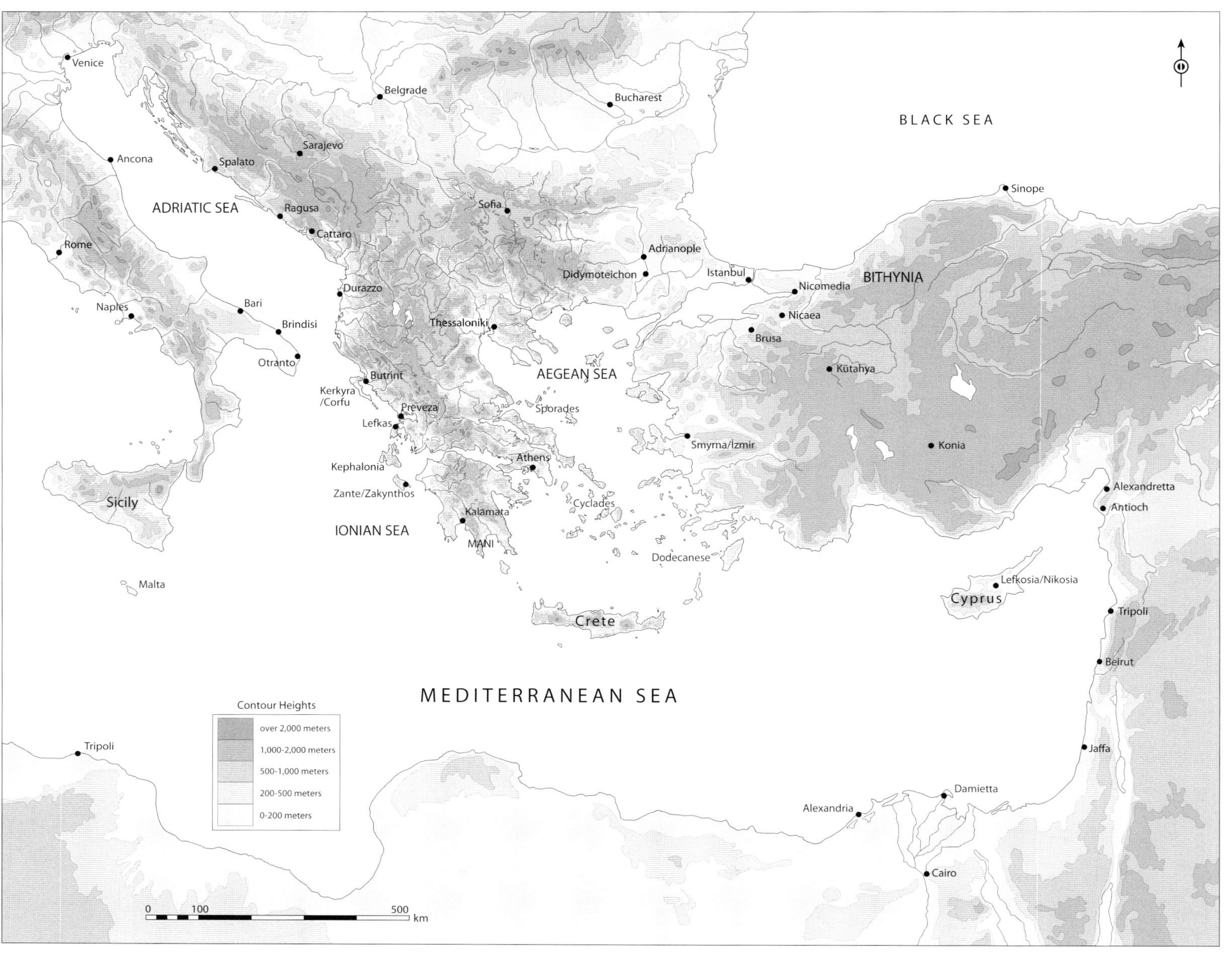

Map 1. The Venetian and Ottoman eastern Mediterranean. R. J. Robertson

patterns and social changes they describe had material consequences that are susceptible to investigation by archaeological methods. The remaining chapters in the volume were written by archaeologists who bring to bear on problems of great interest both archaeological and textual evidence. Like the earlier chapters in this collection, these are all concerned to a greater or lesser extent with the management of empires and the material consequences of the incorporation into them of the regions investigated.

Machiel Kiel, in Chapter 2, considers various Ottoman documents pertaining to the Sporades, the northern Cyclades, and Kythera that were misfiled geographically in the Ottoman archives in Istanbul and have previously been unavailable to scholars. The discovery of these documents has yielded considerable new information concerning the history of settlement and agriculture on these islands, data that complement, but at times contradict, information recorded in the accounts of Western travelers and in Venetian sources. Most significantly for archaeologists, these documents constitute a virtual invitation to integrate this information with the results of regional studies already completed or in progress in the Cyclades and on Kythera.[68]

In Chapter 3, Aglaia Kasdagli considers the potential of another significant source of documentary evidence, notarial documents from Latin and Ottoman Greece. In many parts of Greece, where no other local archival information survives, notarial documents can provide significant information regarding the social and economic organization and management of these areas while they were part of Frankish, Venetian, or Ottoman imperial systems, and their agrarian histories. Among other issues, Kasdagli is concerned with land-management systems that worked to the detriment of small farmers and that were dismantled after Greece achieved independence from the Ottoman Empire. Her conclusions deserve comparison with those of ethnohistorical and archaeological investigations that have already considered the material consequences of such a distribution of control over agricultural resources (we return to this issue later).

Chapter 4, by Joanita Vroom, may be read as complementary to the work of John Bintliff in Chapter 11: in large part, it is her research that has permitted a finer chronological resolution in the interpretation of the archaeological finds from the Boiotia Project. She observes that, after pioneering articles by Frederick Waagé and Allison Frantz in *Hesperia,* interest in Ottoman pottery languished in the period following World War II. Regional studies projects therefore had considerable difficulty in dating surface finds from the more recent Greek past. This chapter describes the results of Vroom's recent refinements in the analysis of Ottoman and contemporary Mediterranean ceramics as they apply to the reconstruction of rural patterns of settlement during the times of Ottoman and Venetian occupation.

In Chapter 5, Alexis Malliaris discusses how, after the conquest of the Peloponnese by the Venetian general Morosini that began in 1685, the Venetian government embarked on a long-term program of state-sponsored colonization of the Peloponnese. As a result of these efforts, many thousands of Greeks moved to the Morea from Ottoman and Venetian territories alike. This study examines the consequences of these migrations for the

68. See Chap. 10, where Bennet discusses the relevance of these newly discovered data for the history of Kythera, and the section, later in this Introduction, in which we consider these new data with reference to Kea.

social and economic history of Greece. The tight chronological resolution and close spatial focus of the data relevant to this significant event in the history of the Morea constitute a challenge to archaeologists to identify its consequences in the material cultural record.

In Chapter 6, Hamish Forbes draws on ethnographic and historical evidence, including local registers of births and deaths, that gives a strong impression of flux and fluidity among populations in premodern Greece. Some patterns are more apparent than real, based as they are on observations in documentary evidence about continuity and discontinuity in personal names that are presumed to be surnames. Forbes suggests that such names may not have been in use for longer than a generation, and therefore are unlikely to be true surnames. Changes in them can give a false impression of a constant movement of households in and out of communities. The tendency of a significant proportion of the population to have multiple residences can also contribute a spurious element of flux and mobility to the interpretation of past landscapes. Such conclusions have obvious implications for how archaeologists might interpret evidence for the size and continuity of settlements, as well as the extent of residence by farmers in dispersed farmhouses.

In Chapter 7, Michael Given notes that most evidence for occupation in the mountainous areas of Cyprus dates to the 12th century and later, to times when the island was controlled by Lusignans, Venetians, and Ottomans. He contrasts the picture of settlement that can be reconstructed from documentary evidence with the material cultural record. He argues that written and archaeological testimonies are indispensable complementary sources of evidence for the reconstruction of the history of rural settlement and land use, and for understanding the various strategies of control that successive imperial powers imposed on the population of the island.

In Chapter 8, Allaire Stallsmith considers Crete, another of the large islands of the eastern Mediterranean contested by Venice and Istanbul. She compares the strategies that the Venetian and Ottoman empires used in the administration of their possessions on the island of Crete. Although the origins of the two regimes and their administrative goals differed, she argues that these imperial powers employed remarkably similar systems to control their peasant populations (i.e., they adapted the status quo). This study focuses on the ways in which policies of Venice and Istanbul affected the crops grown and agricultural techniques favored by the primary cultivators of the island.

In Chapter 9, Timothy Gregory draws on archaeological, historical, and documentary information to address similar themes and to reconstruct pictures of agricultural exploitation in the Ottoman Corinthia and on the Venetian island of Kythera. He concludes that the systems of administration in the two regions differed considerably because the goals set by the Ottoman and Venetian empires varied. The Ottomans wished to capitalize on the rich produce of areas that could easily be manipulated as cash crops. The Venetians, on the other hand, were not primarily interested in the production of cash crops; they insisted on the production of wheat as a means to feed the fleet and to make the island self-sufficient and not dependent on Venetian support.

In Chapter 10, John Bennet outlines examples of how a combination of text, image, and archaeology has facilitated archaeological-historical research in the context of two regional studies projects in which he has been involved: the Pylos Regional Archaeological Project and the Kythera Island Project. Drawing on these examples, he suggests how the use by politically dominant forces of what might broadly be termed "geo-metrical"—that is, land-measuring—techniques may offer insights into the ways in which control over land was conceptualized and enabled by governing elites and indigenous populations.

In Chapter 11, research on the history and archaeology of the Ottoman period in central Greece is reviewed by John Bintliff in the light of archaeological fieldwork and archival studies. He considers the enormous potential for an Ottoman-period archaeology of Greece and defines critical research areas. These include water-management systems, khans and hostels, and vernacular architecture.

Chapter 12, by Björn Forsén, and Chapter 13, by Curtis Runnels and Priscilla Murray, serve as commentaries on the previous chapters.

A CASE STUDY OF THE ISLAND OF KEA

We conclude this Introduction with a case study growing out of the interdisciplinary gathering in Cincinnati. Kiel's presentation at the Cincinnati workshop of entirely new information concerning the economic and social history of the Cycladic island of Kea (published here as Chap. 2) was particularly welcome, since one of the editors of this volume (Davis) had, in 1983–1984, collaborated in organizing a team of archaeologists to explore the northwestern part of the island, an area that was effectively the hinterland both of the prehistoric site of Ayia Irini and of the classical city-state of Korisia.[69] The Ottoman and early modern periods were of particular interest to the project, inasmuch as the former constituted "an extreme example of residential nucleation in the context of increased monopolization of land ownership."[70]

As elsewhere in the Aegean islands under the Latins and Ottomans, control of land on Kea was dominated by a wealthy privileged class that also occupied public offices and served to mediate between the islanders and the Ottoman administration, since few, if any, non-Greeks were generally resident on the island. Much of the land on the island was monopolized by members of this class in large parcels *(voles)*, over which in their totality grazing rights were held by a single owner, while each parcel was in turn broken into myriad smaller fields that could be cultivated but not fenced. Such a system, similar to that described by Kasdagli for Naxos in Chapter 3, would have impeded the consolidation of land by peasants. Thus, there could have been little incentive to live in isolation in the countryside when one's agricultural parcels had been scattered by partible inheritance throughout the island.

With the Greek Revolution of 1821 and the subsequent emergence of a democracy that offered individual citizens a voice in government, the

69. Cherry, Davis, and Mantzourani 1991.

70. Cherry, Davis, and Mantzourani 1991, p. 467 (on the later history of the island, see pp. 467–471).

older system of land ownership that was supported by the elite collapsed. Land in the later 19th and 20th centuries then changed hands readily. Some small farmers were able to consolidate parcels and pursued a more intensive agricultural strategy that included residence amidst their fields. This impressive expansion of settlement outside the town of Chora is readily observable in the distribution of agricultural structures that have been built in the rural landscape in the past 200 years, and in the changing shapes of fields as the older *voles* have been increasingly subdivided.[71]

At the time of publication of archaeological fieldwork in the northwestern part of the island, the earliest published text from Kea that related to Ottoman administration dated to 1770 and emanated from a Greek source.[72] The discovery and transcription by Kiel of relevant Ottoman documents has thus opened a window on an almost entirely unknown stage in the history of Kea from the 15th to the 19th century, a period familiar only from the accounts of foreign visitors.[73] Of particular interest is that this new information appears to confirm what was previously suspected: The only significant settlement was located at the modern capital of the island, Chora (officially Ioulis), and there were no other villages.

At the same time, the Ottoman documents seem to support the notion that there was little in the way of isolated rural settlement prior to the period of Greek independence. The detailed Ottoman register *(mufassal defter)* of 1670/1 divides all inhabitants of the island into 15 *mahalle* (Greek μαχαλάδες—neighborhoods, or wards, or districts).[74] These are identified in relation to churches, all of which appear to have been located in Chora or nearby.[75] The only individuals who are registered as resident elsewhere are the few monks recorded in Appendix 2 of Chapter 2.

Such a highly nucleated pattern of settlement is precisely that suggested by the account of Giuseppe Sebastiani, who visited Kea only three years before the Ottoman register was composed. He wrote in 1667 that "Hoggi ha una sola città dove il Latini hanno una chiesa dedicate a S. Andrea apostolo."[76] That this distribution of population continued to be characteristic of the island in the following century is indicated by an unpublished map (Map 2) drawn immediately following the Greek Revolution by members of the Expédition scientifique de Morée. Aside from Zea (Chora) and its "château," marked elsewhere are only rural seasonal shelters, "magazines," doubtless those used for storage of *velanidi* (acorn caps) awaiting export,

71. Whitelaw 1991.

72. Psyllas 1921, pp. 312–313.

73. Bennet and Voutsaki 1991.

74. This *defter* is among those described by Kiel in Chap. 2.

75. *Tapu ve Kadastro Genel Müdürlüğü* (TKGM), Ankara, no. 105, fols. 91a–100b (A.D. 1670/1). We are grateful to Machiel Kiel for providing us with information extracted from this document. The *mahalle* include: Aya Apostol (Ayioi Apostoloi); Ayo Atanas (Ayios Athanasios); Tirianda (Ayia Triada); [unreadable name]; Ayo Yani Selogo (Ayios Ioannis Theologos); Porodromo (Ayios Ioannis Prodromos); Aya Nikola (Ayios Nikolaos); Hristos (Metamorphosis tou Hristou?); Aya Yorgi (Ayios Yorgios); Panaya Yerusalim (Panayia tou Yerusalim, at present Panayia Rematiani); Ayi Pandi (Ayioi Pantes); Ayo Vasil (Ayios Vasilios); Panaya Arva(nilan?) (Panayia? Arvanitissa); Ayo Andoni (Ayios Antonios); and Panaya Zodoho (Panayia Zoodohos Piyi). The following sources have been especially useful in identifying churches on Kea: Dimitropoulos 1983; Gerola 1921–1922; and Thomopoulos 1963. We are grateful to Eleftherios Lepouras of Kea and to Evi Gorogianni for their assistance in this regard. Only the church of Panaya Zodoho is not attested in Chora itself, but a church of Panayia Zoodohos Piyi is nearby at Sklavonikolas, ca. 2 km to the southwest.

76. Gerola 1921–1922, p. 194.

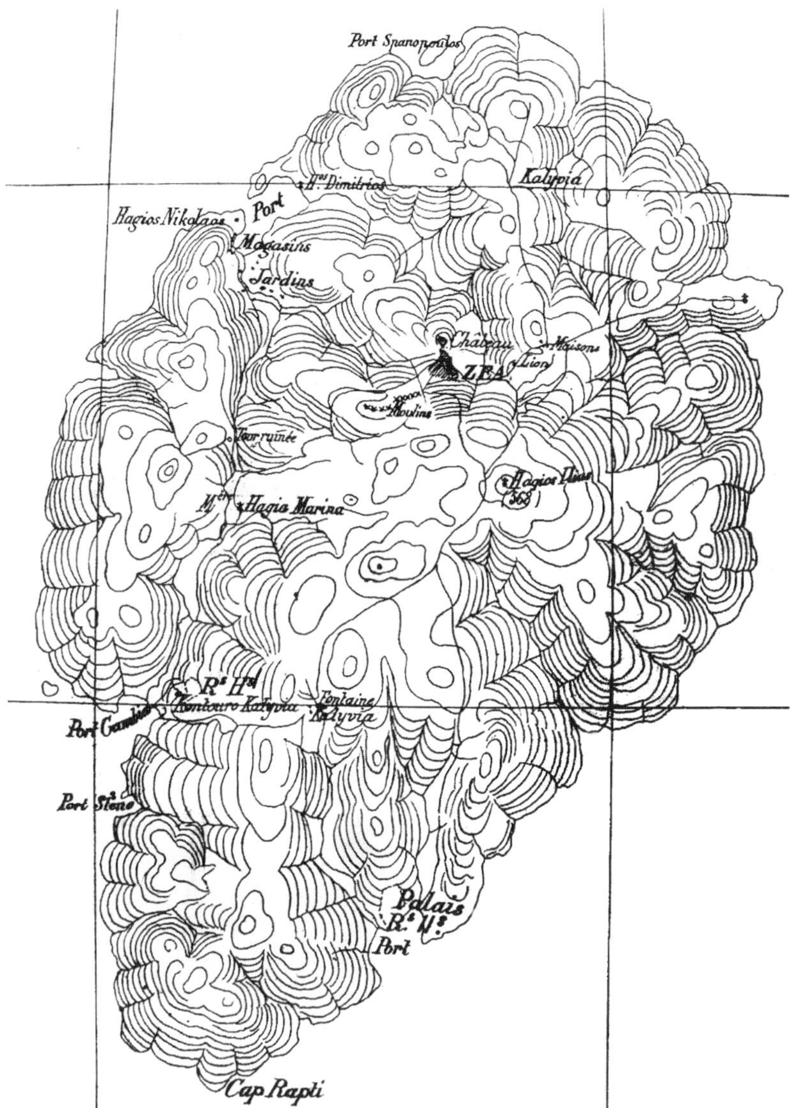

Map 2. Map of Kea by the Expédition scientifique de Morée, "St. Grégoire d'Arbora, Zéa Andros, C 14–19, en trois morceaux, 2ᵉ feuille." With permission of the Board of Directors of the Historical and Ethnological Society of Greece

at the site of the present town of Korisia (Hagios Nikolaos on Map 2), and several houses close to the northeast of Chora.[77]

In the case of Kea, both Western accounts and Ottoman documents point to the existence of a highly nucleated pattern of settlement, at least from the later 17th century until the Greek Revolution. Such a picture is in accord with the results of archaeological investigations in the northwestern part of the island, which were largely unsuccessful in finding artifacts datable to the 16th through early 19th centuries outside Chora, in the rural landscape, despite the fact that the entire ceramic assemblage from the project was examined by archaeologists familiar with the ceramics of these centuries.[78] The archaeological evidence and the map of the Expédition scientifique suggest that the Ottoman data do not conceal a situation in which farmers maintained both urban and rural residences, as Forbes has described for Methana in Chapter 6.

It is important to emphasize that it is only the combination of various threads of evidence that permits us to make the preceding statements with confidence. Data from Ottoman *defter*s can in themselves be misleading

77. "St. Grégoire d'Arbora, Zéa Andros, C 14–19, en trois morceaux, 2ᵉ feuille." The image presented here as Map 2 was made from a copy held in the collection of the National Historical Museum of Athens, and is reproduced with the permission of the Board of Directors of the Historical and Ethnological Society of Greece. We are grateful to Philippos Mazarakis-Ainian of the National Historical Museum of Athens for facilitating our study of it.

78. Cherry, Davis, and Mantzourani 1991, pp. 353–355.

with regard to the pattern of settlement. In Seriphos, for example, it is clear from local Greek taxation records that, in the later 18th century, population was considerably dispersed beyond the capital.[79] Both then and at the end of the 17th century, the accounts of Westerners imply, however, that settlement was very nucleated, with references only to one village that bore the name of the island and to a hamlet.[80] Gerola quotes a report of a Jesuit, Giacomo Saverio Portier: "La principale demeure des Serphiotes est dans un gros bourg, situé sur la pointe d'une montagne fort escarpé, à près d'un lieue de la mer, et dans un village éloigné du bourg d'environ une lieue."[81] Tournefort calls this village San Nicolò; Gerola identifies it with the present town of Pyrgos.[82] The Ottoman *defter* of 1670/1 likewise does not hint at a dispersed pattern of settlement. The population of the island is recorded with reference to seven churches, six of which appear to represent neighborhoods in Chora.[83]

CONCLUSION

The preceding case study illustrates some of the advantages of using different types of evidence, even if it takes 20 years to find it![84] The challenges that can divide the disciplines of archaeology and history require a tremendous amount of dialogue and understanding of the respective methodologies. Perhaps the most basic steps are to agree on examining the same geographical areas, and, for archaeologists, to agree that they must devote more resources to the analysis of post-classical artifacts. Historians of this period may not yet be accustomed to looking to archaeology for answers and are perhaps, through disciplinary traditions, isolated from developments in archaeological thinking. The multiperiod, multidisciplinary projects that have become common in Mediterranean archaeology are perhaps still alien to the traditionally solitary historian who has specialized, perforce, in a narrow time period.

Orser complains that "historical archaeologists are not sought out by scholars in other disciplines."[85] In terms of the confines of this book, there is to date still little published archaeology of this period for Greece or Cyprus. This needs to be remedied to allow historians to access the results and begin to see the potential of cooperation.

79. Liata 1987, p. 40; Davis 1991, pp. 177–180.

80. Di Krienen 1773, p. 105.

81. Gerola 1916–1920, pp. 211, n. 2.

82. Tournefort 1727, vol. 1, p. 215; Gerola 1916–1920, p. 212.

83. All entries are preceded by *kilise-i* (church of) and include Hristos, [illegible], Ayo Yorgi (Ayios Yioryios), Selogo (Ayios Ioannis Theologos), [illegible], Taksiarhi (Taxiarchi), and Kostantino (Ayios Konstantinos). Regarding Ayios Yioryios, Ayios Ioannis Theologos (San Giovanni Evangelista), and Ayios Konstantinos, see Gerola 1916–1920, pp. 217–218. On the use of these three churches and Hristos to describe areas of Chora, see Liata 1987, pp. 41, 183. In addition to these places, seven individuals are recorded at Taksiarhi. These men probably represent laity associated with the Monastery of the Taxiarchi, where 15 monks are recorded separately, although there was also a Church of the Taxiarchi in the village of Pyrgos.

84. It is worth noting that similar reexaminations of data from other published archaeological projects in light of new archival research could be equally rewarding. One thinks, e.g., of the potential for integrating more fully the wealth of Venetian textual and cartographic information available for the Argolid (e.g., Liata 2002, 2003; Topping 2000) with fruits of intensive surface survey in the Hermionid and in Methana (Jameson, Runnels, and van Andel 1994; Mee and Forbes 1997; Sutton 2000).

85. Orser 1996, p. 62.

It was in the hope of starting such a dialogue among historians and archaeologists working in Greece that this volume was conceived. Although not all the chapters are examples of interdisciplinary work, if we have at least made the disciplines more aware of each other and their common interests, then we have taken a step forward.

ACKNOWLEDGMENTS

In closing, it is our pleasure to acknowledge the support we have received in producing this volume. We are grateful to the Semple Fund of the Department of Classics of the University of Cincinnati for underwriting costs of production, and for supporting the workshop in Cincinnati, where most of the chapters in the book were first presented as conference papers. We thank Shari Stocker for her help in organizing that event, and Mark Armstrong, Yuki Furuya, Jody Gordon, Evi Gorogianni, Julie Hruby, Ols Lafe, and Sean Lockwood for their assistance in performing the many duties that are necessarily coincident with such a gathering. Gayle McGarrahan and Ken Gottorff offered much valuable advice regarding planning. Several scholars in attendance at the workshop did not contribute to this volume, but their participation in discussion was no less valuable in promoting the fruitful exchange of ideas. In this regard, we thank Cyprian Broodbank, Elizabeth Frierson, Thurstan Robinson, and Fariba Zarinebaf. Help from Rosemary Robertson and John Wallrodt has, as always, been indispensable in ensuring that illustrations are of the highest standards, Sarah Lima has helped with the assembly of both text and images, and John Schicht with editing. Finally, we thank Victoria Sabetai, Yiannis Saïtas, and the anonymous reviewers of this manuscript for help with bibliography, and the latter also for insightful comments that, we hope, have greatly improved the final product.

REFERENCES

Agora = *The Athenian Agora: Results of Excavations Conducted by the American School of Classical Studies at Athens,* Princeton
IX = G. C. Miles, *The Islamic Coins,* 1962.
XX = A. Frantz, *The Church of the Holy Apostles,* 1971.

Alexander, J. C. 1999. "Counting the Grains: Conceptual and Methodological Issues in Reading the Ottoman *Mufassal Tahrir Defters*," *Al-Majallah al-tarikhiyah al-ʾArabiyah lil-dirasat al-ʾUthmaniyah* (Arab Historical Review for Ottoman Studies) 19–20, pp. 55–70.

Andrews, K. 1953. *Castles of the Morea* (Gennadeion Monographs IV), Princeton.

———. 2006. *Castles of the Morea* (Gennadeion Monographs IV), repr. with an introduction by G. Bugh, Princeton.

Arbel, B. 2000. *Cyprus, the Franks, and Venice,* Burlington, Vt.

Aristeidou, A. 1990. *Ανέκδοτα έγγραφα της κυπριακής ιστορίας από το Αρχείο της Βενετίας,* 4 vols., Nikosia.

Armstrong, P. 1996. "The Survey Area in the Byzantine and Ottoman Periods," in *Continuity and Change in a Greek Rural Landscape: The Laconia Survey,* ed. W. Cavanagh, J. Crouwel, R. W. V. Catling, and G. Shipley, London, pp. 125–140.

Balta, E. 1989. *L'Eubée à la fin du XVe siècle: Économie et population, les registres de l'année 1474,* Athens.

———. 1992. "Rural and Urban Population in the *Sancak* of Euripos in the Early 16th Century," *Αρχείον Ευβοϊκών Μελετών* 29, Athens, pp. 55–185.

———. 1997. *Problèmes et approches de l'histoire ottomane: Un itinéraire scientifique de Kayseri à Eğriboz,* Istanbul.

———. 1999. *Peuple et production: Pour une interpretation des sources ottomanes,* Istanbul.

———. 2003. *Ottoman Studies and Archives in Greece,* Istanbul.

Baram, U. 2000. "Entangled Objects from the Palestinian Past: Archaeological Perspectives for the Ottoman Period, 1500–1900," in Baram and Carroll 2000, pp. 137–159.

Baram, U., and L. Carroll, eds. 2000. *A Historical Archaeology of the Ottoman Empire: Breaking New Ground,* New York.

Bennet, J., and S. Voutsaki. 1991. "A Synopsis and Analysis of Travelers' Accounts of Keos (to 1821)," in Cherry, Davis, and Mantzourani 1991, pp. 365–382.

Bintliff, J. 1996. "The Frankish Countryside in Central Greece: The Evidence from Archaeological Field Survey," in Lock and Sanders 1996, pp. 1–18.

———. 1999. "The Ottoman Era in the Context of Long-Term Settlement History: A Case-Study, the Archaeological Survey of the Valley of the Muses, Boeotia, Greece," *Al-Majallah al-tarikhiyah al-ʾArabiyah lil-dirasat al-ʾUthmaniyah* (Arab Historical Review for Ottoman Studies) 19–20, pp. 203–229.

Bon, A. 1969. *La Morée franque: Recherches historiques, topographiques et archéologiques sur la principauté d'Achaïe (1205–1430),* Paris.

Brumfield, A. 2000. "Agriculture and Rural Settlement in Ottoman Crete, 1669–1898: A Modern Site Survey," in Baram and Carroll 2000, pp. 37–78.

Carroll, L. 2000. "Toward an Archaeology of Non-Elite Consumption in Late Ottoman Anatolia," in Baram and Carroll 2000, pp. 161–180.

Cherry, J. F., J. L. Davis, and E. Mantzourani, eds. 1991. *Landscape Archaeology as Long-Term History: Northern Keos in the Cycladic Islands from Earliest Settlement until Modern Times* (Monumenta archaeologica 16), Los Angeles.

Cohn, B. S. 1996. *Colonialism and Its Forms of Knowledge: The British in India,* Princeton.

Cooper, F., ed. 2002. *Houses of the Morea,* Athens.

Cooper, N. K. 1996. "The Frankish Church of Haghia Sophia at Andravida," in Lock and Sanders 1996, pp. 29–48.

Corinth = *Corinth: Results of the Excavations Conducted by the American*

School of Classical Studies at Athens
III.1 = C. W. Blegen, O. Broneer, R. Stillwell, and A. R. Bellinger, *Acrocorinth: Excavations in 1926,* Cambridge, Mass., 1930.
III.2 = R. Carpenter and A. Bon, *The Defenses of Acrocorinth and the Lower Town,* Cambridge, Mass., 1936.
XI = C. H. Morgan, *The Byzantine Pottery,* Cambridge, Mass., 1942.
XX = C. K. Williams II, and N. Bookidis, eds., *Corinth, The Centenary: 1896–1996,* Princeton 2003.

Coulson, M. L. 1996. "The Dominican Church of Saint Sophia at Andravida," in Lock and Sanders 1996, pp. 49–60.

Curuni, S. A., and L. Donati. 1988. *Creta veneziana,* Venice.

Davies, S. 2004. "Pylos Regional Archaeological Project, Part VI: Administration and Settlement in Venetian Navarino," *Hesperia* 73, pp. 59–120.

Davis, J. L. 1991. "Contributions to a Mediterranean Rural Archaeology: Historical Case Studies from the Ottoman Cyclades," *JMA* 4, pp. 131–216.

———, ed. 1998. *Sandy Pylos: An Architectural History from Nestor to Navarino,* Austin.

di Krienen, Conte H. L. P. 1773. *Breve descrizione del Arcipelago e particolarmente delle diciotto isole sottomesse l'anno 1771 al dominio russo,* Leghorn.

Dimitropoulos, C. P. 1983. "Οι εκκλησίες της Κέας" (diss. Univ. of Thessaloniki).

Dokos, K., and G. Panagopoulos. 1993. *Το βενετικό κτηματολόγιο της Βοστίτσας,* Athens.

Eliot, C. W. J. 1992. *Campaign of the Falieri and Piraeus in the Year 1827, or, Journal of a Volunteer, Being the Personal Account of Captain Thomas Douglas Whitcombe* (Gennadeion Monographs V), Princeton.

Faroqhi, S. 1999. *Approaching Ottoman History: An Introduction to the Sources,* Cambridge.

Finley, M. I. 1976. "Colonies: An Attempt at a Typology," *Transactions of the Royal Historical Society,* ser. 5, vol. 26, pp. 167–188.

Forsén, B. 2003. "The Roman–Early Modern Periods: Conclusions," in *The Asea Valley Survey: An Arcadian Mountain Valley from the Palaeolithic Period until Modern Times,* ed. J. Forsén and B. Forsén, Stockholm, pp. 307–331.

Foutakis, P. 2005. "The Granite Column in Modon: How to Make a Stone Say What You Want It to Say," *OJA* 24, pp. 89–105.

Funari, P. P. A. 1999. "Historical Archaeology from a World Perspective," in Funari, Hall, and Jones 1999, pp. 37–66.

Funari, P. P. A., M. Hall, and S. Jones. 1999. "Introduction: Archaeology in History" in *Historical Archaeology: Back from the Edge,* ed. P. P. A. Funari, M. Hall, and S. Jones, London, pp. 1–20.

Georgopoulou, M. 2001. *Venice's Mediterranean Colonies: Architecture and Urbanism,* Cambridge.

Gerola, G. 1916–1920. "Sèrfino (Sèriphos)," *ASAtene* 3, pp. 203–241.

———. 1921–1922. "Zea (Keos)," *ASAtene* 4–5, pp. 180–221.

———. 1923–1924. "Fermenia (Kythnos-Thermjà)," *ASAtene* 6–7, pp. 43–82.

———. 1930–1931. "Le fortificazioni di Napoli di Romanìa," *ASAtene* 13–14, pp. 347–410.

Gerstel, S. E. J., M. Munn, H. E. Grossman, E. Barnes, A. H. Rohn, and M. Kiel. 2003. "A Late Medieval Settlement at Panakton," *Hesperia* 72, pp. 147–234.

Greene, M. 2000. *A Shared World: Christians and Muslims in the Early Modern Mediterranean,* Princeton.

Gregory, T. E. 1996. "The Medieval Site on Mt. Tsilika near Sophiko," in Lock and Sanders 1996, pp. 61–76.

Herzfeld, M. 1991. *A Place in History: Social and Monumental Time in a Cretan Town,* Princeton.

Hodgetts, C., and P. Lock. 1996. "Some Village Fortifications in the Venetian Peloponnese," in Lock and Sanders 1996, pp. 77–90.

Ivison, E. A. 1996. "Latin Tomb Monuments in the Levant 1204–ca. 1450," in Lock and Sanders 1996, pp. 91–106.

Jameson, M. H., C. N. Runnels, and T. H. van Andel. 1994. *A Greek*

Countryside: The Southern Argolid from Prehistory to the Present Day, Stanford.

Johnson, M. 1999a. "Historical, Archaeology, Capitalism," in *Historical Archaeologies of Capitalism,* ed. M. Leone and P. Potter, New York, pp. 219–231.

———. 1999b. "Rethinking Historical Archaeology," in Funari, Hall, and Jones 1999a, pp. 23–36.

Kasdagli, A. E. 1999. *Land and Marriage Settlements in the Aegean: A Case Study of Seventeenth-Century Naxos,* Venice.

Kiel, M. 1970. "Notes on the History of Some Turkish Monuments in Thessaloniki and Their Founders," *BalkSt* 11, pp. 123–148.

———. 1971. "Observations on the History of Northern Greece during the Turkish Rule: Historical and Architectural Description of the Turkish Monuments of Komotine and Serres, Their Place in the Development of Ottoman Turkish Architecture, and Their Present Condition," *BalkSt* 12, pp. 415–444.

———. 1973. "A Note on the Exact Date of Construction of the White Tower of Thessaloniki," *BalkSt* 14, pp. 352–357.

———. 1981. "Two Little-Known Monuments of Early and Classical Ottoman Architecture in Greek Thrace: Historical and Art Historical Notes on the Hamams of Tumurtas Pasazade Oruç Pasha (1398) and Feridun Ahmed Beg (1571) in Didymoteichon," *BalkSt* 22, pp. 127–146.

———. 1983. "The Oldest Monuments of Ottoman-Turkish Architecture in the Balkans: The Imaret and the Mosque of Ghazi Evrenos Bey in Gümülcine (Komotini) and the Evrenos Bey Khan in the Village of Ilıca/Loutra in Greek Thrace (1370–1390)," *Sanat Tarihi Yıllığı/Kunsthistorische Forschungen* 12, pp. 117–138.

———. 1992. "Central Greece in the Süleymanic Age: Preliminary Notes on Population Growth, Economic Expansion, and Its Influence on the Spread of Greek Christian Culture," in *Soliman le Magnifique et son temps,* ed. G. Veinstein, Paris, pp. 399–424.

———. 1997. "The Rise and Decline of Turkish Boeotia, 15th–19th Century (Remarks on the Settlement Pattern, Demography, and Agricultural Production According to Unpublished Ottoman-Turkish Census and Taxation Records)," in *Recent Developments in the History and Archaeology of Central Greece. Proceedings of the 6th International Boeotian Conference* (*BAR-IS* 666), ed. J. L. Bintliff, Oxford, pp. 315–358.

———. 2000. "The Ottoman Imperial Registers: Central Greece and Northern Bulgaria in the 15th–19th Century: The Demographic Development of Two Areas Compared," in *Reconstructing Past Population Trends in Mediterranean Europe (3000 B.C.–A.D. 1800),* ed. J. Bintliff and K. Sbonias, Oxford, pp. 195–218.

———. 2005. "Construction of the Ottoman Castle of Anavarin-i cedid, According to Orders of the Imperial Council as Preserved in the *Mühimme Defter*s 19–31: From 2 *Safer* A.H. 980 to 10 *Receb* A.H. 985 (June 1572–November 1577)," in Zarinebaf, Bennet, and Davis 2005, pp. 265–281.

Kiel, M., and F. Sauerwein. 1994. *Ost-Lokris in türkischer und neugriechischer Zeit (1460–1981)* (Passauer Mittelmeerstudien 6), Passau.

Koder, J. 1973. *Negroponte: Untersuchungen zur Topographie und Siedlungsgeschichte der Insel Euboia während der Zeit der Venezianerherrschaft,* Vienna.

Koukkou, E. E. 1989. *Οι κοινοτικοί θεσμοί στις Κυκλάδες κατά την Τουρκοκρατία,* Athens.

Kuniholm, P. 2000. "Dendrochronologically Dated Ottoman Monuments," in Baram and Carroll 2000, pp. 90–136.

Liata, E. 1987. *Η Σέριφος κατά την Τουρκοκρατία (17ος–19ος αι.),* Athens.

———. 1998. *Με την αρμάδα στο Μοριά 1684–1687,* Athens.

———. 2002. *Το Ναύπλιο και η ενδοχώρα του από τον 17ο στον 18ο αιώνα,* Athens.

———. 2003. *Αργεία γη: Από το τεριτόριο στο βιλαέτι,* Athens.

Lock, P. 1996. "The Towers of Euboea: Lombard or Venetian; Agrarian or Strategic," in Lock and Sanders 1996, pp. 107–126.

Lock, P., and G. D. R. Sanders, eds. 1996. *The Archaeology of Medieval Greece,* Oxford.

Lowry, H. W. 1992. *Studies in Defterology: Ottoman Society in the Fifteenth and Sixteenth Centuries,* Istanbul.

MacKay, T. S. 1996. "A Group of Renaissance Pottery from Heraklion, Crete: Notes and Questions," in Lock and Sanders 1996, pp. 127–137.

———. 2003. "Pottery of the Frankish Period," in *Corinth* XX, pp. 401–422.

Maltezou, C. A. 1997. *Απογραφές πληθυσμού Κυθήρων (18ος αι.),* 3 vols., Athens.

———. 2002. *Πρακτικά του Διεθνούς Συμποσίου: Κύπρος–Βενετία. Κοινές ιστορικές τύχες. Πρακτικά του Διεθνούς Συμποσίου, Αθήνα, 1–3 Μαρτίου 2001,* Venice.

Maltezou, C. A., and C. E. Papakosta, eds. 2006. *Πρακτικά Διεθνούς Συνεδρίου: Βενετία–Εύβοια από τον Έγριπο στο Νεγροπόντε. Χαλκίδα, 12–14 Νοεμβρίου 2004* (Ελληνικό Ινστιτούτο Βυζαντινών και Μεταβυζαντινών Σπουδών Βενετίας: Εταιρεία Ευβοϊκών Σπουδών, Συνέδρια 10/*Venezia–Euboea: Da Egripos a Negroponte. Atti del convegno internazionale, Chalkida, 12–14 novembre 2004*), Venice/Athens.

McKee, S. 2000. *Uncommon Dominion: Venetian Crete and the Myth of Ethnic Purity,* Philadelphia.

Mee, C., and H. Forbes, eds. 1997. *A Rough and Rocky Place: The Landscape and Settlement History of the Methana Peninsula, Greece. Results of the Methana Survey Project,* Liverpool.

Nikiforou, A. 1999. *Δημόσιες τελετές στην Κέρκυρα κατά την περίοδο της βενετικής κυριαρχίας, 14ος–18ος αι.,* Athens.

Orser, C. E. 1996. *A Historical Archaeology of the Modern World,* New York.

———, ed. 2002. *Encyclopedia of Historical Archaeology,* London.

Parveva, S. 2003. "Agrarian Land and Harvest in South-West Peloponnese in the Early 18th Century, *ÉtBalk* 38, pp. 83–123.

Paton, J. M. 1940. *The Venetians in Athens, 1687–1688, from the* Istoria *of Cristoforo Ivanovich* (Gennnadeion Monographs I), Cambridge, Mass.

Paynter, R. 2000. "Historical and Anthropological Archaeology: Forging Alliances," *Journal of Archaeological Research* 8, pp. 1–37.

Psyllas, I. N. 1921. *Ἱστορία τῆς νήσου Κέας,* Athens.

Robinson, R. C. W. 1985. "Tobacco Pipes of Corinth and of the Athenian Agora," *Hesperia* 54, pp. 149–203.

Robinson, T. 2002. "An Archaeological Survey in Graeco-Roman Pisidia: A Study of Sia, Anassos, and Their Territories" (diss. Oxford Univ.).

Sanders, G. D. R. 1987. "An Assemblage of Frankish Pottery at Corinth," *Hesperia* 56, pp. 159–195.

———. 1996. "Two Kastra on Melos and Their Relations in the Archipelago," in Lock and Sanders 1996, pp. 147–177.

Sbonias, K. 2000. "Investigating the Interface between Regional Survey, Historical Demography, and Paleodemography," in *Reconstructing Past Population Trends in Mediterranean Europe (3000 B.C.–A.D. 1800),* ed. J. Bintliff and K. Sbonias, Oxford, pp. 219–234.

Scott, J. C. 1998. *Seeing Like a State: How Certain Schemes to Improve the Human Condition Have Failed,* New Haven.

Sinopoli, C. M. 1994. "The Archaeology of Empires," *Annual Review of Anthropology* 23, pp. 159–180.

Shelton, K. 2003. "The Early Modern Pottery," in *The Asea Valley Survey: An Arcadian Mountain Valley from the Palaeolithic until Modern Times,* ed. J. Forsén and B. Forsén, Stockholm, pp. 299–304.

Stallsmith, A. B. 2004. "The Settlement History of the Ottoman to Modern Periods: 1669 to 20th Century," in *Reports on the Vrokastro Area, Eastern Crete* 2: *The Settlement History of the Vrokastro Area and Related Studies,* ed. B. J. Hayden, Philadelphia, pp. 279–325.

———. See also Brumfield, A., A. B. Stallsmith.

Stedman, N. 1996. "Land-Use and Settlement in Post-Medieval Central Greece: An Interim Discussion," in Lock and Sanders 1996, pp. 179–192.

Sutton, S. B. 1990. "Anthropological Studies," in "The Nemea Valley Archaeological Project: A Preliminary Report," by J. C. Wright, J. F. Cherry, J. L. Davis, E. Mantzourani, S. B. Sutton, and R. F. Sutton, Jr., *Hesperia* 59, pp. 594–603.

———, ed. 2000. *Contingent Countryside: Settlement, Economy, and Land Use in the Southern Argolid since 1700,* Stanford.

Thomopoulos, I. 1963. "Μελέτη τοπωνυμικὴ τῆς νήσου Κέω," *Επετηρίς Εταιρείας Κυκλαδικών Μελετών* 3, pp. 311–480.

Topping, P. 2000. "The Southern Argolid from Byzantine to Ottoman Times," in Sutton 2000, pp. 25–40.

Tournefort, J. Pitton de. 1727. *Relation d'un voyage du Levant, fait par ordre du Roy,* 3 vols., Lyon.

Van Dommelen, P. 1998. *On Colonial Grounds: A Comparative Study of Colonialism and Rural Settlement in First Millennium B.C. West Central Sardinia,* Leiden.

Vionis, A. K. 2005. "'Crusader' and 'Ottoman' Material Life: The Archaeology of Built Environment and Domestic Material Culture in the Medieval and Post-Medieval Cyclades, Greece (c. 13th–20th A.D.)" (diss. Leiden Univ.).

Vroom, J. 1998. "Early Modern Archaeology in Central Greece: The Contrast of Artefact-Rich and Sherdless Sites," *JMA* 11, pp. 131–164.

———. 2003. *After Antiquity: Ceramics and Society in the Aegean from the 7th to the 20th Century A.C. A Case Study from Boeotia, Central Greece* (Archaeological Studies, Leiden University 10), Leiden.

Whitelaw, T. M. 1991. "The Ethnoarchaeology of Recent Rural Settlement and Land Use in Northwest Keos," in Cherry, Davis, and Mantzourani 1991, pp. 403–454.

Wilkinson, T. J. 2004. *On the Margin of the Euphrates: Settlement and Land Use at Tell es-Sweyhat and in the Upper Tabqa Area, Syria,* Chicago.

Williams, C. K., II. 2003. "Frankish Corinth: An Overview," in *Corinth* XX, pp. 423–434.

Wylie, A. 1999. "Why Should Historical Archaeologists Study Capitalism?" in *Historical Archaeologies of Capitalism,* ed. M. Leone and P. Potter, New York, pp. 23–49.

Yenişchirlioğlou, F. 2005. "L'archeologie historique de l'Empire ottoman: Bilan et perspectives," *Turcica* 37, pp. 245–265.

Zarinebaf, F., J. Bennet, and J. L. Davis. 2005. *A Historical and Economic Geography of Ottoman Greece: The Southwestern Morea in the 18th Century* (*Hesperia* Suppl. 34), Princeton.

Ziadeh-Seely, G. 2000. "The Archaeology of Ottoman Tiʿinnik: An Interdisciplinary Approach," in Baram and Carroll 2000, pp. 79–91.

Greeks, Venice, and the Ottoman Empire

by Siriol Davies and Jack L. Davis

The history of Venice's territorial possessions in the Aegean area begins at the start of the 13th century, when the Republic agreed to transport the Fourth Crusade to the Holy Land. These forces instead attacked and plundered the Byzantine capital of Constantinople, to the ultimate advantage of Venice's economic interests in the Levant. When the city fell to the crusaders in 1204, the Venetian doge, Enrico Dandolo, negotiated for a major share of the spoils of the Byzantine Empire in Greece. The territories which thus came under Latin rule became known in the West as "Romania."

By the mid-15th century, in areas now within the borders of the modern Greek state, Venice held the island of Crete, the fortresses of Koroni (Coron) and Methoni (Modon) in Messenia, Argos and Nauplion, certain of the Aegean islands, the islands of Corfu and Kythera, and Naupaktos (Lepanto). Venice in the 13th century also had acquired virtual sovereignty over the island of Euboia (Negroponte), which it maintained until 1470, when the island was lost to the Ottomans.

Parallel to this expansion of Venice in the Balkans, a fledgling Ottoman Empire whittled away at Byzantine territory in the East. By the beginning of the 14th century, the Byzantines had lost almost all of Asia Minor to several small independent Turkish states. One of these, a small polity in northwestern Asia Minor in the area of Bithynia, was ruled by Osman, founder of the Ottoman dynasty. As he expanded his rule through wars of conquest, coastal Byzantine cities such as Nicaea and Nicomedia soon fell and an Ottoman fleet began to threaten Byzantine island possessions.

In 1354, Ottoman armies entered Europe for the first time; by 1370, Didymoteichon and Adrianople in Thrace had been captured. After the defeat of the Serbs at the Battle of Kosovo in 1389, Constantinople became a Byzantine island surrounded by Ottoman possessions, and the Morea (the Peloponnese) was the only substantial Balkan territory that remained in Byzantine hands. In 1453, Constantinople also fell, and Mehmed the Conqueror transformed it into the Ottoman capital, now Istanbul.

In the course of the next 450 years, the borders of the Ottoman Empire expanded or contracted in the Balkans and the Aegean, as territory was gained or lost through warfare or treaty in lands that once had belonged to the Byzantine Empire or subsequently to various Latin powers

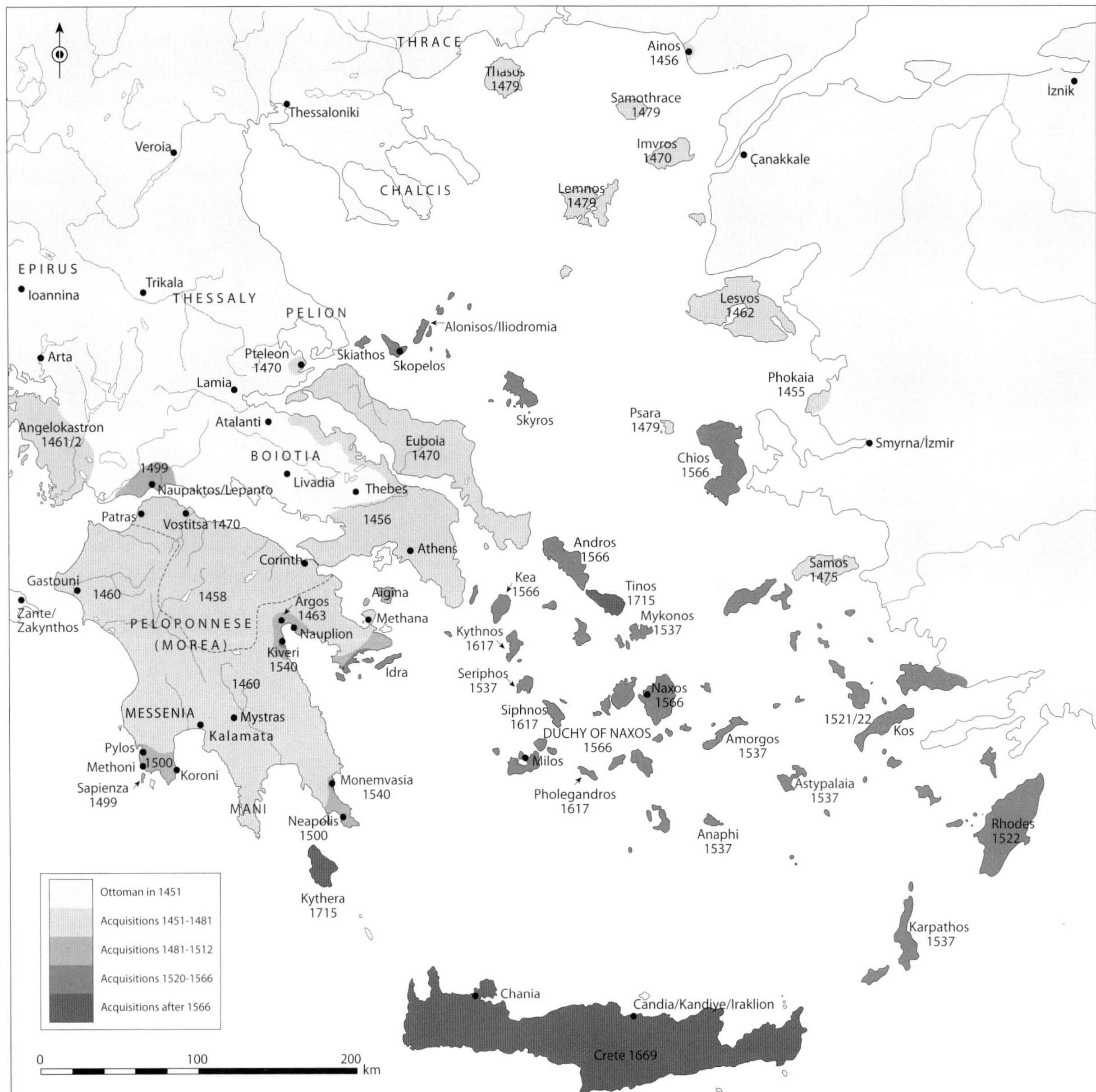

Figure 1.1. Ottoman expansion in the eastern Mediterranean, 15th–17th centuries. R. J. Robertson, after Pitcher 1972, map XIV

(Fig. 1.1). Among the latter, Venice was the most significant force. Apart from territorial possessions in the northern Adriatic, the Venetian overseas empire was mainly insular (Ionian and Cycladic islands, Crete, and Cyprus), reflecting the need for ports of call for Venetian galleys on their voyages to the Black Sea and the eastern Mediterranean. The period was punctuated by Veneto-Ottoman wars in 1463–1479, 1499–1500, 1537–1540, 1570–1571, 1645–1669, 1684–1699, and 1715–1718. In intervals of peace, the longest being that from 1571–1645, the Venetian ambassador in Constantinople did his best to ensure that awkward incidents such as attacks on Ottoman shipping by Venetian subjects did not give cause for the sultan to declare war.

The tale of these years is mainly one of Venetian losses: in 1500, Methoni and Koroni; in 1540, Nauplion and Monemvasia; in 1570, Cyprus;

in 1669, Crete. Rather unexpectedly, the late 17th century brought a revival of Venetian fortunes in the form of the conquest of the Peloponnese, but this late imperial dream was short-lived. For most of the 18th century, until the end of the Republic in 1797, the Venetian empire south of the Adriatic was restricted to the Ionian islands.

The historical geography of the Ottoman Empire is also complicated, and political histories of specific areas often diverge. Thessaly, Boiotia, and Epirus had become Ottoman possessions already by the middle of the 15th century and remained so into the 20th century. But other areas of the Aegean were under Ottoman domination for a much shorter time. Venice lost the island of Tinos to the Ottomans only in 1715. The island of Kythera was Ottoman for fewer than three years (1715–1718). Quickly regained for Venice as a result of the Peace of Passarowitz, Kythera remained a colony of Venice until the Napoleonic wars.

Since it is impossible to offer readers a short and simple narrative history of Ottoman or Venetian Greece, we instead provide the following brief overviews of Ottoman and Venetian rule in those areas of modern Greece and Cyprus relevant to the chapters in this volume—namely, parts of the eastern Mediterranean (the islands of the Aegean, Crete, Kythera, the Morea, and Cyprus) where both the Ottoman Empire and Venice had major political and economic interests.

THE AEGEAN ISLANDS

In 1451, rule of the Aegean islands was extraordinarily fragmented. The Sporades (discussed in Chap. 2 by Machiel Kiel), Limnos, Thasos, Samothrace, and Imvros were nominally Byzantine but paid tribute to the Ottomans; the Genoese controlled Lesbos, Chios, and Samos; the Knights of St. John, the Dodecanese. An independent Duchy of Naxos held the central Cycladic islands, while Kea (discussed in the Introduction to this volume and also by Kiel) was divided among several families of Italian origin who sometimes ruled under the protection of Venice. In the course of the 16th century, however, most of the Aegean islands were brought into the Ottoman Empire, in campaigns by Hayreddin Barbarossa in 1537 (as described by Kiel). The Duchy of Naxos and the island of Chios were annexed in 1566, and only the island of Tinos remained in Latin hands through the 17th century. The Ottoman Empire ruled most of the islands indirectly through the intermediary of local Greek elites, as had the Latins before them (see Chap. 3 by Aglaia Kasdagli). Few Muslims settled there. The Sporades and Cyclades became part of the modern Greek state as a result of the Greek War of Independence.

CRETE

Assaults on Ottoman shipping by Westerners, especially the Knights Hospitallers of Rhodes, provided an excuse for the Ottomans to attack the island of Crete, Venetian since the early 13th century; the culprits often sought refuge there. The final Ottoman conquest of the island began in

April 1645, when a fleet of 78 galleys and various smaller ships set sail from Istanbul under the orders of Sultan İbrahim IV, believing that Crete would be an easy conquest.

Crete was to be the last major territorial gain of the Ottoman Empire and a major loss to Venice. By 1647, Rethymon, Chania, and most of the smaller fortresses had fallen, and Ottoman efforts were focused on Candia (modern Iraklion). By 1669, nearly all of the island was in Muslim hands, and the Ottomans had long since set in place an administration that would persist for more than two centuries. Both Venetian and Ottoman systems of governance on the island are the topics discussed by Allaire B. Stallsmith in Chapter 8. Crete was unified with the modern Greek state in 1913.

KYTHERA

The island of Kythera came under Venetian control after 1204 and was ceded to a Venetian noble family, the Venieri. The family divided the revenues of the island into 24 lots, which were shared among its members. In 1363, however, the Venieri, who also had interests in Crete, participated in a revolt against Venetian rule there, and the Republic decided to seize back control of Kythera from them. Eventually 13 of the shares were returned to the family, but Venice retained direct control of the other 11. The island was governed by an official appointed directly from Venice. This unusual arrangement prevailed until the end of Venetian rule in 1797, being only briefly interrupted by an Ottoman occupation from 1715 to 1718. In 1537, Kythera was sacked by Barbarossa in a devastating raid. Over the years the island was administered variously from Crete (until 1669), the Peloponnese (1687–1715), and Corfu (1718–1797).

THE MOREA

In 1459, a civil war between two Byzantine despots, Thomas and Dimitrios Palaiologos, invited Ottoman interference in the Peloponnese. By March 1462, the Morea had been pacified by the Ottomans. Venice's determination to hold on to its coastal possessions, however, meant that the Ottomans were able to establish firm control only with the campaigns of Sultan Bayezid II between 1499 and 1503. Venice managed to retain Nauplion and Monemvasia until 1540, but after that the Morea remained in Ottoman hands until 1685. Under the Byzantines and Ottomans, large numbers of Albanian immigrants widely settled there, in areas such as the Methana peninsula (Hamish Forbes's topic in Chap. 6).

Soon after Venice lost Iraklion to the Ottomans in 1669, a crusade of the so-called Holy League, an alliance of Venice, Austria, and Poland, was launched under the auspices of the pope. The Venetians, with support from German mercenaries, Maltese forces of the Knights Hospitallers, Slavs, papal troops, and recruits from Tuscany, opened an offensive aimed at recapturing Crete. The project failed in that objective but did result in the total conquest of the Morea between 1685 and 1690.

In 1684, a Venetian naval offensive captured the island of Lefkas and the port of Preveza in Aitolia. In 1685, Koroni, Kalamata, and fortresses in Mani were taken. In 1686, Pylos, Methoni, Argos, and Nauplion were gained, and the conquest of the Morea, except for Monemvasia, was completed the following year with the addition of Patras and Corinth. Venice then set out to organize the administration of its new province. Aspects of its rule there in the late 17th and early 18th centuries are discussed by Alexis Malliaris in Chapter 5, by Timothy E. Gregory in Chapter 9, and by John Bennet in Chapter 10.

Venice's rights to this *Regno di Morea* (Kingdom of the Morea) were recognized in 1699 under the terms of the Treaty of Karlowitz. Venice continued to rule the Morea until 1715, when the Ottomans regained it in its entirety in a brief but bloody campaign. The Morea then remained firmly in Ottoman hands until 1821, when the rebellion began that led to its incorporation into the modern Greek state.

CYPRUS

After 1191, the island of Cyprus was ruled by a dynasty established by Guy de Lusignan, the dispossessed heir to the Latin Kingdom of Jerusalem. Italian merchants gained power on Cyprus, and in the 15th century the island became the property of Venice after one of its noblewomen, Caterina Corner, married the Lusignan king. The island was taken by the Ottomans in 1571, and was held until Great Britain obtained control of it in 1878 through an agreement with the sultan. In Chapter 7, Michael Given discusses the effects of Frankish, Venetian, and Ottoman administrations on patterns of settlement on the island.

FURTHER READING

From the foregoing brief survey it should be clear that the political history of each region varied considerably in this period. Therefore we close this chapter by highlighting some references as good starting points concerning the history of the period. Further specific regional bibliography can be found in each chapter, and should be read in conjunction with relevant works mentioned in the Introduction.

With regard to the borders of the Ottoman Empire and the extent of Venetian possessions in the Aegean, see Pitcher 1972; concerning economic and political treaties between the two empires, see Theunissen 1998. Thiriet 1959 tells the story of the development of the Venetian Empire up to 1500. Shaw and Shaw 1976–1977 is an important source for the history of the Ottoman Empire and modern Turkey, and Hammer-Purgstall 1842 remains indispensable. Gregory 2005 provides a very readable account in English of the interaction between the Ottomans and the Byzantines; for surveys of the history of post-Byzantine Greece see, in particular, Finlay 1856, Vakalopoulos 1973, and Zakythinos 1976. Miller 1908 is still the best description of the complicated history of Western colonization in the

Aegean in the wake of the Fourth Crusade (see also Miller 1921). Lock 1995 is an important supplement that is attentive to material culture as well as documentary evidence. Jacoby 1989 is useful on the transition from Byzantine to Latin rule, and Balard 1998 provides a comprehensive bibliography of recent scholarship on the Latin East. On the incorporation of Ottoman territories into the modern Greek state in the 19th and 20th centuries, see Gallant 2001.

With respect to Ottoman and Venetian rule in particular parts of the Aegean and Cyprus, there is now a wealth of good resources. These include, for the Greek islands, Balta and Spiliotopoulou 1997 (for Santorini), Koder 1973 (for Euboia), Koumanoudi and Maltezou 2003 (for Kythera), and Slot 1982 (for the Cycladic islands); for Crete, Georgopoulou 2001, Greene 2000, and Zachariadou 1983; for the Morea, Davies 2004, Setton 1991, and Zarinebaf, Bennet, and Davis 2005; and for Cyprus, Arbel 2000 and Jennings 1993. On relations between local Orthodox populations and both Venice and Istanbul, see Papadia-Lala 2004, Ploumidis 1985–1992, and Zarinebaf, Bennet, and Davis 2005. Recent scholarship on Venetian Greece is disseminated through *Thesaurismata,* the journal of the Greek Institute of Byzantine and Post-Byzantine Studies in Venice.

REFERENCES

Arbel, B. 2000. *Cyprus, the Franks and Venice, 13th–16th Centuries,* Burlington, Vt.

Balard, M. 1998. "État de la recherche sur la latinocratie en Méditerranée Orientale," in *Ricchi e poveri nella società dell'oriente grecolatino,* ed. C. A. Maltezou, Venice, pp. 17–36.

Balta, E., and M. Spiliotopoulou. 1997. "Landed Property and Taxation in Santorini in the 17th Century," in *Problèmes et approches de l'histoire ottomane,* ed. E. Balta, Istanbul, pp. 115–148.

Davies, S. 2004. "Pylos Regional Archaeological Project, Part VI: Administration and Settlement in Venetian Navarino," *Hesperia* 73, pp. 59–120.

Finlay, G. 1856. *The History of Greece under Othoman and Venetian Domination,* Edinburgh.

Gallant, T. W. 2001. *Modern Greece,* London.

Georgopoulou, M. 2001. *Venice's Mediterranean Colonies: Architecture and Urbanism,* Cambridge.

Greene, M. 2000. *A Shared World: Christians and Muslims in the Early Modern Mediterranean,* Princeton.

Gregory, T. E. 2005. *A History of the Byzantine Empire,* Oxford.

Hammer-Purgstall, J. von. 1842. *Histoire de l'empire ottoman depuis son origine jus'qu à nos jours,* Paris.

Jacoby, D. 1989. "From Byzantium to Latin Romania: Continuity and Change," in *Latins and Greeks in the Eastern Mediterranean after 1204,* ed. B. Arbel, B. Hamilton, and D. Jacoby, London, pp. 1–44.

Jennings, R. 1993. *Christians and Muslims in Ottoman Cyprus and the Mediterranean World, 1571–1640,* New York.

Koder, J. 1973. *Negroponte: Untersuchungen zur Topographie und Siedlungsgeschichte der Insel Euboia während der Zeit der Venezianerherrschaft,* Vienna.

Koumanoudi, M., and C. Maltezou. 2003. *Venezia e Cerigo,* Venice.

Lock, P. 1995. *The Franks in the Aegean, 1204–1500,* London.

Miller, W. 1908. *The Latins in the Levant: A History of Frankish Greece (1204–1566),* Cambridge.

———. 1921. *Essays on the Latin Orient,* Cambridge.

Papadia-Lala, A. 2004. *Ο θεσμός των αστικών κοινοτήτων στον ελληνικό χώρο κατά την περίοδο της Βενετοκρατίας (13ος–18ος αι.): Μία συνθετική προσέγγιση,* Venice.

Pitcher, D. E. 1972. *An Historical Geography of the Ottoman Empire,* Leiden.
Ploumidis, G. S. 1985–1992. *Αιτήματα και πραγματικότητες των Ελλήνων της Βενετοκρατίας,* Ioannina.
Setton, K. M. 1991. *Venice, Austria, and the Turks,* Philadelphia.
Shaw, S. J., and E. K. Shaw. 1976–1977. *History of the Ottoman Empire and Modern Turkey,* Cambridge.
Slot, B. J. 1982. *Archipelagus turbatus: Les Cyclades entre colonisation latine et occupation ottomane c. 1500–1718,* 2 vols., Istanbul.
Theunissen, H. 1998. "Ottoman Venetian Diplomatics: The Ahd-names. The Historical Background and the Development of a Category of Political Commercial Instruments Together with an Annotated Edition of a Corpus of Relevant Documents," *Online Journal of Oriental Studies* 1, pp. 1–698. Posted at www2.let.uu.nl/Solis/anpt/ejos/EJOS-I.2.html.
Thiriet, F. 1959. *La Romanie vénitienne au Moyen Âge: Le développement et l'exploitation du domaine colonial vénitien, XIIe–XVe siècles,* Paris.
Vakalopoulos, A. 1973. *Ὁ Ἑλληνισμὸς ὑπὸ ξένη κυριαρχία: Τουρκοκρατία, Λατινοκρατία, 1453–1669, 1669–1821* (Ἱστορία τοῦ Ἑλληνικοῦ Ἔθνους 10–11), Athens.
Zachariadou, E. 1983. *Trade and Crusade: Venetian Crete and the Emirates of Menteshe and Aydin (1300–1415),* Venice.
Zakythinos, D. 1976. *The Making of Modern Greece: From Byzantium to Independence,* trans. K. Johnstone, Totowa, N.J.
Zarinebaf, F., J. Bennet, and J. L. Davis. 2005. *A Historical and Economic Geography of Ottoman Greece: The Southwestern Morea in the 18th Century* (*Hesperia* Suppl. 34), Princeton.

PART I: SOURCES FOR A LANDSCAPE HISTORY OF EARLY MODERN GREECE

A variety of rich source material—much of it newly available—is at the disposal of archaeologists and historians desiring to study Venetian and Ottoman Greece. Although all of the contributors to this volume employ a wide range of evidence (from archival documents in Italy, Turkey, and Greece, to published accounts of travelers and early modern historians, to the material culture retrieved from archaeological excavations and field surveys), the three chapters that constitute Part I illustrate the richness of particular sources of information, all of which have been relatively neglected by social historians and archaeologists until recently.

In Chapter 2, Machiel Kiel introduces new data, here published for the first time, drawn from Turkish archives. The information he provides not only forces us to reconsider opinions about patterns of settlement in the Aegean islands after the Ottoman conquest, but also can be used in tandem with archaeological data to build an integrated picture of settlement and land use in particular places at particular points in time, as we have attempted to do for Kea in the Introduction and as John Bennet does for Kythera in Chapter 10. As Kiel notes, the information he presents here represents only a sample of the wealth of data available in archival sources.

In Chapter 3, Aglaia Kasdagli reprises and updates her pioneering research on locally notarized legal documents from the Greek islands—wills, dowry agreements, land sales, and the like. Although contemporary information from Ottoman taxation registers is gradually becoming available, they were all composed from the perspective of a central Ottoman administration in Istanbul that was concerned principally with the generation of tax revenue. Notarized documents, in contrast, offer us information from the unique, and often very personal, perspective of the subject population that inhabited the Aegean islands. These Greek territories enjoyed considerable autonomy within the Ottoman empire and, unlike areas such as the Peloponnese, maintained local institutions of governance. The rich descriptions of real and movable property, as Kasdagli notes, reflect social conditions that left material consequences in the landscape subject to archaeological documentation.

Finally, in Chapter 4, Joanita Vroom describes the significant developments that have occurred in the past few years in the study of ceramics and other artifacts of the Venetian and Ottoman periods in Greece. Such finds can now be dated with much greater precision than in the past, and substantially more is known about the function of specific types of artifacts in the societies of early modern Greece. One result is that patterns of settlement and land use in the landscapes of early modern Greece can now be reconstructed by archaeologists with much higher chronological resolution than was possible even a decade ago. The enormous progress these developments have made possible is exemplified by the case studies in Boiotia discussed by John L. Bintliff in Chapter 11.

The Smaller Aegean Islands in the 16th–18th Centuries according to Ottoman Administrative Documents

by Machiel Kiel

The empire of the Ottoman Turks was founded by the sword but kept together by the pen. The Turkish archives in Istanbul contain millions of documents and registers concerning every part of this vast military and bureaucratic complex. These records provide a wealth of information for the historian, the historical geographer, and the demographer, as well as the archaeologist. A small fraction pertaining to some of the Sporades and Cyclades, and the island of Kythera, is here presented as "raw material" for further study, as a contribution to a comparative demographic and economic history of these islands.

THE SPORADES BETWEEN 1540 AND 1670

In the "Frankish" Middle Ages, after 1205, the islands of Skyros, Skiathos, Skopelos, and Alonisos (Hiliodromia) belonged to the Venetian Seigneury of the Ghizi.[1] Besides engaging in agriculture, fishing, and shipping, the residents of these islands also were involved in piracy. In the first decades of the 16th century, they had been particularly active in attacking the Ottoman-controlled mainland opposite northern Euboia, in the Lamia-Stylis area, a subject discussed in preserved Ottoman reports.[2] In the 1530s pirates from Skiathos launched an all-out attack on the coast of Locris in the Atalanti area. They slaughtered the Muslims of Atalanti, including the imam of the Balaban Ağa Mosque there, and also carried off as prisoners many inhabitants of places inhabited by Greeks and Albanians near the coast. The record of this little-known event is preserved in an Ottoman tax register, or *tapu tahrir defter* (TT), number 431, p. 480, dating from A.D. 1539/40, in the Başbakanlık Osmanlı Arşivi in Istanbul (BBA), and describing all the settlements of the *sancak* (provincial subdivision) of Eğriboz/Euripos (Euboia).[3] As a result, the signal system on the coast of Locris, from Longos and Livanates to Malesina, was reorganized.[4] In the same years, the monks of the monastery of Galataki near Limni on Euboia, opposite Locris, asked Istanbul's permission to build a fortified tower in their monastery in order to protect themselves better against pirates.[5] The sultanic government, doubtless with the raid against Atalanti in mind, immediately granted this request. The original *fermân* (imperial edict) is preserved in the archive of the monastery.

1. For the pre-Ottoman history of the Sporades, see Loenertz 1975. The "Gazavat-ı Hayreddin Paşa" contains details of the Ottoman military actions of 1537–1538 (see Galotta 1970), as does Haci Chalfa's *History of the Maritime Wars of the Turks* (see Mitchell 1831).

2. These reports are found in the Topkapı Sarayı Archives and were used by Vatin (1994, pp. 294–310, 466–480).

3. Christian dates have been calculated from the Islamic by means of the conversion page of the University of Zurich, posted online at www.ori.unizh.ch/hegira.html.

4. See Kiel and Sauerwein 1994, p. 43, and p. 44, fig. 5, regarding coastal settlement in Eastern (Opuntian) Locris at this time.

5. See Koder 1973, pp. 158–159, concerning the monastery (now a nunnery) of Ayios Nikolaos tou Galataki.

When in 1538 the dreaded Ottoman admiral Hayreddin Barbarossa (son of a Turkish *sipahi* [fief-holder in the cavalry service] from Yenice-i Vardar in Macedonia and a Greek woman from Lesvos/Mytilini) attacked the Sporades, Skiathos was to receive special treatment.[6] The island suffered a violent conquest and its population was said to have been carried off into captivity. The other northern Sporades were apparently taken without resistance. The first statistics at our disposal date to a year and a half after the conquest and are contained in the previously mentioned register, TT431. Descriptions of the islands of Skiathos and Skopelos are included among the settlements of Euboia, to which they were administratively attached. TT431 is in a very bad state of preservation. The writing on some pages has been wholly or partly destroyed by moisture. The binding had been broken and the various pieces of the manuscript were not reassembled correctly. Sections may be missing, but the register has not yet been studied codicologically.

The summary form of the 1539/40 register, the *icmal* (BBA, TT197), is also preserved. On page 4, where the sultanic domains *(hass-ı hümayun)* are enumerated, more islands are mentioned, including islands of the Cyclades, all of which pay a lump sum *(maktuᶜ)* as tax. Their names are here presented in alphabetical order together with the sum of tax levied from each:

Aigina: "has to be revived"
Andros: 35,000 *akçe* in cash (700 Venetian ducats)
Karpathos: 10,000 *akçe* in cash (200 Venetian ducats)
Naxos and dependencies: 3,000 in Frankish gold coins
Skyros: 35,000 *akçe* in cash (700 Venetian ducats)

The next register containing information on the Sporades is TT474 of the *sancak* of Eğriboz from A.H. 977 (1569/70).[7] The growth of population and of the tax burden (in *akçe*) of Skiathos and Skopelos can be followed in the succeeding century in a detailed *tahrir defter* of 1670/1, made after the conclusion of the long Cretan War (*Tapu ve Kadastro Genel Müdürlüğü* [TKGM] 105, in Ankara). It belongs to a series of documents; the part of the series that concerns the six largest islands of the Cyclades is preserved in Istanbul as TT800 and was previously introduced to the scholarly world by the Dutch archivist and historian Benjamin Slot.[8] The document in Ankara also contains data relating to four of the Sporades: Skiathos, Skopelos, Skyros, and Alonisos. The fragmentary *defter* bears the misleading name *Defter-i Cezire-i Taş Özi* (Register of the Island of Thasos), and is dated to A.H. 1081 (May 21, 1670–May 9, 1671).

Besides this *mufassal,* or "detailed" register, there exists a very well-made *icmal* ("synoptic" register; TKGM 180) of TKGM 105 that leaves out the names of the inhabitants but gives agricultural details. The *icmal* has 62 folios, many of which are left blank, clearly to separate entries for different islands. On the first original page, folio 1v, is a systematic list mentioning all of the islands by name, their total number of households, and the total tax to be paid by them on agricultural production.

Table 2.1 summarizes data for 1539/40, 1569/70, and 1670/1. The numbers for 1539/40 are of particular interest. In 1470, according to Giacomo Rizzardo, Skiathos and Skopelos together had 1,200 inhabitants, that is, some 250–270 households in total.[9] In 1538 there must have been more.

6. For the origins of Barbarossa, see Kiel and Karydis 2000.

7. TT474, fols. 37v–42r.

8. Slot 1982, vol. 1, appendix 4: "Les registres fiscaux turcs de Naxos, Paros, Santorin, Milos, Andros et Syros"; see also Slot 2001 regarding Siphnos. Slot was given a microfilm of this document by the director of the Istanbul archives. Other sections of registers that appear to have covered the entire archipelago are scattered in Ankara, but have yet to be used.

9. Rizzardo's list has been published several times, most recently by Topping (1986, pp. 231–232), who characterized its estimates as "informed and reasonable."

TABLE 2.1. HOUSEHOLDS AND TAXATION ON SKIATHOS, SKOPELOS, SKYROS, AND ALONISOS, 1539/40–1670/1

Island	*Households (1539/40)*	*Tax in* Akçe *(1539/40)*	*Households (1569/70)*	*Bachelors (1569/70)*	*Widows (1569/70)*	*Tax in* Akçe *(1569/70)*	*Households (1670/1)*	*Tax in* Akçe *(1670/1)*
Skiathos	82	–	131	37	14	30,000	76	33,411
Skopelos	89	–	60	9	14	8,500	266	213,014
Skyros	310	35,000	440	151	69	50,000	326	207,248
Alonisos	0	0	20	*	*	4,000	87	66,113
Total	481		651			92,500	755	519,786

Note: A dash signifies an illegible entry in the original document, and an asterisk signifies data not recorded in the original document.

William Miller, in his account of Barbarossa's campaign, maintained that both Skiathos and Skopelos were deserted,[10] but, in fact, the figures from 1539/40 show that sufficient people remained on the islands of the Sporades to ensure their economic recovery, and also that Skyros had escaped the ordeal largely unharmed. Barbarossa had not carried off the entire population.

The figures seem to suggest that between 1569/70 and 1670/1 the tax total of the islands rose dramatically, but what we really see is the effect of drastic inflation in the value of the Ottoman silver coin, the *akçe,* after 1585. In 1569/70, the Venetian gold ducat was worth 60 *akçe,* whereas in 1670/1 it was worth 220, or nearly 3.7 times more. Thus in 1569/70 Alonisos paid 200 *akçe* per household, and in 1670/1, 205 *akçe* of the old value. Skopelos paid more: 142 *akçe* per household in 1569/70 and 216 old *akçe* in 1670/1, which probably reflects a rise in production rather than a higher tax rate. It should be added that, in the 1670/1 register, it is indicated at the beginning of the description of each island that *ḫumus-i ğillât* (one-fifth of the harvest) was taken as tax. In 1569/70 the average household of the four islands paid a total tax of 142 *akçe.* On the island of Euboia, and on the mainland of Attica, Boiotia, and Locris, many villages paid more, depending on the size of their agricultural production.

The numbers of households on the four islands in Table 2.1, when compared to Rizzardo's numbers for 1470, show a remarkable degree of recovery and expansion in spite of the severe trials of 1538 and the strain of the Cretan War. Such a picture seems more realistic than the one sketched by Miller and repeated by those who have followed him.

KYTHERA (CERIGO/ÇUKA ADASI) UNDER THE OTTOMANS

The period during which the island of Kythera, known to the Latin West as Cerigo and to the Ottomans as Çuka or Çuha Adası, belonged to the Ottoman Empire was but a brief interlude in its long history—three years in total (1715–1718), a period about which very little is known.

Kythera/Çuka is a relatively large island. Its surface area of 280 km^2 falls between that of two of the largest of the Cyclades, Naxos (430 km^2) and Paros (196 km^2). Kythera was often described by travelers as particularly mountainous, stony, and infertile,[11] yet all over the island there exist areas of land where agriculture is possible. The absence of an excellent harbor

10. Miller 1908, pp. 628–630.
11. Broodbank, Bennet, and Davis 2004; see also the comments of Ottoman administrators discussed later in this chapter.

or anchorage, which would have encouraged its development as a center of shipping, afforded it some protection against enemy raids. At the same time its geographical position, between the southeastern tip of the Morea and the northwestern promontory of Crete, gave it command over this singularly important sea lane linking the central and eastern parts of the Mediterranean. This is why a naval power such as Venice took pains to dominate the island for many centuries. Kythera was first controlled by indirect rule, via the Venetian family of the Venieri (from 1207), then by direct rule from 1363 to 1797 (with power shared between Venice and the Venier family from 1393), until the very end of the existence of Venice as an independent state.

Under Venetian rule the island supported a relatively large population. The list of Rizzardo from 1470 contains, to the best of my knowledge, the oldest known population numbers for the island.[12] In the course of the 16th century, the Venetians tried on several occasions to increase the population of Kythera by settling colonists from elsewhere. This policy, and a healthy natural increase, elevated the population from 1,850 in 1545 to 7,500 in 1620.[13]

Various Ottoman attacks on the island, the most serious being that of Barbarossa in 1537 during the Venetian-Ottoman war, did not fundamentally alter the upward trend of the island's population. Similarly, the expedition of the admiral Kılıç Ali Pasha in 1580 had no lasting effect, and, during the Cretan War of 1645–1669, Ottoman naval actions were severely curtailed by the Western fleets. All action was concentrated on the long siege of Candia/Iraklion. During the Ottoman reconquest of the Morea, in June 1715, however, the Ottoman fleet under admiral Canım Hoca Haci Mehmed Pasha (in office 1714–1717, 1731, and 1733–1736) succeeded not only in retaking Aigina and finally conquering Tinos (İstendil), but also in capturing Cerigo/Çuka Adası.

What the Ottomans did on the island (besides removing a group of 1,000 people as prisoners), or what they planned to do, has been completely unknown until now. They had evidently come to stay, as the surviving documents demonstrate. When in 1718, however, peace was made at Passarowitz with Venice and its European allies, the Ottomans succeeded in retaining the Morea but had to surrender Çuka Adası. It was to remain Venice's sole outpost in the Aegean until the end of the Serenissima, as marked by the Treaty of Campo Formio in 1797.

In the four years that the Ottomans were masters of the island they tried to lay the foundations for fair rule, based on local autonomy and just taxation. The story of their actions is recorded in an apparently unique manuscript, preserved in a little used and badly catalogued section of the Ankara archive that is, because of its condition, rarely consulted by researchers. The document, catalogued as TKGM, *Vakf* 128, contains 82 pages, each 44 × 16 cm, enclosed in a cover of marbled *(ebru)* boards; the pages are numbered as folios. Ink and paper are preserved in such an excellent state that it appears as if the text had been written only yesterday.

The description of the inhabitants of the island and their agricultural products (fol. 1) is preceded by the copy of a sultanic order to Ali Efendi, the secretary of the Department of Finances *(Maliye Tezkireci)*, that explains how a census on the newly conquered island should be conducted. The order is dated to the "middle ten days of Ramazan 1127" (mid-September 1715).

12. Koder 1972, pp. 232–233.

13. Information concerning the island's population was collected by Richard Leonhard in his excellent monograph (Leonhard 1899). See now Maltezou 1997 for much more detailed statistics from Venetian censuses for the 18th century, and Leontsinis [1987] 2000, pp. 192–211, esp. pp. 193–194 (table 1), for 19th-century figures.

An agent of admiral Canım Hoca had reported to Constantinople that, as was the practice on other nearby islands, it would be good to take all taxes together as one lump sum *(maktuᶜ)*. The Kapudan Pasha (naval commander) also reported that, like the island of Thermia (Kythnos) and others, Çuka Adası was stony and mountainous. Places where agriculture was possible were limited, as were other means of making a livelihood. Therefore, the islanders should not be asked to pay the *ᶜavarız* (extraordinary dues and services used to meet emergency expenses) and the similarly unpopular *nüzûl* tax (provisioning an army on campaign).

The order further explains that the land was not yet registered by the Ottomans, and the precise economic situation of the inhabitants was not known. Ali Efendi, therefore, is instructed to calculate the poll tax not on the basis of the number of adult males (as is required by Islamic law, *shariᶜa*) to whom poll-tax tickets *(evrak)* are given, but, as on other islands, as a lump sum consisting, per household, of three gold coins *(guruş)*, each worth 100 *akçe*, plus cash payments of 60 *akçe* and one *guruş* as tax on their agricultural production. This measure would have cost the imperial treasury a considerable amount of money, since, following the great tax reform of 1691, all adult male non-Muslims of the empire, married or unmarried, had been taxed. Depending on the age structure of the population, this meant that in the case of Kythera one-third fewer people had to pay (see below). For Çuka Adası, the Porte waived its claim to this extra money because of its compassion for the population of the island, so the order notes.

Ali Efendi is instructed to register individually by name the entire adult male population, both those settled and those without fixed residence, whether living in the town or in the villages of the island, and to register carefully the fields, gardens, vineyards, orchards, houses, mills, *çiftlik*s, and fruit-bearing trees. A separate register was to be made listing only the names of the heads of household. The poll tax, together with the tithes on the agricultural production, was to be collected every year by the Kapudan Pasha.

The register ends with a petition, in the form of a report, that asks the sultan to decide to implement the preceding policy. The petition is dated 22 *Rebi ül-Ahir* of the year 1128 (April 15, 1716). The registration of the island's population and all of its agricultural resources was thus completed between mid-September 1715 and mid-April 1716.

On the following 56 pages (fols. 2a–28a) of the register, all the settlements of the island, including the adult male population and its agricultural production, are described individually under the title *Defter-i cezire-i Ada-i Çuka*. The descriptions begin with the *nefs-i kalᶜe-i Çuka* (the castle of Çuka proper), which contains 91 adult males, of whom 60 are heads of household. Next is listed the *varoş* or "open town" *(borgo)* of the castle, consisting of 247 adult males, of whom 161 are heads of household, and a separate group of 8 people who have a privileged status and pay no taxes at all. What then follows are descriptions of 28 villages in the district of Livadi, the town of Mylopotamos and 9 villages in the district, the town of Kastrisianika and 11 villages in its district, and, finally, the borough of Potamos, and 7 other villages. From folio 28b to the end of the register, folio 41b, the households are listed one by one, with the heads recorded first, and then the names of unmarried adult males who live in them—in practice the sons of the heads, as their patronymics indicate.

TABLE 2.2. SOURCES DATING 1470–1981 FOR THE POPULATION OF KYTHERA

Year	*Source*	*Number of Inhabitants*	
1470	Rizzardo (Topping 1986, p. 234)	500	
1545	Quirini (Leonhard 1899, p. 34)	1,850	
1553	Quirini (Leonhard 1899, p. 34)	3,300	
1578	Castrofilaca (Leonhard 1899, p. 35)	3,161	
1590	Leonhard 1899, p. 35	4,000	
1620	Leonhard 1899, p. 35	7,500	
1715/6	Ottoman *tahrir*	5,600–6,000	(+ "1,000" deportees)
1724	Maltezou 1997, vol. 1, p. 222	5,046	
1753	Maltezou 1997, vol. 1, p. 340	5,508	
1760	Maltezou 1997, vol. 1, p. 481	6,347	
1765	Leonhard 1899, p. 35	6,183	
1770	Maltezou 1997, vol. 2, p. 139	6,029	
1772	Maltezou 1997, vol. 2, p. 261	5,021	
1784	Maltezou 1997, vol. 2, p. 418	6,958	
1788	Maltezou 1997, vol. 2, p. 586	7,425	
1826	Davy (1842, p. 37)	13,020	(questionably high)
1836	Kirckwall (Leonhard 1899, p. 37)	12,781	(questionably high)
1858	Kirckwall (Leonhard 1899, p. 37)	13,497	(questionably high)
1878	Leonhard (1899, p. 37)	13,529	
1889	Leonhard (1899, p. 37)	10,920	
1928	Chouliarakis (1988, p. 33)	9,092	
1940	Chouliarakis (1988, p. 33)	8,178	
1951	Chouliarakis (1988, p. 33)	6,507	
1961	Chouliarakis (1988, p. 33)	5,510	
1971	Chouliarakis (1988, p. 33)	4,102	
1981	Εθνική Στατιστική Υπηρεσία της Ελλάδος	3,469	

In addition to the 8 privileged individuals who paid no taxes, there were 1,652 adult males on the island, of whom 1,139 were heads of household. Such figures yield a total of approximately 5,600–6,000 inhabitants of the island, depending on the multiplier one uses, and a population density of 21 or 22 inhabitants per km^2. Fewer than half this number live on the island today.

A sequence of population numbers from the 15th century to recent times would provide a framework for the history of the island. Therefore, I present in Table 2.2 a list of hard numbers, as collected by Leonhard, that have been enriched with data from Ottoman sources and Venetian and modern Greek censuses.

The total agricultural production of the island, calculated on the basis of the numbers provided in the register of 1715/6, is presented in Table 2.3. Although the agricultural production of the villages of Kythera is given in great detail, it is difficult to convert the metrical units used into kilograms because the Ottoman document records tithes in local measures, the values of which are not always clearly understood. The unit for cereals, for example, is given as *muzur,* for flax and cotton, *ledre,* for olive oil, *kilinder;* that for grape must is a unit that cannot be read. There are other problems with the register; for example, 60 *akçe* were levied per head of sheep, but the number of sheep (only 197 animals) appears implausible. In Table 2.3, I have simply

TABLE 2.3. AGRICULTURAL PRODUCTION AND TAXATION ON THE ISLAND OF KYTHERA, 1715/6

Product	*Units*	*Price per Unit* (Akçe)	*Total Value* (Akçe)	*Tax as Percentage of Total Value*
Wheat	524 *muzur*	40	20,960	30
Barley	335 *muzur*	30	10,050	14
Mixed grain	362 *muzur*	30	10,860	16
Olive oil	360 *kilinder*	30	10,800	16
Grape must	650 [illegible]	20	13,000	19
Flax	271 *ledre*	5	1,355	2
Cotton	57 *ledre*	10	570	1
Beehives	58 items	25	1,450	2

set out figures as recorded and, after computing their value in *akçe,* have tried to reconstruct an overview of the agricultural structure of the island by calculating the percentage of tax derived from each source.

The three cereals together give a tithe of 1,221 *muzur.* Assuming the "tithe" to be one-fifth *(ḫumus-i ğillât),* as is written in the register, the total harvest of Kythera would have amounted to 6,105 *muzur.* On other Aegean islands a *muzur* is sometimes said to be the same size as the *binek* or *pinaki* of 38 liters, but employing such an equivalency for Kythera yields a total cereal production of only 238,095 kg, or 209 kg of cereals per household.[14] Asdrachas has suggested that 200 kg of cereals would have been required per individual per year, in addition to 59 kg for seed and 36 kg for tax, a total of about 300 kg per individual.[15] The World Food Organization also employs the figure of 200 kg of cereals per year as the minimum required to feed an individual. Therefore, a family of four or five that was entirely dependent on grain would need 1,200–1,500 kg of cereals per year, five times more than our calculations suggest.

We may perhaps conclude that Ali Efendi, who was ordered to apply *istimalet,* "meeting the other halfway" or "compromise," recorded the tithe of the island as lower than it actually was. We cannot know, and there are other possibilities. It may be that grain production was genuinely low and that islanders survived on a more diversified diet, as seems to have been the case on some Cycladic islands (see below).[16] Another possibility is that the value of the *muzur* on Kythera was much larger than 38 kg, as it appears to have been on Naxos.[17]

By way of comparison with the Ottoman figures, it is worth noting that wheat and barley were sometimes insufficient for the needs of the local population in the 17th century. Coronelli, in his *Description géographique et historique de la Morée,* noted that the island produced little and exported nothing.[18] Such a deficiency has not been the situation in more recent times. Ansted in 1863 mentioned that 77,000 bushels (ca. 28,000 hectoliters) of cereals (for the most part maize) were harvested on the island.[19] Leonhard noted that 400,000 *okka* of wine were produced in 1896 and that, in 1835, an area of 207 hectares had yielded 465 barrels of olive oil (76,000 liters).[20] In 1860, some 5,000 pounds (ca. 2,273 kg) of flax were grown.[21] Finally, Lehmann states that in 1977 the island produced 800 metric tons of olive oil, 90 of almonds, 35 of honey, and had 7,000 sheep, 4,500 goats, 3,000 pigs, and 300 cows.[22]

14. Slot 1982, vol. 1, pp. 295–296, vol. 2, p. 442; see also Petropoulos 1952, pp. 68–69, where the *muzur* is assigned even smaller values, equivalent to 20 *okka* of wheat or 12 *okka* of barley.
15. Asdrachas 1978, p. 90, p. 285, n. 33; see also McGowan 1969; Clark and Haswell 1964, p. 54 (210 kg of unmilled grain per individual as a subsistence minimum in a diet entirely dependent on grain).
16. Studies of Greek diet reviewed by Foxhall and Forbes (1982, pp. 65–68) note that grain at times has supplied less than half the calories required in the diet of modern rural populations; on Crete, actual measured consumption rates of grain in 1947–1948 were only 128 kg per person (Allbaugh 1953, p. 107).
17. On that island, Kasdagli (1999, p. 411) considers the *muzur* to have been equivalent to six *pinakia/binek* of eight *okka* each (ca. 60 kg).
18. Coronelli 1687, p. 180.
19. Ansted 1863, p. 474.
20. Leonhard 1899, p. 38, n. 4, and p. 39.
21. Leonhard 1899, p. 39.
22. Lehmann 1980, p. 160.

TABLE 2.4. POPULATIONS AND TAXATION IN THE WESTERN CYCLADES, 1470–1734/5

	Households (1470)	*Households (1569/70)*	*Bachelors* (1569/70)*	*Widows (1569/70)*	*Poll Tax† (1569/70)*	*Households (1670/1)*	*Poll Tax† (1670/1)*	*Individuals (1734/5)*	*Households (1734/5)*
Kea	60–70	86	–	10	15,000	220	179,783	550	440‡
Kythnos	40‡	50	10	2	5,000	296	186,245	335	268‡
Seriphos	40–45	46	9	2	6,666	101	52,833	230	184‡
Siphnos	200–220	350‡	–	–	12,000	414	138,971	510	408‡
Total	340–375	532			38,666	1,031	557,832	1,625	1,300‡

Note: A dash signifies illegible data in the original document.

*Bachelors are *mücerred,* unmarried young men; individuals *(nefer)* represent the total number of heads of household and unmarried young men. In the original document, Kea is called Mürted and Kythnos is called Thermi.

†Taxes are in *akçe.*

‡Figures represent reconstructed household numbers.

THE WESTERN CYCLADES

The 1569/70 *tahrir* of the *sancak* of Eğriboz also contains information that pertains to the four western islands of the Cyclades. In combination with figures reported by Rizzardo for 1470, data from the 1670/1 register, and information from a poll-tax register, *Kepeci* 2888 (BBA), from A.H. 1147 (1734/5),[23] a general outline of the demographic development of Kea, Kythnos, Seriphos, and Siphnos has been reconstructed in Table 2.4.[24]

The data from 1569/70 are of interest because, in the case of Kea, they confirm Slot's conclusion that Cornaro and Da Millo's reports that the island was depopulated in the 16th century must be regarded with caution.[25] In 1569/70, Kea was certainly not deserted. It recovered vigorously, suffered again during the Cretan War (this time at the hands of the Venetians), but then continued to increase in population. Seriphos, like Kea and Kythnos, was "visited" by Barbarossa in 1537, but by 1569/70 it also had rebounded to a considerable extent.

The Economy of Siphnos

There are no contemporary data from the 16th century that concern the island of Siphnos. The 1569/70 register for the *sancak* of Eğriboz has, however, a brief but interesting remark:

> cezire-i Sifnoz hassa-i müşar alehi, tabi-i Eğriboz
> hasil fi sene 12,000
> Bundḳânîleri ḫavafından rencide olan ahalisi gelüb tahrir olunmağa aḳdarları olmamağın ber vech-i icmal ḳayd olundı

> Island of Siphnos, domain of the aforementioned [Ali Pasha], dependency of Eğriboz, yearly revenue 12,000 *[akçe];* the inhabitants, who had suffered from the terror of the Venetians, came to us. Because a *tahrir* has not [yet] been made and their situation is, therefore, not known, they have been noted only in a summary manner.

23. *Kepeci* 2888 is a register of 55 pages of finely polished paper, now covered by a modern card binding; the original leather binding is preserved inside, adorned with a gilded *şemsiye* (sun symbol). The text is superbly well preserved but is written in very small characters. The introductory notes state explicitly that a new registration has been made and also give the number of days that the census commission spent on each island.

24. Where there are gaps in our information (for Kythnos in 1470 and for Siphnos in 1569/70), estimates have been supplied: 40 for Kythnos in 1470, 350 for Siphnos in 1569/70. The exact numbers might differ slightly but general trends will not be affected. For 1734/5, a conservative estimate of 20% unmarried adult males, a figure characteristic of slow-growing populations in general, has been subtracted from the number of *nefer* (individuals) recorded, in order to estimate the number of households.

25. Slot 1982, vol. 1, pp. 281–282.

TABLE 2.5. TAXATION ON PRINCIPAL CROPS PRODUCED ON SIPHNOS, 1670/1

Crop	*Percentage of Total Tax*
Wine	62
Grains	20
Olive trees	6
Cotton	6
Beans	4
Sheep	2

Here we have a nice example of "the empire strikes back" in the unending propaganda war of those times. The note seems to indicate that the inhabitants of Siphnos placed themselves under Ottoman protection, although until 1617 the administration of the island remained in the hands of their Latin seigneurs of the House of Gozzadini.[26] In the second half of the 17th century and the first half of the 18th, the island of Siphnos had roughly the same population as in recent times (ca. 2,000).

In 1670/1 the island had four sizeable villages, four Greek Orthodox monasteries with 18 monks total, one *metochi* (monastic property) of an Athonite monastery, and one Latin Christian monastery with one monk (Papa Françesko). Curiously enough, the *defter* mentions that the small monasteries of Ayo Yani Theologo (Ayios Ioannis Theologos Monkou) and Chrysostomo were "in the hands of the widows of the monks" *(der yed-i bivehâ-i keşiş);* both were nunneries, in fact, and this must explain such a colorful circumlocution![27] The richest monastery was that of the Panayia "Mavromyrthe," which paid a tax of 5,600 *akçe.*[28] Monastic property on Siphnos was, therefore, but an unimportant fraction of the total. All of Siphnos paid 138,971 *akçe* as tax; the five monasteries paid only 9,330 *akçe,* or less than 7% of the total.

The data in the register also allow us to reconstruct roughly the island's economy. Taken together, the four villages (Kastro with 122 households, Stavro [Stavri] with 86, Artamona [Artemon] with 71, and Afşa Milo [apparently Exambela] with 135) had 2,042 olive trees, 1,020 fig trees, 100 beehives, 24 windmills, 19 olive presses, and 810 head of sheep.[29] The total tax on wheat, barley, mixed grains, beans, cotton, olive trees, sheep, and wine was 89,492 *akçe.* This is distributed as shown in Table 2.5, reflecting the structure of the island's production and economy.

The Economy of Kea/Mürted in 1670/1

Some have believed that Ottoman population and taxation registers for many Cycladic islands are not preserved; for Kea, a local Greek record from 1770 is, in fact, the oldest published taxation register for that island.[30] We do, however, find the island not only in the register of 1569/70 for the *sancak* of Eğriboz, but also in the *mufassal defter,* TKGM 105, and in the *icmal,* TKGM 180. For Kea, on folios 40r–40v of the *icmal* are recorded the total number of households, and complete information regarding agricultural production of the islanders and of its four monasteries and two *metochia.*[31]

26. Slot 1982, vol. 1, pp. 113–115; more in Hopf 1818–1889.

27. Symeonidis (1990, p. 203) describes these places.

28. The reading of the epithet of the Virgin, apparently "Mavromyrthe," is uncertain and cannot obviously be identified with any known institution on the island. Panayia sti Vrisi ("at the spring") was the most prosperous of the monasteries of this date that is attested in Greek and Western sources.

29. See TKGM 180, fols. 25v–27r; Slot (2001) had at his disposal Ottoman data for only the first three of the four villages.

30. Psyllas 1921, pp. 312–313.

31. The monasteries are all familiar from Greek sources, and include Ayia Marina near Mylopotamos, Episkopi near Chora (Ioulis, at present), Ayia Anna near Chora, and Dafni near Chora. The *metochia* are Ayios Panteleimon at Ellinika and Ayios Efstathios; the latter no longer exists, but according to local tradition it was founded by monks from Andros at Chora (Psyllas 1921, p. 198). Psyllas (1921, p. 190) implies that income from the property of Ayios Panteleimon was first presented by the islanders to Patmos in the 19th century, but this tradition seems to be contradicted by the Ottoman document.

This information is nearly identical with that on folios 91–100 of the *mufassal.* In Appendix 1 I provide a transcription of the entire taxation section of the *mufassal* in Latin characters. Parts of the *mufassal* give more information about the monastic property than is included in the *icmal.* A transcription of the relevant text is presented in Appendix 2.

The information in Appendixes 1 and 2 may serve as the basis for an approximate reconstruction of the island's economy as expressed by the monetary value of each product. As on other islands in the Cyclades, one-fifth of the harvest was taken as a "tithe." Because income from most products is derived from three different groups—Christian households, Muslim households, and monastic property—the figures for each product are presented in this order in Table 2.6, which enables the reader to see immediately the proportional importance of the production of each group.

The figures in Table 2.6 suggest that the number of Muslims on the island was limited to a few families, perhaps no more than a half-dozen, of poor crofters (their total production was valued at only 1,588 *akçe*). The figures also show that on Kea the monasteries did not play a large role in the island's economy. Only a little more than 5% of the tax on the three cereals and 7% of the tax on grape must came from the monasteries.

It may come as a surprise that *velanidi* (Ottoman *palamud,* English "acorn caps"), in some periods a major export product of the island, represented only about 10% of the tax.[32] In addition to *velanidi,* Pitton de Tournefort mentions figs as important, but it is clear that in 1670/1 wine and cereals were the major products of Kea.[33]

The metric equivalent of the local measure of capacity for cereals, *axagi,* seems clear, and various threads of evidence suggest that it was equal to one-half of a *kile* of 22 *okka* of wheat, 15 *okka* of mixed grains, or 12 *okka* of barley.[34] Therefore, an *axagi* of barley would have been approximately equivalent to 6 *okka* (ca. 8 kg). A will of 1796 confirms a value of this order.[35] The text of the will requires the executor (the son-in-law of the deceased) to provide for his mother-in-law one-half *axagi* of barley flour per week, or 30 *axagia* (180 *okka,* ca. 230 kg) of barley per year. The latter figure appears to be the notional amount that the author of the will imagines his wife will require, since it is specified that she will receive it only if she is living alone.[36]

Since TKGM 105 records 4,301 *axagia* of all grains as tax (20% of the harvest), the total harvest of Kea may be estimated as about 21,500 *axagia.* Given the 220 Christian households and eight monks recorded in the *defter,* we might imagine that some 900–1,050 individuals resided on the island in 1670/1 (assuming a family size of 4–4.75). There can have been no substantial surplus production of grain.

The fact that the 529 *axagia* of wheat produced by Christians was taxed at a value of 8,992 *akçe* presumes a value of ca. 17 *akçe* per *axagi.* In the later 17th century a *kile* of wheat (ca. 22 *okka* in weight) was selling in Istanbul for between 50 and 80 *akçe.*[37] On Kea, an Istanbul *kile* would have been equal to about 2 *axagia* of 11 *okka;* the value of an *axagi* of wheat in the *defter* therefore was equivalent to about 34 *akçe* per *kile,* considerably lower than it was in cosmopolitan markets.

32. Bennet and Voutsaki 1991, p. 376; Whitelaw 1991, pp. 447–449.

33. On figs, see Tournefort 1717, pp. 334–335, 338–340.

34. Petropoulos 1952, pp. 71–72 (with reference to Euboia). Although elsewhere in the Aegean the measure could be considerably smaller, in Kea older residents of the island still evaluate the size of fields in *axagia* (the amount of seed required to sow a field), and describe the *axagi,* when a measure of capacity, as a *miso-kile* (i.e., a half-*kile*), as in nearby Euboia. I am grateful to Evi Gorogianni for this information.

35. Psyllas 1921, p. 326, no. 362.

36. Figures published by Foxhall and Forbes (1982, pp. 75–81) suggest that a given measure of whole hulled barley will yield, even after grinding, winnowing, and sifting, about 70% of its volume in barley flour.

37. Mantran 1962, p. 273.

TABLE 2.6. VALUE OF PRODUCTS, AND RELIGIOUS AFFILIATIONS OF PRODUCERS, ON KEA, 1670/1

Product	*Religious Affiliation*	*Value in* Akçe
Wheat	Christian	8,992
	Muslim	153
	Monastic	720
Mixed grains	Christian	10,160
	Muslim	276
	Monastic	516
Barley	Christian	21,192
	Muslim	216
	Monastic	1,072
Cowpeas	Christian	288
	Muslim	16
	Monastic	20
Broad beans	Christian	960
	Muslim	36
	Monastic	193
Vetch	Christian	1,141
	Muslim	21
	Monastic	190
Garden tax	Christian	2,500
	Muslim	–
	Monastic	110
Cotton	Christian	792
	Muslim	–
	Monastic	178
Olive oil	Christian	608
	Muslim	15
	Monastic	202
Fruit and figs	Christian	4,570
	Muslim	25
	Monastic	254
Silk cocoons	Christian	6,000
	Muslim	–
	Monastic	200
Beehives	Christian	904
	Muslim	2
	Monastic	110
Flax	Christian	240
Velanidi (acorn caps)	Christian	15,400
Grape must	Christian	65,394
	Muslim	828
	Monastic	5,008
Fish weir	Christian	550
Sheep	Christian	7,005
	Muslim	–
	Monastic	200
Pigs	Christian	300
Mills (total 11)		480
Total		158,037

Note: A dash signifies that no information was recorded in the original document.

TABLE 2.7. TAXATION ON VARIOUS COMMODITIES PRODUCED BY VILLAGES ON SERIPHOS AND AT THE MONASTERY OF THE TAXIARCHI, 1670/1

Product	*Location*	*Tax in* Akçe	*Percentage*
Wheat	Village	2,170	5.5
	Monastery	106	
Barley	Village	3,612	9.1
	Monastery	152	
Mixed grains	Village	3,200	8.0
	Monastery	120	
Subtotal of cereals		9,297	22.6
Cowpeas	Village	808	2.1
	Monastery	48	
Vetch	Village	588	2.8
	Monastery	552	
Flax	Village	480	1.2
Fruits and figs	Village	520	1.5
	Monastery	100	
Sheep	Village	1,720	4.8
	Monastery	264	
Grape must	Village	25,227	65.0
	Monastery	1,858	
Total		41,525	100.0

Note: The right-hand column indicates the percentage of the total tax levied on a commodity produced by the villages and the monastery combined.

The Economy of Seriphos

Finally, TKGM 105 in Ankara presents us with information about the economy of the island of Seriphos in 1670/1. The island is half the size of Kea (73 km^2 vs. 131 km^2) and is stony, arid, and poor. Its impoverished state is clearly reflected in the area of arable land *(tarla)* recorded in the *defter.* Kea has 10,242 *axagia* of *tarla,* Seriphos only 1,778. Seriphos, however, has a much higher proportion of gardens and vineyards: 1,430 *axagia* on Kea versus 627 on Seriphos, numbers that reflect the great importance of viticulture for the island.[38]

Seriphos had one important monastery, that of the Taxiarchi. With 15 monks, it was one of the most populous in the Cyclades. The monastery was founded around 1600 when the island was still under the administration of the Gozzadini.[39] By the second half of the 18th century it had become the greatest landowner on the island, and the compound today preserves 60 cells for monks, attesting its former importance. By 1980, however, only one monk lived in the entire building.

Divided among the 101 households of the island and the monastery with its 15 monks, products of the island are expressed in Table 2.7 in terms of the monetary value of the tax on a "tithe" of one-fifth of the harvest.

It is clear that in 1670/1 the monastery was still far from being the principal economic factor on the island. Only 4% of the cereals were produced on the monastic lands, and only 3.5% of the arable land belonged

38. On this aspect of the economy of the island, see Liata 1987; Davis 1991, pp. 174–193, 197. In these instances, *axagi* refers to the extent of the land that could be sown with a measure of grain of this size.

39. For the date of its founding, see Evangelidis 1909, p. 132.

to it. This picture contrasts strongly with that reflected in detailed local records of the later 18th century.[40]

In the case of Seriphos, we know from local sources that the capacity measure used on the island, the *pinaki,* or *binek* as it is written in Ottoman sources, was equivalent to 8 *okka* of wheat.[41] The island would have produced 5 × 996.5 *binek* as a total harvest of the three cereals grown there, or 4,982.5 *binek* × 10.24 kg = 51,021 kg of cereals—a maximum of only 505 kg per household, since a *pinaki* of mixed grain or barley would have weighed considerably less than one of wheat.

It must have been the great wine production that made life bearable for the roughly 500 inhabitants of Seriphos. A second significant source of income would have been the 992 sheep (almost 10 per household). With regard to the monastery, it is important to note that the uninhabited little island of Serphopoula, 8 km northeast of the main island, was worked by the monks of the Taxiarchi Monastery. They paid 60 *akçe* as tax for its small area of agricultural land, 100 *akçe* as tax for fruits and figs, and 264 *akçe* as tax for sheep. Sheep were taxed at two *akçe* per head; therefore it can be calculated that the monks grazed 132 sheep there.

CONCLUSION

The new data offered in this chapter should, of course, be compared with those of other islands, and with the information given by travelers, especially the valuable account of Pitton de Tournefort, who traveled to the Levant in 1700. To identify and transcribe all of the information scattered in the Turkish archives that might be useful for composing a history of the Aegean islands in Ottoman times, and to process it in an appropriate format, would take years of painstaking work, but would certainly be worthwhile, as I hope is demonstrated by this brief introduction to the sources.

40. Liata 1987; Davis 1991, pp. 174–193.
41. Liata 1987, p. 137, n. 17; cf. Petropoulos 1952, pp. 66, 70.

APPENDIX 1

TRANSCRIPTION OF FOLIOS 40R–40V OF MUFASSAL REGISTER TKGM 105 REGARDING THE TAXATION OF KEA, 1670/1

Note: TKGM 105 contains names of Christian residents on the island of Kea, descriptions of their property, and indications of the sizes of their harvests; similar information is recorded for owners living elsewhere, for monks, and for Muslims. The transcription omits some clichés that are repetitive in the document.

[Defter-i harac-i arazi-i zimmiyân-i cezire-i Mürted der Livâ-i Cezair ba emr-i şerif-i ᶜali tahrir şüdde fi 20 Safer sene 1081][1]

Ḥaṣṣa [Kapudan Paşa]

tarla, aḳṣâya	bağ, aḳṣâya	esçâr-i zeytun	esçâr-i incir
9,792	1,297½	aded 206	aded 1,290

esçar-i meyve	asyâb-i mîrî	asyâb al-ᶜame	esçâr-i dut
aded 340	6 bâb	5 bâb	aded 316

Ḥâṣilât, humus-i ğillât

İspence, ḫâne	ḥinṭa, aḳṣâya	maḫlût, aḳṣâya	şaᶜir, aḳṣâya
220	529	847	2,649
baha 5,500	baha 8,992	baha 10,160	baha 21,192

böğrülce, aḳṣâya	baḳla, aḳṣâya	fîk, aḳṣâya	resm-i bostân
18	60	61½	132
baha 288	baha 960	baha 1,141	baha 792

pembe, . . .	maḥsulât-i revğân-i zeyt	maḳtuᶜ-i ᶜöşr-i esçar-i
132	608	fi sene 3,870
baha 792		

maḥṣûlât-i esçâr-i meyve-i saire	resm-i gögül, ledre	resm-i küvare
700	50	baha 904
	baha 6,000	

resm-i gerdek	kesm-i tapu-i	resm-i esçâr-i palamud
baha 300	zemin maᶜ destiban	ḳanṭâr 350
	baha 2,000	baha 15,400

1. This heading is supplied by the *icmal,* TKGM 180.

resm-i ketan, 20 . . .	maḥṣûlat-i bağat gayr ez-müslümanan ve manastıran
baha 240	şire, mestâne 3,633 . . . 32,697, baha 65,394

asyab-i abi, bab 4, harab	maḥṣûlât-i mandra-i
asyab-i abi, bab 5, baha 120	500

resm-i . . . -i mahi der uhde-i cezire-i mezbûr 550

otlaḳ-i ağnâm muḳabele-i ḫarac-i arazi
7,000

maḳtu ʿat-i bahçe fi sene 50	bid ʿat-i hınzır maʿ božik
resm-i asyab-i badi, bab 6, baha 360	baha 300
asyab-i badi harab, bab 2	

bâd-i havva ve cürm-i cinâyet ve beyt ül-mal . . .
maʿ gömrük-i iskele ber vech-i emanet
fi sene 8,000

YEKÛN 163,320 [Akçe]

Muteṣarrifât-i arâzi ez-ḫaric yekûn

tarla aḳṣâya	bağ	bostan	esçâr-i meyve-i müterevvia	esçâr-i incir
70½	10	½	adet 6	adet 3

Ḥâṣilât, ḥumus-i ğillât

ḥinṭa aḳṣâya 5	maḫlût, aḳṣâya 11	ṣaʿir, aḳṣâya 11	baḳla, aḳṣâya 1
baha 85	baha 132	baha 88	baha 16

bostan 20 maktu-i ʿöṣr-i esçâr-i meyve-i
sayre maʿ incir ve gayri
fi sene 30

mahsul-i bağat şire mestâne 28 . . .
baha 504

YEKÛN
875

Muteṣarrifât-i arâzi-i müslümanân der cezire-i mezbûr [3 *zemin*s of Muslims]

tarla, aḳṣâyî	bağ	esçâr-i meyve-i saire	esçâr-i incir
220	23	aded 8	aded 11

esçâr-i meyve	kovan	asıyâb-i bâdî	asıyâb-i abî
aded 5	aded 1	bâb 1	bâb 1

Ḥâṣilât, ḥumus-i ğillât min el-sebʿî

resm-i bennâk	ḥinṭa, aḳṣâya 9	maḫlût, aḳṣâya 23	ṣaʿir, aḳṣâya 27
36	baha 153	baha 276	baha 216

baḳla, aḳṣâya 1	fik, aḳṣâya 1½	böğrülce, aḳṣâya 1	meyve ve incir
baha 16	baha 21	baha 16	25

resm-i zeytun	resm-i küvâra	asıyâb-i bâdî	asıyâb-i âbî
baha 15	baha 2	aded 1 fî 60	aded 1 fî 60

mahsûlât-i bağat-i şire, mestâne 46 bağçe 75 incir ve meyve 24
baha 828

Maktuᶜat-i manastırân

Manastır-i Aya Marina Manastır-i Panaya Peskopi
5,100 [Akçe] 2,600 [Akçe]

Manastır Aya Anna Manastır-i Panaya Astirdafi[?]
2,300 [Akçe] 1,440 [Akçe]

Metoh-i Ayo Estatio Metoh-i Ayo Pandeleymon
320 [Akçe] 1,400 [Akçe]

[maktuᶜat-i cezire-i Bibercik der kurb-i Mürted, halî ez-reᶜayet, der uhde-i ahâli-i cezire-i mezbûr ber vech-i maktuᶜ fî sene 600][2]

YEKÛN 197,783

2. This closing statement is supplied by the *icmal,* TKGM 180.

APPENDIX 2

TRANSCRIPTION OF PARTS OF MUFASSAL REGISTER TKGM 105 PERTAINING TO THE PROPERTY OF THE MONASTERIES OF KEA, 1670/1

Manastır-i Aya Marina, raḥibân 7 [all mentioned by name]

tarla, ḳaṭki 63	bağ, ḳaṭki 11	esçâr-i zeytun	esçâr-i dut
aḳṣâya 260	aḳṣâya 36	aded 50	aded 7

esçâr-i meyve-i saire	incir 38	kovan 30	ağnam 80 reʿs
aded 23			

[Maḥṣûlât]

ḥinṭa, aḳṣâya 14	maḫlût, aḳṣâya 20	şaʿir, aḳṣâya 44
baha 252	baha 280	baha 396

böğrülce, aḳṣâya 2	baḳla, aḳṣâya 5	fiğ, aḳṣâya 6	pembe, ledre 10
baha 40	baha 75	baha 90	baha 60

esçâr-i zeytun	incir	resm-i kovan	resm-i otlaḳ
baha 150	baha 110	baha 60	160

gögül, [ledre 1]	meyve 90	bostan 50	şire, 101 mestâne . . . 909
baha 120			baha 1,818

hane-i rahiban
neferan 7
baha 1,330

Yekûn ber vech-i maktuʿ
5100

Manastır-i Panaya Peskopi, râhibân 3

tarla, ḳaṭki 20	bağ, ḳaṭki 9	esçâr-i zeytun	meyve-i saire
aḳṣâya 115½	aḳṣâya 19½	2	15

esçâr-i incir 14 esçâr-i dut 3 ağnam 20 reʿs kovan 10

asıyâb-i badi bâb 1

[Maḥṣûlât] humus-ı ğillat

ḫinṭa, aḳṣâya 8	maḫlût, aḳṣâya 17½	şaʿir, aḳṣâya 17½
baha 144	baha 245	baha 196

baḳla, aḳṣâya 4	pembe	asıyâb, bâb 1	kovan	escâr-i zeytun
baha 60	4	60	20	5

escâr-i incir	escâr-i meyve	resm-i otlaḳ	resm-i bostan
45	50	40	20

şire, mestâne 53½	gögül, öki 4
baha 980	baha 40

Yekûn ber vech-i maktuʿ, fi sene 2,600

Manastır-i Aya Anna râhibân 3

yekûn: tarla, ḳafḳî 23	bağ, ḳafḳî 9	esçâr-i incir	esçâr-i zeytun
aḳṣâya 90	19½ aḳṣâya	aded 5	aded 7

esçâr-i dud	esçâr-i meyve	asıyâb-i abî
3	2	1

Hasilât humus al-ğillât

hane-i rahibân	ḫinṭa, aḳṣâya 6 ½	maḫlût, aḳṣâya 13	baḳla, aḳṣâya 1
neferan 3	baha 117	baha 203	baha 15
baha 570			

fiğ, aḳṣâya 1	escar-i incir	escar-i zeytun	resm-i meyve
baha 30	15	22	15

mahsul-i bagat şire, mestâne 54½	gögül, öki 4	pembe, 4 . . .
. . . baha 980	baha 40	baha 24

Yekun ber vech-i maktuʿ fi sene 2,300

Manastır Panaya Astirdafni[?] râhib 1

yekûn tarla, ḳafḳi 36	bağ, ḳafḳi 3	esçâr-i zeytun	esçâr-i incir
aḳṣâya 94	aḳṣâya 11	aded 4	aded 22

esçâr-i meyve	asıyâb, . . . 1
aded 6	

Hasilât humus al-ğillât

ḫinṭa, aḳṣâya 6½	maḫlût, 14½	şaʿir, aḳṣâya 14½	baḳla, aḳṣâya 1½
baha 117	baha 203	baha 130	baha 22

resm-i meyve	asıyâb-i abi bâb 1	resm-i bagat-i şire, mestâne 3
18	5	baha 558

mahsul-i bostan	resm pembe, . . . 4
20	baha 26

yekûn ber vech-i maktuʿ fi sene 1,400

Metoḫ-i Ayo Estatio, der cezire-i Andra râhib 1

tarla, ḳatḳi 1 aḳṣâya 1½ m	bağ, ḳatḳi 1 aḳṣâya 1½

ḫinṭa, aḳṣâya 1 baha 18	şire, mestâne 4½ baha 78	MAKTU[c] 320

Manastır Ayo Panteleymon, der Manastır-i S̲eloġo der cezire-i Patnos râhib 1

yekûn tarla, ḳatḳi 17 aḳsâya, 124	bağ, ḳatḳi 4 aḳsâya 12	esçâr-i incir aded 8	esçar-i zeytun aded 5
esçar-i meyve aded 5			

Hasilât humus al-ğillât

ḫinṭa, aḳṣâya 4 baha 72	maḫlût, aḳṣâya 12 baha 168	şair, aḳṣâya 24 baha 216	baḳla, aḳṣâya 2 baha 30
fiğ, aḳṣâya 2 baha 30	böğrülce, aḳṣâya 1 baha 20	pembe, . . . 6 baha 36	resm-i escar-i incir 24
escar-i zeytun 15	meyve	bostan	şire, mestâne 33 baha 594

YEKÛN 1,400

REFERENCES

Allbaugh, L. G. 1953. *Crete: A Case Study of an Underdeveloped Area,* Princeton.

Ansted, D. T. 1863. *The Ionian Islands in the Year 1863,* London.

Asdrachas, S. 1978. *Mécanismes de l'économie rurale dans l'empire ottoman, 15ᵉ–16ᵉ siècles,* Athens.

Bennet, J., and S. Voutsaki. 1991. "A Synopsis and Analysis of Travelers' Accounts of Keos (to 1821)," in *Landscape Archaeology as Long-Term History: Northern Keos in the Cycladic Islands from Earliest Settlement until Modern Times* (Monumenta archaeologica 16), ed. J. F. Cherry, J. L. Davis, and E. Mantzourani, Los Angeles, pp. 365–382.

Broodbank, C., J. Bennet, and J. L. Davis. 2004. "Aphrodite Observed: Insularity and Antiquities on Kythera through Outsiders' Eyes," in *Explaining Social Change: Studies in Honour of Colin Renfrew,* ed. J. Cherry, C. Scarre, and S. Shennan, Cambridge, pp. 227–239.

Chouliarakis, M. 1988. *Εξελίξεις του πληθυσμού των αγροτικών περιοχών της Ελλάδος, 1920–1981,* Athens.

Clark, C., and M. Haswell. 1964. *The Economics of Subsistence Agriculture,* London.

Coronelli, V. 1687. *Description géographique et historique de la Morée reconquise par les Venitiens, du royaume de Negrepont, et autres lieux circonvoisins: Enrichie de plusieurs plans, & vûës de places des mêmes païs,* Paris.

Davis, J. L. 1991. "Contributions to a Mediterranean Rural Archaeology: Historical Case Studies from the Ottoman Cyclades," *JMA* 4, pp. 131–216.

Davy, J. 1842. *Notes and Observations on the Ionian Islands and Malta* 2, London.

Evangelidis, T. E. 1909. *Ἡ νῆσος Σέριφος καὶ αἱ περὶ αὐτὴν νησίδες,* Hermoupolis, Syros.

Foxhall, L., and H. Forbes. 1982. "Sitometreia: The Role of Grain as a Staple Food in Classical Antiquity," *Chiron* 12, pp. 41–90.

Galotta, A. 1970. "Le gazavat di Hayreddin Barbarossa," *Studi Magrebini* 3, pp. 79–160.

Hopf, K. 1818–1889. "Gozzadini in Griechenland," in *Allgemeine Encyklopädie der Wissenschaften und Künste* 76, ed. J. S. Ersch and J. G. Gruber, Leipzig, pp. 415–426.

Kasdagli, A. E. 1999. *Land and Marriage Settlements in the Aegean: A Case Study of Seventeenth-Century Naxos,* Venice.

Kiel, M., and D. N. Karydis. 2000. *Μυτιλήνης αστυγραφία και Λέσβου χωρογραφία,* Athens.

Kiel, M., and F. Sauerwein. 1994. *Ost-Lokris in türkischer und neugriechischer Zeit (1460–1981)* (Passauer Mittelmeerstudien 6), Passau.

Koder, J. 1972. "Topographie und Bevölkerung der Ägäis-Inseln in spätbyzantinischer Zeit: Probleme der Quellen," *Byzantinische Forschungen* 5, pp. 217–234.

———. 1973. *Negroponte: Untersuchungen zur Topographie und Siedlungsgeschichte der Insel Euboia während der Zeit der Venezianerherrschaft,* Vienna.

Lehmann, I. 1980. *Griechische Inseln* 1: *West Aegäis,* Leichlingen.

Leonhard, R. 1899. *Die Insel Kythera: Eine geographische Monographie,* Gotha.

Leontsinis, G. N. [1987] 2000. *The Island of Kythera: A Social History (1700–1863),* repr. Athens.

Liata, E. D. 1987. *Η Σέριφος κατά την Τουρκοκρατία (17ος–19ος αι.),* Athens.

Loenertz, R. 1975. *Les Ghizi: Dynastes vénitiens dans l'Archipel 1207–1390,* Florence.

Maltezou, C. A. 1997. *Απογραφές πληθυσμού Κυθήρων (18ος αι.),* 3 vols., Athens.

Mantran, R. 1962. *Istanbul dans la seconde moitié du XVIIᵉ siècle* (Bibliothèque archéologique et historique de l'Institut français d'archéologie d'Istanbul 12), Paris.

McGowan, B. 1969. "Food Supply and Taxation on the Middle Danube," *Archivum Ottomanicum* 1, pp. 153–157.

Miller, W. 1908. *The Latins in the Levant,* New York.

Mitchell, J. 1831. *The History of the Maritime Wars of the Turks,* London.

Petropoulos, D. A. 1952. "Συμβολὴ εἰς τὴν ἔρευναν τῶν λαϊκῶν μέτρων καὶ σταθμῶν," *Ἐπετηρὶς τοῦ Λαογραφικοῦ Ἀρχείου* 7, pp. 57–101.

Psyllas, I. N. 1921. *Ἱστορία τῆς νήσου Κέας,* Athens.

Slot, B. J. 1982. *Archipelagus turbatus: Les Cyclades entre colonisation latine et occupation ottomane c. 1500–1718,* 2 vols., Istanbul.

———. 2001. "Η Σίφνος: Μία ειδική νησιωτική οικονομία (15ος–17ος αιώνας)," in *Πρακτικά Α΄ Διεθνούς Σιφναϊκού Συμποσίου, Σίφνος 25–28 Ιουνίου 1998,* Athens, pp. 59–72.

Symeonidis, S. M. 1990. *Ιστορία της Σίφνου,* Athens.

Topping, P. 1986. "Latins on Lemnos before and after 1453," in *Continuity and Change in Late Byzantine and Early Ottoman Society,* ed. A. Bryer and H. Lowry, Birmingham, pp. 217–234.

Tournefort, J. Pitton de. 1717. *Relation d'un voyage du Levant* 1, Lyon.

Vatin, N. 1994. *L'ordre de Saint-Jean-de-Jerusalem, l'Empire ottoman et la Méditerranée orientale entre les deux sièges de Rhodes, 1480–1522,* Paris.

Whitelaw, T. M. 1991. "The Ethnoarchaeology of Recent Rural Settlement and Land Use in Northwest Keos," in *Landscape Archaeology as Long-Term History: Northern Keos in the Cycladic Islands from Earliest Settlement until Modern Times* (Monumenta archaeologica 16), ed. J. F. Cherry, J. L. Davis, and E. Mantzourani, Los Angeles, pp. 403–454.

Notarial Documents as a Source for Agrarian History

by Aglaia Kasdagli

In this chapter I discuss the value of the notarial acts that have survived from Greek lands into the early modern period, the vast majority of which come from the islands. The focus is on the 16th and 17th centuries, with Naxos as the primary example, in an attempt to investigate the insights that these documents offer for agrarian history. The advantages and disadvantages of this type of source are addressed first, followed by examples of the types of relevant information that can be retrieved. This discussion also examines other investigations that attempt to use the largest number of notarial documents available and combine that data with other types of textual and archaeological evidence.

Notarial acts appeared in the Byzantine or former Byzantine lands by the late Middle Ages, as they did in other countries of Mediterranean Europe. Few documents of legal practice have come down to us from the Byzantine period, and evidence suggests that the tradition died out in most areas after their integration into the Ottoman Empire.[1] This, however, was not the case in regions that experienced long-term Latin, and in particular Venetian, rule. The most notable example is Crete; its local archives included thousands of notarial and other documents dating from the 14th to the 17th centuries that the Venetians considered worth carrying away when they lost the island to the Ottomans.[2] A wealth of material—as yet even less explored—is also to be found in the Ionian islands, most of which never became part of the Ottoman Empire.[3]

1. For the Byzantine notarial system, see Saradi-Mendelovici 1991.

2. In the last 100 years or so a great number of scattered notarial acts from Venetian Crete have appeared in print. The most substantial recent collections of the late Venetokratia are Bakker and van Gemert 1987; Mavromatis 1994; Iliakis and Chronaki 2002; Kaklamanis and Lampakis 2003; Drakakis 2004; and Drakakis and Marmareli 2005. Examples from the earlier period (in Latin) are in McKee 1998 and Gasparis 1999, where bibliography of older editions can be found.

3. The rich archives of Zakynthos were destroyed by fire following the 1953 earthquake, but a small sample is in Vagiakakos 1954 and 1955. To the notarial documents from Kephalonia and Paxoi published some decades ago (Petropoulos 1958, 1962) can be added a number of recent publications concerning Kerkyra (Paparriga-Artemiadi and Rodolakis 1996; Paparriga-Artemiadi, Rodolakis, and Karaboulas 1997), Kephalonia (Zapanti 1999), Ithaki (Zapanti 2002), and Kythera (Drakakis 1999). For references to older collections of notarial acts from other parts of Greece, see bibliography in Kasdagli 1999. Another good starting point is the collection of legal documents of post-Byzantine law in Yinis 1966. Extremely useful is the Web site Post-Byzantine Law (currently at www.geo-cities.com/ekeied/index.html); although yet far from exhaustive, it is being systematically updated and expanded. Many notarial acts may be found in specialized journals such as *Επετηρίς του Αρχείου της Ιστορίας του Ελληνικού Δικαίου* and *Επετηρίς του Κέντρου Ερεύνης της Ιστορίας του Ελληνικού Δικαίου*, or in local periodicals.

Chios and the Cyclades fall into a category of their own. They both remained under Western control (the former under the Genoese, the latter under various lords closely associated with Venice) until 1566 and gained privileged status as soon as they became part of the Ottoman Empire.[4] This meant that existing practices, including a well-developed notarial tradition, were well preserved, especially so in the case of the Cyclades, where Muslims never settled in any large numbers.

My original research involving notarial documents took place long ago and was part of a wider study of the economic and social history of the island of Naxos, the largest of the Cyclades, examined mostly from the relatively plentiful but rather scattered extant notarial documents. Searching archives in Naxos, Athens, and Rome, I collected records of more than 3,000 acts.[5] Most abundant are the acts of sale, which make up 30%–35% of all acts. They are mostly sales of land but also involve houses, and a few deal with the sale of miscellaneous items such as olive presses, mills, water rights, and boats. Another large category of acts is that related to family and inheritance: marriage contracts (concerning 403 individuals of all social classes), wills (209 in all, 31 of which were made by peasants), and also disputes, which more often than not were intrafamilial and involved property. Other contracts are related to agreements for the exploitation of land and other resources, the majority involving land leases in perpetuity (250 agreements). Also to be found are contracts for shared animals or shared exploitation of mills, a few contracts of service or apprenticeship, dozens of transactions relating to credit (which were much more common in the town), and a few other miscellaneous acts.

Throughout the 16th and 17th centuries, indeed until the 1960s, Naxos was basically an agrarian society and other economic activities (trade, navigation, and crafts) were decidedly of secondary importance. The island had 6,000–7,000 people dispersed among the town of Naxos and some 40 villages and hamlets. The vast majority of the population belonged to the Greek Orthodox Church; these were Greek-speaking people and they referred to themselves as Ρωμιοί, meaning that they followed the Orthodox or Romaic creed. There were only a few Muslims, and these were forced to flee during the Turco-Venetian wars that ravaged the Aegean for about 40 years during the 17th century (1645–1669 and 1684–1699).

4. Hayreddin Barbarossa's expedition in 1537 resulted in the islands becoming tributary to the sultan while retaining more or less their previous internal regime; in 1566, the islands were formally incorporated into the Ottoman Empire (see Slot 1982 for details). All documents from the town of Chios were lost in the desolation wreaked by the Ottoman fleet during the Greek War of Independence (1822), but examples of notarial acts from the villages have been published by Kanelakis (1890) and, more recently, in several slim volumes by Kavvadas (1950, 1956, 1966, and 1976).

5. The richest surviving sources are the two registers of the notary Ioannis Miniatis (covering the years 1668–1674 and 1680–1689), one of which has been published (see Siphoniou-Karapa, Rodolakis, and Artemiadi 1991, 914 deeds). Of the other material, only fragments—remnants of various archives—have been published sporadically. Major examples are the Αρχείον της Καθολικής Αρχιεπισκοπής Νάξου (Archive of the Catholic Archbishopric of Naxos), containing, among other things, 120 acts of the register of the notary Markos Soummaripas and the unique register of the *topos* of Filoti; the register of the Jesuits (*Repertorio de' beni della Kiura Kapela,* in private hands); the collection of documents from the countryside kept at the Historical and Ethnological Museum, Athens (Ναξιακόν Αρχείον); those of the National Library of Greece, Athens (Department of Manuscripts, Ξ); the Vatican Library *(Codices Vaticanae Graecae);* and the General State Archives (ΓΑΚ) in Athens and its branch on Naxos, the Historical Archive of Naxos (Ιστορικό Αρχείο της Νάξου). For more detailed information, see Kasdagli 1999.

Approximately 5% of the population was Catholic (Latins or "Franks," Φράγκοι), some of them descendants of Westerners who had occupied the islands since the 13th century or had come subsequently from other parts of the Aegean or from Western Europe. A few were relatively recent converts, or merchants and sailors whose stay on the island was temporary. All Latins lived in the town; they had succeeded in maintaining the power and wealth they had enjoyed at the time of the Dukes, exploiting the peculiar "privileged" position of the islands to their own benefit. Most big landowners and holders of seigneurial rights came from this group, whereas all peasants and the majority of townspeople (craftsmen, petty officials, and the like) were Greek Orthodox. By the second half of the 17th century, a middling stratum of "new men" had begun to emerge. They were Greek Orthodox, lived mostly in the town, engaged in entrepreneurial activities, and used some of the proceeds to invest in land. The evolution and proliferation of this rising middling group destined it to transform the economic basis and eventually the structure of Naxian society over the next two centuries.

The notarial acts have some distinctive advantages as historical sources. For example, they allow insight into the personal experience of people of all social classes, including some marginal elements of society about whom other types of documentation, such as fiscal records, have nothing to say.[6] Also, the acts refer to matters directly relevant to vital interests of the major part of the population, and consequently go to the heart of the mechanisms of society. Myriad details remain to be retrieved, classified, and interpreted on a wide range of issues. The picture that emerges is in no way complete, but on the positive side, all evidence is linked to a specific time and place. In most cases there is a good indication of the socioeconomic status of the main participants, as well as a built-in check on the information provided, because all transactions involve more than one person, and the interests of the parties, if not directly clashing, nevertheless contain an element of antagonism. On the negative side, statistical data are almost impossible to retrieve from notarial evidence, especially when the evidence does not consist of continuous series of registers.

A vital key for the interpretation of the information gleaned from the notarial acts for historical purposes is the legal system prevalent in each case: Venetian law in territories held by Venice; customary law, which regulated most legal relations in regions such as the Cyclades; and other influences, such as the Assizes of Romania[7] or Islamic law.[8] Another point, which may be irrelevant when one deals with, for example, land use or lists of material objects, but which may become crucial if one is interested in narratives and the attempt to reconstruct perceptions and feelings rather than economic data, is that notarial documents at times purport to record the views of the actors themselves, or even to quote their very words. This is notably encountered in wills and marriage contracts or in eyewitness accounts of various incidents, and is in effect a mixed blessing. Sources of this type may offer rare and exciting insight into the actors as individuals or as representatives of specific social groups. We may discover an undoubted approximation to the reactions of real people that cannot be found in sources such as administrative or fiscal registers. Yet this advantage may be counterbalanced by other factors. For instance, the notary's interference is impossible to determine accurately;[9] moreover, there is the problem of the

6. By definition, the very poor and marginalized have no place in transactions involving real property, but their presence in the documents may be associated with antisocial behavior, such as involvement in affrays and petty crime. They may also act as witnesses to various incidents.

7. "Romania" was the name given by Westerners to the former Byzantine Greek lands. The Assizes of Romania consisted of the Frankish or "feudal" code imposed by the French rulers in Achaia, but later also adopted in the Venetian territories. The final version was written up in the 14th century, and in the islands there are references to its use until the late 16th century (Jacoby 1971).

8. This was pronounced only on islands with substantial Muslim minorities, such as Chios and Rhodes.

9. On this, see the observations of Poisson (1985, p. 117) regarding a French case. There is rich bibliography by French scholars, and in particular Poisson, concerning the theory and practice of *notariologie* (a term coined by Poisson himself). It should, however, be emphasized that the French studies, though liable to provoke questions of comparative interest, cannot be used as a guide when researching the Greek paradigm because they are the product of a substantially different social organization.

abundance of notarial formulas. As a result, researchers should be keenly aware of the difficulty in discerning which expressions are formulaic; which formulas are empty formalities representing a standard requirement to secure the legality of certain types of transactions; and, which ones are used as a standard subterfuge. Among several detectable cases of spurious evidence is the example of a Naxian will that seems to make a strong statement for family solidarity, but appears in quite a different light when seen in conjunction with other documents concerning the same family.[10]

Furthermore, any attempt to interpret the people's "own words" needs to take into account the commonplace observation that historical written texts reflect the concerns of the society that created them rather than those of the historians who study them. Notarial deeds are documents drawn up for specific practical purposes, in accordance with rigid legal and normative rules, and regarding matters of the utmost importance to the parties concerned. It is probable that the researcher, who will not have a personal stake in the proceedings, will not even be aware of the background of most cases, of veiled nuances, or of unwritten expectations. He or she may not even understand fully, let alone share, the values of the actors. What all this emphasizes is that the historian has to be inventive if he or she is to extract information that may yield some answers to the questions asked. Also, it is necessary that information retrieved from the notarial records should be used in conjunction with, and checked against, as many other types of evidence as possible—public or private, folk or literary, material or archaeological.

To illustrate the point, consider my recent investigation concerning literacy and education in the Aegean during the "dark" 17th century.[11] My aim was, first, to demonstrate that the sparseness of our knowledge about various aspects of the social and cultural history of the 17th century is attributable more to the failure of researchers to explore and collate all available sources than to any insurmountable or absolute lack of documentary evidence, and second, to suggest that the notarial archives are a source that up to now have been underexplored. Nevertheless, on the subject of literacy, my quest showed that the records available could not provide direct, quantitative answers to the question. They do, however, give us some indication of the categories of people who at least were able to sign their names. Also, it appears that in the islands, this basic writing ability (which presupposes reading ability) was diffused among wider sections of the population than seems to have been the case in agrarian communities of continental Greece at the same time and even at a much later date. More than that, the extensive use by most segments of the island populations of documents such as deeds of sale, marriage contracts, and wills highlights the important role of written documents in that particular society. In other words, there was an obvious need—and an ensuing tendency—to replace oral customary law with written legal codes, which were deemed to be more objective and more difficult to dispute. Indeed, the first extant written customs date from the 17th century and were issued by the ruling groups of local communities, with the direct—if not always explicit—aim of serving their own needs.

10. Kasdagli 1999, p. 67.
11. Kasdagli 2004.

THE EXPLOITATION OF LAND

Let us now examine the value and uses of notarial documents in exploring issues associated with the exploitation of the land in Romania in the early modern period. My first point of reference will be the Cyclades, but I also will refer to examples from elsewhere.

Land exploitation was obviously an issue of the greatest importance to these primarily agrarian societies. This assumption is not affected by the fact that there was some urban development on Crete, Kerkyra, and Kephalonia, and that one comes across busy commercial ports even on small islands such as Milos.

Records of land sales are a treasure of information. In most cases, these records are the most common type among all extant acts, which is not surprising given that they served as title deeds and were likely to be copied and kept with great care for generations. The standard contract of a land sale would describe the type of land and cultivation in varying levels of detail. Vineyards, for example, are always described as such, maybe with a further specification that the site is a new plantation or an old vineyard, or that the land also has trees. Trees were also common on arable land, and it seems that coplantation or intercropping was the norm. To find an indication of the total proportion of land under each type of cultivation, however, the best indexes at our disposal, at least for the Cyclades, are the lands transferred through marriage contracts. This is because, in contrast to what happened on Crete or the Ionian islands (where most land was passed from father to son, whereas only the marriage portion of women was listed in detail), in the Cyclades marriage was the critical point at which both women and men were endowed with property. By the same token, the bulk of property transfers occurred upon marriage under a bilateral dotal system. In this case, therefore, the surviving 17th-century marriage contracts and wills provide the most detailed and standardized information, and they are a reasonably accurate source of information about land use.[12]

On Naxos, of the 3,700 plots or so that, according to the extant documentation, were transferred in this way in the course of the 17th century, one-fourth were vineyards, 8% of which were young plantations not yet bearing fruit and some others were plantations of neglected vines in need of vigorous restorative measures. It is clear from the sources that every effort was made to have a winepress on the spot, as this saved on transportation costs and facilitated the monitoring of the cultivator to prevent his cheating the landowner of his rightful share of the produce. When a vineyard did not have its own press, it is likely that the owner had access to that of an adjacent plot, which more often than not had belonged to a previously single holding subsequently fragmented through inheritance or sale.

Even though wheat was produced on all types of land, intermixed with other crops, more than half of the plots given away upon death or marriage were simple arable fields, with perhaps a few interspersed trees, on which dry-land farming was practiced. Presumably these plots were fairly standard in appearance and quality because there is a stock of different terms used to describe fields with distinguishing characteristics relating to soil and terrain,

12. Most of the traits mentioned here can also be found in other parts of Romania from which similar notarial documents survive. I use this example simply because I have worked out all details systematically.

size, irrigation, and crops. Thus, we have different terms for irrigated plots, waste, permanent enclosures, vegetable patches, inferior fields in rocky or sandy ground, strips of land next to streams and liable to flooding, fields used mainly for beans, and so on. It is interesting to note that such terms were often peculiar to a single island or even a region of an island.

Following an ancient tradition, the custom in all Greek lands allowed for ownership of trees separate from that of the land. Terraced fields were not commonly described as such, though fields or areas described as strips of mountainous land were probably found on terraced slopes.

Fencing was of paramount importance for all types of land. Building and maintaining fences were tasks that no cultivator could ignore. Makeshift hedges made of reeds, posts, and twigs were the most common fences. They were the only ones suitable for grain fields (which would remain open after harvest and until the land was plowed for the next crop), but because they were inexpensive and relatively easy to build, they were also used to protect vineyards, which were kept enclosed throughout the year. Permanent drystone walls, however, surrounded other areas; ditches with elevated sides also were common.

Whatever the material of which they were made, fences had to be high enough to keep animals out. That the cultivators were successful in their efforts is to be doubted, given the frequency with which landowners pressed the point and the many examples of friction caused by stray animals. On one such occasion the holder of the land killed an ass that had ravaged a field. The communal notables to whom the case was referred dispatched four peasants to inspect the plot and see whether it was enclosed and fenced "like any well-tended sown field." The verdict was that it was not, because the hedge was low and easy to climb over. This (in conjunction with the fact that the ass was tethered at the time and that his owners had not received any warning) presumably meant that the landholder was liable for damages for the loss of the animal.[13]

Other means of marking boundaries were streams and irrigation channels, trees and bushes, large stones, rocks, or other natural features. In most cases (e.g., in contracts of alienation), however, a plot was identified in reference to adjacent properties and/or the public thoroughfare. Plots formed as a result of relatively recent subdivision were often considered to be fragments of the original field, especially since neighboring landholders frequently had to share rights of access or resources such as water rights, a threshing floor, or a winepress.

The size of a plot is seldom given in the notarial documents of the period, presumably because this would not serve any practical purpose. When it is, the reason is frequently obvious, namely, that the land involved was a specific part of a larger holding. This is especially true in the case of a measure denoting the amount of land that a pair of draft animals could plow in a single day (ζευγαριά), a measure similar to those common in other European societies. A different unit of measure (encountered also on Crete) is based on the number of laborers required to work the land: "a vineyard of five workers."

Availability of water is always noted, as this determined the type of cultivation (and to some extent the productivity of the land) as well as the

13. April 4, 1666, Archives of the Catholic Archbishopric, Naxos, cartulary of the notary Markos Soummaripas.

comfort of the cultivators and their animals. Evidence for the abundance or lack of water also can be seen in the numbers of water mills, wells, fountains, and cisterns (a cistern was a valued dowry item on arid Santorini). In most cases, however, there were rights to either seigneurial or communal running waters, which were distributed through a network of specially constructed channels. The vital importance and relative scarcity of water is illustrated not only by the minute listing of watering rights but also by various disputes over it recorded in our documents.

As for the improvement of the soil, only casual information is found about the methods adopted. The most widespread method was to leave part of the land fallow and sow another part with pulses. On one occasion, peasants who had allegedly left some lands uncultivated for 30 years were asked to burn them over first—a method of fertilization widely practiced in the Cyclades. In another instance there is an explicit requirement for drains around the field. This was in the swampy plain where drainage could be a problem, but ditches were a common feature everywhere and served as boundaries and fences as well as drains.

Animal droppings were a well-known fertilizer. The large estates (τόποι) followed a pattern also common elsewhere (cf. medieval English open fields): the temporary fences were brought down after the harvest and the animals of the village (including the landlord's herds) were left to roam freely, feed on the stubble, and leave their droppings behind. The domestic gardens next to the house were called κοπριές (dung-heaps), a term suggesting that they were probably used as a repository for animal, household, and yard refuse.

The notarial documents do not have much to offer about specific crops; nevertheless, other sources such as Ottoman fiscal documents, memoranda kept by the Jesuits, and descriptions by European travelers yield information about all the varieties of produce. Disparities between notarial evidence and what is known from other sources also can be suggestive. For example, our documents contain more references to pure wheat than to any other grain, quite out of proportion to its actual availability. Conversely, barley is least mentioned, far less than mixed grains and unspecified grain. The latter is sometimes referred to simply as "bread," which likewise probably indicated mixed grains. The many references to wheat highlight its role as a particularly valuable commodity, usually reserved for those of better means. It is often mentioned in association with the payment of rents and debts, whereas barley, being the most abundant and thus exportable grain, does not appear as frequently in the day-to-day transactions, in which mixed grains played a major role.

In arboriculture, olive trees and fig trees were ubiquitous and in a class of their own; this is confirmed in the Ottoman fiscal register of 1670/1.[14] The importance of olives and olive oil does not require comment, and figs (fresh, sun-dried, or oven-baked) were a staple food throughout the year. There was a variety of other fruit trees and nut trees, but these were much less abundant and do not seem to have been considered essential.

Throughout Romania the agricultural system was mixed husbandry, and the notarial documents give some rather fragmented information about the pastoral sector of the economy. Cows and oxen are the animals mentioned

14. For selective use of the Ottoman data, see Slot 1982. Large parts of the 1670/1 assessment have not yet been discussed in print; but cf. Chap. 2 in this volume, where additional data from it are presented.

most frequently, as they were indispensable to agriculture. Donkeys were much more numerous than horses or mules, and pigs are hardly ever mentioned separately. One or two pigs must have been common in peasant households, and their presence was probably implied among the unspecified "small animals"—that is, with the sheep and goats. The latter must have been so common that no separate word for them was used; they were simply known as "animals" or "productive animals" (ζώα καματερά).

Marriage contracts give a good indication of differences in livestock ownership according to economic and social class. For Naxos, more than half of all surviving dowry arrangements mention livestock settled on the young couple, but the manner of listing and describing the animals involved is far from standard and at times fairly vague: "a share of all stock, equal to that of his brother"; "half of the female donkeys kept at the pasture of Lord *x*"; "the cows that *x* keeps for me." On the other hand, small proprietors tended to be much more specific and provide details such as "the youngest ox of the team"; "half my share of the spotted cow I hold with *x*"; "15 of my goats with their kids, half female, half male."

Among the peasantry and the upper landowning classes, livestock was an equally common item in dowries, even though the scale and mode of exploitation were vastly different. That is, about three-quarters of the individuals in each group brought animals into the marriage. This is a striking contrast with the middling group of townspeople, since slightly more than three-quarters of them did not get any animals at all.

The widespread sharing of large animals was partly due to the common practice of leasing animals to peasants in long-term contracts under which the peasant eventually gained a half-ownership right to the animal. Furthermore, it was an option adopted by peasants themselves, especially when they wanted to set up their children but could not afford to give them all of the animal power required for agricultural operations. On such occasions it was certainly more efficient to share the full capacity of any animals available than to divide the existing livestock in a manner that would leave the parents' holdings and/or those of the young people inadequately supplied. Therefore a peasant woman, instead of imparting to each of her two sons half of her livestock (consisting of two oxen, a cow with its calf, and a female and a male donkey), gave all of the animals to the two sons to hold jointly.[15]

Such examples show that securing the sharing of animals in a binding way was a response to the universal problem of the poorer sector in any peasant society: an inability to support a sufficient number of animals and, in particular, those required for traction and transportation. Contracts for shared use of large animals were common on Crete as well as Kythera. In all likelihood there were other solutions (e.g., informal cooperation among peasants or perhaps loans of beasts in exchange for other services), but no arrangements of this type are found in the records. The couple, however, who started their married life with no lands whatsoever, a one-room house, and a total of two oxen, two shared cows, three donkeys, and three sheep, might well have been offering their services and those of their animals to larger landholders.[16]

15. June 21, 1667, Ναξιακόν Αρχείον, Historical and Ethnological Museum, Athens.

16. January 9, 1672, ΓΑΚ, codex 85, fol. 360v.

LAND TENURE

All this information about land use and agricultural activities, which I can only sketch here, is the necessary background for proceeding to the examination of the prevalent institutions of land tenure and the relationship between land and social structure. For example, who owned and who worked the land? What was the relative position of direct producers and those who enjoyed the surplus of their labor? What was the relationship between the two groups? By addressing such questions one may hope to move toward a reconstruction of the system of land tenure and exploitation in any given society during a particular period. Given the range of regional variation and the often imperceptible but nevertheless ever-present changes over time, the specificity of place and time cannot be overemphasized.[17]

In order to consider the issues of land exploitation, land tenure, and the relationship between land and social structure, I return to the example of 17th-century Naxos, which satisfies the criterion of being based on the greatest possible number of surviving contemporary documents. The bulk of information came from all types of notarial acts, including arbitrations of disputes, reports by witnesses to various incidents, documents relating to credit, delineations of landed properties, contracts for the exploitation of the land or of livestock, sales of land, and, of course, wills, donations, and marriage contracts.

First, I distinguish the different types of rights to the land enjoyed by various groups of people in the 17th-century context. These were rights of free property, conditional rights of ownership, and seigneurial rights. Then I examine leases in perpetuity, which are the best documented, although they were not the most common, mode of land exploitation on 17th-century Naxos.

Free Property

Land could belong to an individual absolutely during his or her lifetime. In practice, after the owner's death it would normally be entailed to someone else, usually a member of a younger generation, because custom was strongly opposed to the alienation of family property. The property involved was said to be "free, absolutely free, except for the tax of the kingdom." It could be of any size and its owner might equally be either a poor peasant or a powerful lord. It was cultivated predominantly either by family labor, that is, labor provided from within the household of the direct producer, or by temporary tenants who were paid with a share of the harvest. The evidence available is insufficient to allow us to determine the role of wage labor in detail, but in general terms, it was limited and employed mostly on a seasonal basis.

Conditional or Limited Ownership

Conditional or limited ownership mostly involved lands cultivated under a perpetual contract of sharecropping-in-half. The sharecropper was required

17. My attempt to assess the value of published notarial archives in the study of major aspects of economic and social history showed that even a cursory glance may lead to interesting observations, on this occasion concerning the agrarian society as revealed by the land leases found in the published register of a Cretan notary of the turn of the 17th century (Kasdagli 2000).

to surrender half of the produce of the plot to the "master of the land," who was not necessarily a lord with seigneurial rights. The tenant was also the actual owner of one-fourth of the specific plot, which he was free to alienate under the same terms of tenure. His rights to it, however, could be revoked at any time if he had not fulfilled his obligations to the landlord's satisfaction. From the lessor's point of view, ownership was also limited, because he or she could neither replace the tenant nor change the terms of the contract at will, nor could he choose to cultivate the land, even his own three-fourths of it, in any other way (e.g., on his own behalf with the intention of realizing all the profit).

From the tenant's point of view, lands held in εντριτία (see the next section) can also be regarded as of this type of land rights, in the sense that these too were customary tenures for which a fixed share of the revenues was handed over to the master of the land, who reserved the right of justifiable eviction. By the 17th century, arrangements for εντριτία concluded by a written contract had been largely assimilated into the logic of sharecropping; it will, however, be seen that differences between the latter and εντριτία proper were significant.

Seigneurial Rights

Seigneurial rights generally involved the big landlords—mostly aristocratic Latins, addressed as "lords" and "ladies." One of their most important privileges was the right to levy εντριτίες—payments in kind of a fixed share of the harvest, claimed by virtue of lordship over the estate, or τόπος, on which the land was situated. Admittedly, by the 17th century the original feudal character of the εντριτία had been significantly adulterated, so that the resulting revenue was often almost indistinguishable from a land rent.

Even though the term εντριτία implies a share equal to one-third of the produce, common practice at the time seems to have involved one-fourth of the winter crop only. Variants were probably fixed by the custom of each estate, sometimes also by special arrangement, and ranged between one-third and one-tenth of the harvest.

The justification for the levying of εντριτίες, as presented by the Latin lords to the Ottoman government in Constantinople, was that their ancestors had owned the lands ever since the island had become tributary to the sultan. (In reality, however, the Ottomans had merely accepted the status quo.) The lords argued that they had always paid taxes for the lands, and that as they could not cultivate them themselves, they had leased them to villagers for a share of the crop, a share that varied according to contracts agreed upon for each τόπος. This familiar argument possibly hints at an earlier development by which land managed directly by the lord of the τόπος ("home farm") was parceled out and leased to various peasants in return for a share of the harvest. Because little is known about the manner of exploitation of seigneurial lands in the Duchy of Naxos, the hypothesis cannot be verified, but it is nevertheless supported by parallels in the development of sharecropping systems elsewhere.[18]

In all probability then, the institution was originally a strictly seigneurial prerogative. By the 17th century, however, it seems that the system of εντριτία had largely become a simple land rent. Even so, the privilege still

18. The term τόπος, employed with a similar meaning, is also documented for 16th-century Andros (Polemis 1995).

retained class connotations, and the clear majority of those who enjoyed it were Latin aristocrats. The remainder were Greek townspeople, most of them of well-established and well-off families, the Jesuits and other members of the Latin clergy, and one or two Greek religious foundations.

The spread implies a disintegration of the coherence of the system of the τόποι, of which there are other signs, too. Partible inheritance must have been an important factor in this, because not only were the great estates divided and subdivided among heirs, but also seigneurial rights at times were detached and alienated separately.

A rent of unequivocally feudal origin was the τέλος, a fixed payment in cash or kind, usually small and resembling a quit-rent (i.e., a payment in lieu of required services). It could be a measure of wine, oil, or grain, one or two hens or cocks, a quantity of wax, or a small sum of money. By the 17th century a τέλος could designate a number of different payments. In most cases the common link among them lies in the original meaning of the rent, which was clearly in acknowledgment of the lord's superior authority over property and even persons. With the passage of time other payments were presented as τέλη, having been gradually assimilated into the original feudal rent. By then, however, the rights to τέλη were (or became) alienable effects.

A simple description of the different sets of rights relating to land is useful, but it cannot explain the system in any satisfactory way unless the relative importance of each can be established. A very crude indication is given by marriage contracts listing real property and often including information about types of tenure.

Peasant contracts are not particularly informative in this respect. Parcels of land are more often than not described as "a share of" a field or vineyard, but this could mean one of several things: the quarter to which a perpetual sharecropper was entitled, co-ownership (with a sibling, another relative, or an apparently unrelated individual), or even that the "portion" was a strip of an open field. In addition, we find peasant lands owing εντριτία, and a few charged with a τέλος. Well-off peasants unable to work all their lands themselves leased them to others as permanent sharecropping-in-half, or cultivated them by employing temporary tenants or wage laborers.

Among artisans or lower-class townspeople in general, the average number of plots is low. Some instances of permanent sharecropping are encountered, but in most cases no details pertaining to tenure are given. It is plausible that such people mostly held lands situated not far from where they lived, which they cultivated, or at least supervised, personally.

There is better evidence for the lands of those who were not direct producers, but it should be stressed that it is not clear either how scrupulously the details of tenure were written down or what the relative quality and size of various lands were. Nevertheless, a few examples may reveal something about the extent of different methods of land exploitation.

Combined evidence suggests that middling landowners were probably the most likely to have a high proportion of lands in perpetual leases. This would be consistent with limited opportunities for direct involvement in production and close supervision of the cultivators throughout the year. In contrast, the landed property of great aristocratic landlords consisted of seigneurial τόποι and various εντριτίες, but few of their many and varied pieces of land appear to have been in perpetual leases. It seems that such landowners were actively involved in the process of production, and although details of their direct management have not survived, this would undoubtedly mean that the lords made decisions about crops to be sown, the course of rotation to be followed, and any improvements such as enclosing the land properly, planting trees, irrigation, and fertilization.

Leases in Perpetuity

Because contracts concluding leases in perpetuity reveal much about relations of production in general, it is useful to examine the available documentation in some detail. Much of the information derives from the 250 surviving agreements of perpetual leases-in-half, in which the produce was divided equally between the owner of the land and the cultivator, who usually bore all expenses. This arrangement involved three basic types of agricultural land: (1) arable fields, about 46% of all contracts, one-fifth of which concerned irrigated enclosures; (2) vineyards, about 45% of all contracts, 18% of which involved fields that were to be planted and turned into vineyards; and (3) waste or marginal land to be reclaimed and cultivated, about 9% of the remaining contracts.

A comparison between early and late documents reveals a noticeable differentiation: wheat fields make up 54% of all lands leased until 1668 but only 43% in the subsequent period; viticulture is the concern of 39% of the earlier contracts and 47% of the later ones, which suggests an expansion of wine production, probably in response to growing market demand. Lands to be reclaimed make up 7.5% and 10% of the total, respectively.

These figures do not at once reflect the strong link between agreements for sharecropping and major land clearance that has been observed in other European societies. Nevertheless, it is clear that this type of contract was particularly effective when land exploitation required extra labor for operations such as the reclaiming of waste or the planting of vines. Furthermore, in almost all cases relating to irrigated fields, major improvements were stipulated—usually the planting of trees, but also clearing uncultivated patches, preparing a vegetable garden, and erecting permanent enclosures. If to these labor-intensive undertakings is added the demanding cultivation of mature vines, we see that fewer than one-third of all contracts involve relatively straightforward labor on prepared arable land. Though there is no evidence that plots in this last category were disadvantaged (e.g., because of their location or inferior soil), the possibility cannot be ruled out. This would explain the special status of lands leased in perpetuity and the apparently better terms under which holders of such tenancies labored.

An indication of the relative importance of sharecropped lands could be found by considering the price paid by the lessee, the so-called entry fine (μπατίκι), which, as the century advanced, was increasingly seen as representing the price of the quarter of the land over which the cultivator would obtain property rights. In some instances the two parties even appointed assessors to value the land as if the agreement were a proper sale, with the prospective tenant being asked to pay one-fourth of the assessed value. This was not a common practice, however. Usually the lessor and lessee came to a mutual agreement on a price. It is probable that the negotiated sum differed appreciably from the actual value of the land, since the relative bargaining power of the contracting parties was affected by several factors: the indebtedness of either (usually the cultivator); the seigneurial authority exercised by the lessor; and the scarcity of desirable land or, conversely, of the workforce at the time.

Price was also linked to the type and amount of work required, so that labor and expenses pledged by the tenant were often regarded—implicitly or explicitly—as the entry fine. All in all, between the years 1600 and 1668, entry fines in whatever form were paid in approximately 60% of all agreements, but the proportion falls to 45% in the subsequent period. This sharp drop would seem to indicate a strengthening of the bargaining position of the peasant vis-à-vis the landowner, but while I cannot go into further detail here, complete analysis of the terms of tenure suggests the contrary, that the tenant's position actually deteriorated in the later period. It is therefore probable that the decline in entry fines was due, at least in part, to the proliferation of more labor-intensive agriculture. In other words, fines may have been reduced to counteract heavier demands that were being imposed on tenants.

CONCLUSION

My aim has been to demonstrate that the number of questions one may pose to the sources is virtually unlimited and that tentative answers, suggesting points to consider and spurring further investigation, may be given to many of them. An issue worth discussing is how we proceed from here. With regard to textual evidence, is it really satisfactory for scholars to spend years of isolated, tireless study poring over the same texts that perhaps someone else also has spent a long time examining closely while researching a different issue? Could there be ways for people working on different sets of documents, or referring to different localities but interested in similar questions, to exchange data and conclusions and come to a better understanding of wider issues that go beyond the confines of a single monograph, however erudite and perceptive it may be? In my experience, historians tend to work in isolation, and these days limited funds do not favor large projects. An exchange of ideas and experiences, however, might lead to a qualitatively different type of work.

Starting with the premise that increasingly more archives are becoming accessible and that several bodies of notarial registers have been or are about to be published, while more and more people are working on unpublished records, I felt it was high time that a systematic effort be made to tame and make usable the wealth of information these documents hold in their totality. Notwithstanding the inherent difficulties presented by this vast and far from homogeneous material, the ideal would be to collect all data that can be retrieved from all extant notarial acts, in the hope that a quantitative analysis, followed by attempts at interpretation, might permit the mapping of important issues of medieval and early modern Greek history. The tentative conclusions, combined with information drawn from other available sources, could subsequently be compared with data from countries of Mediterranean Europe in which similar primary sources have been preserved.

In this context, and given that what I have just outlined seems an unattainable vision at present, I opted for a small-scale pilot research project that could be realized in a relatively short time. A database has been constructed that is being filled with information drawn from marriage contracts, wherever in the Greek world they may be found, pertaining to the family and the transmission of property. The first phase—which is now virtually complete—involved the collection and processing of the published documents from 1500 to 1831, in the belief that the establishment of a Greek state in the 1830s was an important turning point in the history of many aspects of Greek society. There are provisions for unpublished material to be incorporated in due course, however. Funds permitting, the early (14th- to 15th-century) documents and the more recent ones should also be included at a later stage. The database is in English, and since it pertains to social, economic, and cultural history, it may be of interest to scholars of different disciplines (e.g., history, social anthropology, law), in Greece and abroad. In 2007 it became accessible through the Internet, on the Web site of the Institute of Mediterranean Studies (www.ims.forth.gr), which has supported this project. Also available, copyrights permitting, will be the collected marriage contracts that have been scanned electronically and provide a valuable point of reference for scholars interested in other types of information (e.g., linguistic, legal, sociological).

I hope that the result will provide a sound basis for the reconstruction of inheritance systems and the early modern Greek family in much of its variability, for tracing changes through time, and for interpreting the findings before proceeding to comparisons with societies that are geographically, chronologically, and culturally distinct. As the work of a number of archaeologists and historians has shown in the past decades,[19] and as the chapters in this volume amply demonstrate, however, textual evidence is (or should be) only part of the story. The people involved in these innovative projects have proven how much interdisciplinary work has to offer, highlighting the main approaches and the contribution and correlated problems of each. Going through this exciting material, one cannot help but envisage how far our knowledge about the early modern Cyclades would advance were we to examine it "through image, text, and archaeology." Naxos and Andros, for instance, offer themselves admirably to an interdisciplinary approach. The rural landscape can still reveal much about the past, but it is fast disappearing under pressure from tourist-related development. Evidence gathered from rarely explored sites of medieval settlements and material remains (houses, mills, olive presses, agricultural implements, items of jewelry, embroidery, etc.) may be combined with the relatively abundant notarial documents from the 16th century onward and supplemented by other narrative or normative sources as well as texts of high and folk culture.

With such grand visions, I have just embarked on yet another small-scale, realistic project. This one is more focused in time and place and its purpose is to investigate geographic mobility and the transmission of knowledge in the Aegean islands during the 17th century.

19. Recent developments in the archaeology of medieval Greece have been outlined in Bintliff 2001. Much of this work concerns mainland Greece, but see Davis 1991 for specific examples from the Cyclades.

REFERENCES

Bakker, W., and A. van Gemert, eds. 1987. *Μανόλης Βαρούχας νοταριακές πράξεις—Μοναστηράκι Αμαρίου (1597–1613),* Rethymnon.

Bintliff, J. L. 2001. "Recent Developments and New Approaches to the Archaeology of Medieval Greece," in *IV European Symposium for Teachers of Medieval Archaeology, Sevilla–Cordoba, 29th September–2nd October 1999,* ed. M. Valor and A. Carmona, Seville, pp. 33–44.

Davis, J. L. 1991. "Contributions to a Mediterranean Rural Archaeology: Historical Case Studies from the Ottoman Cyclades," *JMA* 4, pp. 131–216.

Drakakis, M. G., ed. 1999. *Εμμανουήλ Κασιμάτης, νοτάριος Κυθήρων, 1560–1582,* Athens.

———, ed. 2004. *Μιχαήλ Μαράς, νοτάριος Χάνδακα: Κατάστιχο 149* 1 [January 16–March 30, 1549], Iraklion.

Drakakis, M. G., and T. Marmareli, eds. 2005. *Μιχαήλ Μαράς, νοτάριος Χάνδακα: Κατάστιχο 149* 2 [April 1–June 28, 1549], Iraklion.

Gasparis, C. 1999. *Franciscus de Cruce, νοτάριος στον Χάνδακα,* Venice.

Iliakis, K., and D. Chronaki, eds. 2002. *Πέτρος Πατσιδιώτης, νοτάριος Καινούργιου Χωριού των Καρών,* Neapoli, Crete.

Jacoby, D. 1971. *La féodalité en Grèce médiévale: Les "Assises de Romanie," source, application et diffusion,* Paris.

Kaklamanis, S., and S. Lampakis, eds. 2003. *Μανουήλ Γρηγορόπουλος, νοτάριος Χάνδακα 1506–1532: Διαθήκες, απογραφές, εκτιμήσεις,* Iraklion.

Kanelakis, K. N. 1890. *Χιακὰ ἀνάλεκτα,* Athens.

Kasdagli, A. E. 1999. *Land and Marriage Settlements in the Aegean: A Case Study of Seventeenth-Century Naxos,* Venice.

———. 2000. "Οι πολύχρωμες ψηφίδες των δημοσιευμένων νοταριακών εγγράφων και η επίπονη διαδικασία της ανάπλασης του ψηφιδωτού: Συμβάσεις αγροληψίας στην Κρήτη της ύστερης Βενετοκρατίας," in *Ενθύμησις Νικολάου Μ. Παναγιωτάκη,* ed. S. Kaklamanis, A. Markopoulos, and Y. Mavromatis, Iraklion, pp. 311–322.

———. 2004. "Εγγραμματοσύνη και παιδεία στο Αιγαίο κατά τον 'σκοτεινό' 17ο αιώνα από τις μαρτυρίες των νοταριακών εγγράφων: Μία πρώτη προσέγγιση," in *Η Ελλάδα των νησιών από τη Φραγκοκρατία ως σήμερα* 2, Athens, pp. 535–548.

Kavvadas, S. 1950. *Οἱ κώδικες τῆς Χίου,* Chios.

———. 1956. *Θημιανούσικα ἔγγραφα,* Chios.

———. 1966. *Νοταριακοὶ κώδικες τῆς Βολισσοῦ Χίου,* Athens.

———. 1976. *Ἁρμολούσικα: Ἀπὸ χειρογράφους κώδικας,* Athens.

Mavromatis, Y. K. 1994. *Ιωάννης Ολόκαλος, νοτάριος Ιεράπετρας: Κατάστιχο, 1496–1543,* Venice.

McKee, S., ed. 1998. *Wills from Late Medieval Venetian Crete, 1312–1420,* 3 vols., Washington, D.C.

Paparriga-Artemiadi, L., and G. Rodolakis, eds. 1996. *Οι πράξεις του νοταρίου Αγίου Ματθαίου Κερκύρας, Πέτρου Βαράγκα (1541–1545)* (Επετηρίς του Κέντρου Ερεύνης της Ιστορίας του Ελληνικού Δικαίου 32), Athens.

Paparriga-Artemiadi, L., G. Rodolakis, and D. Karaboulas, eds. 1997. *Οι πράξεις του νοταρίου Καρουσάδων Κερκύρας, πρωτοπαπά Φιλίππου Κατωιμέρη (1503–1507)* (Επετηρίς του Κέντρου Ερεύνης της Ιστορίας του Ελληνικού Δικαίου 33), Athens.

Petropoulos, G. A. 1958. *Νοταριακαὶ πράξεις Παξῶν διαφόρων νοταρίων τῶν ἐτῶν 1658–1810,* Athens.

———, ed. 1962. *Νοταριακαὶ πράξεις Κεφαλληνίας τῆς συλλογῆς Ε. Μπλέσσα τῶν ἐτῶν 1701–1856,* Athens.

Poisson, J.-P. 1985. *Notaires et société: Travaux d'histoire et de sociologie notariales,* Paris.

Polemis, D. I., ed. 1995. *Οι αφεντότοποι της Άνδρου: Συμβολή εις την έρευναν των καταλοίπων των φεουδαλικών θεσμών εις τας νήσους κατά τον δέκατον έκτον αιώνα,* Andros.

Saradi-Mendelovici, H. 1991. *Le notariat byzantin du IXe au XVe siècles*, Athens.

Siphoniou-Karapa, A., G. Rodolakis, and L. Artemiadi, eds. 1991. *Ο κώδικας του νοταρίου Νάξου Ιωάννου Μηνιάτη 1680–1689*, Athens (offprint of *Επετηρίς του Κέντρου Ερεύνης της Ιστορίας του Ελληνικού Δικαίου*), Athens.

Slot, B. J. 1982. *Archipelagus turbatus: Les Cyclades entre colonisation latine et occupation ottomane c. 1500–1715*, 2 vols., Istanbul.

Vagiakakos, D. 1954. "Μανιάται εἰς Ζάκυνθον," *Επετηρίς του Κέντρου Ερεύνης της Ιστορίας του Ελληνικού Δικαίου* 5, pp. 3–96.

———. 1955. "Μανιάται εἰς Ζάκυνθον," *Επετηρίς του Κέντρου Ερεύνης της Ιστορίας του Ελληνικού Δικαίου* 6, pp. 3–92.

Yinis, D. S., ed. 1966. *Περίγραμμα ἱστορίας τοῦ μεταβυζαντινοῦ δικαίου*, Athens.

Zapanti, S., ed. 1999. *Γιακουμάκης Σουριάνος, νοτάριος Κάστρου, Κατάστιχο 1570–1598*, Thessaloniki.

———, ed. 2002. *Γεώργιος Βλασόπουλος, νοτάριος Βαθέος Ιθάκης 1636–1648*, Ithaka.

Kütahya between the Lines: Post-Medieval Ceramics as Historical Information

by Joanita Vroom

Interest in post-medieval ceramics in Greece from a purely archaeological perspective began in the first half of the 20th century with the pioneering articles of Frederick Waagé and Allison Frantz in *Hesperia* (1933 and 1942, respectively). Although useful publications have appeared since then, much remains to be accomplished in the field of post-medieval archaeology in this part of the Mediterranean. It should be noted that until 1950 the archaeological legislation in Greece protected only antiquities dating before 1453, the year of the "fall" of Constantinople.

The designation "post-medieval ceramics" used in this chapter refers to pottery of the mid-15th century through the 18th, when most of the Greek lands were part of the Ottoman Empire or under Venetian domination. Note that the designation "Ottoman pottery" is not used here, although this term is sometimes associated with the production of fine wares in 16th- to 19th-century Turkey (e.g., in İznik, Kütahya, and Çanakkale). Instead, I prefer the more neutral term "post-medieval ceramics" as a general designation for pottery finds from about the mid-15th through the 18th centuries. Here I focus on these centuries, omitting ceramic finds of the 19th and 20th centuries, which are, of course, interesting in their own right.

In the first part of this chapter I present an overview of the history of research concerning post-medieval ceramic finds from excavations in the Aegean area (by which I mean the Greek mainland and islands, Cyprus, and parts of western Turkey). I briefly discuss the publications that have been most important for the study of post-medieval pottery, with emphasis on studies relating to excavations on the Greek mainland, in Constantinople/Istanbul, and in the Greek islands and Cyprus. Furthermore, I try as much as possible to refer to the most recent publications on this subject.

Next, I discuss some recent pottery finds from current archaeological projects (excavations and surveys) in the Aegean. At these projects the ceramics were approached strictly from an archaeological point of view and studied from the perspective of type, date, and quantity.[1] On the basis of that information, I explore the possibilities of acquiring historical information from post-medieval ceramics in general. Work remains in progress, however, and the subject is still riddled with uncertainties. It should be noted that I do not focus attention here on the relationship between changing pottery

1. I thank the following people for allowing me to study and publish the post-medieval material from their excavations and surveys: Richard Hodges of the Butrint Project in southern Albania; Vassilis Aravantinos, Director of the 9th Ephorate of Prehistoric and Classical Antiquities; John Bintliff and Anthony Snodgrass of the Boiotia Project; Cyprian Broodbank and Evangelia Kiriatzi of the Kythera Island Project; Bernard Knapp and Michael Given of the Troodos Archaeological and Environmental Survey Project on Cyprus; and Peter Doorn and Sebastiaan Bommeljé of the Aetolia Project. Furthermore, I thank Machiel Kiel, John Hayes, Jack Davis, and Siriol Davies for their valuable suggestions. My research was supported financially by the Packard Humanities Institute.

shapes and the history of dining habits during post-medieval times, a topic that I have explored elsewhere and that presents an excellent opportunity to combine evidence from the analysis of archaeological artifacts, from written sources, and from the pictorial representation of dining scenes.[2] Instead, I concentrate more on the fundamental practice of studying post-medieval ceramics as a part of field research, carefully considering the possible but problematic relationship between archaeology and text.

RESEARCH ON POST-MEDIEVAL CERAMICS IN THE AEGEAN

The First Pioneers: Waagé and Frantz

The first "archaeological" study of post-medieval pottery in Greece was the publication by Frederick Waagé of ceramic finds from the first season of work by the American School of Classical Studies in the Athenian Agora in 1933.[3] The study embraced the wares used in Athens from about the 1st century B.C. (Late Hellenistic times) through the 18th century (Late Ottoman times), and included, therefore, discussion of a number of new wares not previously described by excavators. Waagé introduced, for instance, the general term "Turkish painted ware." Information about the stratigraphy of the excavation was minimal, however, and as a result, no attention could be given by Waagé to unglazed coarse wares; all the published vessels were glazed.

More valuable was an article written nine years later by Allison Frantz on other post-medieval pottery finds from the Athenian Agora excavations.[4] Here, for the first time, archaeological attention was paid solely to the centuries following the conquest of Greek lands by the Ottomans. However, the 16th- to 18th-century levels at Athens had been so severely disturbed that the material (from 10 different deposits in the Agora) was presented by Frantz with only tentative suggestions for dating. The groups she discussed offered only a few indications of absolute dates, but the coincidence of different wares allowed her to determine their relative chronology. Most important was Frantz's recognition of a locally made type of tin-glazed majolica that she called "blue and white painted ware," but which today is known as local "majolica from Greece" (discussed in more detail later in this chapter).[5]

More Recent Ceramic Finds of the Post-Medieval Period on the Greek Mainland

After the pioneering articles of Waagé and Frantz there ensued a long period of apparent lack of interest by archaeologists in post-medieval pottery in Greece. This relative silence lasted 30 years, until 1977. At that time, excavations by the Greek archaeologist Charalambos Bakirtzis in Macedonia and Thrace provided a new stimulus to the study of pottery from this period on the Greek mainland. In particular, his publications of

2. See Vroom 1996; 1997, pp. 210–211; 1998b, pp. 540–545; 2000; 2003, pp. 229–239, 303–357.
3. Waagé 1933.
4. Frantz 1942.
5. See also Vroom 2003, p. 173.

Figure 4.1. Thebes: Fragments of a slip-painted dish from Didymoteichon found during excavations in the city center. J. Vroom. Scale 1:2

ceramics from Didymoteichon, an important Thracian production center during the post-medieval period, were groundbreaking.[6]

Here, for the first time, previously unknown locally produced wares dating from the 15th century to the 19th century were presented. Most vessels found at Didymoteichon were made in a "Byzantine" style, using traditional decorative techniques from the Byzantine period in Greece, such as sgraffito and slip-painting (Fig. 4.1). Previously unknown wares in Bakirtzis's publications included monochrome green-glazed vessels in various shapes and unglazed domestic vessels, such as chamber pots and jugs with spouts on the shoulder. Two glazed jugs with rosettes in relief on the outside looked similar to types produced at Çanakkale in western Turkey. An unfinished jug of this type demonstrated, however, that these wares also must have been made at Didymoteichon. Local production at Didymoteichon was confirmed by the discovery of two kilns, several potter's tools, and much kiln waste datable to the early 19th century in a building site just outside the town walls.

Bakirtzis's article on "post-Byzantine" wares from Didymoteichon spawned a group of articles published in Greek in the 1980s, mainly in popular periodicals such as *Αρχαιολογία* and *Εθνογραφικά*. Pottery production centers of fine and domestic wares were located, for instance, in 16th- to 18th-century Larissa, in 17th- to 19th-century Athens, and in 17th- to 18th-century Arta.[7]

These publications showed that the production centers of glazed wares in post-medieval Greece did not change their pottery repertoire and decoration methods radically from those of Byzantine and medieval times. In fact, the two main decorative techniques employed by the Greek potters during the post-medieval period were painting and incision (sgraffito), and they closely followed the conservative Byzantine color palette of green and ochre-yellow brushstrokes (Fig. 4.2). Decoration was limited to winding lines and circles and the wares were covered with a transparent lead glaze, as in the medieval period.

6. Bakirtzis 1980, 1984; see also Vroom 2003, p. 184, with further literature.

7. Vroom 2003, p. 71, with further literature.

Figure 4.2. Athens: Brown and green sgraffito bowl from the Dimitris Oikonomopoulos Collection.
Reproduced with the permission of the Greek Ministry of Culture

Figure 4.3. Arta: Locally produced jug with the year of production, 1791, painted on the shoulder.
Reproduced with the permission of the Benaki Museum

Arta was one such production center of glazed wares where traditional methods managed to survive in post-medieval times. Its red-bodied, lead-glazed products included slip-painted ware, colored sgraffito ware, and brown and green painted ware.[8] Noteworthy is a locally produced jug from Arta in brown and green painted colors with the exact production year, 1791, and the Greek letters ΔΗ and ΜΟ, probably the initials or the beginning of the potter's name, painted on the shoulder of the vessel (Fig. 4.3).

8. Vavylopoulou-Charitonidou 1981–1982, 1984.

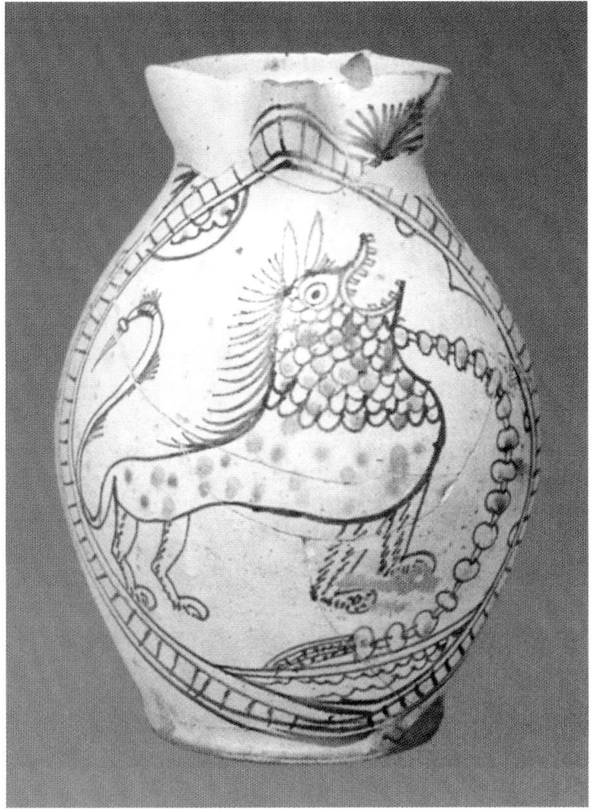

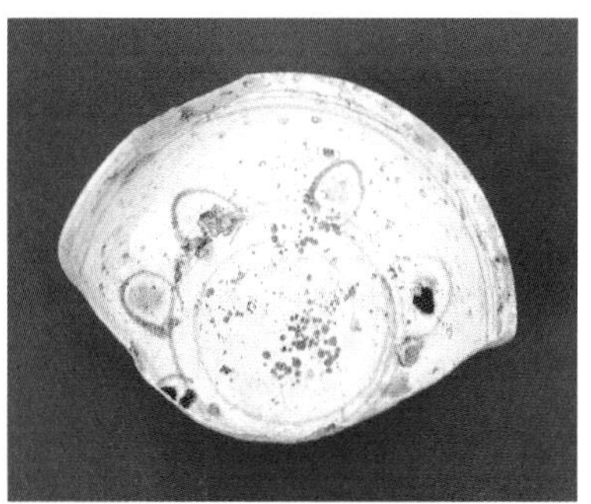

Figure 4.4 ***(above)*****. Athens: Local imitation of a majolica trefoil-mouth jug (Athenian Agora P 1902).** Courtesy of the Trustees of the American School of Classical Studies at Athens

Figure 4.5 ***(upper right)*****. Thebes: Locally produced majolica bowl found during excavations at Pelopidou Street.** J. Vroom. Scale 1:3

Figure 4.6 ***(lower right)*****. Boiotia: Locally produced majolica fragments from rural sites, recovered by the Boeotia Project.** J. Vroom. Scale 1:4

Other production centers in Greece using Byzantine and medieval techniques included Thessaloniki, Veroia, and Trikala, where unfinished products, potter's tools, and wasters of the post-medieval period were found during rescue excavations in the city centers.[9]

In most of the locally produced post-medieval ceramics in Greece, one can distinguish the influence of Italian pottery technology of the Renaissance period (such as tin-glazed majolica from northern Italy or polychrome sgraffito ware from the region around Venice). The Italian majolica even appears to be imitated in Greece. Finds of imitations of Italian blue-and-white majolica in Athens, published by Frantz in 1942, were found together with two potter's kilns, wasters, and potter's stilts (Fig. 4.4).[10] The most characteristic shapes of this locally produced majolica from Greece are small bowls, plates, and trefoil-mouth jugs. Fragments of this local majolica were found during excavations at Corinth and at Thebes (Fig. 4.5), as well as on rural sites in Boiotia (Fig. 4.6).[11]

In all, two main types of locally produced ceramics of the post-medieval period have been found during excavations on the Greek mainland: painted and sgraffito wares in a traditional Byzantine style, and imitations of Italian majolica. Archaeologists working in northwestern Greece published these two main types of post-medieval wares that were found during excavations at the castle of Rogon near Arta, and during excavations at the Castle of Ioannina in Epirus.[12] The stratigraphy of these excavations, however, is not always clear.

9. See Papanikola-Bakirtzi 1999, pp. 249–265.

10. Frantz 1942, p. 2.

11. See Vroom 2003, p. 173 (ware 28), figs. 6.33 and 6.44, for the Boiotian examples; see Vroom (forthcoming) for the Theban examples.

12. Vavylopoulou-Charitonidou 1986–1987; Tsouris 1982.

Ceramic Finds of the Post-Medieval Period in Constantinople/Istanbul

The modern standard for defining and dating glazed and domestic wares of the post-medieval period from stratigraphical excavations at Constantinople/Istanbul was set more recently by John Hayes. His first preliminary report on these wares concerned finds from excavations of the Bodrum Camii (or the Myrelaion), followed by a more detailed publication of material from the Saraçhane excavations 11 years later.[13]

In excavations of the Bodrum Camii, a 16th-century fill overlying a Late Byzantine tiled floor yielded some 90% of the finds. The great bulk of the material was uniform, comprising fragments of İznik ware (and other fine sherds) as well as local domestic pottery prevalent during the first half of the 16th century. In addition, a small amount of 18th-century pottery was recovered, of types characteristic of a higher fill. The date of this later fill was provided by fragments of well-dated 18th-century Kütahya ware. In addition, a few pieces of modern china came from the surface of this deposit.

In the excavations at Saraçhane, most of the post-medieval finds came from 15 groups from pits and wells; these provided an excellent range of pottery types prevalent between 1500 and 1650. The period from 1700 to 1850 was poorly represented. This phase, however, provided a convenient break between the earlier ceramic finds (late 15th to mid-17th centuries) and the later ceramic finds (18th to early 20th centuries).

In the absence of numismatic evidence, it was mainly the fine wares (e.g., porcelain, İznik ware, and majolica) that served as a dating tool for the coarse wares of the late 15th to 17th centuries. Some 20 wares of the latter, glazed as well as unglazed, were identified by Hayes. According to him, most were locally produced in Istanbul. About 190 types of vessels were listed in a preliminary conspectus of those used in Istanbul during Early Ottoman times (ca. late 15th to mid-17th centuries). Unfortunately, transitional shapes of the late 17th and early 18th centuries were underrepresented in these samples.

Post-medieval coarse wares produced and used in Istanbul appear not to have differed significantly from their medieval predecessors, displaying no markedly new technical features in fabric and manufacture. Nevertheless, one of the most striking new features in the post-medieval deposits was the total absence of large amphoras, which were probably replaced by wooden barrels. Noteworthy also was the replacement of thin-walled, unglazed cooking pots by simple lead-glazed types. As a result, the proportion of glazed wares in the later assemblages increased substantially, to around 35%–40% of finds in Early Ottoman contexts of the late 15th to mid-17th centuries, with a further rise in the 18th–19th centuries, when glazed wares came to predominate (ca. 60%–80% of finds). The glazes of the local wares were generally dark-toned and applied directly to the clay body (though a white slip occurs on some wares). Decoration was not common on the domestic wares.

A breakdown of the chief classes present in late 15th- to early 17th-century deposits at Saraçhane shows the following pattern: (1) fine wares (İznik, porcelain, etc.), some 1%–10% of total sherds; (2) plain glazed

13. Hayes 1981, 1992.

Figure 4.7. Iraklion: Polychrome sgraffito bowl from Italy; rim Diam. 0.24 m, base Diam. 0.10 m, H. 0.09 m (lower left is profile view). Reproduced with the permission of the Greek Ministry of Culture

wares, about 25%–35%; (3) unglazed tablewares, about 15%–20%; and (4) unglazed coarse wares (mainly drinking cups and spouted jugs), about 50%, and declining in the 17th century.[14]

The 18th-century increase in the proportion of glazed wares from the Saraçhane excavations is largely explained by the partial glazing of formerly unglazed spouted jugs from this time onward. New shapes, however, were mostly unglazed: for example, high-stemmed drinking bowls (goblets), spouted jugs (the so-called *ibrik*), and tall, two-handled flagons.

Ceramic Finds of the Post-Medieval Period in the Greek Islands and on Cyprus

Little is known about the pottery used in southern Greece and in the Greek islands from the late 14th century to the 17th, when these parts of Greece were under Venetian rule. One might expect to find imported pottery from Italy in these Venetian outposts and colonies of this period. Very few Renaissance ceramics from the West have been published until now, however, although one can suspect that ceramics of the Renaissance period were exported from Italy to the Aegean. Exceptions are publications of some occasional pieces of 15th- to 16th-century *graffita arcaica* and 16th-century majolica found on Rhodes and on Crete (for instance, at Malia, Chania, and Iraklion; Fig. 4.7), as well as two recent publications on fortresses in the Cyclades (e.g., Kos and Andros) that include imported post-medieval pottery finds from Italy and Turkey.[15]

14. Hayes 1992, p. 233.

15. Vroom 2003, p. 73, with further literature. See also Kontoyiannis 2002 for the post-medieval pottery finds on the island of Kos (e.g., majolica, İznik ware, marbled ware, Kütahya ware, Çanakkale ware); and Deliyianni-Dori, Velissariou, and Michailidis 2003 for the post-medieval pottery finds on the island of Andros (e.g., majolica, Miletus ware, İznik ware, marbled ware, Çanakkale ware).

On Crete, the Greek-Swedish Kastelli excavations at Chania provided good stratified layers and sealed deposits of post-Byzantine finds (including kitchenware as well as imported tableware from Italy and Turkey), but the material was unfortunately very fragmentary.[16] A helpful addition was the publication of six well-preserved 15th- to 16th-century tin-glazed jugs found in western Crete, now in the collection of the Archaeological Museum of Chania.[17] Although these jugs were all stray finds from villages near Chania, and information about exact provenance and context was scarce, they provided the excavators of Chania with entire profiles to help them in their study of the smaller fragments.

Another 15th- to 16th-century group of published material was recovered in the course of public works in Iraklion.[18] The finds, which are now stored in the Iraklion Historical Museum, included a lustre bowl from Spain (Valencia), majolica from northern Italy, and one piece of a polychrome painted ware, the so-called RMR (for the colors *ramina, manganese, rosso*) ware from southern Italy, as well as undecorated glazed wares and unglazed wares (cooking pots). Unfortunately, the photographs are not well reproduced in the publication of the finds and there is no information about the find circumstances of these vessels.

With regard to Cyprus, the only serious publication dealing with 14th- to 16th-century imports from Italy is Peter Megaw's pre–World War II (but published in 1951) article concerning three closed deposits of tableware and kitchenware from rubbish pits excavated in Nikosia.[19] These finds were the result of random discoveries during building operations. The pits contained majolica from Faenza, Padua, and Venice, as well as Italian polychrome sgraffito ware from the Veneto. Apart from these Italian imports, some pieces from the East, such as İznik ware from Turkey, Chinese porcelain, and painted bowls from Syria, also were found in the pits. According to Megaw, the Syrian finds illustrated the flourishing trade between Cyprus and the Near East, "when Syrian merchants, circumventing the Papal Edicts which prohibited Christians from trading in the ports of the Saracen enemy, transported their merchandise to Cyprus for re-shipment in Christian vessels to the West."[20]

More recently, the archaeologist Marie-Louise von Wartburg-Maier published additional imported tablewares of the Ottoman period found on Cyprus, this time in Swiss excavations at Kouklia.[21] She distinguished 15 groups of imported wares, among them pottery from Italy (Pisa, Montelupo, Albisola), as well as imports from Thrace, western Turkey, and China.

In summary, we can conclude, even from this preliminary survey of publications, that the main archaeological projects in the Aegean have yielded little knowledge about the types and dates of post-medieval ceramics in the Aegean. Until now, most publications of excavated pottery finds have focused exclusively on glazed wares (mainly imports and usually complete pots). Little attention has been paid to the fragmentary unglazed coarse wares, which constitute the main body of ceramic evidence of surface surveys (see, e.g., Fig. 4.8). This particularly limits the usefulness of previous published work for the interpretation of finds from surveys. When there are no easily recognizable fragments of İznik ware or Kütahya ware in surface pottery assemblages of post-medieval material, we simply cannot closely

16. Hahn 1989, 1997.

17. Hahn 1991.

18. MacKay 1996.

19. Megaw 1951.

20. Megaw 1951, p. 145.

21. Von Wartburg-Maier 2001. See also Gabrieli 2001; Cook and Green 2002 for a few post-medieval ceramic finds from excavations at the theater site at Nea Paphos in western Cyprus; as well as François and Vallauri 2001, pp. 539–546, for post-medieval ceramic finds from a survey around Potamia-Ayios Sozomenos in central Cyprus.

Figure 4.8. Kythera: Fragment of a post-medieval storage jar in a local fabric, recovered by the Kythera Island Project. J. Vroom. Scale 1:3

date the remainder of the ceramics. It is therefore very difficult—if not quite premature—to speak with any certainty about the distribution and the quantities of pottery finds of the 15th–18th centuries in the Aegean area, let alone to compare the results from various survey projects in Greece.

In addition, hardly any attention has been paid until now to ceramics that were imported during the post-medieval period into the Aegean region from other parts of the Mediterranean, such as majolica from Italy. We know that Italian majolica probably reached the Aegean in large quantities, but because of lack of publication we do not have insight into its distribution.

Nevertheless, recently I have made an effort to classify the most commonly found post-medieval wares in the Aegean that exhibit clear stylistic and technological similarities. These wares have been categorized on the basis of their fabric, surface treatment, decoration, shape, origin, distribution, and date range.[22] Also, I have argued that within this preliminary classification system it is preferable to date post-medieval pottery finds in the Aegean only by century, and abandon traditional designations such as "Early Ottoman" or "Late Ottoman." In fact, dates lack the historical and cultural connotations attached to conventional periodization and provide a clearer basis for discussion.

POST-MEDIEVAL CERAMICS AS A SOURCE OF HISTORICAL INFORMATION

Literature dealing with post-medieval ceramics from Turkey in general, and in particular with the famous colorful tablewares produced in İznik (Fig. 4.9), Kütahya, and Çanakkale in western Turkey, is, of course, quite extensive. Research into these wares, however, was until recently not conducted from an archaeological perspective, and it strongly emphasized variations in decorative styles, which were often influenced by styles from the East, especially from Syria, Iran, and China. The technical aspects of the production processes of these wares or their distribution and use throughout the Ottoman empire were hardly examined.[23] The publication of the excavation of some pottery kilns at İznik (with emphasis on kiln equipment and deformed or unfinished products) appears until now to be the only example of a different approach to post-medieval ceramics in the eastern Mediterranean.[24]

Another consequence of a concentration of scholarship on the well-known wares from the large-scale production centers in İznik, Kütahya, and Çanakkale is that other types of decorated ware or domestic wares, which were produced throughout the Ottoman empire at medium-sized centers or in small local workshops, have remained unpublished and therefore are unknown. As has been demonstrated in the first part of this chapter, we now have evidence for pottery production during Ottoman times in Athens, Didymoteichon, Arta, Thessaloniki, Veroia, and Trikala, but this distribution, of course, only hints of the places where we may find evidence of production in the future.

The picture is not entirely gloomy, however. Post-medieval ceramics have been and can be successfully used as a source of historical information.

22. Vroom 2005, pp. 138–177.
23. Laudable exceptions are Tite 1989; Atasoy and Raby 1994; and Carroll 2000. See also Baram and Carroll 2000a for the multiple pathways to an Ottoman archaeology.
24. Aslanapa, Yetkin, and Altun 1989.

Figure 4.9. Athens: Polychrome painted vessel from İznik, second half of the 16th century. Reproduced with the permission of the Benaki Museum

When properly analyzed and dated they may offer us new views on the material culture of the post-medieval past. Taken a step further, they may also shed light on aspects of life such as trade, dining habits, and the symbolism of consumption.

In the remainder of this section I will introduce three examples of such an approach. First, I discuss two sherds of pottery from the University of East Anglia and the Institute of Archaeology in Tirana excavations at Butrint in southern Albania.[25] Found there were two body fragments of a majolica jug of the early 16th century that were decorated on the outside with an image of a lion, probably the Lion of St. Mark representing the Venetian Republic (Fig. 4.10). We already know from ample documentary evidence that Butrint was at that time in Venetian hands, but these pieces seem to suggest something more—namely, that the political and military expansion of the Venetian Republic was explicitly symbolized through the distribution of its material culture.[26] The Lion of St. Mark is widely found as a symbol of the Venetian Republic in various parts of the Mediterranean that were under Venetian domination. These lions are normally incorporated into gateways and conspicuous parts of Venetian fortifications and public buildings, their purpose being to denote the authority of Venice.

25. See, e.g., Hodges et al. 2000; Gilkes et al. 2002.

26. Soustal 2004.

Figure 4.10 *(above, left)*. Butrint: Two fragments of a majolica jug with an image of a lion, found during excavations in the lower city. J. Vroom

Figure 4.11 *(above, right)*. Serres: *Bacini* from Ottoman and early modern (20th century) times in a wall of the 13th-century Monastery of Timios Prodromos (St. John the Baptist). J. Vroom

It is therefore interesting to note that other post-medieval ceramics include depictions of the Lion of St. Mark as well (among various examples, one might note a majolica plate from Stari Bar in Montenegro and two sgraffito fragments, which are now in the Ca' d'Oro in Venice and in the Museo dei Grandi Fiumi di Rovigo in the Veneto region). Consequently, what we see here may very well be the archaeological and iconographical side of an expanding mercantile power. We know from written sources that during the 16th century the production and distribution of majolica was organized in an early capitalistic manner, and it seems that the expansion of this system did not leave Greek lands untouched.[27]

A second example of the potential that ceramics hold as a source of historical information is provided by the so-called *bacini*. These are often colorful, decorated bowls that were embedded in the facades and walls of churches or other buildings from the 11th century onward. In the Aegean, the custom remained popular through Ottoman and even modern times (Fig. 4.11). *Bacini* of the 16th–20th centuries were, for instance, set into the walls of several churches in Attica and on the islands of Salamis and Hydra, in Methana, on Mt. Pelion, on the island of Euboia, and in the Cyclades.[28] Since the 1960s these *bacini* have been recognized as a tool for establishing the chronology of these buildings, and therefore may function as a sort of control for the written sources that refer to them. Machiel Kiel, however, is one of the few who has written about *bacini* of the post-medieval period in Greek churches.[29]

A third way that pottery can be used as a source of historical information is illustrated by the results of an excavation in 1993 and 1994 in the city center of Thebes. The excavation was conducted by the Archaeological Museum of Thebes under the direction of Vassilis Aravantinos. During this excavation, 14 rubbish pits and 1 well were discovered. Three of the pits contained closed deposits of the Ottoman period.[30]

27. See, e.g., Goldthwaite 1989; Vroom 2003, pp. 293–295.

28. Vroom 2003, p. 45, with further literature; see also Korre-Zographou 1995, pp. 69–76, for some examples of *bacini* of the post-medieval period in Greece.

29. Kiel 1991.

30. E.g., Aravantinos, Godart, and Sacconi 1995, 2001, 2002; Vroom 2006.

Figure 4.12. Thebes: Fragments of İznik ware found during excavations at Pelopidou Street. J. Vroom. Scale 1:3

Figure 4.13. Thebes: Fragments of Kütahya coffee cups found during excavations at Pelopidou Street. J. Vroom. Scale 1:3

Present in all three rubbish pits were brightly colored tin-glazed tablewares. The majority of the sherds came from İznik and Kütahya in western Turkey (Figs. 4.12, 4.13). These high-quality imported wares were the result of improved ceramic technology, leading to better durability and better glaze techniques, and were designed for the table or status display.

Imports from more eastern regions also are among the finds. One is a blue-and-white painted bowl with Chinese-inspired designs on the exterior and interior (Fig. 4.14). A Chinese calligraphic mark painted on the bottom of the bowl suggests that it is a late-16th-century porcelain bowl from the Ming period, or at least a very good imitation of Ming porcelain manufactured in Turkey or Persia. Whatever the case, the variety of imported vessels in these rubbish pits suggests that Thebes thrived economically during Ottoman times.

Figure 4.14. Thebes: Blue-and-white Ming porcelain bowl (or imitation) found during excavations at Pelopidou Street. J. Vroom. Scale 1:3

The relatively rich and varied contents of these rubbish pits contrast sharply with earlier observations about the material culture of Thebes during Ottoman times. The Greek archaeologist Sarantis Symeonoglou, for instance, wrote that the Turkish period in Thebes "is recognizable through the poor quality of its pottery, which rarely includes glazed examples."[31]

Census and tax registers for 15th- and 16th-century Boiotia that have been translated and studied by Machiel Kiel (described in part in Table 4.1), however, offer a picture that is more in line with the finds from the rubbish pits. According to these registers, Thebes appears to have been one of the largest and most densely populated cities in central Greece at the time.[32] The Theban economy was based on the production of wheat, wine, cotton, wool, and silk, and on the breeding of sheep. From about 1506 to

31. Symeonoglou 1985, p. 170.
32. Kiel 1992, p. 406 and table 3; 1999a, p. 226.

TABLE 4.1. CITY OF THEBES: OTTOMAN REVENUE IN THE 15TH AND 16TH CENTURIES

Households			
1466	487		
Ca. 1506	900		
1540	1,467		
1570	1,497		
Wheat Production (per Household)			
1540	660 kg	229 *akçe*	
1570	666 kg	296 *akçe*	
Sheep			
1506	1,100	22,000 *akçe*	24 per household
1540	2,100	50,400 *akçe*	34 per household
1570	12,000	336,000 *akçe*	224 per household
Cotton Production			
1540	2,460 bales	12,300 *akçe*	9 bales per household
1570	4,060 bales	24,360 *akçe*	16 bales per household
Silk Production			
1540	361 *ledre*	11,200 *akçe*	
1570	770 *ledre*	35,000 *akçe*	
Mills			
1505	17 mills		
1540	22 mills		
1570	31 mills (of which 20 were wool presses)		
Market Dues and Revenue of Public Weighing-House			
1506		14,000 *akçe*	
1540		19,000 *akçe*	
1570		30,000 *akçe*	

Source: After Kiel 1991, p. 446.

1570, cotton production increased enormously and production of wine and silk doubled, as did the number of water mills, and market dues and the revenue from the public weighing-house.[33] At the same time, Thebes produced its own school of icon and fresco painters, whose surviving works can be found all over Greece.[34]

The excavated pottery from the three rubbish pits offers an important perspective on the apparently rich material culture of Thebes during Ottoman times. It would be interesting to discover the extent to which İznik and Kütahya wares were used in normal households and in well-to-do households in towns and in the countryside. (References to household objects, especially pottery, in documentary evidence such as notarial documents or inventory lists also will be of great assistance to research in post-medieval ceramics in the future.)

33. Kiel 1991, p. 433, n. 8, and p. 446; 1992, table 5b.
34. Kiel 1991, pp. 431–433.

Dating Post-Medieval Ceramics by Tobacco Pipes and Coffee Cups

Apart from finds of tin-glazed pottery fragments, clay tobacco pipes of the *chibouk* style have become a new dating tool in the Aegean since the 1980s. Such pipes consist of a mouthpiece, a long wooden stem, and a molded ceramic bowl (Fig. 4.15).

Today it is acknowledged that the study of clay tobacco pipes may contribute to the resolution of the problems encountered in excavations and surface surveys in establishing a tentative type chronology for the "difficult" ceramics of post-medieval times.[35] According to Rebecca Robinson in her publications of tobacco pipes from Athens and Corinth, these pipes may have been used in the Aegean after 1605 (subsequent to the introduction of pipe smoking to the Ottoman empire—an event that may have occurred as early as 1599). Their development can be followed with some accuracy through the following centuries.[36] Women, as well as men, smoked this type of pipe in Ottoman times (Fig. 4.16).

John Hayes's preliminary report on post-medieval clay pipes from the Saraçhane excavations, published in 1980, first established a chronology for pipe bowls of the *chibouk* style.[37] Based on associated finds, he constructed a provisional typology and chronology that divided them into 27 types, which became vital for dating other materials from the Aegean. Hayes's report inspired other articles about post-medieval clay pipes, specifically those published by Rebecca Robinson and Uzi Baram concerning examples found in Athens and Corinth in Greece, on Cyprus, and in Palestine.[38]

Coffee cups are also easily identifiable in ceramic assemblages from surface surveys and excavations; their production typologies offer another valuable chronological tool.[39] Toward the end of the post-medieval period (probably in the 18th century), a new type of glazed tableware made its way to Greece—namely, small thin-walled cups from Kütahya in Turkey, made of a fine, buff-colored fabric (Fig. 4.13). Polychrome painted designs in blue, green, red, purple, and yellow were usually geometrical, floral, or figural. This tableware from Kütahya was strongly influenced by Chinese porcelain, and is therefore sometimes described as a cheap substitute for real porcelain or as "peasant-porcelain."[40] The small Kütahya cups are clearly related to the spread of coffee consumption, and their shape was probably

35. See Simpson 1990, p. 10, and 1998, p. 17; Ziadeh 1995, pp. 210–211; and Ziadeh-Seely 2000, p. 86, for such an approach in the Near East (although Ziadeh's dating and interpretation of the pottery finds fromTiᶜinnik are questionable: the Early Ottoman pottery finds from stratum 6 might also be of the 14th–15th centuries and, therefore, Mamluk).

36. Robinson 1985, p. 151. See Robinson 1983, p. 266 and n. 7 on Thomas Dallam's diary regarding the exchange of tobacco and tobacco pipes between an English ship and a Turkish galley at the Dardanelles. Simpson (1998, p. 15) suggests that smoking was introduced to the Middle East by English sailors docking at Istanbul or at Egyptian ports between 1599 and 1606. Baram (2000, p. 149) refers to a text about tobacco use in Istanbul in the 1590s, and states that the Dutch used a treaty from 1612 as an opportunity to launch tobacco into Turkish social life.

37. Hayes 1980; see Hayes 1992, pp. 391–395 for his revisions to the chronology. See also Simpson's review (1993) of these publications, with critical comments on Hayes's typology.

38. Robinson 1983, 1985; Baram 1995, 2002.

39. Vroom 1996, with further literature; see also Ward 2000, pp. 189–191, fig. 7.1, for a more archaeological approach to the study of 18th-century coffee cups found on the Sadana Island shipwreck off the coast of Egypt.

40. Lane 1957, p. 65; see Vroom 2003, p. 178 (ware 36).

Figure 4.15 *(above)*. Athens: Ceramic pipe bowl of the *chibouk* style (Athenian Agora MC 1279). Courtesy of the Trustees of the American School of Classical Studies at Athens. Scale 1:1

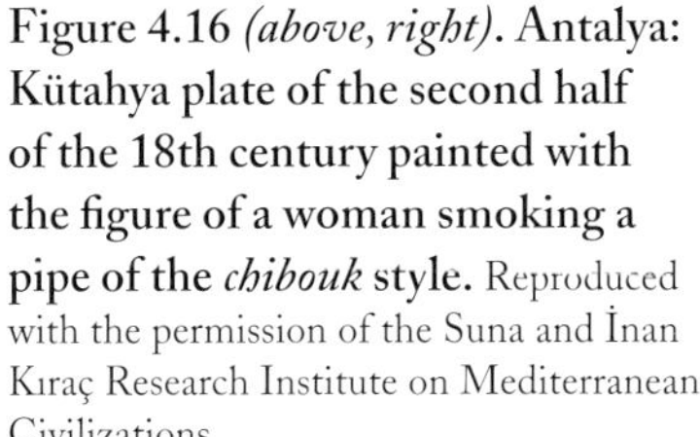

Figure 4.16 *(above, right)*. Antalya: Kütahya plate of the second half of the 18th century painted with the figure of a woman smoking a pipe of the *chibouk* style. Reproduced with the permission of the Suna and İnan Kıraç Research Institute on Mediterranean Civilizations

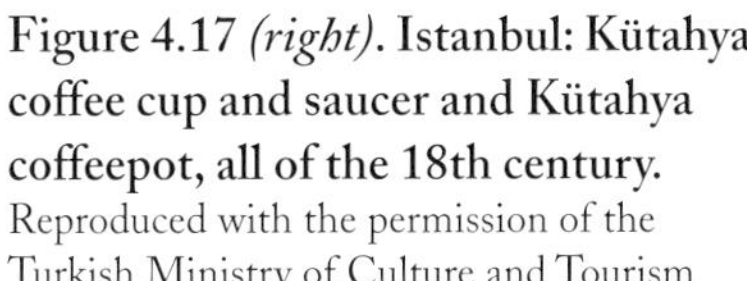

Figure 4.17 *(right)*. Istanbul: Kütahya coffee cup and saucer and Kütahya coffeepot, all of the 18th century. Reproduced with the permission of the Turkish Ministry of Culture and Tourism

derived from that of porcelain coffee cups made in Vienna and Meissen (Germany) ca. 1730–1740 (Fig. 4.17).[41]

According to the archaeologist and anthropologist Uzi Baram, in the Ottoman empire of the 17th and 18th centuries, coffee cups and tobacco pipes embodied "the new, the modern, the rebellion against the social order." He suggests that by the end of the 19th century and the beginning of the 20th, these items had become old-fashioned or, in his words, "the vestiges of an old empire," and were eventually to be "replaced by tea, cigarettes, and nationalism" arriving from the West.[42] Smoking cigarettes indeed became much more convenient than pipe-smoking for all social classes at the

41. Lane 1939, p. 236; 1957, p. 65.

42. Baram 1999, p. 151; these ideas are further developed in Baram 2000, in which tobacco pipes are regarded as "entangled objects" that show patterns of material changes in the Ottoman past.

beginning of the 20th century, and this change in consumption manners had far-reaching effects on the tobacco pipe industry in the East. Although tobacco was still grown in Turkey and in Palestine, pipes were replaced by Western-styled and -produced cigarettes. According to Simpson, "the last pipe-maker in Istanbul died in A.D. 1928, although others appear to have lingered on as late as the 1950s in other parts of the Middle East."[43]

Apart from providing Kütahya coffee cups and tobacco pipes as dating tools, examination of the history of consumption patterns (such as those of coffee drinking and smoking) has the potential to shed further light on the origins, spread, and social acceptance of the use of these stimulants. This point is illustrated by a map that shows the density and spread of coffeehouses in Anatolian villages between 1945 and 1960 (Fig. 4.18).[44]

Other Means of Dating Post-Medieval Ceramics

In the dating of post-medieval ceramics found in excavations and surveys, important chronological anchors can also be provided by the detailed tax records (*defters*) from the Ottoman Imperial Archives.[45] These registers range in date from the 15th century to the 18th and provide all kinds of information. The interaction between these historical sources and archaeological finds can operate in more than one way. Archaeological discoveries may help to identify place-names mentioned in the *defters*, and the textual information can sometimes aid in dating the post-medieval ceramics found in such places by providing archaeologists with their history. Several archaeological projects in the Mediterranean have indeed benefited enormously from the work of Ottomanists such as Machiel Kiel, Fariba Zarinebaf, Thurstan Robinson, and Marios Hadjianastassi. This has allowed information from the Ottoman archives to be linked to archaeological data.[46]

Still, the data from the Ottoman registers provide no easy or straightforward solution to the many problems we face in post-medieval archaeology. The Ottomanist Suraiya Faroqhi has warned scholars to be careful in the interpretation of these tax registers. She suggests that one must take into account distorting factors such as the conditions of transportation and communication during the 16th century, as certain taxpayers may well have hidden and thus avoided registration. Other problems are connected with the fact that in most parts of the Ottoman empire the tax registers of the 16th century record very high rates of population growth. Some of these increases, she argues, may simply reflect more effective counting procedures. Finally, historians trying to arrive at estimates of rural population for the 17th and 18th centuries—a period in which the registers seem much less detailed than before—are obliged to work "with a rather intractable documentation."[47]

Although Faroqhi's warnings are perhaps too pessimistic,[48] it is a challenge to combine the information obtained from the Ottoman tax registers with actual archaeological data from the sites recorded in them. In this regard, the information provided by the tax registers sometimes can be amplified and verified by accounts of Western travelers who regularly passed through Greece from the late 15th century onward. Some of these

43. Simpson 1998, p. 17.

44. Beeley 1970, fig. 1. Hattox (1985) introduces the Ottoman coffeehouse as a new type of place in the Near East, where people come together to engage in social activities. See also Given 2000, p. 214, for the importance of the coffeehouse in the social organization of villages on Ottoman Cyprus.

45. Kiel 1997.

46. Cf. Kiel's studies on behalf of various projects in the Aegean (Kiel 1991, 1992, 1999a, 1999b); see also Zarinebaf's contribution to the historical and economic geography of Messenia in the early 18th century in Zarinebaf, Bennet, and Davis 2005. Unpublished yet are Robinson's work in Turkey (e.g., Pisidia) and in Albania (e.g., for the British-Albanian excavations at Butrint and for the Mallakastra Regional Archaeological Project around Apollonia), as well as Hadjianastassi's work on Cyprus (e.g., for the Troodos Archaeological and Environmental Survey Project).

47. Cf. Faroqhi (1999, p. 89) versus Kiel (1999b), who recognizes the dangers but also the potential profits in using the tax registers.

48. In fact, the registers for Crete at the end of the 17th century, as those for the Morea in 1715, are among the most detailed ever compiled by the Ottomans, as is shown in Greene 2000 and in Zarinebaf, Bennet, and Davis 2005.

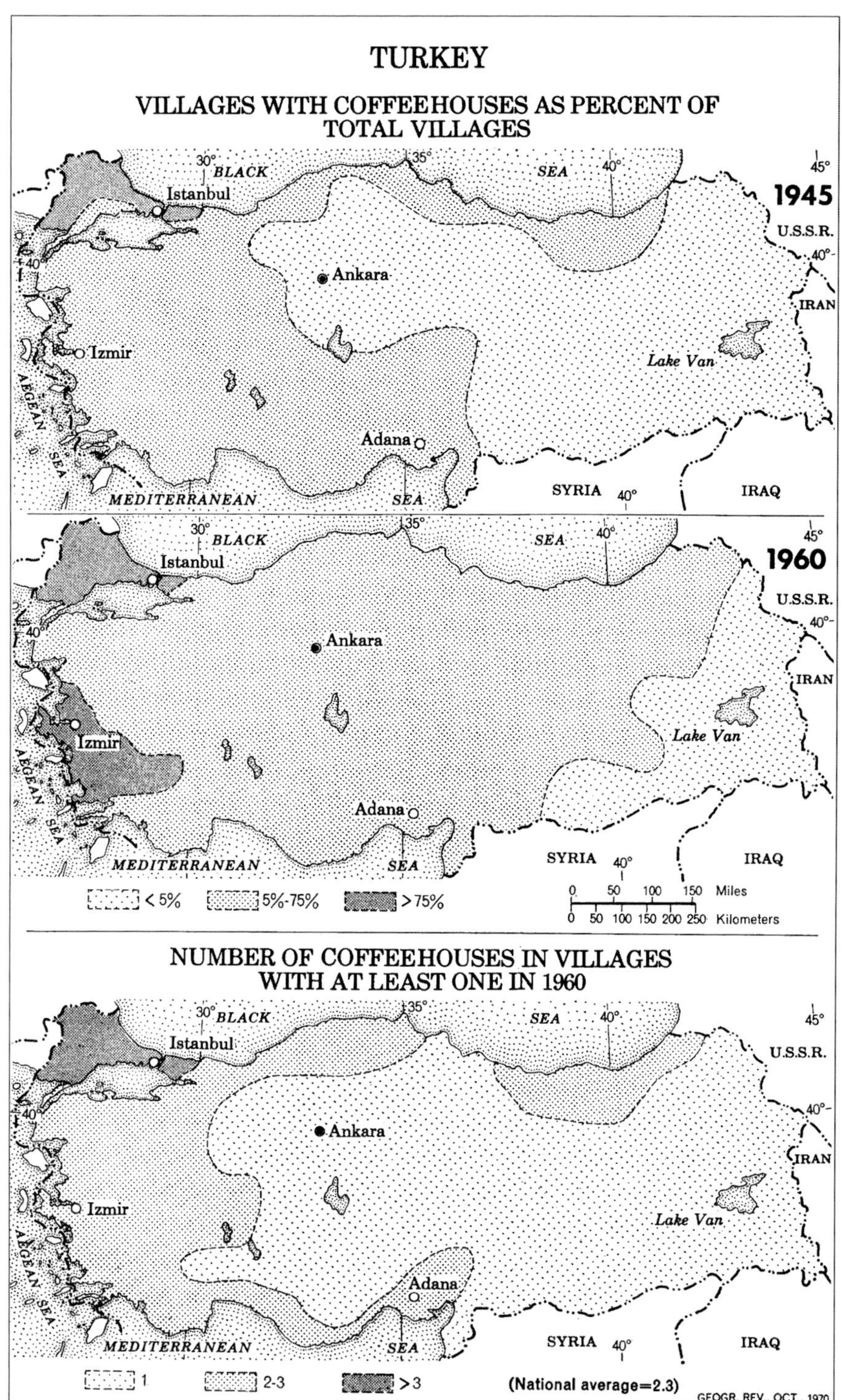

Figure 4.18. Spread of coffeehouses in Anatolian villages, 1945–1960. Beeley 1970, p. 477; reproduced with permission of the American Geographical Society

travelers were trained scholars and antiquarians visiting the ancient sites and classical monuments of Greece; others were more casual travelers and observers. The antiquarian perspective was expressed, for instance, by the canon of Durham Cathedral, George Wheler, who traveled with his companion, the French physician Jacob Spon, through Greece in 1676.[49] Where relevant, general observations about the Greek landscape and sites

49. See Constantine 1984, pp. 7–33, with further literature.

TABLE 4.2. IDENTIFIED AND UNIDENTIFIED VILLAGES IN TAX REGISTERS FOR THE DISTRICTS OF LIDORIKI AND VITRINITSA, EASTERN AITOLIA

Villages	*1466*	*1506*	*1521*	*1540*	*1570*	*ca. 1780*
Identified	38	38	38	38	41	55
Unidentified	14	14	15	11	16	8
Problematic	4	4	3	5	6	3
Total	56	56	56	54	63	66

Source: After Doorn 1989, table 2.

Figure 4.19. Kythera: Fragment of a 19th-century transfer-printed plate from England with willow tree design, recovered by the Kythera Island Project. J. Vroom. Scale 1:1

by such travelers, as well as their specific comments on contemporary villages and settlements, can be used to support the dating and interpretation of the sherds we now find in the fields.[50]

We must also face, however, the difficult practical problems of relating ceramics to these written sources. Do we just stop asking questions after we think we have "identified" a place-name that is mentioned in the *defters*? And if we "identify" an Ottoman site in the landscape, how can we judge the relationship between a broad spectrum of post-medieval pottery finds and a written source describing conditions at one specific point in time? How much pottery of what period should we find in order to be certain of "identifying" a settlement mentioned in the sources? In the end, we try to merge two very different types of sources in one argument.

Furthermore, the problem of identification varies substantially from one region to another. This point may be illustrated by the case of Aitolia, a Greek mountain landscape that forms quite a contrast to the low-lying, easily accessible regions in which most surface surveys have been conducted.[51] Although there are, thanks to Machiel Kiel, detailed Ottoman *defters* available for Aitolia from about the mid-15th century onward, it proves quite another matter to identify the listed settlements archaeologically in the landscape or to associate the 15th- and 16th-century toponyms with currently existing villages or surviving toponyms.[52] In general, virtually no post-medieval pottery is to be found in the Aitolian mountains, and identification of the many listed settlements is possible only by recourse to toponyms on old maps, to names mentioned in travel accounts, or to oral information provided by locals. About one-third of the settlements mentioned in the *defters* remain without certain identification (see Table 4.2).

Another problem, this one not exclusive to Aitolia, is the contrast between the great detail provided in census lists of the late 15th and 16th centuries and the more summary character of those of the 17th and 18th centuries. All kinds of changes can be observed in the lists that are apparently not reflected in the material finds recovered by archaeologists in the field.

Yet another elusive problem is posed by the many new Albanian settlements that are listed in the *defters* of the 15th century. Can we see social and ethnic differences reflected in the pottery finds from these villages and those described as "Greek"?

50. Studies using Western travelers' accounts in combination with contemporary archaeological approaches are, e.g., Bennet and Voutsaki 1991; Davis, Zarinebaf, and Bennet 2000; Vroom 2003; Broodbank, Bennet, and Davis 2004.

51. E.g., Bommeljé et al. 1987; see also Vroom 1998a, pp. 147–158, with further literature.

52. See Doorn 1989 for the possibilities and difficulties of processing data from Ottoman *defters* and identifying settlements in the districts of Lidoriki and Vitrinitsa (in the eastern part of the research area investigated by Doorn's team in Aitolia) that were recorded in 15th- and 16th-century Ottoman registers. See also Kiel 1999b, fig. 15.8, for settlements recorded in the district of Agrafa (in the northern part of the research area).

In general, we cannot explain the contrast between the relative abundance of the easily recognized glazed post-medieval ceramics of the 15th and 16th centuries and the scarcity of later finds, even in settlements that, according to the *defters*, remained inhabited. We have seen such scarcity in Timothy Gregory's surveys in the Corinthia and on Kythera, and apparently there is also a lack of post-medieval pottery on sites in Palestine.[53]

Several hypotheses that might explain this lack of pottery were discussed during the workshop in Cincinnati: shifts in site use, shifts in land use, population movements, and relocations of villages. This absence of archaeological artifacts perhaps can also be explained by the phenomenon of the "sherdless site," a term I introduced in a previous article on early modern ceramics in Greece. There I noted that in some parts of the Mediterranean, and in some periods, people used in their households nonceramic objects made of materials such as wood, stone, basketry, and metal.[54] This could also have been the practice in some parts of Greece (particularly in rural areas) during Ottoman times, especially in the 17th and 18th centuries, reflecting poorer standards of living. In Aitolia, for instance, we know from village interviews and from written sources that transporting ceramics into the mountains was difficult and expensive.[55] People therefore ate from wooden bowls with wooden spoons. Furthermore, metal objects were very much in favor (especially in transhumant households). Over time they were cheaper because, when broken, they could be repaired easily and reused several times.

It is only with the introduction of industrially manufactured wares in the 19th century, which were cheaper and mass-produced in the West, that consumption patterns in Greece began to change.[56] A 19th-century transfer-printed plate with a willow tree design from England, found on the island of Kythera by the Kythera Island Project (Fig. 4.19), is typical of this type of pottery.[57] The introduction of these industrially manufactured wares was accompanied by socioeconomic changes (e.g., by an increase in consumer purchasing power, and by new means of distribution such as steamships), as well as by changes in dining habits. Today these changes are reflected in the large quantities of early modern ceramics (mainly of the 19th and 20th centuries) that archaeological survey teams discover on the surface.

CONCLUSION: THE CURRENT STATE OF AFFAIRS AND FUTURE PROSPECTS

Interest in post-medieval pottery in the Aegean is a fairly recent phenomenon. In fact, excavations in the Aegean have yielded more systematically collected stratigraphical information on medieval and post-medieval ceramics during the past 10 years than was produced in the previous century.

John Hayes's 1992 publication of the pottery from the Saraçhane excavations in Istanbul is a landmark for the study of post-Roman pottery in the eastern Mediterranean for several reasons: (1) the multiperiod nature of the excavation; (2) the comprehensive and detailed presentation of the finds; and (3) the exhaustive comparisons with material from other excavations.

53. For the Corinthia and Kythera, see Chap. 9 in this volume; see Ziadeh 1995, p. 223, and Baram 2002, pp. 20–21, for the Palestinian sites.

54. Vroom 1998a, pp. 151–158.

55. See Bommeljé and Doorn 1996 on the intricate network of roads and khans that existed for the transportation of goods across the Aitolian landscape.

56. Vroom 2003, pp. 236–237.

57. E.g., Broodbank 1999.

We must not cheer too early, however. With regard to post-medieval pottery, the situation is still far from ideal. Although there now exists a basic chronology for fine wares, there is still much uncertainty about the relative dating of many ceramic types. For example, little is known about the local production and dating of glazed wares, and especially of unglazed domestic wares, from parts of the eastern Mediterranean outside Istanbul.

Most recent publications of post-medieval pottery offer few new type-series for the material examined, and little progress has been made in understanding patterns of exchange. The emphasis in most publications continues to be the presentation of complete pots from private or museum collections, and these almost always lack stratigraphical context. As far as post-medieval ceramics in the Aegean are concerned, it seems that the more recent the pottery, the more art-historical and ethnographic the study of it has been. For pottery from the post-medieval period, systematic archaeological research has been done in northern Greece (Macedonia and Thrace), but pottery from excavations in the large urban centers in Greece (e.g., Athens, Corinth, and Thessaloniki) has not been thoroughly studied and little has been published with its stratigraphical context. Studies of the distribution and use of ceramics of the Ottoman and Venetian periods in the Aegean area are lacking altogether.

We need more information about production centers and kilns in the Aegean area. We need more examinations of closed deposits from excavations in the large urban centers, including all excavated material (fine wares as well as cooking wares). In short, we need more scholars pursuing archaeological approaches to research concerning pottery of the Ottoman and Venetian periods in Greece and the Aegean.

In addition, as I have argued before, translations of the Ottoman tax registers have opened up a world of new possibilities, but also a host of new problems. This is because, in the end, one has to admit that it remains difficult to make the jump from the sherd on the surface to the written text in the archives. It is a stimulating, but perhaps also questionable, characteristic of some archaeological projects in Greece that theory building tends to advance far more rapidly than the slow, tedious, less spectacular work of establishing solid typologies and chronologies for ceramic types (not least for coarse wares). So, far from advocating less theory, I believe that the main task of post-medieval archaeology remains the fundamental work of further refining the analysis and documentation of pottery finds. Every new text that becomes available demonstrates the urgency of that task.

REFERENCES

Aravantinos, V., L. Godart, and A. Sacconi. 1995. "Sui nuovi testi del palazzo di Cadmo a Tebe," *RendLinc* 9, no. 6, pp. 809–845.

———, eds. 2001. *Thèbes. Fouilles de la Cadmée* 1: *Les tablettes en linéaire B de la odos Pelopidou: Edition et commentaire,* Pisa.

———, eds. 2002. *Thèbes: Fouilles de la Cadmée* 1: *Les tablettes en linéaire B de la odos Pelopidou,* Pisa.

Aslanapa, O., S. Yetkin, and A. Altun, eds. 1989. *The İznik Tile Excavation,* Istanbul.

Atasoy, N., and J. Raby. 1994. *İznik: The Pottery of Ottoman Turkey,* London.

Bakirtzis, C. 1980. "Didymoteichon: Un centre de céramique post-byzantine," *BalkSt* 21, pp. 147–153.

———. 1984. "Διδυμότειχο," *ArchDelt* 32, B′2 (1977), pp. 284–287.

Baram, U. 1995. "Notes on the Preliminary Typologies of Production and Chronology for the Clay Tobacco Pipes of Cyprus," *RDAC* 1995, pp. 299–309.

———. 1999. "Clay Tobacco Pipes and Coffee Cup Sherds in the Archaeology of the Middle East: Artefacts of Social Tensions from the Ottoman Past," *International Journal of Historical Archaeology* 3, pp. 137–151.

———. 2000. "Entangled Objects from the Palestinian Past: Archaeological Perspectives for the Ottoman Period, 1500–1900," in Baram and Carroll 2000b, pp. 137–159.

———. 2002. "The Development of Historical Archaeology in Israel: An Overview and Prospects," *Historical Archaeology* 36, pp. 12–29.

Baram, U., and L. Carroll. 2000a. "The Future of the Ottoman Past," in Baram and Carroll 2000b, pp. 3–32.

———, eds. 2000b. *A Historical Archaeology of the Ottoman Empire: Breaking New Ground,* New York.

Beeley, B. W. 1970. "The Turkish Village Coffeehouse as a Social Institution," *Geographical Review* 60, pp. 475–493.

Bennet, J., and S. Voutsaki. 1991. "A Synopsis and Analysis of Travelers' Accounts of Keos (to 1821)," in *Landscape Archaeology as Long-Term History: Northern Keos in the Cycladic Islands from Earliest Settlement until Modern Times* (Monumenta archaeologica 16), ed. J. F. Cherry, J. L. Davis, and E. Mantzourani, Los Angeles, pp. 365–382.

Bommeljé, Y., and P. Doorn. 1996. "The Long and Winding Road: Land Routes in Aetolia (Greece) since Byzantine Times," in *Interfacing the Past,* ed. H. Kamermans and K. Fennema, Leiden, pp. 343–351.

Bommeljé, S., P. Doorn, M. Deylius, J. Vroom, Y. Bommeljé, R. Fagel, and H. van Wijngaarden. 1987. *Aetolia and the Aetolians: Towards the Interdisciplinary Study of a Greek Region* (Studia aetolica 1), Utrecht.

Broodbank, C. 1999. "Kythera Survey: Preliminary Report on the 1998 Season," *BSA* 94, pp. 191–214.

Broodbank, C., J. Bennet, and J. L. Davis. 2004. "Aphrodite Observed: Insularity and Antiquities on Kythera through Outsiders' Eyes," in *Explaining Social Change: Studies in Honour of Colin Renfrew,* ed. J. Cherry, C. Scarre, and S. Shennan, Cambridge, pp. 227–239.

Carroll, L. 2000. "Toward an Archaeology of Non-Elite Consumption in Late Ottoman Anatolia," in Baram and Carroll 2000b, pp. 161–183.

Constantine, D. 1984. *Early Greek Travellers and the Hellenic Ideal,* Cambridge.

Cook, H. K. A., and J. R. Green. 2002. "Medieval Glazed Wares from the Theatre Site at Nea Pafos, Cyprus: Preliminary Report," *RDAC* 2002, pp. 413–426.

Davis, J. L., F. Zarinebaf, and J. Bennet. 2000. "The Pylos Regional Archaeological Project III: Sir William Gell's Itinerary in the Pylia and Regional Landscapes in the Morea in the Second Ottoman Period," *Hesperia* 69, pp. 343–380.

Deliyianni-Dori, E., P. Velissariou, and M. Michailidis. 2003. *Κάτω Κάστρο* (*Ανδριακά Χρονικά* 34), Andros.

Doorn, P. 1989. "Population and Settlements in Central Greece: Computer Analysis of Ottoman Registers of the Fifteenth and Sixteenth

Centuries," in *History and Computing* II, ed. P. Denley, S. Fogelvik, and C. Harvey, Manchester, pp. 19–208.

Faroqhi, S. 1999. *Approaching Ottoman History: An Introduction to the Sources,* Cambridge.

François, V., and L. Vallauri. 2001. "Production et consommation de céramiques à Potamia (Chypre) de l'époque franque à l'époque ottomane," *BCH* 125, pp. 523–546.

Frantz, M. A. 1942. "Turkish Pottery from the Agora," *Hesperia* 11, pp. 1–28.

Gabrieli, R. S., B. McCall, and J. R. Green. 2001. "Medieval Kitchen Wares from the Theatre Site at Nea Pafos," *RDAC* 2001, pp. 335–356.

Gilkes, O., A. Crowson, R. Hodges, K. Lako, and J. Vroom. 2002. "Medieval Butrint: Excavations at the Triconch Palace 2000 and 2001," *Archeologia medievale* 29, pp. 343–353.

Given, M. 2000. "Agriculture, Settlement, and Landscape in Ottoman Cyprus," *Levant* 32, pp. 209–230.

Goldthwaite, R. A. 1989. "The Economic and Social World of Italian Renaissance Maiolica," *Renaissance Quarterly* 42, pp. 1–32.

Greene, M. 2000. *A Shared World: Christians and Muslims in the Early Modern Mediterranean,* Princeton.

Hahn, M. 1989. "Byzantine and Post-Byzantine Pottery from the Greek-Swedish Excavations at Khania, Crete," in *Recherches sur la céramique byzantine* (*BCH* Suppl. 18), ed. V. Déroche and J. M. Spieser, Athens, pp. 227–232.

———. 1991. "A Group of 15th–16th-Century Jugs from Western Crete," *Acta Hyperborea* 3, pp. 311–320.

———. 1997. "Modern Greek, Turkish, and Venetian Periods: The Pottery and the Finds," in *The Greek-Swedish Excavations at the Agia Aikaterini Square, Kastelli, Khania, 1970–1987,* ed. E. Hallager and B. P. Hallager, Stockholm, pp. 170–196.

Hattox, R. S. 1985. *Coffee and Coffeehouses: The Origins of a Social Beverage in the Medieval Near East,* Seattle.

Hayes, J. W. 1980. "Turkish Clay Pipes: A Provisional Typology," in *The Archaeology of the Clay Tobacco Pipe* 4, ed. P. Davey, 2nd ed., rev., Oxford, pp. 233–395.

———. 1981. "The Excavated Pottery from the Bodrum Camii," in *The Myrelaion (Bodrum Camii) in Istanbul,* ed. C. L. Striker, Princeton, pp. 36–41.

———. 1992. *Excavations at Saraçhane in Istanbul* 2: *The Pottery,* Princeton.

Hodges, R., W. Bowden, O. J. Gilkes, and K. Lako. 2000. "Late Roman Butrint, Albania: Survey and Excavations," *Archeologia medievale* 27, pp. 241–257.

Kiel, M. 1991. "Byzantine Architecture and Painting in Central Greece 1460–1570: Its Demographic and Economic Basis According to the Ottoman Census and Taxation Registers for Central Greece Preserved in Istanbul and Ankara," *Byzantinische Forschungen* 16, pp. 429–446.

———. 1992. "Central Greece in the Süleymanic Age: Preliminary Notes on Population Growth, Economic Expansion, and Its Influence on the Spread of Greek Christian Culture," in *Soliman le Magnifique et son temps,* ed. G. Veinstein, Paris, pp. 399–424.

———. 1997. "The Rise and Decline of Turkish Boeotia, 15th–19th Century (Remarks on the Settlement Pattern, Demography, and Agricultural Production According to Unpublished Ottoman-Turkish Census and Taxation Records)," in *Recent Developments in the History and Archaeology of Central Greece. Proceedings of the 6th International Boeotian Conference* (*BAR-IS* 666), ed. J. L. Bintliff, Oxford, pp. 315–358.

———. 1999a. "The Icon and the Mosque: Orthodox Christian Art as a Source to Retrieve the Lost Monuments of Ottoman Architecture of Southern Greece, the Case of İstife/Thebes," in *Essays in Honor of Aptullah Kuran,* ed. Ç. Kafescioğlu and L. Thys-Senocak, Istanbul, pp. 223–232.

———. 1999b. "The Ottoman Imperial Registers: Central Greece and Northern Bulgaria in the 15th–19th Century, the Demographic Development of Two Areas Compared," in *Reconstructing Past Population Trends in Mediterranean Europe*

(3000 B.C.–A.D. 1800), ed. J. F. Bintliff and K. Sbonias, Oxford, pp. 195–218.

Kontoyiannis, N. 2002. *Μεσαιωνικά κάστρα και οχυρώσεις της Κω,* Athens.

Korre-Zographou, K. 1995. *Τα κεραμεικά του ελληνικού χώρου,* Athens.

Lane, A. 1939. "Turkish Peasant Pottery from Chanak and Kutahia," *The Connoisseur* 104, pp. 232–259.

———. 1957. *Later Islamic Pottery: Persia, Syria, Turkey, Egypt,* 2nd ed., London.

MacKay, T. S. 1996. "A Group of Renaissance Pottery from Heraklion, Crete: Notes and Questions," in *The Archaeology of Medieval Greece,* ed. P. Lock and G. D. R. Sanders, Oxford, pp. 127–137.

Megaw, A. H. S. 1951. "Three Medieval Pit-Groups from Nicosia," *RDAC* 1937–1939, pp. 145–162.

Papanikola-Bakirtzi, D., ed. 1999. *Byzantine Glazed Ceramics: The Art of Sgraffito,* Athens.

Robinson, R. C. W. 1983. "Clay Tobacco Pipes from the Kerameikos," *AM* 98, pp. 265–285.

———. 1985. "Tobacco Pipes of Corinth and of the Athenian Agora," *Hesperia* 54, pp. 149–203.

Simpson, St. J. 1990. "Ottoman Clay Pipes from Jerusalem and the Levant: A Critical Review of the Published Evidence," *Society for Clay Pipe Research Newsletter* 28, pp. 6–16.

———. 1993. "Turkish Clay Pipes: A Review," *Society for Clay Pipe Research Newsletter* 39, pp. 17–23.

———. 1998. "'Where There's Smoke, There's Fire . . .' Pipe-Smoking in the Ottoman Empire," *British Museum Magazine* 31, pp. 15–17.

Soustal, P. 2004. "The History of Butrint in the Middle Ages," in *Butrint: Excavations and Survey 1994–1999,* ed. W. Bowden, R. Hodges, and K. Lako, Oxford.

Symeonoglou, S. 1985. *The Topography of Thebes from Bronze Age to Modern Times,* Princeton.

Tite, M. S. 1989. "İznik Pottery: An Investigation of the Methods of Production," *Archaeometry* 31, pp. 115–132.

Tsouris, K. E. 1982. "Κεραμεικά Ιωαννίνων από το τέλος του 18ου αιώνα," *Ηπειρωτικά Χρονικά* 24, pp. 267–281.

Vavylopoulou-Charitonidou, A. 1981–1982. "Νεοελληνική κεραμεική στην Άρτα επί Τουρκοκρατίας," *Εθνογραφικά* 3, pp. 5–22.

———. 1984. "Βυζαντινά κεραμεικά στην Άρτα," *Δελτίον της Χριστιανικής Αρχαιολογικής Εταιρείας* 4, pp. 453–472.

———. 1986–1987. "Μεταβυζαντινά αγγεία από το κάστρο των Ρωγών," *Ηπειρωτικά Χρονικά* 28, pp. 37–42.

von Wartburg-Maier, M.-L. 2001. "Types of Imported Table Ware at Kouklia in the Ottoman Period," *RDAC* 2001, pp. 361–396.

Vroom, J. 1996. "Coffee and Archaeology: A Note on a Kütahya Ware Find in Boeotia, Greece," *Pharos* 4, pp. 5–19.

———. 1997. "Pots and Pans: New Perspectives on the Medieval Ceramics of Greece," in *Material Culture in Medieval Europe: Papers of the "Medieval Europe Brugge 1997" Conference* 7, ed. G. De Boe and F. Verhaeghe, Zellik, pp. 203–213.

———. 1998a. "Early Modern Archaeology in Central Greece: The Contrast of Artefact-Rich and Sherdless Sites," *JMA* 11, pp. 131–164.

———. 1998b. "Medieval and Post-Medieval Pottery from a Site in Boeotia: A Case Study Example of Post-Classical Archaeology in Greece," *BSA* 93, pp. 513–546.

———. 2000. "Byzantine Garlic and Turkish Delight: Dining Habits and Cultural Change in Central Greece from Byzantine to Ottoman Times," *Archaeological Dialogues* 7, pp. 129–216.

———. 2003. *After Antiquity: Ceramics and Society in the Aegean from the Seventh to the Twentieth Century A.C. A Case Study from Boeotia, Central Greece* (Archaeological Studies, Leiden University 10), Leiden.

———. 2005. *Byzantine to Modern Pottery in the Aegean: An Introduction and Field Guide,* Utrecht.

———. 2006. "Byzantine Garbage and Ottoman Waste," in *Thèbes. Fouilles de la Cadmée* II.2: *Les tablettes en Linéaire B de la "Odos Pelopidou." La céramique de la Odos Pelopidou et la chronologie du Linéaire B,* E. Andrikou, V. L. Aravantinos, L. Godard, A. Sacconi, and J. Vroom, Pisa and Rome, pp. 181–233.

Waagé, F. O. 1933. "Excavations in the Athenian Agora: The Roman and Byzantine Pottery," *Hesperia* 2, pp. 279–328.

Ward, C. 2000. "The Sadana Island Shipwreck: A Mid-Eighteenth-Century Treasure Trove," in Baram and Carroll 2000b, pp. 185–202.

Zarinebaf, F., J. Bennet, and J. L. Davis. 2005. *A Historical and Economic Geography of Ottoman Greece: The Southwestern Morea in the 18th Century* (*Hesperia* Suppl. 34), Princeton.

Ziadeh, G. 1995. "Ottoman Ceramics from Ti'innik, Palestine," *Levant* 27, pp. 209–245.

Ziadeh-Seeley, G. 2000. "The Archaeology of Ottoman Ti'innik: An Interdisciplinary Approach," in Baram and Carroll 2000, pp. 79–91.

PART II: ETHNICITY AND POPULATION STABILITY IN SOUTHERN GREECE AND ON CYPRUS

Questions raised by the sheer magnitude of the population shifts documented in areas that now fall within the borders of Greece must be confronted by all scholars of the early modern Balkans. Have we been viewing the history of settlement in these lands from an overly narrow perspective, one shaped by policies of the centralized state government of the modern Greek state? Are there alternative, more nuanced histories yet to be written—those that emphasize regional distinctions and relationships between local populations that may not always have identified themselves as Greek and central imperial governments that have dominated them economically, socially, and politically?

Both material culture and text may be brought to bear on questions of identity in early modern Greece, yet ethnicity too rarely has been the focus of scholarly investigations. In part, this situation must reflect a still commonly found belief among scholars of Greek history—that since classical antiquity a Greek race, speaking the Greek language, has remained dominant and stable in both the rural and the urban populations throughout the lands that now constitute the Greek nation.

Such a notion is clearly mistaken. Ottoman texts document, for example, the wide and dense distribution of Albanian settlement in areas such as the Corinthia as early as the 15th century. There are interesting questions to be posed. Through what forces has the Greek state succeeded in incorporating into a homogeneous Greek society peoples who once did not speak Greek, observe the Orthodox faith, or identify themselves as Greek? Archaeological and documentary information also can threaten the concept of the timeless village by working in synergy to permit the composition of histories of individual settlements. At the same time, it is clear that documentary evidence, in and of itself, is not sufficient to monitor population growth and decline.

Alexis Malliaris, a historian of early modern Greece who specializes in the period of Venetian ascendancy in the Morea (1687–1715), in Chapter 5 draws on material explored in his dissertation regarding settlement in the north of the peninsula. Here he explains the Venetian government's strategy of encouraging immigrants to settle on land deserted by Muslims, and explores the interaction between native and immigrant communities and particularly the social structure of immigrant groups. Although the general outline of these developments is known to historians, Malliaris's very original contribution is to demonstrate how immigrants gained economic and social status through the Venetian use of quasi-feudal, or, as he calls them, para-feudal, institutions to create a new landed class. This instance is, of course, only one of many in which various states (Ottoman, Byzantine, Frankish, and Venetian) either promoted or forced migration into lands now belonging to modern Greece.

In Chapter 6, Hamish Forbes, an anthropologist and archaeologist who has conducted research in the northeastern Peloponnese for more than 30 years, examines the population history of one Orthodox, almost entirely Albanian-speaking, village on the Saronic Gulf peninsula of Methana. He finds that the interpretation of evidence, as documented in official records of the modern Greek state, must be approached with caution. In particular, that households and individuals sometimes were recorded under nicknames, not stable surnames, often giving a false impression of discontinuity in population. After the establishment of the modern Greek state, political and economic instability was a significant factor in encouraging migration to Methana from Ottoman territories, but Forbes draws the important conclusion, on the basis of his study of sources from the 19th century that date to after the nation of Greece was established, that fluidity and instability of rural populations are likely to have been the norm in early modern Greek lands.

Both Malliaris and Forbes found their conclusions on documentary and historical evidence. In contrast, in Chapter 7, Michael Given, an archaeologist prominent in two recent significant regional studies of mountainous, frequently marginal, uplands on Cyprus, establishes a dialectical relationship among (1) material cultural remains documented by his own research projects; (2) the written testimonia of archived bureaucratic documents commissioned by the various imperial powers that in succession controlled that island (most recently, Great Britain); and (3) more casual comments extracted from the travelogues of Western visitors. Above all, his observations emphasize once again the need to be critical, even at times skeptical, in our use of archival sources. In particular, it is dangerous to assume that early modern censuses can be employed unequivocally to reconstruct past patterns of settlement and premodern distributions of population.

Population Exchange and Integration of Immigrant Communities in the Venetian Morea, 1687–1715

by Alexis Malliaris

THE VENETIAN OCCUPATION OF THE PELOPONNESE

The occupation of the Peloponnese (Morea) by Venetian troops under Francesco Morosini was part of the extended turbulence caused by the European alliances against the Ottomans during the second half of the 17th century. The siege of Vienna by the Ottomans in 1683 alarmed the entire European world and changed dramatically the way the Christian states of the West would confront the Ottoman danger. In 1684 the Holy Roman Empire, Poland, and Venice joined to form the Holy League of Linz, which launched the defense of Europe on two fronts: one in central Europe and the northern Balkans, on the initiative of the Hapsburgs, and one in the Greek sphere under the Venetians.[1] The conquest of the Peloponnese by the Venetian military, which was not a planned political and military goal but rather an accidental event, led to the annexation of the peninsula by the Venetian state.[2]

The country was conquered in stages from 1685 to 1687, although Monemvasia did not fall until 1690. The Treaty of Karlowitz, in 1699, granted posession of the Morea to Venice. The Venetian presence there was destined to be short, however; the Ottomans, following a violent invasion in 1715, reoccupied the area, limiting Venice's territorial possessions in Greece to the Ionian Sea.

1. I am indebted to Siriol Davies and Jack Davis for their unlimited generosity and compassion. Abbreviations used are as follows: ASV = Archivio di Stato di Venezia; b. = *busta* (a large file); f. = *filza* (an independently numbered subsection of a *busta*); fol. = folio; r = recto; v = verso. On this period in general, see Eickoff 1991; Cessi 1981; Lane 1978.

2. For a general view of the Venetian conquest of the Peloponnese and the period of the second Venetian rule in the Morea, see Kalligas 1998; Liata and Tsiknakis 1998; Dokos and Panagopoulos 1993; Cozzi 1985a, 1985b; Guida 1989; Davies 1996, 2004; and Malliaris 2001, 2002. The last three works include complete bibliography concerning the entire period. With regard to the war in the Morea in particular, see Stouraiti 2001 for published archival material from the Querini Stampalia Library in Venice.

VENETIAN IMMIGRATION POLICY

The most important consequence of Venice's establishment in the area came as a result of its colonization policy. Taking over a wasteland, the Venetians urgently needed to fill major gaps in the population of the countryside. To that end, they induced massive population movements from various Greek areas toward these abandoned regions, which had to accept a vast number of immigrants.[3]

Inhabitants of Athens, Thebes, Livadia, Lepanto, Euboia, Chios, and Crete followed the defeated Venetians into the Peloponnese after enduring military conflict in their own regions. Inhabitants of the Venetian Ionian islands, Epirus (mainly Ioannina), and Macedonia, areas that were under Ottoman domination, as well as people from Constantinople and Smyrna with Peloponnesian origins, came to the new Venetian colony looking for a better life. Italians, Croatians, Dalmatians, and Germans, mercenaries of the Venetian army, found themselves in the Peloponnese after the cessation of hostilities, which in many instances was concurrent with the end of their military careers.[4]

The first immigrants, apart from those who had already reached the area during the Veneto-Ottoman conflicts, started arriving immediately after the occupation of the Peloponnesian fort-cities by Venetian troops and the expulsion of the Ottomans in 1687. From 1687 to 1700 the arrival of the immigrants was significant, as thousands of refugees and inhabitants from the mainland and islands were drawn to the Morea, fleeing protracted atrocities in various parts of what is now Greece.

The Venetian authorities, from the first year of the occupation, strove to welcome and settle the foreigners. Venice had extensive experience in moving populations from one place to another, as similar measures had to be taken in the broader Greek world every time one of its colonies was taken by the Ottomans, a process that began with Venetian losses in the 15th century. In the case of the Peloponnese, however, the massive settlement of immigrants who were in fact refugees fleeing violence presented situations that differed from those previously handled by Venice.

First, the majority of immigrants did not emerge from Venetian-controlled areas and were not moving to a place with a long-established history of Venetian dominion. These people were unfamiliar with the Venetian system of governance, its codes, and its institutions. The Venetians welcomed the immigrants to a region that was only nominally theirs and in which they had not had time to establish control. Moreover, the fact

3. The Venetians described the Morea on their arrival as underpopulated, perhaps a result of the 16th-century economic crisis in the Ottoman Empire. In 1689 they estimated the population to be 89,000 (excluding Corinth and Mani), and 250,000 by 1709, although neither figure is entirely reliable (Topping 1972, pp. 71–72). For general accounts of migration in preindustrial Europe, see Page-Moch 1992, and Lucassen and Lucassen 1997.

4. For a discussion of migration to the Venetian Peloponnese, see Malliaris 2001, with all the related bibliography. On the mobility of peasant populations as a reaction to crisis, see Chap. 6 in this volume.

that their occupation of the Peloponnese was relatively recent, and that the country was emerging from a long period of Ottoman domination that had determined its identity, prevented the Venetian administration from managing the situation adequately.

The enduring efforts of the Venetian authorities to distinguish between public and private property in order to supply immigrants with land proves that they were not familiar with the economic structures of their new dominion.[5] The country's Ottoman past, which had left a decisive stamp, could not easily be acknowledged by the new Venetian power, which, despite its long presence in the Greek world, had never before experienced a similar succession. The Peloponnese and Lefkas (Santa Maura) were the only instances in the history of the Venetian Levant in which the Venetians took territory from the Ottomans rather than vice versa. (Elsewhere, only in the northern Balkans and the Slavophonic world were areas under Ottoman control transferred to Venice; in the case of Dalmatia, Venetians enforced a similar practice that involved the transfer of populations from Ottoman areas to their newly conquered territories.)

The settlement of immigrants in the newly conquered area and the way in which the Venetians dealt with the different population groups reveal different expectations. To the Athenians the Venetians were generous in allotting land; they were expecting from them a substantial contribution to the financial recovery of the area because many of them were of a superior economic and social class and were involved in commercial activities.[6]

The vast numbers of immigrants from the rest of central Greece were dealt with in a different way. These people, who formed the basic population element, especially in the area of the northern Peloponnese, were mainly farmers and shepherds. As they were predestined to cultivate the land, they were scattered along the lowlands of the north, northwest, and northeast Peloponnese from Gastouni, Patras, and Vostitsa to Corinth, Argos, and Nauplion (Napoli di Romania), where they lived mainly in the villages. In contrast, the cities of Patras and Nauplion also received a large proportion of "first-class" immigrants, according to the unofficial categorization of the Venetian administration, which reflected the immigrants' previous situation in their places of origin.[7]

It seems that in the first years of the Venetian occupation, the settlement of the population in particular areas of the country where there were large areas of deserted territory was accomplished mainly on the initiative of the immigrants themselves. The Athenians, the most powerful group, favored the cities and settled in Patras, Gastouni, and Nauplion as well as in Mystras. Patras also was chosen by the powerful people of central Greece, and the same city was a center for the activities of islanders from the Ionian Sea, mainly from Kephalonia and Zante. The Catholic families from Chios who left their island in 1694, after the failure of Venetian troops to capture it, settled mainly in Methoni, although some of them preferred Nauplion. Finally, a number of Cretans reached Lakonia and settled mostly in Monemvasia and Molaoi.

After the first years of the Venetian conquest, when the most favorable areas—that is, the lowlands—had already been occupied, the Venetian

5. For further discussion of public and private land, see Malliaris 2001, pp. 91–113; Davies 2004, pp. 86–90. For a general overview, see Malliaris 2003.

6. Malliaris 2001, pp. 26–37. For the activities of the Athenians in Corinth, see Davies 2002.

7. Dokos 1975; Malliaris 2001, pp. 38–48. Immigrants were divided into three classes for the purposes of determining their allotments of public land and revenues.

authorities tried in some instances to plan settlement, situating the newcomers in places that were still only partially inhabited. This was done with people from Ioannina and Ayios Donatos (Paramythia) of Epirus, who were placed in the lowlands of Messenia, where large tracts of land were still uncultivated. In contrast, the areas of Patras and Gastouni were excluded because they were already occupied by a considerable number of people from Athens and the rest of Roumeli (central Greece).

INTERACTION OF IMMIGRANT AND NATIVE POPULATIONS AND THE FORMATION OF NEW IDENTITIES

The fact that various population groups coming from the wider Ottoman-dominated Greek world had to live together created problems for the construction of a well-integrated society. These groups had different social and financial backgrounds, cultural perceptions, and religious creeds, as in the case of the Chios Catholics. This often led to tension and disputes not only among the immigrants, but also in their relationship with the native populations.

The new immigrants to the Peloponnese met not only the native Greeks and Albanians (Arvanites), but also Christianized Muslims *(Turchi fatti Cristiani),* who had stayed in the country when the Ottomans left.[8] In some cases, for example in Achaia and Messenia, grants of land from the Venetian authorities of the Morea to foreigners provoked a reaction on the part of the natives, who claimed that their fathers' land was being usurped by the newcomers with the tolerance of the Venetian administration. Similar claims also were made by the Christianized Muslims, who, whether Orthodox or Catholic, claimed part of their paternal property. Some of these were descendants of Ottoman officeholders in the Morea who had cultivated large pieces of land.

The immigrants were compelled to cope with the native groups and eventually their interrelationships came to form new social, economic, and political structures. The mutual confrontation of the immigrants and the natives as groups presupposed that each group would participate in the formation of the identities of the others. Different social organizations and symbols of status, as well as self-determination and external recognition, were elements that resulted in the formulation of an image and identity for each population group.[9]

The blending of the population groups ultimately imparted a cosmopolitan image to the cities of Nauplion and Patras. This marked these cities as important administrative and commercial centers of the Peloponnese and attracted others to them. People of Greek origin from different parts of the wider Greek world, as well as those of Italian, Venetian, and Slavic origin who had been mercenaries in the Venetian army, mingled and lived together in all possible combinations. Natives and foreigners, Greeks and Italians, Orthodox and Catholic, as well as Christianized Muslims, coexisted during the entire Venetian period.[10]

8. For the *Turchi fatti Cristiani,* see Nikolaou 1997, pp. 55–80; Malliaris 2001, pp. 72–77.

9. For discussion of the construction of group identities, see Malliaris 2001, pp. 22–25.

10. A general account can be found in Malliaris 1997a.

Mixed marriages were a significant factor in this integration. Immigrants married not only native individuals, but also immigrants from the same or different areas as well as people of Venetian or Slavic origin. Marriages between people of Greek and Venetian origin are particularly interesting not only because they involved individuals of different religious creeds, but also because of the unequal relationship between the dominated Greeks and the dominant Italians.

Examination of the Venetian documents relating to mixed marriages offers information about this custom and also reveals the attitude of the people, women in particular, toward it. We have, for instance, data for the population of the city of Patras, where there lived a large number of foreigners, Greek immigrants from the Ottoman empire, and Italians. This city, as an important harbor for Venetian commerce and a center of vital economic interest, attracted a significant number of immigrants and merchants who settled in the region. As a result, mixed marriages were frequent, and documents from the *Archivio Grimani ai Servi* provide us with information about them.[11] The following couples are listed for the year 1700:

woman from Thebes and man from Patras
woman from Thebes and man from the Peloponnese
woman from Salona and man from the Ionian islands
woman from Salona and man from Patras
woman from Salona and man of Italian origin
woman from Thebes and man from Athens
woman from Roumeli and man from Patras
woman from Roumeli and man from Crete.[12]

We have further information on the subject from the archive of the Carmelitani Scalzi, the Catholic monastery of St. Andrew of Patras. Among the archival materials of the monastery are several marriage licenses signed between 1705 and 1715 by the Catholic archbishop of the Peloponnese, Angelo Maria Carlini. There are seven marriages between Greek women and Italian men:

Antonius Bona and Maria Atheniensi
Jacobus Baruvier and Ioanna Psaromilico
Nicolaus Sandri and Anna Magodi
Johannes Riccius and Anastasia Pilasopula
Johannes Benetto and Assimina Vimacci
Ippolitus Barbieri and Despina de Maria
Antonius Alberti and Panoria da Salona.[13]

These cases as well as others from the peninsula as a whole reveal a certain ease in relations among the various groups that lived in the new Venetian region, at least after the formal establishment of Venetian rule in 1699. Such interaction is only to be expected, given the opportunities offered by the circumstances, the effort of the Venetian authorities to increase the population of the Morea, and the subsequent influx of immigrants.

11. Francesco Grimani was governor general of the Morea from 1698 to 1700.

12. ASV, *Archivio Grimani ai Servi,* b.32, f.86, fol. 134v–141r; see also Malliaris 2001, p. 195.

13. ASV, *Materie ecclesiastiche,* b.7, fol. 125r–138r; see also Malliaris 2001, pp. 196–197.

THE SOCIAL ORGANIZATION OF IMMIGRANT GROUPS

The immigration and settlement of the various population groups in the Peloponnese had important consequences not only for the demographics of the Morea, but also for other parts of the Aegean.[14] The following data concerning household types were drawn from the lists of land distributions and grants of public land *(concessioni di beni)* to immigrants by the Venetian authorities of the Peloponnese.

The dominant domestic or household demographic type was that of the nuclear family, although there were other, more complicated varieties of familial organization that themselves present internal variations (mainly in the groups of Christianized Muslims who stayed in the Peloponnese after the Ottomans had departed).[15] For instance, in a list of public lands granted to immigrants in the province of Achaia during the years 1699–1701, we recognize a high percentage of nuclear families; in second place is a type of household consisting of only a single individual; and in third place is that of the extended nuclear family.[16] In the last case, the data offer some detailed information about the structure of these families, their size, and, in particular, the nature of their composition. The following variations can be seen:

the couple, their children, and the man's mother
the couple and the man's father
the couple and the man's sister
the couple, their children, and the man's brother
the couple and the man's nephew
a widower, his children, and his mother
an adult son, his mother, and his brothers
an adult son and his mother
a widow and her brother

It is clear that all family members living with a couple were relatives of the man of the couple. This is not coincidence, given the fixed structures characteristic of preindustrial families. Further, an unmarried adult son who lived with his mother was the head of the family, not the widowed mother.

Another registration of immigrants, from Livadia (Roumeli) to Vostitsa (1700), also demonstrates the predominance of the nuclear family. Of 25 households, 22 are of the nuclear type of family, two are of the extended nuclear type (a son with his mother; a widower with his children and his mother), and one consists of a household without parental or conjugal bond (unmarried brothers).[17] Finally, a registration of the immigrants of Chios at Methoni (1699) yields the following information: of 75 families, 47 are nuclear families, 12 consist of a single member, 11 lack a parental or conjugal bond, and 5 are extended nuclear families.[18]

14. For the size of the total population of the Peloponnese and other demographic issues pertaining to the Venetian censuses, see Panayiotopoulos 1987, pp. 135–206.

15. For a detailed discussion of demographic issues and the types of households, see Malliaris 2001, pp. 199–215; in the classification of the various types of households, I used the typological model proposed by Peter Laslett (Laslett and Wall 1972).

16. Dokos 1975, pp. 176–206.

17. ASV, *Archivio Grimani ai Servi,* b.35, fol. 453r–454v; see also Malliaris 2001, p. 204.

18. ASV, *Archivio Grimani ai Servi,* b.30, fol. 898r–909r.

The various forms of the family result not only from the circumstances of immigration (the long distance between the homeland and the Morea; the effects of diseases—plague in particular—and the resulting high death rate of older people during the displacement), but also from the attitude of immigrants who, in many cases, preferred to move to the Morea alone, without their families, in order to investigate the opportunities for permanent settlement. This strategy explains the fact that many men are registered as single in households of which they are the only member, as they most likely belonged to larger family units in their homelands.

THE ROLE OF IMMIGRANTS IN TRANSFORMING PELOPONNESIAN SOCIETY

The immigrants quickly incorporated themselves into the local social structures and transformed them significantly, as demonstrated by an analysis of land grants and the membership of communal institutions in the Morea. The instability of the period provided many possibilities for economic and social advancement, a situation that many of the immigrants took advantage of in order to improve their status.

Despite the fact that some of the immigrants in the end simply "transmitted" their previous social and economic status to the Morea, chances for social mobility granted by the era contributed to a change of social status for many of the immigrants as well as for many of the natives. Mountain-dwellers, peasants, and shepherds settled in the city, where they received land grants from the administration, leased land, and farmed taxes, which lent them urban characteristics and an important presence with regard to local issues.

Over time and after continual grants of public land from the Venetian authorities, many newcomers acquired huge parcels of land. The distinction of some of them as landowners, their immediate attachment to the Venetian authority, their acquisition of honorary titles, and their participation with special privileges in the constituted *comunità* (communal institutions; see the next section)[19] had immediate consequences for the social body.

With regard to landowning in the Peloponnese, the phenomenon of the *contea* (land under the jurisdiction of a count) is of special interest.[20] The Venetian authorities, in order to recompense some of the new residents who had provided important military services against the Ottomans, assigned them large parcels of land under the *contea* regime, conferring upon them at the same time the hereditary honorary title of *conte* (count). The land allotted as *contea* was similar to a fief, but came with certain limitations: it could not be sold and, although granted in perpetuity, could be assigned only to male descendants of the *conte*.[21]

The *contea* in the Morea was totally unknown to Venetian historiography until my research in the Archivio di Stato di Venezia. Archival material, in the form of letters *(dispacci)* written by the Venetian authorities of the Peloponnese, as well as records of the *provveditori sopra feudi* (magistrates responsible for feudal grants), offers an abundance of information concerning the establishment of this institution. The earliest evidence for the

19. For discussion of the *comunità* in more detail, see the next section. On the institution of the *comunità* in the Greco-Venetian Levant, see Papadia-Lala 1993 and 2004.

20. For the terms of landowning in the Venetian Peloponnese, see the introduction to Dokos and Panagopoulos 1993; Davies 2004, pp. 86–100; and Malliaris 2001, pp. 91–143.

21. For the establishment of the *contea* in the Morea and the families that held this title, see details in Malliaris 2001, pp. 144–184. The families who acquired the title *conte* in the northwestern Peloponnese were the Macola, Bosichi, Dousmani, Perouli, and Logotheti, all Athenian except for the Logotheti, who came from Zante; see ASV, *Provveditori sopra feudi*, b.1039 (file of the Bosichi family).

existence of the *contea* is provided by *Provveditore* Francesco Grimani, in a letter dated 1699, and the first application of this institution was for the benefit of the Athenian family Macola, immigrants to Patras.[22]

The obligations to the state were the payment of a one-time sum known as *laudemio,*[23] and the tithe per annum.[24] There were also some variations on the obligations. In addition to the *laudemio* and the tithe, the Venetian administration, after 1701, fixed another sum to be paid annually as *livello perpetuo* (permanent lease) in order to increase the public revenues and, in so doing, offset loss of revenues from the concession of the *contea.*

For the renewal *(investitura)* of the *contea,* it was obligatory that the new holder be able to verify that he was a legal descendant of the first recipient and that he was a permanent resident of the Morea. In addition, the state demanded from the new count an expression of faith and devotion *(fedeltà)* to the Venetian government.[25]

All these conditions meant that the *contea* was similar to a fief, except that it did not entail any future obligation for military service. The use of terms such as *contea, laudemio, investitura,* and *fedeltà* in the documents points to a connection with the feudal part of Europe's history, but in the period of Venetian rule in the Morea at the beginning of the 18th century, the feudal past was already distant. It would be more correct to refer to institutions in the Venetian Morea as parafeudal, echoing the old feudal world of Western Europe.[26]

The grant of the title *conte* and the declaration of large grants of land as *contea* to certain individuals (mainly to the Athenian immigrants of Achaia, but also to other immigrants elsewhere in the Peloponnese, and to some natives) clearly distinguished these persons from the rest of the population. They were placed by the Venetian authorities at a higher social level, and often, especially in the case of the prominent Athenians who received the title of *conte* in Achaia, they functioned at a local level as agents of the Venetian administration and as intermediaries between Venetians and Greeks.

In the city of Patras, for example, the Athenian families Macola and Bosichi, families with a powerful social and economic presence, were both possessors of *contea* (which included entire villages and their inhabitants), the Macola family having been granted the title before the Bosichi. It is worth noting that both, in essence, were appointed to replace former Ottoman landowners at the local level, as, through land grants and the renting of public lands, they occupied lands that certain Ottomans had possessed during the previous period.

22. ASV, *Provveditori da Terra e da Mar,* b.849, no. 58, July 26, 1699, Tripolitsa.

23. *Laudemio* is a feudal term and was in use during the Middle Ages in Western Europe. For an analysis of it see Malliaris 2001, pp. 153–154; Gasparis 1997, p. 161.

24. On the issue of the tithe in the Venetian Morea, see Davies 1994, 1996.

25. ASV, *Provveditori da Terra e da Mar,* b.854, no. 7, March 9, 1709, Kalamata.

26. For an interpretation of feudal institutions in Europe, see Hilton 1976; 1983, pp. 166–170. On feudalism in Latin Greece, see Jacoby 1971; Topping 1977; Kasdagli 1999, pp. 161–194. For the phenomenon of *contea* in the Venetian Terraferma, see Zamperetti 1991.

THE VENETIAN COMUNITÀ

The establishment of the institution known as *comunità* (a citizen body responsible for urban governance whose members were eligible for offices relating to justice, policing, market trading, hygiene, etc.) was one of the most important novelties introduced during the Venetian occupation of the Morea. Initially it was a factor of utmost importance in the integration of the immigrants into the new Venetian possession, and afterward in emphasizing their social distinction. The inception of this institution marked, in every city, the creation of a new local class of powerful families whose supremacy rested on land ownership, on participation in the *comunità,* and on a direct relationship with the Venetian authorities that resulted in their release from any obligation to provide public service.

Study of the *comunità* of Patras has shown that local families that had social importance during the previous Ottoman period maintained their high status in the new Venetian era, and coexisted in the *consiglio* (council) of the *comunità* with the families of the immigrants who had managed to become a part of it with the support of the Venetian authorities. The Athenian families (again with the Macola and Bosichi families preeminent) prevailed in the *comunità* as the most prominent *cittadini* (citizens); in other Peloponnesian *comunità* as well, new inhabitants managed to become members and to acquire an exceptional position in the local communities, which allowed them to take advantage of native individuals.[27]

Communal groups oligarchic and hereditary in nature were in this way created; their restricted membership led to the hardening of distinctions between social groups. With the establishment of the *comunità,* there was an immediate segregation of the social body into two groups, one with a specific number of people and the other with more numerous members. The first group comprised a specific and limited number of families *(cittadini),* quite often foreigners, who were members of the *comunità* and whose privileges depended on the Venetian administration. They received relief from various burdens (immunity from public service, for instance), which were transferred to the majority of the native and immigrant population that was not a part of the *comunità.*[28]

SOCIAL STRATIFICATION AND THE FLIGHT OF PEASANTS

As time passed, the groups diverged more radically and the agrarian population was even more burdened, since it had become completely responsible for the local population's financial obligations to the state. The weaker part of the population had to suffer arbitrary actions from officials and army officers, the members of the *comunità,* the tenants of public lands, and the tax collectors, especially those who collected the tithe. Disappointment with the Peloponnesian environment, and the oppression under which the common people suffered, led many ex-refugees, especially in the northern and northwestern Peloponnese, to abandon their new homes and return to their Ottoman-controlled native lands in central Greece.[29]

27. Malliaris 2001, pp. 230–246; Papadia-Lala 2004, pp. 480–489.

28. See Dokos 1999–2000; Malliaris 2001, pp. 250–261; and Davies 2004, pp. 72–75.

29. For this phenomenon, see Malliaris 2001, pp. 262–276; Davies 2004, p. 105.

The Venetian authorities of the Morea, and especially those of Achaia and Romania (the province of the capital city of Nauplion), took steps to stop the flight of immigrants, a phenomenon that created serious problems for the Venetian administration during the entire period that they occupied the Peloponnese. Among these steps were posting guards along the Peloponnesian coasts from Corinth to Patras, instituting sea patrols, and arresting any suspected fugitives.[30] On the other side, the Ottomans secretly collaborated with immigrants to the Peloponnese who were willing to abandon the Morea, offering them assistance with transportation and spreading propaganda that promised amnesty and the return of all property in Ottoman lands that the immigrants had abandoned.[31]

Even when flight was a necessity, however, it was a choice that was not viable for immigrants in most parts of the Peloponnese. For those on the northern Peloponnesian coast it was relatively easy to cross the Gulf of Patras, the Corinthian Gulf, or the Gulf of Aigina to lands under Ottoman domination, and from there to return to their places of origin. Other immigrants, especially those in the southern Peloponnese, were far from such departure points.

These circumstances highlight the fact that the ability of the peasantry, both native and immigrant, to react to situations that affected both differed markedly. Immigrants in the northern Peloponnese who had come from Roumeli were in a more advantageous position than natives in that area because they could choose to stay or leave. If they left the Morea, they would find families and relatives in their native lands, easing their reintegration.

The fact that the less favored mass of people, and especially the immigrants, had begun to emigrate from the Venetian Morea must be interpreted as an act of disapproval of the situation that had begun to prevail in that area. According to *Provveditore* Francesco Grimani in 1698, the primary motivation for emigration was that the great number of members in the *comunità* burdened the peasantry with excessive requirements for public service and *angarie* (labor services). This in turn resulted in a great degree of social differentiation within the population of the Morea.[32] Another important factor was the scarcity of land, especially after the first two decades of Venetian government in the Morea. In addition, debts to the *camera fiscale* (treasury) forced many immigrants, as well as locals, to flee.[33]

30. ASV, *Provveditori da Terra e da Mar,* b.849, no. 3, March 19, 1698, Argos.

31. ASV, *Provveditori da Terra e da Mar,* b.851, no. 6, February 2, 1701, Napoli di Romania.

32. ASV, *Provveditori da Terra e da Mar,* b.849, no. 3, March 19, 1698, Argos. For the connection between the *comunità* and the *angarie,* see Dokos 1999–2000; and Malliaris 2001, pp. 250–261.

33. ASV, *Archivio Grimani ai Servi,* b.36, f.92, fol. 477v. It is worth noting that the Venetian army's doctor in Napoli di Romania, the Florentine Alessandro Pini, states in his description of the Peloponnese, written in 1703, that the immigrants were *di natura* unwilling to stay permanently in the Morea, and also that during their sojourn in the Peloponnese they usually gave birth to only one child, whereas in their homelands they had numerous descendants; see Malliaris 1997b, pp. 33–34.

The movement of populations between the Venetian Peloponnese and Ottoman central Greece sheds light on, among other things, the perceptions Greeks had of the two empires. Religious choice between the Christian Venetians and the Muslim Ottomans seems to have been a low priority. Their first and most important necessity was to survive; secondarily, they strove for better living conditions.

ISTANBUL VERSUS VENICE

The Ottoman invasion and reconquest of the Venetian *regno di Morea* in 1715 offers further insights regarding the social status of the population of the Venetian Peloponnese. It is no coincidence that the Venetians were helped by almost all the landowning families, the possessors of *contea* and members of the *comunità*, and especially by those families who came as refugees to the Morea. These are the people who followed the Venetians when they left the Peloponnese after the victory of the Ottomans, and, in so doing, left a country in which they had prospered.[34] For the remainder of the immigrant and native population, the change of authority from Venetian to Ottoman was perhaps not of great importance, as it did not anticipate any dramatic change in its quality of life.

A period of important population movements in the territory of the Peloponnese thus came to an end. Immigration and emigration had modified the social and economic structures of the Morea. An important next step for researchers is to consider the ramifications of the Venetian era for the next period of Peloponnesian history, beginning in 1716, after the Ottoman reconquest, and extending to the Greek Revolution at the beginning of the 19th century.

34. For the attitude of the Greek population (the peasantry and the upper social classes) toward the Ottoman invasion, see Malliaris 2001–2002.

PRIMARY SOURCES

Archivio di Stato di Venezia (ASV)

Archivio Grimani ai Servi

b.30 Carte diverse relative agli affari di Morea, 1698–1700
b.32, f.86 Filza de primati e relationi di Morea, fine secolo XVII
b.35 Filza di lettere a Francesco Grimani da varie cariche e privati, 1700
b.36, f.92 Filza di lettere a Francesco Grimani, 1699–1700

Materie ecclesiastiche

b.7 Fascio di carte relative all' amministratione del convento di San Andrea di Patrasso (Carmelitani Scalzi)

Provveditori sopra feudi

b.1039 Filza famiglia Bosichi

Provveditori da Terra e da Mar

b.849 Dispacci Francesco Grimani, 1697–1699
b.851 Dispacci Giacomo da Mosto, 1700–1703
b.854 Dispacci Marco Loredan, 1708–1711

PUBLISHED SCHOLARSHIP

Cessi, R. 1981. *Storia della Repubblica di Venezia,* Florence.

Cozzi, G. 1985a. "La politica del diritto della Repubblica di Venezia nel Regno di Morea (1687–1715)," in *Diritto comune, diritto commerciale, diritto veneziano,* ed. K. Nehlsen von Stryk and D. Nörr, Venice, pp. 155–161.

———. 1985b. "La Repubblica di Venezia in Morea: Un diritto per il nuovo Regno (1685–1715)," in *L'età dei lumi: Studi storici sul settecento europeo in onore di Franco Venturi* 2, Naples, pp. 739–789.

Davies, S. 1994. "Tithe-Collection in the Venetian Peloponnese, 1696–1705," *BSA* 89, pp. 433–455.

———. 1996. "The Fiscal System of the Venetian Peloponnese: The Province of Romania, 1688–1715" (diss. Univ. of Birmingham).

———. 2002. "Venetian Corinth in 1700: The Letters of Argirò Besagni," *Θησαυρίσματα* 32, pp. 235–250.

———. 2004. "Pylos Regional Archaeological Project, Part VI: Administration and Settlement in Venetian Navarino," *Hesperia* 73, pp. 59–120.

Dokos, K. 1975. *Ἡ Στερεὰ Ἑλλὰς κατὰ τὸν ἐνετοτουρκικὸν πόλεμον, 1684–1699, καὶ ὁ Σαλόνων Φιλόθεος,* Athens.

———. 1999–2000. "Οι αστικές κοινότητες και οι αγγαρείες του δημοσίου στη βενετοκρατούμενη Πελοπόννησο," *Εώα και Εσπέρια* 4, pp. 243–280.

Dokos, K., and G. Panagopoulos. 1993. *Το βενετικό κτηματολόγιο της Βοστίτσας,* Athens.

Eickoff, E. 1991. *Venezia, Vienna e i Turchi: Bufera nel Sud-Est Europeo 1645–1700,* Milan.

Gasparis, C. 1997. *Η γη και οι αγρότες στη μεσαιωνική Κρήτη. 13ος–14ος αι.,* Athens.

Guida, F. 1989. "L'ultima esperienza 'imperiale' di Venezia: La Morea dopo la pace di Carlovitz," in *Studi balcanici, pubblicati in occasione del VI Congresso internazionale dell' Association internationale d' Études Sud-Est Européennes, Sofia, 30 agosto–5 settembre* (Quaderni di Clio 8), ed. F. Guida and L. Valmarin, Rome, pp. 107–136.

Hilton, R., ed. 1976. *The Transition from Feudalism to Capitalism,* London.

———. 1983. *Dictionary of Marxist Thought*, Oxford.

Jacoby, D. 1971. *La féodalité en Grèce médiévale: Les "Assises de Romanie," sources, application et diffusion*, Paris.

Kalligas, H., ed. 1998. *Η εκστρατεία του Morosini και το Regno di Morea: Μονεμβασιώτικος Όμιλος, Γ΄ Συμπόσιο Ιστορίας και Τέχνης, 20–22 Ιουλίου 1990*, Athens.

Kasdagli, A. E. 1999. *Land and Marriage Settlements in the Aegean: A Case Study of Seventeenth-Century Naxos*, Venice.

Lane, F. C. 1978. *Storia di Venezia*, Turin.

Laslett, P., and R. Wall, eds. 1972. *Household and Family in Past Time*, Cambridge.

Liata, E., and K. Tsiknakis, eds. 1998. *Με την αρμάδα στο Μοριά 1684–1687*, Athens.

Lucassen, J., and L. Lucassen, eds. 1997. *Migration, Migration History, History: Old Paradigms and New Perspectives*, Bern.

Malliaris, A. 1997a. "Όψεις συμβίωσης πληθυσμιακών ομάδων στην Πελοπόννησο κατά τη Δεύτερη Βενετοκρατία (1685–1715)," in *Πρακτικά Ε΄ Διεθνούς Συνεδρίου Πελοποννησιακών Σπουδών, Άργος–Ναύπλιο 6–10 Σεπτεμβρίου 1995* 4, Athens, pp. 39–48.

———. 1997b. *Alessandro Pini: Ανέκδοτη περιγραφή της Πελοποννήσου (1703)*, Venice.

———. 2001. "Η συγκρότηση του κοινωνικού χώρου στη Β.Δ. Πελοπόννησο την περίοδο της βενετικής κυριαρχίας (1687–1715)" (diss. Ionian Univ., Corfu).

———. 2001–2002. "Η τουρκική εισβολή στη βενετική Πελοπόννησο (1715): Η στάση του ελληνικού πληθυσμού έναντι Βενετών και Τούρκων και η διασπορά του ελληνικού και του βενετικού στοιχείου," in *Πρακτικά ΣΤ΄ Διεθνούς Συνεδρίου Πελοποννησιακών Σπουδών, Τρίπολη 24–30 Σεπτεμβρίου 2003*, Athens, pp. 420–436.

———. 2002. "La formazione dello spazio sociale in un nuovo posedimento veneziano: Veneziani, coloni e nativi nel Peloponneso del nordovest (territorio di Patrasso) 1687–1715," *Θησαυρίσματα* 32, pp. 219–234.

———. 2003. "La mobilizzazione della terra in un paese di nuova conquista: Lo stato fondiario nel Peloponneso veneziano agli inizi del XVIII secolo," in *Il Mercato della Terra secc. XIII–XVIII*, ed. S. Cavaciocchi, Prato, pp. 499–505.

Nikolaou, G. 1997. "Islamisation et Christianisation dans le Péloponnèse (1715–ca. 1832)" (diss. Univ. of Strasbourg).

Page-Moch, L. 1992. *Moving Europeans: Migration in Western Europe since 1650*, Bloomington.

Panayiotopoulos, V. 1987. *Πληθυσμός και οικισμοί της Πελοποννήσου: 13ος–18ος αιώνας*, Athens.

Papadia-Lala, A. 1993. "Οι Έλληνες και η βενετική πραγματικότητα: Ιδεολογική και κοινωνική συγκρότηση," in *Όψεις της ιστορίας του βενετοκρατούμενου ελληνισμού*, ed. C. A. Maltezou, Athens, pp. 173–276.

———. 2004. *Ο θεσμός των αστικών κοινοτήτων στον ελληνικό χώρο κατά την περίοδο της Βενετοκρατίας (13ος–18ος αι.): Μία συνθετική προσέγγιση*, Venice.

Stouraiti, A. 2001. *Memorie di un ritorno: La guerra di Morea (1684–1699) nei manoscritti della Querini Stampalia*, Venice.

Topping, P. 1972. "The Post-Classical Documents," in *The Minnesota Messenia Expedition: Reconstructing a Bronze Age Regional Environment*, ed. W. A. McDonald, G. R. Rapp, Jr., Minneapolis, pp. 64–80.

———. 1977. "Feudal Institutions as Revealed in the Assises of Romania: The Law Code of Frankish Greece," in *Studies on Latin Greece, A.D. 1205–1715*, London, pp. 1–192.

Zamperetti, S. 1991. "Stato regionale e autonomie locali: Signorie e feudi nel dominio veneziano di terraferma," *Studi Veneziani* n.s. 21, pp. 111–136.

Early Modern Greece: Liquid Landscapes and Fluid Populations

by Hamish Forbes

> Peasants do not decamp readily. . . . When they do flee, it means that life has become so burdensome or dangerous as to justify . . . the sacrifice . . . and the risks of leaving everything behind.[1]

This chapter addresses issues relating to the ways in which scholars use documents to understand landscapes and their populations in early modern Greece.[2] Many of the documents that are increasingly being studied, such as censuses and tax registers, indicate the populations of particular settlements at particular times—even listing named individuals in specific locations.[3] It is therefore possible to consider them as presenting quasi pictures of premodern Greek landscapes. The effect of such documents is to provide an essentially static picture, in which individuals and communities are fixed in time and space. One goal of this chapter is to evaluate whether these documents can give genuine views of these landscapes or whether they are more akin to caricatures or even mirages.[4]

The underlying issue is that of stability and permanence in premodern Greek rural populations. For the kinds of documents noted above, the central factors are recorded family names (surnames) and places of residence. Many studies of premodern rural populations in Europe assume that the great majority had long-term residential stability.[5] For the Mediterranean lands, however, historians have long been aware that both individuals and populations have had a degree of mobility for millennia. For Braudel, much of the rural population mobility observable in the historical record results from the juxtaposition of mountain and plain.[6]

1. McGowan 1994, pp. 680–681.

2. Research on archival sources on Methana in 1998 was made possible by a travel grant from the Leverhulme Foundation, part of a Leverhulme Fellowship in 1997–1998. I am most grateful to the president of the Dimos of Methana, Panayiotis Lambrou, for permission to study and copy the archival sources held in the Dimarchio, and to the secretary and the assistant secretary of the dimos for their help, advice, and hospitality while I was working on these materials. I also thank all the Methanites who, over the years, have offered me hospitality and information.

My thanks also to Lena Cavanagh for information on names, to Jack Davis, John Bennet, and Fariba Zarinebaf for allowing me to see a prepublication copy of their research on *Tapu Tahrir* 880, to Siriol Davies and Jack Davis for inviting me to the "Between Venice and Istanbul" workshop and for their perspicacious comments, suggestions, and pointers to additional sources that I exploited in subsequent drafts of this chapter. Of course, any flaws and infelicities are my responsibility alone.

3. E.g., Topping 1976, 2000; Panayiotopoulos 1985; Zarinebaf, Bennet, and Davis 2005.

4. See the Introduction on tax records.

5. E.g., McGowan 1994, pp. 680–681.

6. Braudel 1972.

He notes as an example the uninterrupted flow of immigrants onto the plains of Languedoc from neighboring mountainous regions: "landless peasants, unemployed artisans, casual agricultural workers, . . . outcasts of society, beggars and beggar-women, travelling preachers, *gyrovagues*, . . . vagabonds, . . . street musicians, and shepherds with their flocks."[7] The pump for the immigrant stream, Braudel argues, was the clear disparity between the poverty of the mountain areas and the relative wealth of the plains.[8] Alternatively, he suggests, mountainous areas could also be the sources of sporadic but not uncommon migrations of whole populations. He points to Albania as an example: in the 16th century, Albanians could be found on Cyprus, in Venice, Rome, Naples, on Sicily, in Greece, and in large numbers in the service of the Sublime Porte.[9] Above all, though, for Braudel population mobility is related to pastoralism, to which he devotes a whole chapter.[10] In the European Mediterranean lands, pastoral mobility very rarely has taken the form of nomadism. Transhumance involves the movements of families with their flocks and herds between the plains and the mountains. Thus the mountains are again an essential ingredient in this form of mobility.[11] It is a patterned and stable system in which there are essentially two "homes" rather than one; it is not a form of migration. Nevertheless, it may well have been an important ingredient in the fluid social structures to be discussed later in this chapter.

In a more recent but equally magisterial overview of Mediterranean history, Horden and Purcell likewise devote a substantial chapter to the movement of goods and people.[12] Referring to Macfarlane, they note the disjunction between older views of peasant immobility and the evidence for a wide variety of types of mobility in the Mediterranean area.[13] Especially important is their observation that, although Braudel linked vagrancy and casual mobility with employment, "the common denominator may be no more than the knowledge that movement is an option, and the means, psychological and physical, to undertake it."[14]

The title of this chapter indicates my debt to Susan B. Sutton's recent work.[15] Paralleling Horden and Purcell's views, Sutton confronts older views of Greek rural populations as conservative "peasantries" tied to their lands and changeless in culture over centuries, with an alternative model of communities as dynamic entities in which people readily react to changing circumstances. Migration, even over relatively short distances, she notes, is an important element in a repertoire of such reactions.[16] Thus Sutton's work in the Ermionida echoes the views of Horden and Purcell and provides important social and cultural background to issues of demographic and settlement pattern change in the Venetian and Ottoman periods.[17]

In this chapter I argue that the option of mobility had not simply an economic dimension, but sometimes also a political one. Quite apart from any other reasons for moving, mobility could be employed to deal with the forces of colonializing governments' agents if their actions or effects became unduly severe. At the same time, I will argue that another cultural element—the fluidity of surnames between generations—may give an impression of a population that was more mobile than may actually have been the case.

7. Braudel 1972, p. 47.

8. Braudel 1972, p. 47; cf. Le Roy Ladurie 1966, p. 97.

9. Braudel 1972, pp. 48–49. For a specific example of an earlier movement of Albanian settlers, see Chap. 11 in this volume.

10. Braudel 1972, pp. 85–102.

11. Braudel 1972, pp. 85–87.

12. Horden and Purcell 2000, pp. 342–400.

13. Macfarlane 1984, p. 342; Horden and Purcell 2000, pp. 383–387.

14. Horden and Purcell 2000, p. 385.

15. Sutton 2000a, 2000b.

16. Sutton 2000b, pp. 84–85.

17. See, e.g., Chaps. 5 and 11 in this volume.

A major element in the intervention of governments in people's lives is taxation.[18] Possibly more than any other type of government activity, taxation requires detailed documentation of populations in the form of registers, censuses, or cadasters, indicating households or individuals and the places in which they live. In the context of Greece under the control of the Venetians and the Ottomans, such documents relating directly or indirectly to taxation provide some of the most interesting and detailed historical sources for the state of the contemporary human landscape. Most studies of these documents seem to assume that the surnames of the individuals thus registered were essentially immutable, being automatically handed down through the generations with minimal change.[19] For example, Eva Topping discusses *noms de famille* (surnames) without any suggestion that they might not last for as many generations as there were male offspring.[20]

In the discussion that follows I shall suggest that in the period from the 15th to the early 19th century, surnames—at least for the ordinary populations of the Greek countryside—were less stable than is generally assumed, contributing an important additional element to the physical fluidity of premodern Greek populations, and that a knowledge of the Greek kinship system helps in understanding both of these aspects of fluidity.

Along with Sutton's work on population mobility, a second major stimulus behind this chapter was the publication of part of *Tapu Tahrir* 880, an Ottoman cadaster of 1716.[21] One of the difficulties the document presents to modern scholars is that of determining whether "surnames" given to individuals in addition to their personal names indicate patronymics (e.g., son of Yeoryios), genuine surnames, or even nicknames. Sometimes a combination of more than one of these possible alternatives seems to occur. The two stimuli just described resonated with elements of my research into 19th-century population documents from Methana in the eastern Peloponnese.

METHANA: SOME BACKGROUND

Methana is a small volcanic peninsula on the southwestern (Peloponnesian) side of the Saronic Gulf. It has been the main focus of my research since 1972. A period of ethnographic fieldwork in 1972–1974 was followed by three seasons of archaeological field survey in 1984–1986. A further research visit occurred in 1998, during which I studied two important 19th-century documents that provide much of the historical data for the present chapter.

One of these documents comprises the original returns of the census of 1879 for most, but not all, of the villages on the peninsula. Each household is listed, with ages and relationships of family members usually indicated. All members of a household apparently were accounted for, including regular members who were elsewhere at the time—for example, in domestic service. Internal evidence suggests that the census-takers went from house to house in sequence along the streets in many villages, on occasion progressing from one side of the street to the other.[22]

18. E.g., Davies 1994; Zarinebaf, Bennet, and Davis 2005.
19. E.g., Lowry 2002.
20. Topping 1969.
21. Zarinebaf, Bennet, and Davis 2005.
22. Forbes, forthcoming.

The other document, a *mitroon arrenon* (register of males), is a running list of male births apparently kept for military call-up purposes. The entries, begun in 1809, are sporadic until regular recording starts in 1844. The document that I studied in detail ends in 1878. Internal evidence in the form of occasional apparent duplications, and the fact that it had been specially printed, suggest that the document had been produced from several earlier originals, probably in conjunction with the 1879 census.

In common with the rest of the Argolic Peninsula, to which it is attached, Methana's history from the later medieval period until the early 19th century was almost exclusively one of domination by foreign powers. For much of the 14th century Methana was controlled by the Franks. It was recovered by the Byzantine Despotate of the Morea toward the end of the century, only to fall into the hands of the Ottomans in the mid-15th century.[23] It continued to be ruled by the Ottomans until the outbreak of the Greek War of Independence in 1821, apart from the relatively brief Second Venetian Occupation of 1685–1715.[24]

From the end of the medieval period until the beginning of the 19th century, Methana seems to have had a meager population and a single small settlement, also called Methana. By 1830, however, at the end of the Greek War of Independence, there were at least five additional villages on the peninsula, with two or three more appearing in succeeding decades. These new villages seem to have been founded by refugees from the fighting during the War of Independence.[25] The 19th-century documents shed indirect light on the contexts of the mobility indicated by these apparent refugees.

NAMES AND NAMING

At the heart of this section is the question: What is meant by the word "surname"? In modern Western societies, a person has a "first name" ("personal name," "given name") that he or she is assigned shortly after birth. In Christian communities this may also be termed the "baptismal name." First names serve, inter alia, to distinguish different members within a household. The first name is followed by another name: the surname. The expectation, at least by the 19th and 20th centuries, has been that the surname will be shared by all members of the same family and handed down through the male line to all members of succeeding generations, continuing for as long as there are male offspring. However, the word "surname" in English has had other meanings. In 16th- and 17th-century English, "surname" was sometimes used as if it meant "sire-name"—that is, father's first name = patronym (see below). It could even mean "nickname."[26] In other words, "surname" has meant no more than the name used to identify all members of a family at a particular point in time, with no inbuilt assumption of generational continuity. Here, however, I shall use the term in its normally accepted modern meaning, that of a family name handed down indefinitely through the male line as long as there are males to carry it.

Some writers use the term "patronym" (i.e., "father's name") as a direct equivalent of "surname." In this chapter, however, I shall use the term

23. Jameson, Runnels, and van Andel 1994, p. 116.

24. Davies 1994, p. 443.

25. Forbes 1997, pp. 107–110; 2000b, p. 214.

26. Webster's 1913 dictionary, posted online at www.hyperdictionary.com/dictionary/surname.

"patronym" in its other sense: the use of a father's given name (first name) as an identifier for the whole family, in addition to a person's own given name. Depending on the culture and historical period, a patronym in this sense may be the only name in use other than the given name, or it may be used in addition to some other form of family name.

In both of the 19th-century documents from Methana, the naming system is the one customary in Greece throughout much of the 20th century. Men are identified by a baptismal (given) name, a surname, and their father's baptismal name. Women are identified by their baptismal name, with their father's surname and baptismal name if unmarried, or their husband's surname and baptismal name if married.

To give an actual example, the census lists a Vasilios Konstandinou Gkikas (i.e., Vasilios Gkikas, son of Konstandinos Gkikas), living with his wife Elenio Vasiliou (i.e., wife of Vasilios) Gkikas, and Vasilios's unmarried younger brother, Nikolaos Konstandinou Gkikas. Additional notes in the census indicate that Nikolaos was a brother of the head of household; the use of the patronym shared with Vasilios confirms this fact. If Nikolaos had been a son of Vasilios, he would have been Nikolaos Vasiliou Gkikas.[27]

A striking feature in the census is the predominance of surnames derived from baptismal (given) names. For example, in a village of 53 households, many of which shared the same surnames, there were 13 different surnames based on Greek or Albanian baptismal names, two names that were, broadly speaking, descriptive names or nicknames, two that indicated an occupation, one that indicated a place of origin, and three of unknown derivation.[28] In another village, three different surnames that could be considered as deriving from nicknames were associated with nine households. The remainder of the 42 households had surnames derived from baptismal names.

Many surnames derived from baptismal names are in the genitive: for example, Ioannou, Dimitriou, Yeoryiou, the normal form used to indicate "son of *x*." As a specific example, one entry in the census lists Eleni Andreou, *chira tou Andreou Ioannou Andreou* (Eleni Andreou, widow of Andreas, son of Ioannis Andreou). Crucially, in yet another village, one individual had no surname. There is a comment that he is "from Turkey," and his occupation is listed as a σχοινάς (*schoinas,* rope-maker) rather than a farmer. He was also officially recorded as the only speaker of Greek in the village, all the others being listed as speaking Albanian.

A second noticeable feature associated with surnames is their mutability in the written sources. When the *mitroon arrenon* and census documents are studied together, it is plain that spellings (and therefore presumably pronunciations) of certain names were not always clear. For example, one household in the census is listed with alternative pronunciations of the same basic name: Tzinaris or Tsinaris. There is a similar instance in the *mitroon arrenon:* Liakos or Lakos. Yet another surname is written one way in the census, but differently in the *mitroon arrenon.* At present it is spelled slightly differently again. These are interesting but understandable differences. Less understandable are entries in the *mitroon arrenon* for two sons of a man with the surname "Ambatis or Ilias." He was listed simply as Ambatis when a further son was born.[29] There are also two examples

27. Most of those named in the documents have relatives still living on Methana. Normal anthropological practice, requiring that individuals remain anonymous, is at odds with historians' requirements for accurate documentation. As a compromise, because all named individuals are long since dead, I have not changed any names, but wherever possible I have kept village names anonymous.

28. An Albanian dialect has traditionally been spoken in the area.

29. There is no record of the family in the census lists; perhaps the family changed its surname yet again, or moved away.

of households that apparently changed their surname by the addition of the suffix "-opoulos" between the 1840s and 1879, leaving two other households with the original name unchanged.[30] The most likely cause of the change was the division of a single kin-group (*soi*—see the section on kinship organization later in this chapter) into two.

There are indications of a continuation of the use of a patronymic to define a family in a few cases. A man inscribed variably as "Anastasiou or Gkionis" or "Anastasiou or Gkioni" appears several times in the *mitroon arrenon*, and the family is visible in the census using the surname Gkionis. Although there is a certain amount of ambiguity in the records, it seems more than likely that the man's father's name was Anastasios, and that therefore the "surname" Anastasiou was actually a patronymic.

Clearer evidence of the widespread use of patronymics comes from references to the clergy. Frequently, in priests' families the father's personal name is used as a patronymic for the next generation (for an exception, see Table 6.2 below). Thus the sons registered to a priest with the personal name Matthaios have the surname "Papa Matthaiou," spelled as two words. Similarly, a priest whose personal name is given in the register as "Papa-Ioannis" had a son who was registered with the surname written "Papa Ioannou." When Papa Athanasios Spyrou registered a son called Spyros, the compilers of the *mitroon arrenon* were confused about whether the son's surname should be Papathanasiou or Spyrou. As no other sons were registered to this father, the son Spyros was presumably named after Papa Athanasios's own father, indicating in turn that Papa Athanasios's "surname" was in effect simply a patronymic.[31] Evidently the confusion in the *mitroon arrenon* arose because the compilers were unsure whether to continue the system of using the patronymic as a family name for the son (Papathanasiou), or to give him the father's patronymic, Spyrou, as a proper surname.

It is evident that "surnames" in records in the mid-19th century were rather more flexible and mutable than one would expect true surnames to be today. At the very least, such a feature causes problems in discerning the mobility (or otherwise) of households over the longer term. Indeed, is it correct to treat these names as "true" surnames, with an indefinite permanence through the generations for as long as there were male offspring to continue them? The case of Ioannis "from Turkey," who lacked any other distinguishing name, highlights the fact that Ottoman law at the time, and in the period before independence, did not require the use of surnames. Normal official Ottoman practice, as indicated in TT880, was to use patronymics.[32]

Surnames were not completely stable even in the later 19th and earlier 20th centuries. In his description of Methana, its history, and its people, Athanasiou describes a family that changed its name from Christodoulou to Tzavellas in the period sometime after 1850, but there is no evidence in the archival sources that the change of name had occurred by 1879.[33] Later in this chapter, I describe an example of a change of name in the earlier 20th century.

It is evident from documents dating to centuries before the Greek War of Independence (1821–1829) that Greeks generally used another name as well as their baptismal name. Although many of these second names

30. The suffix "-opoulos," although usually treated as a diminutive form, seems, when attached to a name, to have originally denoted a patronymic. During the Ottoman period, the Turkish suffix "-oğlu" (son of) was used to translate the Greek "-opoulos" suffix (see, e.g., Alexander 1985, p. 80; Topping 1969, pp. 224–225).

31. The normal tradition in Greece is that the oldest son and daughter take their names from the relevant paternal grandparent.

32. Zarinebaf, Bennet, and Davis 2005.

33. Athanasiou 1998, p. 85.

are clearly patronymics, or were originally patronymics, others do not appear to be.[34] While it might be tempting to treat these nonpatronymics as "true" surnames with long intergenerational histories, as defined above, Laiou-Thomadakis indicates that in earlier periods they could be highly ephemeral.[35] Her findings for the Late Byzantine period raise the question of when "true" surnames became a standard feature of Greek society. Is it possible that not all Greeks possessed one even at the beginning of the 19th century? It is arguable that, although wealthy families may have kept the same surname for many generations, a significant proportion of the apparent surnames of ordinary Greeks found in pre-19th-century, and even early-19th-century, documents were in actuality either patronymics or else descriptive family names, closer in nature to nicknames than to immutable surnames.[36]

One difficulty is that Greece was a colonial possession, primarily of either Venice or the Ottoman Empire, for many centuries. The official documentation of individuals was thus undertaken in terms of cultural and administrative ideals that were potentially alien to Greece. It is recognized that Ottoman official practice tended to prefer patronymics, but there has been little active debate over whether Venetian practice assumed that the population had "true" surnames (although Lowry, e.g., seems to assume that Venetian usage in Greece was based on permanent surnames).[37]

Close examination of a substantial number of apparent surnames from the centuries before Greek independence indicates that many seem similar to nicknames. Eva Topping lists several examples, such as Georgius Zilapodi (Γεώργιος Ξυλοπόδης, George Woodenleg) and Theodore Maroulis ditto Agriotropos (Theodore Lettuce, called Wild-Manners). A substantial number of other "surnames" described agricultural or other craft specialisms.[38]

Laiou-Thomadakis is explicit that among members of small farming communities in Late Byzantine Macedonia there was flexibility in the use of "surnames"; many were derived from crafts or from family relationships.[39] In some census documents the largest percentage of "surnames" is derived from crafts or professions (e.g., potter, smith) or from what are clearly nicknames, such as Theodoros Avrakotos (Theodore Sans-culottes),[40] although "over time the most constant, common, and viable form of identification was stated or unstated family relationship."[41]

Although the Byzantine aristocracy had family names that remained stable over centuries, the majority of the rural masses discussed by Laiou-Thomadakis had a second identifying name, which could be an indicator of a family relationship or of a profession or even a nickname, and which might or might not endure for more than one generation.[42] When family names did continue through two or three generations, they were not exclusively passed through the male line. Upon marriage, some men became identified by their father-in-law's name.[43] Significantly, in view of the discussion of nicknames below, family names were attached primarily to heads of households or heads of families. Equally significant, some individuals in rural communities were identified by baptismal name only.[44]

Evidently, in Late Byzantine Macedonia a family name was neither immutable nor legally obligatory, nor even necessary in all circumstances.

34. E.g., Laiou-Thomadakis 1977, pp. 118–141; Lowry 2002, pp. 40–55; Topping 1969, pp. 221, 225–231; Zarinebaf, Bennet, and Davis 2005, concordance 1.
35. Laiou-Thomadakis 1977, pp. 118–141.
36. E.g., Laiou-Thomadakis 1977, p. 118.
37. Lewis 1961, p. 283, and see above; Lowry 2002.
38. Topping 1969, pp. 225–230.
39. Laiou-Thomadakis 1977, pp. 118–141.
40. Laiou-Thomadakis 1977, pp. 119–127.
41. Laiou-Thomadakis 1977, p. 140.
42. Laiou-Thomadakis 1977, pp. 118–119.
43. Laiou-Thomadakis 1977, pp. 123–124. See also below for some early-19th-century examples of identification via affinal links.
44. Laiou-Thomadakis 1977, pp. 120, 141.

Although family names were the norm rather than the exception, they seem to have functioned in much the same way as bynames in recent rural communities in many parts of Europe. Bynames are locally used names that identify individuals or households via well-known characteristics, such as occupation, physical or behavioral peculiarities, or kinship links to other well-known individuals in the community (see below).

I believe that the 19th-century documents from Methana are most easily understandable when viewed in the light of similarities prevalent in previous centuries. There is of course a gap of several centuries between the Late Byzantine period and the 19th century. As Herzfeld has indicated, however, the kinship system has been one of the most stable elements of Greek culture, continuing with remarkably little change for millennia, despite the domination of the society by other cultures over that long period.[45] It would seem that the naming system used by ordinary Greeks into the earlier 19th century derives not from something imposed via the Ottoman administrative system but rather from preexisting Byzantine administrative structures.

Little ethnographic research has been published on bynames or nicknames in Greece.[46] In later 20th-century Methana, however, the use of nicknames was still a vital social institution. Nicknames, rather than official surnames, were the primary means of distinguishing individuals in everyday conversations among villagers. Nicknames were indispensable for identifying individuals and households in communities where there was a limited range of personal names, and where it was normal for several people to share both the same baptismal name and the same surname. For example, on one occasion during my ethnographic fieldwork, an outsider arrived seeking a particular individual whom he did not know. The combination of baptismal name and surname that was given was shared by three different adult men, so he was asked to state if he wanted "Solon," "the President," or "Rockefeller," the standard nicknames used for these men.

A substantial number of nicknames in 20th-century Methana were derived from a distinctive occupation (e.g., "Resin-tapper," "Dynamite-fisherman"). Others derived from a physical characteristic (e.g., "Freckles"), personality type (e.g., "Headlong"), habit (e.g., "Slurper"), historical incident, and so forth. They were also heritable to a certain degree, continuing as long as the name served to distinguish a few closely related households from all others.[47] Nicknames were almost invariably assigned to male heads of household; other members of the household would bear the same nickname.[48] I am aware of examples that had been passed through three generations. In due course, however, some more immediately recognizable feature would arise and the nickname would change.

The use of a nickname as the normal household signifier almost certainly explains the man with the twin surnames "Ambatis or Ilias." The name Ambatis is best interpreted as deriving from *ambas,* a form of cloth; the word *ambatzis* signifies a person who makes or sells clothes. Ambatis is thus presumably a nickname derived from a craft or profession associated with cloth or clothing. Athanasiou describes the life of a well-known *rebetika* singer from a Methana family. Born Yeoryios Tsoros in the 1880s, he was given the nickname Batis or Ambatis. Eventually he became known

45. Herzfeld 1983, p. 158.

46. Clark (1988, pp. 415–416) has a long footnote on the use of nicknames on Methana. Gerald Durrell's description in *My Family and Other Animals* of the taxi driver Spyros, who was known to everyone on Corfu by his nickname rather than his surname, is an anecdotal example of exactly the situation on Methana.

47. During my initial fieldwork on Methana I was regularly asked who my landlord was. People in other villages generally failed to identify him when I used his baptismal name and official surname, even though no one else on the peninsula had the same combination of names. Almost all, however, instantly identified him when I used the nickname that he and his brother had inherited from their father.

48. Clark 1988, p. 393, n. 14, and pp. 415–416.

nationally as Yeoryios Batis, or simply Batis.[49] Thus it is possible to see the recurrence of the name Ambatis as a nickname, and the way in which a nickname could become a surname, even in the earlier 20th century.

General Yiannis Makriyannis, of the Greek War of Independence, normally referred to simply as Makriyannis, is a famous example from elsewhere in the Peloponnese of someone assuming a nickname as a surname. Makriyannis was born Yiannis Triandafyllou in 1797. He became known as Makriyannis (i.e., "Tall John") because of his height.[50] His name is thus directly comparable to several surnames on Methana: Megaloyannis ("Big John"), Kondoyannis ("Short John"), Mastroyannis ("Craftsman John"), and Kondoyannopoulos ("Son or descendant of Short John").

Research on Methanites who participated in military action during the War of Independence strengthens the impression of surname flexibility. Of 10 individuals named by Athanasiou, four had the surname Methenitis *(sic)*.[51] One of these, Nikolaos Methenitis, also had an alternative surname derived from a patronymic, Paulis, a name still found on Methana. The name Methenitis or Methanitis, however, is not found in any of the demographic documents from Methana that I have examined for the period from the War of Independence to 1879. Therefore the name Methenitis clearly was used as an ethnic (i.e., a name indicating place of origin) for Methanites when they were away from Methana, although they would seem to have used different names when they were in their own villages.

That naming elsewhere in Greece in the early 19th century was highly flexible is borne out by archival sources dating to the 1820s from the island of Psara in the northern Aegean. These sources are especially important for understanding how Greeks at the time named and identified one another, because they were written by Psariani themselves for their own use. In the surviving financial accounts relating to the war effort against the Ottomans during the Greek War of Independence, a very large number of ordinary individuals are named. Although many were listed using a baptismal name plus an apparent surname (but see the discussion later in this chapter), this is far from universal. Sometimes a single name is used, either a first name, or more often a "surname" that may actually be a nickname. Examples of such nonstandard names are given in Table 6.1.

Most revealing of all are the entries dealing with records of money donations from non-Psariani. Large numbers of entries refer to single names only, or else to ethnics on their own, for example, the Mykoniatis (from Mykonos), the Poriotis (from Poros). Alternatively, a baptismal name is followed by an ethnic, for example, Yiannis Zagoraios (from Zagora), mastro-Andonis Roumeliotis (craftsman-Andonis from Roumeli [= central Greece]), Nikolis Skopelitis (from Skopelos), Petros Kranidiotis (from Kranidi), Braïm [İbrahim] the Cretan captain.[52] Entries with a "standard" combination of baptismal name plus identifiable family name are rare in this section.

The overwhelming impression given by these names is that the naming system even as late as the early 19th century was designed primarily for local use and that surnames in the Western sense of family names enduring through the generations were not obligatory. Enough information was provided to ensure that local people reading these documents would be able to identify other local people. Evidently, the names Marinaina, Nadas,

49. Athanasiou 1998, pp. 117–119. The Greek word *batis* refers to a particular kind of sea breeze.

50. Athanasiou 1998, p. 46.

51. Athanasiou 1998, pp. 43–44.

52. Sphyroeras 1974, pp. 500, 504.

TABLE 6.1. SELECTED NONSTANDARD NAMES FROM ARCHIVAL SOURCES, PSARA, 1821–1824

Savvas the son-in-law *(gamvros)* of Kali [wife—? or daughter] of Boutzaras (από Σάββα της Καλής του Μπούτζαρα γαμβρός) (p. 493)
The child of Andonis son of Kakomounis (από του Αντώνη του Κακομούνη το παιδί) (p. 493)
Craftsman-Andonis Diniakos (από μαστρο-Αντώνη Ντηνιακό) (p. 493)
Skyrianos—the Skyrian (named after the island of Skyros)—(από Σκυριανό) (p. 493)
The widow *(chira)* of Bourekas (από τη χήρα του Μπουρέκα) (p. 494)
Old-Nikolis Simos (από γερο-Νικολή Σίμο) (p. 494)
Marinaina—a woman's name—(από τη Μαρίναινα) (two entries) (p. 494)
The children of Yianni the son of the Chiote (από του Γιάννη του Χιώτη τα παιδιά) (p. 494)
Nadas (από τα ζώα του Ναδά) (p. 494)
Apostolis (από τον Αποστόλη) (p. 494)
The child of Konstandis Bouzounas (από του Κωνσταντή Μπουζούνα το παιδί) (p. 494)
Dimitris the son of Sideris Bournou (or Bournos) (από Δημήτρη του Σιδερή Μπουρνού) (p. 494)
Nikolis the son of Yialouris the son of the priest (από Νικολή του Γιαλούρη του παπά) (p. 495)
Yeoryis the tavern-keeper (από Γεώργη ταβερνάρη (p. 519*), Γεώργη Ταβερνάρη (p. 495)
Paulopoulis (από Παυλοπούλη) (two entries for this person) (p. 496)
The father-in-law *(petheros)* of Androulis (από του Ανδρουλή . . . του πεθερού του) (p. 498)
Theodoris the son of Andriana (από Θεοδωρή της Ανδριάνας) (p. 514)
Yiannis the son of Andriana (από Γιάννη της Ανδριάνας) (p. 528)
Dimitris the son of Yiannis the son of Malamatenia† (από Δημήτρη του Γιάννη της Μαλαματένιας) (p. 528)
Anagnostis the son of Andreas the widow's son (από Αναγνώστη του Ανδρέα της χήρας) (p. 515)
Yiannis the son of Andreas the widow's son (από Γιάννη του Ανδρέα της χήρας) (p. 518)
Craftsman-Lazaros the painter‡ (από μαστρο-Λάζαρο μπογατζή) (p. 515)
Chatzi-Anagnostis (από Χατζη-Αναγνώστη) (p. 513)
The *gamvros* of Chatzi-Manoli Yiannitzis (από Χατζη-Μανόλη Γιαννίτζη . . . και γαμβρός του) (p. 513)
Panayiotis, the *gamvros* of Theophilis (από Παναγιώτη, του Θεοφίλη γαμβρός) (p. 516)
Yiannis Burnt-arse (από Γιάννη Καψόκωλο) (p. 513)
The son of Manolis (από τον υιόν του Μανόλη) (p. 513)
The son of Andreas (από τον υιόν του Ανδρέα) (p. 513)
Auyerinos the *gamvros* of Maria Gypsy (από Αυγερινό της Μαρίας Κατζιβέλου γαμβρός) (p. 523)

Note: Page numbers in parentheses refer to Sphyroeras 1974.
*The page number is misprinted as 319.
†Presumably derived from μάλαμα = gold; a kind-hearted person.
‡The word could also mean dyer.

Apostolis, Paulopoulis, and Androulis (see Table 6.1) were distinctive enough that additional names were unnecessary for identifying a particular individual. A significant minority of individuals are identified by their affinal (i.e., marriage) links, as the father-in-law *(petheros)* of *x*, or the son-in-law *(gamvros)* of *y* (Table 6.1). Such a feature emphasizes that surnames handed down through the male line were not considered obligatory. It directly parallels the feature of naming observed by Laiou-Thomadakis: that the use of a range of different forms of relationship was the most common means of personal identification in late medieval Macedonia.[53] We also can see the alternative from the observations described above regarding Methanites who took, or were given, the ethnic Methenitis. "Proper" surnames seem to have been considered entirely unnecessary for non-Psariani: a baptismal name and an indication of origin seem to have been sufficient in most cases to identify people who were not local.

Under these circumstances it seems very likely that other apparent surnames of Psariani, such as those belonging to Konstandis Yianni Katzikoyanni (*katziko-* = *katsiko-* [goat]);[54] Konstandis Samiotis (the Samian); Dimitris Koutzoukou (?son of the lame man); Anagnostis son of Papa-Koutzoyeorgis (father-lame-George); Yiannis son of Nikolis Koutzodondis (a man with a crooked tooth or teeth); mastro-Dimitris Skyrianos (craftsman-Dimitris the Skyrian); Yiannis the son of Yeoryis Mytaras (Bignose); Yiannis Kapsokolos (Γιάννη Καψόκωλο, Burnt-arse); and Galanis the *gamvros* of Yeoryis the gypsy (Γαλάνη του Γεώργη κατζιβέλου γαμπρό)[55] were actually nicknames, used as local identifiers.[56]

In drawing this section to a close, I must point out that the issue of surnames has wider implications for the histories both of Greece and of small-scale societies in Europe generally during the premodern period. If one assumes that Greeks had mostly immutable surnames comparable to those in Western Europe in the centuries prior to the War of Independence, one also imputes a considerable level of Western-ness, or European-ness, to the ordinary population of Greece. On the other hand, a presumption that there was a lack of surnames, as we currently understand them, among a large proportion of the population of Greece during those centuries could be interpreted as imputing an essential non-Western-ness to premodern Greek populations. These observations potentially have direct historical implications, given that Greece was dominated alternately by Western (and European—especially Venetian) and Eastern (non-European—Ottoman) powers, particularly because there is a tendency to presume that the use of "true" surnames has a very long history in more "developed" parts of Europe, such as Italy.

The assumption of a long history of the use of "true" surnames in Venice in particular, and Italy more generally, is contradicted by a number of sources, however. The 15th-century manuscript Cotton Titus A.XXVI was written in a Venetian form of Italian by Zorzi Trombetta da Modon (Yeoryis the trumpeter from Methoni). The internal evidence indicates that he was a naval trumpeter, as his name suggests. That he was named for his profession rather than having a "true" surname might be explained by the fact that he was evidently Greek in origin, rather than Venetian. But the personal names of two other musician members of the same naval squadron mentioned by Zorzi, Girardo Pifaro and Borttolamio Pifaro

53. Laiou-Thomadakis 1977, p. 140.

54. It is possible that this nickname played on use of the prefix "Chatzi-," meaning someone who had made a pilgrimage, such as Chatzi-Yiannis. Katzikoyannis (Goat-John) could also be seen as a play on the name Koutzoyannis (Lame-John) (e.g., Sphyroeras 1974, p. 529).

55. In Sphyroeras 1974, p. 494, there is a reference to a Γεώργη Κατζίβελο.

56. Sphyroeras 1974, pp. 495, 513, 515, 517, 520, 523.

(*pifaro* = musical pipe), indicate that they were not Greek.[57] The evidence therefore suggests that the use of "true" surnames by ordinary people was not commonplace in Italy at this time.

The use of nicknames rather than surnames as identifiers was still dominant in some parts of Italy in the earlier 20th century. Norman Douglas points out that nicknames were almost universally used instead of official surnames in rural communities in southern Italy fewer than 100 years ago.[58] Although surnames were technically obligatory, often people did not even know their own. As Douglas notes, the use of nicknames was associated with life in small isolated communities. In the early 20th century the practice was beginning to disappear in rural Italy as a result of the increasing intrusion of the state into village life.[59]

It could be argued that the use of nicknames rather than surnames in southern Italy might be a vestige of a Greek-dominated past. A directly comparable usage has been documented in the later 20th century in the Scottish Highlands, however, where everyday life was impossible without knowledge of nicknames.[60] Nicknaming relied primarily on family relationships through either male or female links, but physical characteristics and occupations, places of origin, occupations, and personal attributes—often derisive—were also employed.[61] Although "official" surnames existed, they were rarely used. The critical features associated with the dependence on nicknames were the inward-looking nature of the communities involved (Gaelic-speaking in a predominantly Anglophone region), the limited range of personal names in use, the high levels of interrelatedness and intermarriage, and relatively low levels of in- and out-migration.

In light of the comparative evidence presented above, it is perhaps best to visualize the premodern naming systems in use among rural Greek populations in terms of the ways in which people within the communities actually distinguished individuals and their households. A system using a baptismal name plus a patronymic or nickname to identify individual households works well in a largely inward-looking world of semiclosed small-scale societies in which everyone knows everyone else and all their relatives.[62] Although small rural villages provide obvious paradigms for such societies, the examples from the island of Psara indicate that other, rather larger communities seem to have functioned satisfactorily on the same principles.

The evidence presented here indicates that the issue of the use of permanent surnames versus relatively ephemeral identifiers relates to levels of interaction and relative levels of political centralization of power, rather than to a cultural context of East versus West, or "primitive" versus "developed" societies. As long as most interaction is generally restricted to small, largely inward-looking communities, and the power of the state remains relatively weak and decentralized, with most governmental functions carried out at a local level, a system using a baptismal name plus a patronymic or nickname to identify individual households works well.[63]

Davies shows clearly that during the Second Venetian Occupation of the Peloponnese, responsibility for collection and delivery of taxes was devolved by the central government on whole communities, under the government of their own elders.[64] Such a situation was simply an intensi-

57. Leech-Wilkinson 1978.
58. Douglas [1915] 2001, pp. 67–70.
59. Douglas [1915] 2001, p. 67.
60. Dorian 1970.
61. Dorian 1970, pp. 306–312.
62. A point made by Laiou-Thomadakis (1977, pp. 120, 141) in the context of 14th-century Macedonian villages.
63. Laiou-Thomadakis 1977, pp. 120, 141.
64. Davies 1994.

fication of an ethos that permeated elements of Ottoman administration over several centuries. Already in the 15th century the taxes of peasants who had illegally abandoned their lands were made partially the responsibility of those who remained. The introduction in the 16th and 17th centuries of the *maktu*ᶜ (lump sum) method of assessing tax imposed the liability on villages collectively. Seventeenth-century documents also indicate high levels of collective indebtedness of villages in some parts of the empire.[65] During the 18th century, when the Ottomans returned to the Peloponnese after the expulsion of the Venetians, their rule was becoming increasingly decentralized, with a proliferation of power bases.[66] These are exactly the conditions in which one could expect local-level naming systems to have primacy.

As states become more powerful and centralized, however, such relatively ad hoc local-level approaches to naming would be insufficient for more centralized recording systems. Under these circumstances, perhaps the most economical interpretation of the way "surnames" were being treated on Methana in the 19th century is that a system of permanently enduring surnames was being imposed in the newly independent Greece on small-scale communities whose traditions involved more flexible and locally effective means of defining families and households by a centralizing bureaucracy.

If a significant proportion of the ordinary population was distinguished prior to the 19th century only by the equivalent of a family relationship or a nickname, then sequences of population documents for an area will not be very helpful in identifying whether populations were relatively stable or relatively mobile. Changes in "surnames" could well mask long-term population stability. Furthermore, when individuals or households relocated, they might well take on new "surnames" to distinguish them from others in their new community, as noted earlier with the use of the nickname Methenitis.

KINSHIP ORGANIZATION

If "surnames" were frequently flexible descriptive names, there is a greater likelihood that all those sharing the same identifying name were genuinely related. On Methana, the majority of individual nicknames were restricted to at most a small handful of households, all within the *soi*—a group of related households extending as far as second cousins.[67]

The term *soi* is regularly used in Greece to define a group of people related to an individual bilaterally, that is, through male and female lines. The limit of the group generally extends to second cousins, although regional variations occur.[68] An alternative meaning of *soi*, frequently used on Methana and elsewhere, identifies a group of households related agnatically (i.e., through the male line), extending to second cousins.[69] That is, they all shared the same father's father's father (i.e., great grandfather). I shall demonstrate the potential importance of the agnatically related *soi* later. Here I wish to explore how the clustering of family names may indicate a significant degree of kin-based organization within the settlement.

65. Adanır 1998, pp. 282, 296, 300.
66. Alexander 1985, p. 36, n. 23, p. 39. For Crete, see Chap. 8 in this volume.
67. Clark 1988, p. 242, notes significant differences in the definition of the word *soi* in three different Greek dictionaries, but the common theme behind all of them is "origin." Here I use the term in the ways it was mainly used on Methana and is reported as being used in other rural communities.
68. See, e.g., Aschenbrenner 1986, p. 49.
69. Aschenbrenner 1986, pp. 48–50.

According to Methanites, their villages expanded from small nuclei because sons in succeeding generations stayed and built houses for themselves, usually adjacent to the parental home. Because residence after marriage was overwhelmingly virilocal (i.e., the newly married couple lived in or close to the groom's parents' house), whole neighborhoods of agnatically related households developed as sons in succeeding generations built new houses.[70] This phenomenon is visible on Methana in the 1879 census. Sequences of households with the same surname are common. Because fathers' baptismal names are also given, it is often possible to identify groups of brothers living adjacent to one another. Sometimes it seems that different kin groups lived on opposite sides of the village street, facing each other.

Table 6.2 presents a sequence of households with a shared surname. Anastasios, the founder of the cluster, lived in household 42 with what was probably his youngest son and the son's family. Households 44 and 45 were headed by older sons, as indicated by the evidence of their father's baptismal name. The head of household 43 was presumably another son, although his patronymic was omitted. Yet another son lived as a *sogamvros* elsewhere in the village.[71] In the same village seven households, numbered consecutively, comprised individuals or families with the same surname. The cluster included descendants of Michail, Ioannis, and Andonios, all apparently dead. The relationship of these ancestors to one another is unclear; they were most likely brothers, but could have been cousins. That they shared a common bond of kinship is further suggested by marginal notes in the census: the children of Andonios and Ioannis had unspecified connections with the nearby Plain of Troizinia. The most extreme example occurred in a neighboring village. Of 53 households, 10 had interchangeable forms of the same name. In the census their households run almost entirely in sequence, with three groups of brothers accounting for seven households.

The first point to be made is that it is highly unlikely that Methana is unique in the way in which settlements have a tendency to contain kin-clusters. Similar kin-clusters within settlements may be identifiable in documents from other parts of Greece deriving from periods prior to 1800 if it is accepted that "surnames" were essentially mutable; in that case, shared identifying names would be indicators of close kinship relationships. The second point is that in many instances kinship was more than an important principle governing the organization of settlement space. Spaces within settlements organized on the basis of kinship have traditionally also been the arenas for a wide variety of joint activities.

Although the households of a closely related kin group may have been physically separate, there may still have been a single familial organization, especially while the parents of a group of brothers were alive. Informant data from Methana suggest the widespread existence of joint enterprises in the late 19th and early 20th centuries, comprising an elderly couple and several married sons with their families living in a cluster of houses.[72] Even if closely related neighboring households did not always act as a single organizational unit, they doubtless constantly exchanged labor, equipment, draft animals, and the like, as they did in the later 20th century. Indeed, there was an ethic that even if neighbors were not close relatives, they should behave as though they were.

70. Clark 1988, pp. 221–223.

71. A *sogamvros* is a man who moves to his wife's household upon marriage.

72. Segalen (1984, p. 164) and Wilk and Netting (1984, esp. pp. 17–19) note that task-oriented units need not be the same as co-residing groups.

TABLE 6.2. SEQUENCE OF RELATED HOUSEHOLDS IN THE 1879 CENSUS OF METHANA

Household No.	*Surname*	*Name*	*Father (or Husband)*	*Age*	*Family Relationship*
42	Politis	Anastasios	A.	82	Household head
42	Politis	Petroula	Anastasios	73	Wife
42	Politis	Ioannis	Anastasios	35	His married son
42	Politis	Marigo	Ioannis	30	Ioannis's wife
42	Politis	Anastasios	Ioannis	12	Ioannis's son
42	Politis	[illegible]	Ioannis	10	Ioannis's child
42	Politis	Yeorgoula	Ioannis	8	Ioannis's daughter
42	Politis	Bilio	Ioannis	6	Ioannis's daughter
42	Politis	Irinio	Ioannis	3	Ioannis's daughter
43	Politis	Papa Yeoryios		45	Household head: widower
43	Politis	Petroula	Yeoryios	20	Daughter
43	Politis	Irini	Yeoryios	18	Daughter
43	Politis	Maria	Yeoryios	15	Daughter
43	Politis	Malta	Yeoryios	13	Daughter
44	Politis	Athanasios	Anastasios	38	Household head
44	Politis	Maria	Athanasios	34	Wife
44	Politis	Ekaterini	Athanasios	13	Daughter
44	Politis	Anastasios	Athanasios	11	Son
44	Politis	Stamato	Athanasios	9	Daughter
44	Politis	Nikolaos	Athanasios	6	Son
44	Politis	Yeoryios	Athanasios	4	Son
44	Politis	Ioannis	Athanasios	2	Son
45	Politis	Dimitrios	Anastasios	45	Household head
45	Politis	Stamato	Dimitrios	42	Wife
45	Politis	Anastasios	Dimitrios	22	Son
45	Politis	Phlora	Dimitrios	19	Daughter
45	Politis	Ekaterini	Dimitrios	14	Daughter
45	Politis	Ioannis	Dimitrios	7	Son
45	Politis	Eleni	Dimitrios	4	Daughter

Suprahousehold cooperating groups *(tselingata)* have not been restricted to the Epirote Sarakatsani described by Campbell.[73] They are, for instance, also documented in the Peloponnese.[74] There is also historical evidence for similar arrangements among agriculturalists in earlier periods. In 14th-century Macedonia, although the nuclear family was always statistically predominant, there was a significant minority of laterally extended households, consisting of a number of married siblings and their families. In some documents these constitute 20%–30% of all households, and overall this form was as common as the vertically extended household composed of an elderly couple with a married son or daughter.[75]

The observation that kinship was an important principle for organizing both action and the spatial layout of settlement in previous centuries has important ramifications. It may also have been a crucial mobilizing

73. Campbell 1964.

74. A *tselingato* was a cooperating group of herders, generally with an agnatically related core; see Koster and Koster 1976, p. 280; Koster 1976, p. 20.

75. Laiou-Thomadakis 1977, pp. 80–81.

TABLE 6.3. EXTRACTS FROM THE *MITROON ARRENON*, 1849–1872

Year	*Surname*	*Boy's Name*	*Father's Name*	*Village*
1849	Daremas	Christos	Yeoryios	Kypseli
1850	*Daremas*	*Spyridon*	*Andonios*	*Kolliani*
1851	Daremas	Andonios	Yeoryios	Kypseli
1851	Lissaios	Christos	Anastasios	Kypseli
1852	*Maltezos*	*Emmanouil*	*Vasilios*	*Methana*
1852	Maltezou	Emmanouil	Vasilios	Kypseli
1852	Paulis	Vasilios	Ioannis	Kypseli
1853	Gkikas	Christos	Ioannis	Kypseli
1853	Maltezou	Christos	Dimitrios	Kypseli
1854	Daremas	Athanasios	Yeoryios	Kypseli
1854	Daremas	Yeoryios	Lambros	Kypseli
1854	Maltezou	Vasilios	Athanasios	Kypseli
1854	Maltezou	Petros	Anagnostis	Kypseli
1854	Maltezou	Petros	Yeoryios	Kypseli
1856	Daremas	Dimitrios	Lambros	Kypseli
1857	Maltezos	Yeoryios	Athanasios	Kypseli
1857	Maltezou	Yeoryios	Dimitrios	Kypseli
1857	*Paulis*	*Paulos*	*Ioannis D.*	*Megalo Chori*
1859	*Paulou*	*Ioannis*	*Dimitrios*	*Vromolimni*
1859	Maltezou	Nikolaos	Vasilios	Kypseli
1860	Daremas	Spyridon	Andonios	Kypseli
1860	Maltezou	Dimitrios	Yeoryios	Kypseli
1861	Lissaios	Ioannis	Anastasios	Kypseli
1861	*Paulis*	*Yeoryios*	*Ioannis*	*Megalo Chori*
1862	*Paulou*	*Yeoryios*	*Dimitrios*	*Vromolimni*
1862	Daremas	Yeoryios	Nikolaos	Kypseli
1862	Daremas	Stamatios	Yeoryios	Kypseli
1862	Maltezou	Nikolaos	Yeoryios	Kypseli
1862	Paulis	Athanasios	Alexandros	Kypseli
1863	Lissaios	Ilias	Anastasios	Kypseli
1864	Gkikas	Andonios	Ioannis	Kypseli
1864	Daremas	Ioannis	Yeoryios	Kypseli
1864	Maltezou	Vasilios	Ioannis	Kypseli
1864	*Paulis*	*Nikolaos*	*Ioannis*	*Megalo Chori*
1865	Maltezou	Andreas	Anagnostis	Kypseli
1865	Maltezou	Vasilios	Yeoryios	Kypseli
1866	Daremas	Andonios	Nikolaos	Kypseli
1866	Daremas	Nikolaos	Yeoryios	Kypseli
1867	Maltezou	Ioannis	Ioannis	Kypseli
1867	Maltezou	Ioannis	Yeoryios	Kypseli
1867	Maltezou	Christos	Yeoryios	Kypseli
1867	Paulis	Ioannis	Argyrios	Kypseli
1868	Paulis	Nikolaos	Athanasios	Kypseli
1869	Daremas	Andonios	Yeoryios	Kypseli
1869	Daremas	Stamatios	Ioannis	Kypseli
1869	Maltezos	Anastasios	Yeoryios	Kypseli
1869	Maltezos	Vasilios	Michail	Kypseli
1869	Paulis	Yeoryios	Alexandros	Kypseli

TABLE 6.3—*Continued*

Year	*Surname*	*Boy's Name*	*Father's Name*	*Village*
1870	Maltezos	Angelis	Yeoryios	Kypseli
1871	Paulis	Ioannis	Yeoryios	Kypseli
1871	Paulis	Christos	Alexandros	Kypseli
1872	Maltezos	Andonios	Yeoryios	Kypseli
1872	Paulis	Ioannis	Dimitrios	Kypseli
1872	Paulis	Christos	Athanasios	Kypseli

Note: Entries in italics indicate residence not in Kypseli.

force in the population movements that caused the establishment of the current settlement pattern on Methana. The village of Kypseli is a good example. The original church was built, or extended, in 1848.[76] The first male birth was recorded for the village in the following year. Within four years, each of the five surname groups that still made up the community in the later 20th century had registered a son. Why the village was apparently founded at least 20 years after the end of hostilities cannot presently be explained, but the *way* in which it seems to have been founded is of considerable significance.

Yeoryios Daremas was the first in Kypseli to register the birth of a son, in 1849 (see Table 6.3). The following year Andonios Daremas registered his son Spyridon. His residence, however, is recorded as a seasonally occupied cluster of houses that never became a permanent settlement, not far from one of the peninsula's harbors. In 1860 an Andonios Daremas from Kypseli also registered a son named Spyridon. A reasonable assumption is that this was the same father who had since moved to a permanent residence in Kypseli, and whose first son called Spyridon had died.

In 1852 Vasilios Maltezos registered his son Emmanouil. His residence is listed simply as "Methana," although at that stage there was no village with that name. A Vasilios Maltezou, listed as residing in Kypseli, also registered a son Emmanouil in the same year. Almost certainly he and Vasilios Maltezos were the same person and were accidentally entered twice when the *mitroon arrenon* document was compiled from a number of different records in 1879 (see the discussion earlier in this chapter). A few other fathers registering sons are also recorded as residing in "Methana." In no case, however, is there a second registration to a father residing in "Methana." The best interpretation of this phenomenon is that the small number of households (nine in all, out of more than 800 entries up to 1878) for which "Methana" or the seasonal settlement is given as their residence were newly arrived and were not as yet considered to be permanently settled.

If we assume that families with the same surname are closely related, it becomes clear that many refugees did not arrive on Methana as isolated individuals or even as single households. In the 20-year period between 1849 and 1868, four different households with the surname Daremas registered the birth of at least one son, and at least seven different households with the name of Maltezou or Maltezos registered sons. With the two exceptions already noted, they were all described as resident in Kypseli. Over the same period six different households with the surname Paulis

76. Koukoulis 1997, p. 246.

or Paulou registered sons, although two of them were resident in villages elsewhere on Methana. Because the *mitroon arrenon* registered only male children, any other households having only girls during this period would simply not appear in the record.

The evidence from Kypseli therefore suggests that its founding was not the result of a random collection of individual refugees settling in a particular location and slowly becoming an organized community. It would seem that the founders of the village comprised at least three groups of related families. Much the same phenomenon seems to have occurred in the founding of another village on the peninsula. In the 1879 census records for the village, eight out of 17 households had the name Gkotzias. Tangential evidence supports Methanites's belief that the village was founded by refugees from the Aegean island of Psara, which was devastated by the Ottomans during the War of Independence. A Greek government document dated to October 1828 mentions that 2,000 people from Psara were quartered on the island of Aigina, just across the Saronic Gulf from Methana.[77] Furthermore, archival documents from Psara refer to several individuals with the surname Gkotzias or a version of it.[78] Internal evidence from the 1879 census indicates that the eight households that shared this surname were derived from a group of five or possibly six men, the dates of birth of whose offspring range from 1821 to 1843. The evidence is consistent with a group of relatively young men, presumably all brothers and/or cousins and their families. If this surmise is correct, everyone with this surname was probably related at the level of second cousin or closer (i.e., members of a single agnatic *soi*) when they arrived on Methana.

POPULATION MOBILITY

In these demographic documents we can see something of the social organization of population mobility in the early 19th century. Suprahousehold cooperating groups and "companies" of households, normally although not exclusively recruited along close agnatic lines, have been widely used by herder groups in many parts of Greece.[79] Significantly, Koster documents the formation (or re-formation) of a temporary agnatically organized company when the exigencies of the moment demanded it.[80] In fact, such multifamily units have not been confined to Greek pastoralists; they also have been documented historically among Slavic-speaking and Albanian-speaking groups, both pastoralist and agriculturalist, in southeastern Europe.[81] In reality they represent no more than "a product of patrilocal extension and virifocality" embedded in traditional Greek social structure.[82]

There is no clear explanation as to how or why Kypseli came to be settled so long after the end of the War of Independence. Nor is there information on the origins of the families concerned. When people were asked where their ancestors had come from, they generally were unable to give a definite answer. Significantly, however, one elderly Kypseli resident, when asked where the people with his surname came from, stated that before their arrival at Methana they had had a different name. It is difficult, however, to explain the episode in terms of small groups washed

77. Chouliarakis 1973, p. 32.

78. E.g., Νίκολης Χατζη-Δημητράκη Κοτζιά (Sphyroeras 1974, pp. 18, 81), Δημήτριος Ιω. Κοντζιά (Sphyroeras 1974, p. 464), Νικόλαος Κ. Κοντζιά (Sphyroeras 1974, p. 467), Δημήτριος Χατζη-Γεωργίου Κοτζιά (Sphyroeras 1974, p. 482).

79. Campbell 1964; Koster 1977, p. 77, n. 1.

80. Koster 1976, p. 20.

81. Hammel 1972; Forbes 1982, pp. 464–467.

82. Hammel 1972, p. 339.

ashore, either metaphorically or literally, at Methana as part of the human flotsam and jetsam resulting from tragedies or other incidents associated with the war. Nor was the founding of Kypseli the last occasion when "refugee" families seem to have arrived on Methana. The last mention of "Methana" in the *mitroon arrenon* as a place of birth is 1856, when two or possibly three different families were so registered.[83]

The evidence from Methana therefore suggests that the wholesale movement of groups of families could occur at times other than during periods of direct hostilities. The information derived from census materials suggests that considerable numbers of such groups may have been on the move at this time, a situation that seems to have continued into the 1850s at least. The suggestion is supported by a 2.4% per annum crude population increase on Methana in the period 1830–1848, in sharp contrast with the negligible increase on the adjacent mainland. The high rate of increase is likely to have been caused in part by continued in-migration.[84]

It seems probable that the main period of the readjustment of populations displaced by the war occurred in the late 1820s and early 1830s. There are also reports from the early 1830s of marauding armed bands of disgruntled ex-soldiers.[85] It is hard to interpret the movement of groups of whole households some 20 to 30 years after the cessation of hostilities in this light, however. An alternative explanation is that the relatively ready mobility of households, somewhat in the way identified here, was a recognizable element in the culture of premodern Greece and elsewhere in the Mediterranean.[86]

Sutton's observations on the mobility of Greek rural populations in previous centuries, in opposition to older models of "peasantries" deeply rooted in the landscape, were noted earlier.[87] The same phenomenon is observable in 14th-century Macedonia, where approximately 20%–30% of households disappeared from their communities between censuses some 20 years apart, while broadly comparable numbers of new families appeared. Because the censuses are quite detailed, continuity of households by succession of members of the next generation is usually identifiable. Losses of this magnitude cannot be explained by death through disease or major disasters. It has been suggested that mobility of households was the prime cause of both the disappearance of households and the appearance of new ones.[88]

Despite the substantial differences between the situation in Late Byzantine Macedonia and that in the early-19th-century Peloponnese, some features of the earlier situation may be relevant to most periods in premodern Greece. It would seem that in the 14th century, peasant mobility was more prevalent when political and economic conditions were unstable. In addition, mobility was greatest among those households that were the poorest and therefore presumably had the least to lose by migrating elsewhere. It is clear, however, that household mobility was significant even during periods of relative stability.[89] The fact that in 14th-century Macedonia it was the poorest who tended to be the most likely to migrate returns us to a previous observation, also relating to 14th-century Macedonia: people without any surname were generally those with little or no property, and those who seem in a number of cases to have been the most recent arrivals in the village.

83. Two different entries show fathers with identical baptismal names and surnames registering boys with the same baptismal name, suggesting that a single birth was given duplicate entries.

84. Forbes 1997, p. 110.

85. Frangakis-Syrett and Wagstaff 1992, p. 441.

86. As noted by Horden and Purcell (2000.)

87. Sutton 2000a, 2000b.

88. Laiou-Thomadakis 1977, pp. 247–251, 259.

89. Laiou-Thomadakis 1977, pp. 247–266.

High levels of population mobility were also inherent in Ottoman society over many centuries. Although Ottoman law did not allow peasants to abandon their land at will, the law does not seem to have been enforced systematically, and peasant mobility or flight seems to have been a widespread phenomenon.[90] Estate holders encouraged movement of farmers onto their territories because labor was the most important component of the means of rural production. A number of scholars have observed, moreover, that rural populations were notably ready to abandon one settlement and move elsewhere for a wide variety of reasons.[91] Adanır argues that changes in the Ottoman tax-collection system during the 16th and 17th centuries that made payment of tax the collective liability of whole communities were antithetical to the very idea of a settled peasantry.[92]

During the Second Venetian Occupation (1685–1715), the effectiveness of the Venetians in bringing new settlers to the Peloponnese, causing a substantial population increase in 20 years, may also be in part an indicator of the readiness of premodern populations to move. Such observations resonate with the situation on Methana.[93]

During the 18th century, lawlessness and corruption under Ottoman rule occurred at all levels in the Peloponnese. Corruption among senior administrators was rife and all sorts of banditry and semibanditry were recognized as both a fact of life and a way of life.[94] For the ordinary Christian population, "the period meant an increased vulnerability to extortion, de facto definition of their land titles and labor responsibilities, and possible peonage."[95] Flight was a commonly exercised option; it could take the form of moving elsewhere to find better conditions, or of joining a brigand band.[96]

Another important issue is the tendency for families in rural populations to be seasonally mobile. Quite apart from the mobility of pastoral groups, seasonal movement was a regular occurrence for agricultural households in many parts of Greece prior to the mid-20th century, frequently involving stays of varying lengths in field houses out in the countryside.[97] Seasonal mobility is an understandable response to a landscape in which areas of cultivable land are restricted and separated by tracts of bare mountain or other uncultivable land surface, and in which agriculture was traditionally mostly extensive rather than intensive.[98]

Archaeological survey data from Methana indicate the existence of a number of seasonally occupied sites with dates ranging from the medieval period to the 20th century.[99] The majority of these seem to date to the period before 1800, when all the land resources of the peninsula were exploited from a single main settlement. Given the wide variety of microenvironments in different parts of the peninsula, suited to a wide variety of different crops, it is quite possible that a number of households had more than one temporary base away from the main village.

Seasonal population mobility and residential flexibility also seem to have been a recurrent feature of the Ermionida region of the Argolic peninsula, as suggested by details in some of the documentary sources, especially those from the Second Venetian Occupation of the Peloponnese. In referring to some settlements, the Venetian documents use different terms (e.g., *zevgolatio, boaria*) that seem broadly comparable in a number of aspects for settlements that are not described by the standard name of

90. Adanır 1998, pp. 281–282, 291.

91. İnalcık 1994b, pp. 31, 165; Faroqhi 1994, pp. 436–437; McGowan 1994, pp. 680–681.

92. Adanır 1998, p. 296.

93. Topping 1976, pp. 93–95. See also Chap. 5 in this volume.

94. Alexander 1985.

95. Alexander 1985, p. 39.

96. Alexander 1985, pp. 39–40.

97. See, e.g., Brumfield 2000, pp. 56–60; Jameson, Runnels, and van Andel 1994, pp. 133–134; Wagstaff and Augustson 1982, p. 110; Whitelaw 1991, pp. 403–405, 413–424; Chap. 7 in this volume.

98. Forbes 2000a, pp. 50–51.

99. Forbes 1997, pp. 101–105.

villa (village).[100] The extent to which the different terms indicate differences in meaning is not completely clear. It is evident, however, that they were in some sense satellites to village settlements. The most likely interpretation is that some, at least, were seasonally occupied—a practice that has antecedents in the medieval period.[101]

The evidence from oral histories on Methana suggests that whole families would decamp from their main villages to temporary residences with all their livestock for the duration of whatever agricultural task was involved. In the 19th and 20th centuries, their temporary residences (*kalivia,* huts) were built of stone. The *catastico ordinario* for the territory of Nauplion, a cadaster produced during the Second Venetian Occupation of the Peloponnese, mentions "hovels of straw" that served as "habitations for the agriculturalists" at one seasonal settlement in the Ermionida.[102] It is possible that some households lived temporarily in rough brushwood shelters or in tents during the summer months. Given the apparently temporary nature of many *kalivia* in this period, it is not surprising that, following their abandonment, few physical traces remain to indicate their locations.[103]

There are three other significant features of these seasonal settlements. The first is their generally small size. The second is the way in which they are variously listed in the Venetian documents as inhabited or uninhabited: they sometimes appear in lists of inhabited settlements and sometimes do not. Their small size might suggest that the census-takers sometimes missed them, but the efficiency visible elsewhere in the census documents makes this seem unlikely.[104] More likely, they were simply uninhabited at the time of year when the census was conducted.[105] The third feature is the apparently low status of the inhabitants. One possibility is that they were not fully free and were in some way legally tied to their landlords. Alternatively, they may have been technically free, but landless, and therefore entirely dependent on their landlords for their livelihood. Indeed, one possible translation of the Italian term *boaria,* used to describe some of these settlements, is a place where tenants or sharecroppers live or farm.[106]

CONCLUSION

How do the observations derived primarily from Methana in the 19th century affect our understanding of Greece in previous centuries? First and foremost, the evidence presented here gives a strong impression of flux and fluidity among rural populations. Some of this is more apparent

100. The term *metochi* is also used; it relates to a seasonally occupied settlement on lands owned by a monastery.

101. Forbes 2000a, pp. 48–53; but now see also Davies 2004, pp. 98–100.

102. Forbes 2000a, p. 52. The Italian word *paglia* is probably a mistranslation of the Greek *kalamia* (reeds); shelters built from the giant reed *Arundo donax* could have been quite substantial structures.

103. Jameson, Runnels, and van Andel 1994, pp. 131–134.

104. Topping 2000, p. 34.

105. Forbes 2000a, pp. 43–45, 48–53; Topping 2000, p. 34.

106. Forbes 2000a, pp. 51–52, 54–55.

than real. The observation that the apparent "surnames" of people in the general population might not last beyond a single generation makes the identification of long-term continuity of households potentially difficult. Changing "surnames" could give a spurious impression of a constant movement of households in and out of communities in each generation, even in situations in which population stability might have been the norm. The tendency of a significant proportion of the population to have multiple residences can also contribute a somewhat spurious element of flux and mobility in the interpretation of past Greek landscapes. Reports of uninhabited settlements, especially in periods of instability, can lead to the assumption of "abandonment" if documents do not identify them as seasonally inhabited.

The fact that movement between different locations in the landscape may have been normal practice for many households should be linked to an ethos of mobility and impermanence of residence. Such an ethos might well have been behind the apparent readiness with which households seem to have changed their main residence from one village to another, even in times of relative stability. It is possible that a significant proportion of those who tended to be found moving between seasonal settlements were landless, whatever their exact legal status. It would have been these people who had least to lose by moving elsewhere.

The situation described for Methana also emphasizes the importance of kinship. Although the possibility that "surnames" may frequently not have been surnames in the modern sense presents a potential problem for researchers, from another point of view it allows the distinct possibility that those living in a particular community who shared a "surname" may have been closely related. Furthermore, although it is usually hard to be sure exactly how particular censuses were compiled, it is worth bearing in mind that the order in which households were listed may be linked in some way to their physical locations, as seems to have been the case with the 1879 census on Methana. On occasion, therefore, it may be possible to investigate the kinship organization of space, and presumably also activity, discussed for 19th-century Methana.

Kinship was also important as an organizational framework for managing the movement of groups of people. The tradition of the suprahousehold unit, based on a nucleus of agnatically related kin, is well documented. The example noted earlier of its functioning on an ad hoc basis to address contingencies is relevant here.[107] Nevertheless, the evidence that it governed the movement of groups of related families indicates that their mobility was unlikely to have been a spur-of-the-moment decision. Presumably consultation, discussion, and planning among households were involved prior to any such coordinated move. It again highlights the fact that populations did not move only in the face of imminent disaster.

Mention of kinship involvement in mobility returns us to the core of this chapter: that flux and fluidity, at least, should be considered the norm in a substantial proportion of the Greek population before 1800, not an untoward result of occasional catastrophic events. Underlying this phenomenon, however, were culturally embedded structures that provided stable parameters to socially acceptable instability. One of these is the tradition of multiple settlement locations and seasonal mobility. The other

107. Koster 1976, p. 20.

is the contribution of kinship in the arena of economic activity and the organization of mobility.

Finally, the picture of flux and fluidity set within kinship solidarity in pre-independence Greece can be placed in a wider context within the Ottoman Empire, and presumably other empires, such as that of Venice. In Transjordan, kin-based networks have been identified as the primary element in a repertoire of behaviors involved in resistance to Ottoman domination.[108] Also included were several other cultural features, equally at home in Greece and in the Near East, such as well-developed ethics of hospitality and of honor. Another critical cultural feature in Ottoman period Transjordan was residential flexibility. As with the Greek situation, alternative shelters in Transjordan frequently required minimal labor.[109] Thus the behaviors identified among rural populations in Ottoman and Venetian Greece can be fitted into a political as well as a historical and social context that transcends present-day national borders.

108. LaBianca 2000, pp. 209–210.
109. LaBianca 2000, pp. 210–212.

REFERENCES

Adanır, F. 1998. "The Ottoman Peasantries, c. 1360–1860," in *The Peasantries of Europe: From the Fourteenth to the Eighteen Centuries,* ed. T. Scott, London, pp. 269–310.

Alexander, J. C. 1985. *Brigandage and Public Order in the Morea, 1685–1806,* Athens.

Aschenbrenner, S. 1986. *Life in a Changing Greek Village: Karpofora and Its Reluctant Farmers,* Dubuque.

Athanasiou, S. N. 1998. *Μέθανα από το 10.000 π.Χ. μέχρι το 2.000 μ.Χ.: Ο ήλιος, η θάλασσα, το ψωμί, το λάδι και το κρασί είναι η ζωή μας . . . ,* Piraeus.

Braudel, F. 1972. *The Mediterranean and the Mediterranean World in the Age of Philip II* 1, trans. S. Reynolds, London.

Brumfield, A. 2000. "Agriculture and Rural Settlement in Ottoman Crete, 1669–1898: A Modern Site Survey," in *A Historical Archaeology of the Ottoman Empire: Breaking New Ground,* ed. U. Baram and L. Carroll, New York, pp. 37–78.

Campbell, J. 1964. *Honour, Family, and Patronage: A Study of Institutions and Moral Values in a Greek Mountain Village,* Oxford.

Chouliarakis, M. 1973. *Γεωγραφικὴ, διοικητικὴ, καὶ πληθυσμιακὴ ἐξέλιξις τῆς Ἑλλάδος, 1821–1971* 1, Athens.

Clark, M. H. 1988. "The Transformation of Households on Methana, Greece, 1931–1987" (diss. Univ. of North Carolina at Chapel Hill).

Davies, S. 1994. "Tithe-Collection in the Venetian Peloponnese, 1696–1705," *BSA* 89, pp. 433–455.

———. 2004. "Pylos Regional Archaeological Project, Part VI: Administration and Settlement in Venetian Navarino," *Hesperia* 73, pp. 59–120.

Dorian, N. 1970. "A Substitute Name System in the Scottish Highlands," *American Anthropologist* 72, pp. 303–319.

Douglas, N. [1915] 2001. *Old Calabria,* with an introduction by J. Keates, repr. London.

Durrel, G. 1999. *My Family and Other Animals,* London.

Faroqhi, S. 1994. "Crisis and Change, 1590–1699," in İnalcık 1994a, pp. 411–636.

Forbes, H. A. 1982. "Strategies and Soils: Technology, Production, and Environment in the Peninsula of Methana, Greece" (diss. Univ. of Pennsylvania).

———. 1997. "Turkish and Modern Methana," in *A Rough and Rocky Place: The Landscape and Settlement History of the Methana Peninsula, Greece. Results of the Methana Survey Project,* ed. C. Mee and H. Forbes, Liverpool, pp. 101–117.

———. 2000a. "The Agrarian Economy of the Ermionida around 1700: An Ethnohistorical Reconstruction," in Sutton 2000a, pp. 41–70.
———. 2000b. "Security and Settlement in the Medieval and Post-Medieval Peloponnesos, Greece: 'Hard' History versus Oral History," *JMA* 13, pp. 204–224.
———. Forthcoming. "Connecting the Archaeological Past with the Ethnographic Present: Local Population Records and Settlement Development on 19th-Century Methana," in *New Approaches to the Archaeology and Material Culture of Medieval and Post-Medieval Greece,* ed. J. Bintliff, E. Tsoungarakis, and D. Tsoungarakis, Athens.
Frangakis-Syrett, E., and J. M. Wagstaff. 1992. "The Height Zonation of Population in the Morea, c. 1830," *BSA* 87, pp. 439–446.
Hammel, E. 1972. "The Zadruga as Process," in *Household and Family in Past Time,* ed. P. Laslett and R. Wall, Cambridge, pp. 335–374.
Herzfeld, M. 1983. "Interpreting Kinship Terminology: The Problem of Patriliny in Rural Greece," *Anthropological Quarterly* 54, pp. 157–166.
Horden, P., and N. Purcell. 2000. *The Corrupting Sea: A Study of Mediterranean History,* Oxford.
İnalcık, H., ed. 1994a. *An Economic and Social History of the Ottoman Empire, 1300–1914,* Cambridge.
———. 1994b. "The Ottoman State: Economy and Society, 1300–1600," in İnalcık 1994a, pp. 9–410.
Jameson, M. H., C. N. Runnels, and T. H. van Andel. 1994. *A Greek Countryside: The Southern Argolid from Prehistory to the Present Day,* Stanford.
Koster, H. A. 1976. "The Thousand-Year Road," *Expedition* 19, pp. 19–28.
———. 1977. "The Ecology of Pastoralism in Relation to Changing Patterns of Land Use in the Northeast Peloponnese" (diss. Univ. of Pennsylvania).
Koster, H. A., and J. B. Koster. 1976. "Competition or Symbiosis? Pastoral Adaptive Strategies in the Southern Argolid," in *Regional Variation in Modern Greece and Cyprus: Toward a Perspective on the Ethnography of Greece* (Annals of the New York Academy of Sciences 268), ed. M. Dimen and E. Friedl, New York, pp. 275–285.
Koukoulis, T. 1997. "Catalogue of Churches," in *A Rough and Rocky Place: The Landscape and Settlement History of the Methana Peninsula, Greece. Results of the Methana Survey Project,* ed. C. Mee and H. Forbes, Liverpool, pp. 211–256.
LaBianca, Ø. 2000. "Daily Life in the Shadow of Empire: A Food Systems Approach to the Archaeology of the Ottoman Period," in *A Historical Archaeology of the Ottoman Empire: Breaking New Ground,* ed. U. Baram and L. Carroll, New York, pp. 203–219.
Laiou-Thomadakis, A. E. 1977. *Peasant Society in the Late Byzantine Empire: A Social and Demographic Study,* Princeton.
Leech-Wilkinson, D. 1978. "The Notebook of a Fifteenth-Century Trumpeter: London, British Library, Cotton Titus A.XXVI," posted online at www.kcl.ac.uk/kis/schools/hums/music/dlw/tit.htm.
Le Roy Ladurie, E. 1966. *Les paysans de Languedoc,* 2 vols., Paris.
Lewis, B. 1961. *The Emergence of Modern Turkey,* Oxford.
Lowry, H. W. 2002. *Fifteenth-Century Ottoman Realities: Christian Peasant Life on the Aegean Island of Limnos,* Istanbul.
Macfarlane, A. 1984. "The Myth of the Peasantry: Family and Economy in a Northern Parish," in *Land, Kinship, and Life-Cycle,* ed. R. M. Smith, Cambridge, pp. 333–349.
McGowan, B. 1994. "The Age of the Ayans, 1699–1812," in İnalcık 1994a, pp. 637–758.
Panayiotopoulos, V. 1985. *Πληθυσμός και οικισμοί της Πελοποννήσου: 13ος–18ος αιώνας,* Athens.
Segalen, M. 1984. "Nuclear Is Not Independent: Organisation of the Household in the Pays Bigouden Sud in the Nineteenth and Twentieth Centuries," in *Households: Comparative and Historical Studies of the Domestic Group,* ed. R. M. Netting,

R. R. Wilk, and E. J. Arnold, Berkeley, pp. 163–186.

Sphyroeras, V. V. 1974. *Ἀρχεῖον Ψαρῶν* 1: *Ἔγγραφα τῶν ἐτῶν 1821–1824,* Athens.

Sutton, S. B. 2000a. "Introduction: Past and Present in Rural Greece," in Sutton 2000c, pp. 1–24.

———. 2000b. "Liquid Landscapes: Demographic Transitions in the Ermionida," in Sutton 2000c, pp. 84–106.

———, ed. 2000c. *Contingent Countryside: Settlement, Economy, and Land Use in the Southern Argolid since 1700,* Stanford.

Topping, E. 1969. "Appendix I: Noms de personne," in *Documents sur le régime des terres dans la principauté de Morée, au XIVe siècle,* ed. J. Longnon and P. Topping, Paris, pp. 221–231.

———. 1976. "Premodern Peloponnesus: The Land and People under Venetian Rule," in *Regional Variation in Modern Greece and Cyprus: Toward a Perspective on the Ethnography of Greece* (Annals of the New York Academy of Sciences 268), ed. M. Dimen and E. Friedl, New York, pp. 92–108.

———. 2000. "The Southern Argolid from Byzantine to Ottoman Times," in Sutton 2000a, pp. 25–40.

Wagstaff, J. M., and S. Augustson. 1982. "Traditional Land Use," in *An Island Polity: The Archaeology of Exploitation in Melos,* ed. C. Renfrew and J. M. Wagstaff, Cambridge, pp. 106–133.

Whitelaw, T. M. 1991. "The Ethnoarchaeology of Recent Rural Settlement and Land Use in Northwest Keos," in *Landscape Archaeology as Long-Term History: Northern Keos in the Cycladic Islands from Earliest Settlement until Modern Times* (Monumenta archaeologica 16), ed. J. F. Cherry, J. L. Davis, and E. Mantzourani, Los Angeles, pp. 403–454.

Wilk, R. R., and R. M. Netting. 1984. "Households: Changing Forms and Functions," in *Households: Comparative and Historical Studies of the Domestic Group,* ed. R. M. Netting, R. R.Wilk, and E. J. Arnold, Berkeley, pp. 1–28.

Zarinebaf, F., J. Bennet, and J. L. Davis. 2005. *A Historical and Economic Geography of Ottoman Greece: The Southwestern Morea in the 18th Century* (*Hesperia* Suppl. 34), Princeton.

Mountain Landscapes on Early Modern Cyprus

by Michael Given

At 761 m above sea level, the view from the forest-fire lookout on Kakos Anemos is panoramic.[1] Far below to the west is the Asinou Valley, with an abandoned settlement and the Byzantine church of Panayia Phorviotissa. To the north are the fields, roads, and villages of the densely settled and cultivated Mesaoria Plain. To the south and east, and beyond the Asinou Valley to the west, are the pine-clad diabase ridges of the northern Troodos Mountains. This area seems to be devoid of any sort of human activity, apart from that indicated by the dirt roads that scar the forest.

The archaeological distribution maps show the same pattern. The plains are richly populated with "sites" of various periods, and thanks to the bias toward copper production in Cypriot archaeology, these sites continue into the ore-carrying pillow lavas of the Troodos foothills. Cross into the diabase and the forests of *Pinus brutia,* and the archaeology stops. There is nothing in the mountains, runs the logic, so there is no need to look.

Part of the reason for this apparent lack of material has been the definition and scope of archaeology on Cyprus. It is indeed true that no prehistoric sites have been found above about 600 m, and only rarely above 300 m. Archaic to Roman sites have been found at higher altitudes, though references to them are few.[2] The great wealth of material from the mountains consists of finds from the Lusignan (1191–1489), Venetian (1489–1571), Ottoman (1571–1878), and modern (1878–present) periods. Apart from architectural history and some isolated analyses of sgraffito pottery and sugar mills, it is only in the past 10 years or so that these periods have started to become respectable areas of study in Cypriot archaeology.[3]

1. Much of the information in this chapter was collected as part of the Sydney Cyprus Survey Project (SCSP) and the Troodos Archaeological and Environmental Survey Project (TAESP). I am grateful to the specialists, team leaders, and fieldwalkers of those projects, especially Erin Gibson, Timothy Gregory, Jay Noller, Luke Sollars, and Joanita Vroom. SCSP was directed by A. Bernard Knapp, and TAESP is co-directed by Michael Given, Vasiliki Kassianidou, A. Bernard Knapp, and Jay Noller. TAESP works with a permit from the Department of Antiquities of Cyprus, and its principal source of funding is the Arts and Humanities Research Council of the United Kingdom. I am grateful to the organizers and participants of the "Between Venice and Istanbul" workshop for their helpful comments and stimulating discussion.

2. Ellis Burnet 2004, chap. 9; Karageorghis 1977; Klerides 1948, pp. 15–17.

3. See, e.g., Baram 1995; Gabrieli, McCall, and Green 2001; Given 2000.

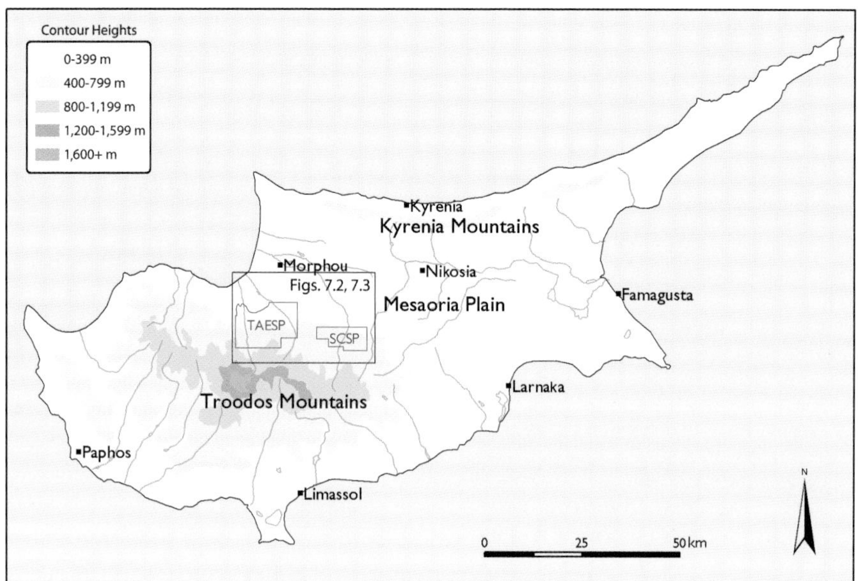

Figure 7.1. Map of Cyprus showing the study area and the TAESP and SCSP survey areas. M. Given

Historical research, of course, reveals a far different picture, and a range of studies of census records and other documentation shows hundreds of villages at all altitudes up to 1400 m.[4] To restrict our analysis to villages, however, or even to archaeological "sites," does no justice to the complexity of settlement and movement within the landscape and the full range of activities that takes place there. Is there a role here for landscape archaeology in complementing the historical records and filling the gap left by decades of archaeological phobia about the mountains?

This approach is particularly important for the analysis of imperialism. Archaeologists have long been able to detect its impact in the cities and plains by investigating the construction of fortifications and infrastructure, the appropriation of land for new estates, and the large-scale extraction of surplus.[5] But this approach views imperialism as a monolithic system imposed on a passive population. What about the individual reactions, initiatives, resilience, and new identities of particular individuals and groups among the colonized?

The mountains can often provide much more interesting opportunities for this type of analysis than the plains. This is not because mountain-dwellers are automatically more independent, which is a perspective tantamount to environmental determinism.[6] Rather, the difficult topography of a mountain landscape makes extensive local knowledge absolutely essential for any kind of relationship or activity among its inhabitants. Mountain landscapes provide opportunities and arenas for resistance, resilience, and a wide range of practices by which people continue to build their own communities and identities.

The overall aim of this volume is to examine the colonial landscapes of the early modern period in Greece and on Cyprus by integrating historical texts and material culture. I address that aim here by contrasting the picture of mountain society given by census and taxation records with that provided by landscape archaeology. My area of focus is the northern Troodos Mountains

4. Grivaud 1998; Papadopoullos 1965.

5. See, e.g., Rizakis 1997; cf. Given 2004, pp. 50–68.

6. See, e.g., Shaw 1990.

of Cyprus (Fig. 7.1), and the period I investigate is the 16th–19th centuries. Much of my data is taken from SCSP and TAESP.[7] Like many other projects of the 1980s and 1990s, SCSP realized the importance of the post-Roman period only in the course of carrying out fieldwork. TAESP, however, was designed to investigate later periods as much as earlier ones, and the material from the Asinou Valley and surrounding mountains is directly relevant to the issues discussed in this chapter.

SETTLEMENTS AND CENSUS RECORDS

Censuses carried out by states to facilitate the taxation of their subjects are invaluable sources for the analysis of regional settlement patterns and productivity. This is why studies of Ottoman tax registers have become so important in landscape archaeology projects in Greece and, increasingly, elsewhere.[8] Although such census and tax records can provide statistical validity far above that of any archaeological estimate of population or agricultural production, it is important to remember that they also represent the intrusions of the state into local communities.

Census officials were by no means entirely efficient and incorruptible. We cannot assume that their censuses were both fully comprehensive and entirely accurate, particularly on no other evidence than their own declarations. In their census of Cyprus in the mid-16th century, for example, the Venetians had difficulties with different local definitions of the term *francomati* (free peasants, as opposed to *paroici,* serfs);[9] the reality behind the tidy lists of figures was clearly much more complex than the officials admitted. Similarly, the surveyors of the Ottoman census in 1572 gave no estimate of the accuracy or thoroughness of their work.[10] An Ottoman legislative decree *(kanunname)* of the same date summarized the preceding Venetian tax regulations, mainly to make pointed contrasts with the fairer new regime. This summary has a number of substantial mistakes and omissions, and illustrates that Ottoman official records are not entirely accurate, either.[11]

Nonofficial sources are more likely to be critical of the accuracy of census records. One such criticism comes from a Spanish nobleman who traveled in Cyprus in 1806 under the pseudonym Ali Bey. Even though many such Europeans exaggerated the inefficiency and corruption of Ottoman administration, it is clear that the government was by no means infallible and omniscient:

> The government has never succeeded in learning how many Greeks there are in the island. They own to a total of thirty-two thousand souls: but well informed persons raise this number to a hundred thousand. Last year a commissioner was sent to make an exact enumeration of the Greek families, but he was "got at," loaded with gold, and went away—his task unfulfilled.[12]

It may be that archaeology can point out some activities, situations, or even entire settlements that were missed by the census-takers.

7. For SCSP, see Given and Knapp 2003; for TAESP, see Given et al. 2002.
8. See, e.g., Bintliff 1997; Forbes 1997; and Chap. 2 in this volume.
9. Grivaud 1998, p. 77.
10. Jennings 1986, p. 176.
11. See Arbel and Veinstein 1986.
12. Quoted in Cobham 1908, p. 396.

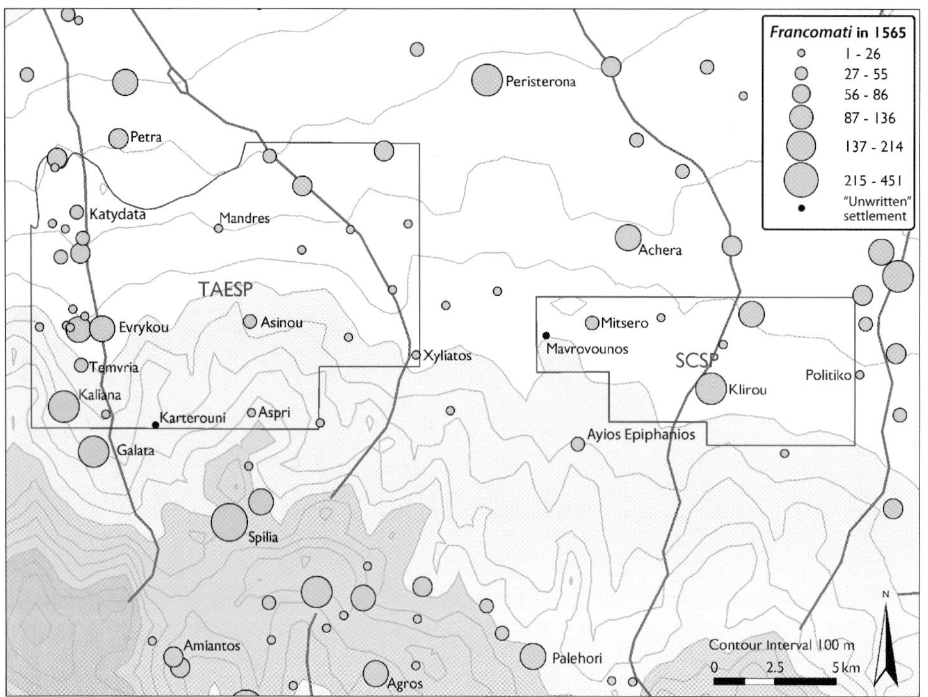

Figure 7.2. Villages in the northern Troodos Mountains with numbers of *francomati* in 1565. M. Given; figures from Grivaud 1998, pp. 445–472

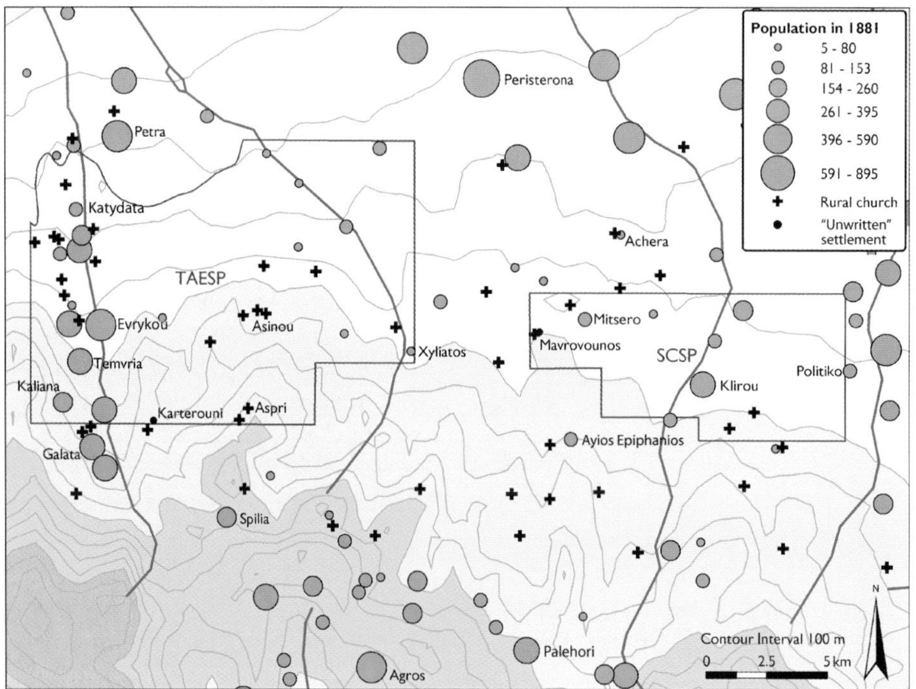

Figure 7.3. Villages in the northern Troodos Mountains with rural churches and population figures for 1881. M. Given; figures from *Census 1881*

Figures 7.2 and 7.3 show population figures in the northern Troodos Mountains from two censuses, those of 1565 and 1881. The Venetian census *(pratico)* of 1565 was intended to record all adult male *francomati,* along with some extra groups such as boys and priests. Unfortunately, no indication is given of household sizes or numbers of *paroici,* which would have allowed us to extrapolate figures for the total population. This census was intended specifically for the imposition of military taxes for finishing the Famagusta and Nikosia fortifications, and for funding the peasant militias created seven years earlier. The British census of 1881, taken three years after Britain's occupation of the island, recorded the inhabitants and houses of each town, village, estate, and monastery, distinguishing males from females, and inhabited from uninhabited buildings.[13]

Obviously the two maps differ, the first indicating the number of free adult males, the second, the total population. What both maps also demonstrate, however, is the general relationship between large and small settlements and their location patterns, and how those changed over time. In both periods the largest river valleys were densely settled and very productive, especially the Solea Valley running down the western side of the TAESP survey area. Gaudry commented in 1855 that this valley was particularly fertile because of the silt brought down by the annual floods, especially after the abandonment of the Venetian system of irrigation channels, and that it produced the best cotton in Cyprus.[14]

The topographical zone that was apparently far less settled and exploited in both periods consists of the steep-sided and deeply incised valleys of the diabase between 500 m and 1,000 m above sea level, excluding the Solea Valley. Below that zone is a series of small villages in the foothills, especially in 1881, with a few such as Ayios Theodoros Soleas and Xyliatos lying in deep river valleys that cut into the mountains. Above 1,000 m there is again a substantial scatter of villages up to about 1,300 m (most of them off the map to the south). These mostly lie on the gabbro ridge top, which is much more broken up than the massive ridges and valleys of the diabase below.

A striking difference between the maps is the substantial size of some of the mountain villages in 1565, compared to those of the river valleys, foothills, and even plains. Galata (which includes the census figures for Kakopetria) and Kaliana in the Solea Valley lie on a major route into the mountains, and the valley is still wide enough for substantial agricultural production. These population figures are supported by the impressive number of churches, seven in all, in Galata and Kakopetria; one was built in the 11th century and the rest in the 16th. Spilia with its 386 *francomati* is the largest village on the map, even though it lies on a steep mountainside with poor access to major communication routes and minimal agricultural land, requiring labor-intensive terracing.

In terms of people's lives and experiences, these spots on the map represent intrusions of census officials and the tax collectors who would follow them. Those 386 *francomati* recorded by the 1565 census in Spilia were all individuals who had to give up substantial proportions of their surplus crops to support the Venetian military. It was no honor to be counted and incorporated into the imperial domain. This made the visit of the census official, like that of the tax collector, part of the theater of domination.[15]

13. For the Venetian census, see Grivaud 1998, pp. 77–78, 445–472; and cf. Davies 1994. For the British census, see *Census 1881.*

14. Gaudry 1855, pp. 96–97, 159–160.

15. Cf. Gosden and Knowles 2001, pp. 15–16.

A particularly clear example of this is the Ottoman "census master" and his commission arriving in a Greek village. The entire population had to appear before them, headed by the priests and notables. This communal act of submission was then repeated at an individual level as the name of every male older than 13 was formally inscribed into the register.[16]

The maps in Figures 7.2 and 7.3 are not so much representations of social organization or community identity, as illustrations of imperialist exploitation and the urge to classify, categorize, and demarcate.[17] To investigate issues such as resistance to imperial rule, local identities, perceptions of the landscape, and the complexities of a mountain economy, we must examine the spaces between the spots on the map. This is exactly what interdisciplinary landscape archaeology tries to do by studying the traces of human activity in very specific social and topographical contexts.

MOUNTAIN LANDSCAPES IN THE NORTHERN TROODOS

Maurovounos, on the western edge of the SCSP survey area, is not atypical of the smaller settlements from the medieval and Ottoman periods, and it illustrates the contribution of a broader perspective from landscape archaeology. It is not listed in the 1565 census, but it appears in three other Venetian village lists from about 1550. In the late 15th century it belonged to the Grand Commandery of the Knights of St. John.[18] According to local tradition, Maurovounos was abandoned some 300 years ago because of a plague.

The settlement lies on a small spur in the upper part of a tributary valley leading down to the Mitsero basin and the Kryon Neron River (Fig. 7.4). Immediately adjacent is the Late Roman copper slag heap from which it clearly derived its name, Maurovounos (Black Hill). The summit and slopes of the spur are covered with lines and piles of rubble, with only two clear enough to distinguish the outlines of the original structures. The glazed pottery suggests a lifespan stretching continuously from the 14th to the 17th or 18th centuries, with a clear peak in the 16th.[19] It is abundantly clear that Maurovounos was a substantial settlement in 1565, in spite of its omission from the census.

The economy of the settlement can be investigated by analyzing the function of the artifacts found and mapping the land use potential of the surrounding area. Arable land is scarce, with a few limited areas preserved by check dams from the erosion that has devastated this valley. Two threshing sledge blades from just above the settlement show there was at least some production of cereals. In contrast to contemporary settlements with better soil and water, there are no olive trees more than 200 years old around Maurovounos. It is clear that the arable sector of the settlement's economy would have provided little more than basic subsistence needs.

The most striking aspect of the pottery assemblage is the large quantities of *pitharia* (storage jars) and *galeuteria* (milking bowls). The storage jars could have been for cereals, wine, or oil, but the milking bowls, with their characteristic broad spouts, strongly suggest a major pastoral

16. Kiel 1997, p. 317.

17. Cohn 1996, pp. 7–8; Given 2002.

18. Grivaud 1998, p. 462; de Mas Latrie 1855, pp. 502–503.

19. Given and Knapp 2003, pp. 104–107.

Figure 7.4. Maurovounos from the south. The medieval settlement lies on the low terraced hill in the middle ground on the right. M. Given

component. The forests surrounding Maurovounos, though now rather depleted on the northern side, provide extensive grazing land. There are two certain goatfolds in its immediate area, and a group of small undated structures on the ridgeline above Maurovounos that may have functioned as goatherds' shelters. One of the goatfolds, Klouvaes, consists of a small semicircular enclosure and a two-room shelter dating to the 19th and early 20th centuries. Late medieval pottery found in the vicinity may have been in use earlier.

More interesting is the goatfold and associated structures at Kalorka, on a high spur on the opposite side of the valley from Maurovounos, 750 m to its south. Where the spur line flattens out is a subrectangular enclosure measuring 47 × 40 m. On its western and southern sides are large rubble piles that conceivably could be field clearance cairns, but are more likely to represent collapsed stone huts or shelters. On the south, leading up the spur, is a series of small hillslope terraces. Where a track has been bulldozed just beyond the western edge of the enclosure, considerable quantities of 14th- to 16th-century pottery have been exposed.

Although this complex is well positioned to serve the largely pastoral economy of Maurovounos, it is clearly more than a shepherds' camp. Its inhabitants were also carrying out small-scale agriculture, and they could exploit the numerous edible resources of the surrounding forest. Whether it was continuously inhabited or seasonal, its inhabitants lived there for sufficiently long periods of time to justify bringing up substantial amounts of sgraffito tableware over some two centuries. This tiny settlement does not appear in any censuses or village lists. Its inhabitants may have been registered as part of Maurovounos and had their goats taxed there, or they might not have been registered at all, safe on their high ridgeline from the tax collectors. What is clear from this one area is that settlement and production, regarded as human activities, were much wider and more complex and fluid than is implied by the census records and "spots" on settlement maps.[20]

20. Cf. Chap. 6 in this volume.

If we now step back from Maurovounos and look at the northern Troodos as a whole, we see the same complexity of settlement and production across this entire mountain region. Terraces, check dams, field shelters, and light pottery scatters show that there were pockets of cultivation penetrating deep into the mountain valleys. Often these pockets are visible in the forest boundaries drawn by the British colonial government in the 1880s, whose officials had to skirt the narrow alluvial terraces and the rows of check dams.[21] Others can be mapped only by combined archaeological and geomorphological survey.

The pastoral economy of Venetian and Ottoman Cyprus clearly was substantial, even though it did not produce major exports of the sort recorded by the foreign consuls; much of the pastoral activity took place in hard-to-access mountains and forests where travelers rarely went. Church records show that many monasteries had substantial flocks. In 1773, for example, the monastery of Ayios Irakleidios outside Politiko village owned 302 goats at the monastery itself, and another 190 sheep and goats at its goatfolds in other villages.[22] The reports by the colonial forest officials after the British occupation in 1878 firmly blame widespread and unrestrained goat-grazing for what they saw as the devastation of the forests.[23] Some of the goatfolds in Macheras Forest are substantial complexes of enclosures, pens, and shelters.[24] As well as their economic importance, such structures are significant for being focuses of settlement and local knowledge, and for being arenas of activity that could easily take place out of the reach of the census official or tax collector.

More than goatfolds were beyond the reach of the tax collector. As we have seen, censuses are by no means a fully accurate and complete representation of the complexity of human society and activity. One expression of the fallibility of census-takers would appear to be the tradition of "unwritten villages" in the Agrapha area of the Pindus Mountains in Greece. These areas supposedly were either given semiautonomy, being taxed as a whole rather than each village being individually inscribed in the register, or else they managed to escape central taxation entirely.[25] But, to some extent, such claims derive ultimately from the nationalist mythology of the 19th and 20th centuries, which used them to celebrate Greek resistance to Ottoman oppression.[26] Such mythology is in itself a form of resistance and a means of maintaining pride and a semblance of independence. It may be, however, that archaeology can find some real examples of "unwritten villages." Tax evasion is by definition secretive and hard to find in the historical record, but in the northern Troodos a systematic pattern of small settlements do not appear in the censuses.

At first sight, the 1565 map (Fig. 7.2) shows impressive coverage by the Venetian census officials, even along the ridgeline of the Troodos Mountains in the south. There is a clear gap, however, along the steep-sided mountain valleys of the northern face of the Troodos massif, and also along the foothills other than the well-watered alluvial valley bottoms. This is exactly where TAESP and SCSP found evidence for small-scale settlements from the 16th century to the 19th, often consisting only of the remnants of a handful of houses, and appearing in neither the 1565 nor the 1881 census. These are indicated as "Unwritten" settlements in Figure 7.2.

21. Given 2002, pp. 12–16.

22. Tsiknopoulos 1967, pp. 62–63.

23. Thirgood 1987, pp. 77–85.

24. Ellis Burnet 2004, chap. 9; Given 2000, pp. 221–223.

25. Clogg 1986, p. 21; Forbes 2000, p. 208; Leake 1835, p. 266.

26. Kiel 1996; see also p. 86, n. 52, in this volume.

Others are known from the survey work of Luke Sollars in the Asinou area and Julia Ellis Burnet to the south of Xyliatos and in the Macheras Mountains to the southeast.[27]

To take a specific area as an example, the 1881 British census recorded no settlements in the Asinou Valley (Fig. 7.3). By contrast, TAESP's systematic transect survey, combined with some purposive survey, shows a busy landscape during this period. There are two rather diffuse areas of settlement and four ruined or functioning churches within 2.5 km, as well as evidence of agriculture, goat-grazing, and resin-tapping (the last two activities mainly carried out in defiance of colonial forest regulations). Another related phenomenon is that of the seasonal settlement, such as Mandres and the two settlements in Figure 7.2 lying between Maurovounos and Xyliatos. These were used by people from different mountain villages for the summer cultivation of cereals, and were well-known problems for the census officials and taxation authorities, who had to extract tithes in one settlement from people registered in another.[28]

Rural churches are a highly visible feature of the mountain landscape, particularly because of their perceived cultural significance, which leads to their inclusion on maps more often than goatfolds and field shelters. It is precisely this cultural significance that is of interest here, as it survives even when the ruins of the church are barely visible on the ground. These churches are among the most striking carriers of memory within the Cypriot landscape. In some 10 seasons of doing various types of survey in the northern Troodos, I have talked to many villagers about archaeological remains in the landscape. In almost every case they talk first about the churches, and have the most stories and details about them.

These memories and deep-seated knowledge can also be seen in specific artifacts and structures. The ruined church of Ayios Yeoryios opposite Karterouni has a substantial deposit of glass bottles in its apse. These date to the mid-to-late 20th century, well after the church fell into ruins, and presumably held oil for dedications. Other churches such as Ayios Kournoutas, north of Agrokipia, are unrecognizable now but were obviously well known during the first cadastral surveys of the 1910s to 1920s. What is striking is the continuity of the knowledge. Some churches clearly have been abandoned for some 300 years, but the name and often stories about the saint, the icons, or an associated settlement survive across this gap. The social memory that these churches carried clearly was active throughout the Ottoman period.

Figure 7.3 shows the "rural" churches of the northern Troodos, defined arbitrarily as churches more than 500 m from a currently inhabited village. The churches within the two survey areas have been found by relatively thorough purposive survey, particularly by using maps of various scales and periods, and all have been visited and described. Those outside the survey areas were mostly recorded on 1:50,000 topographical maps, and only about half have been visited.

The distribution of these churches shows three distinct patterns: very few on the plains; considerable numbers in the mountains, even in apparently remote areas; and an even greater concentration in the Solea Valley to the west. Intensive agriculture on the plains may have caused the destruction

27. Sollars 2005, pp. 135–142; Ellis Burnet (pers. comm.).
28. Given 2000, pp. 217–218.

of several, though it is normal for farmers to respect such ruins when they are identified as churches. The churches in the mountains are commonly in valley bottoms or else on spurs halfway up the side of the valley. There are almost no hilltop churches.

A high proportion of these churches, when visited, have proved to mark the sites of earlier settlements. They are clearly community churches whose life and memory have outlasted the settlement. All four rural churches in the SCSP area, for example, mark the sites of abandoned settlements, or in one case a monastery. There is a notable correlation between settlements on the 1565 map that were subsequently abandoned and the rural churches that remained to mark them. This is particularly clear in the Solea and Asinou valleys in the TAESP survey area, particularly when 16th- and 17th-century settlements not recorded in the 1565 census are added (compare Figs. 7.2 and 7.3).

CONCLUSION

This chapter has summarized four aspects of the mountain landscapes of early modern Cyprus: census-taking and its avoidance, settlement, pastoralism, and the memories inspired by rural churches. Both material and documentary records are enormously rich, and the tensions and disagreements between them are highly stimulating for an analysis of local knowledge and colonial rule.

It turns out that the mountain landscape as viewed from the forest-fire lookout on Kakos Anemos is not so barren after all. There are settlements dating back at least to the 16th century, with a wide range of morphologies and roles within the landscape. There are material traces of agriculture, pastoralism, resin-tapping, pitch production, traveling, and even tax evasion. This is a rich landscape and a rich period for investigating topics such as mountain economies and the continuing creation of local identities under colonial rule.

There are many different types of sources, and anyone looking for a nuanced understanding of the past clearly needs to investigate all of them: official censuses, travelers' accounts, architectural studies of elite sites, and intensive survey in rural areas. This integration of different types of information is one of the aims of this volume. Understanding the context is important in the study of artifacts, structures, and historical documents alike. A census is not just a document in a modern library. It is also the material outcome of a series of expeditions and activities, including the all-important encounter between colonial official and colonized villager. This encounter took place in a very real landscape of meaningful communities, communication routes, activities, and stories, all of which can be reconstructed by the archaeologist and historian working together.

REFERENCES

Arbel, B., and G. Veinstein. 1986. "La fiscalité vénéto-chypriote au miroir de la législation ottomane: Le *qānūnnāme* de 1572," *Turcica* 18, pp. 7–51.

Baram, U. 1995. "Notes on the Preliminary Typologies of Production and Chronology for the Clay Tobacco Pipes of Cyprus," *RDAC* 1995, pp. 299–309.

Bintliff, J. L. 1997. "The Archaeological Investigation of Deserted Medieval and Post-Medieval Villages in Greece," in *Rural Settlements in Medieval Europe: Papers of the "Medieval Europe Brugge 1997" Conference* 6, ed. G. De Boe and F. Verhaeghe, Zellik, pp. 21–34.

Census 1881 = Report on the Census of Population, 1881, Cyprus, London 1882.

Clogg, R. 1986. *A Short History of Modern Greece,* 2nd ed., Cambridge.

Cobham, C. D., ed. 1908. Excerpta Cypria: *Materials for a History of Cyprus,* Cambridge.

Cohn, B. S. 1996. *Colonialism and Its Forms of Knowledge: The British in India,* Princeton.

Davies, S. 1994. "Tithe-Collection in the Venetian Peloponnese, 1696–1705," *BSA* 89, pp. 433–455.

de Mas Latrie, M. L. 1855. *Histoire de l'île de Chypre sous le règne des princes de la maison de Lusignan* 3, Paris.

Ellis Burnet, J. 2004. *Forest Bioresource Utilisation in the Eastern Mediterranean since Antiquity: A Case Study of the Makheras,* Oxford.

Forbes, H. 1997. "A 'Waste' of Resources: Aspects of Landscape Exploitation in Lowland Greek Agriculture," in *Aegean Strategies: Studies of Culture and Environment on the European Fringe,* ed. P. N. Kardulias and M. T. Shutes, Lanham, pp. 187–213.

———. 2000. "Security and Settlement in the Medieval and Post-Medieval Peloponnesos, Greece: 'Hard' History versus Oral History," *JMA* 13, pp. 204–224.

Gabrieli, R. S., B. McCall, and J. R. Green. 2001. "Medieval Kitchen Wares from the Theatre Site at Nea Pafos," *RDAC* 2001, pp. 335–356.

Gaudry, A. 1855. *Recherches scientifiques en Orient entreprises par les ordres du gouvernement, pendant les années 1853–1854: Partie agricole,* Paris.

Given, M. 2000. "Agriculture, Settlement, and Landscape in Ottoman Cyprus," *Levant* 32, pp. 209–230.

———. 2002. "Maps, Fields, and Boundary Cairns: Demarcation and Resistance in Colonial Cyprus," *International Journal of Historical Archaeology* 6, pp. 1–22.

———. 2004. *The Archaeology of the Colonized,* London.

Given, M., V. Kassianidou, A. B. Knapp, and J. Noller. 2002. "Troodos Archaeological and Environmental Survey Project, Cyprus: Report on the 2001 Season," *Levant* 34, pp. 25–38.

Given, M., and A. B. Knapp. 2003. *The Sydney Cyprus Survey Project: Social Approaches to Regional Archaeological Survey* (Monumenta archaeologica 21), Los Angeles.

Gosden, C., and C. Knowles. 2001. *Collecting Colonialism: Material Culture and Colonial Change,* Oxford.

Grivaud, G. 1998. *Villages désertes à Chypre (fin XII*[e]*–fin XIX*[e] *siècle)* (Μελέται καὶ Ὑπομνήματα 3), Nikosia.

Jennings, R. 1986. "The Population, Taxation, and Wealth in the Cities and Villages of Cyprus, According to the Detailed Population Survey *(Defter-i Mufassal)* of 1572," *Raiyyet Rusumu Essays Presented to Halil İnalcık* (*Journal of Turkish Studies* 10), pp. 175–189.

Karageorghis, V. 1977. "A 'Favissa' at Kakopetria," *RDAC* 1977, pp. 178–201.

Kiel, M. 1996. "Das türkische Thessalien: Etabliertes Geschichtsbild versus osmanische Quellen. Ein Beitrag zur Entmythologisierung der Geschichte Griechenlands," in *Die Kultur Griechenlands in Mittelalter und Neuzeit. Bericht über das Kolloquium der Südosteuropa-Kommission 28.–31. Oktober 1992* (*AbhGött,* Philologisch-Historische Klasse, 3rd ser., no. 212), ed. R. Lauer and P. Schreiner, Göttingen, pp. 109–196.

———. 1997. "The Rise and Decline of Turkish Boeotia, 15th–19th Century (Remarks on the Settlement Pattern, Demography, and Agricultural Production According to Unpublished Ottoman-Turkish Census and Taxation Records)," in *Recent Developments in the History and Archaeology of Central Greece. Proceedings of the 6th International Boeotian Conference* (*BAR-IS* 666), ed. J. L. Bintliff, Oxford, pp. 315–358.

Klerides, N. 1948. *Συμβολὴ στὴν ἱστορία τῆς Πιτσιλιᾶς: Ἡ μονὴ τοῦ Μεγάλου Ἀγροῦ,* Nikosia.

Leake, W. M. 1835. *Travels in Northern Greece* 4, London.

Papadopoullos, T. 1965. *Social and Historical Data on Population (1570–1881),* Nikosia.

Rizakis, A. D. 1997. "Roman Colonies in the Province of Achaia: Territories, Land, and Population," in *The Early Roman Empire in the East,* ed. S. E. Alcock, Oxford, pp. 15–36.

Shaw, B. D. 1990. "Bandit Highlands and Lowland Peace: The Mountains of Isauria-Cilicia," *JESHO* 33, pp. 199–270.

Sollars, L. 2005. "Settlement and Community: Their Location, Limits, and Movement through the Landscape of Historical Cyprus" (diss. Univ. of Glasgow).

Thirgood, J. V. 1987. *Cyprus: A Chronicle of Its Forests, Land, and People,* Vancouver.

Tsiknopoulos, I. P. 1967. *Ὁ ἅγιος Ἡρακλείδιος: Ἡ ἱερὰ αὐτοῦ μονὴ καὶ ἡ ἀκολουθία,* Nikosia.

PART III: CONTRASTING STRATEGIES OF LAND USE IN OTTOMAN AND VENETIAN GREECE

One of the enormous advantages of conducting historical and archaeological research in Greece and Cyprus is that it offers scholars the opportunity to engage in research that can be cross-cultural and comparative. This is particularly true for the Peloponnese and Crete, where rich administrative archives survive from both Venetian and Ottoman times. The different ways in which chapters in this part of our book exploit the potential for comparison among and between subregions of early modern Greece illustrate the vast, but still largely underutilized, significance of the material remains, maps, and written culture of Venetian and Ottoman occupation for archaeologists, anthropologists, and geographers.

Both powers had a tendency to accept the status quo in regard to matters such as landholding regimes in their new conquests; this fact can account for apparent similarities in administrative practices in the same territories. It is also true that their economic policies varied according to geography, terrain, and period, so that any general conclusions about them may differ according to which region is examined and what chronological time frame is the object of the inquiry.

Allaire Stallsmith, a historian of modern and ancient agriculture as well as of ancient religion, for more than a decade has worked in association with regional studies projects organized by archaeologists in eastern Crete. There, she has been principally engaged in documenting the material remnants of early modern rural settlement and archaeological activities in the landscape of the island. In Chapter 8, she brings various types of evidence to bear in illustrating differences in the ways the Venetians and the Ottomans organized the rural economy of the island. Understanding the effects of imperal policies on landscape is an important aid in interpreting material remains.

Timothy Gregory, in Chapter 9, adds richness to the picture by considering the variable manner in which Ottoman and Venetian administrations were exploiting contemporaneously two very different landscapes: one, an area of the mainland east of Corinth; the other, Kythera (Venetian Cerigo), a small island off the southern coast between the Morea and Crete. Gregory, a historian of the Byzantine Empire and an archaeologist specializing in the study of the material culture of Byzantine and post-Byzantine Greek lands, has organized and participated in archaeological excavations and regional studies in Greece, Turkey, and on Cyprus. Here he draws on the rich sets of data collected in the course of his recent fieldwork.

In Chapter 10, John Bennet takes a very different tack, emphasizing how textual and archaeological information together describe the remarkably similar ways in which Venetian and Ottoman administrators, as well as local Greek farmers, mentally organized the agricultural resources of two territories of Greece in which he himself has conducted archaeological and historical research. The relationship between text and material culture, and the conceptualization of rural landscapes by tax authorities, have been central topics in Bennet's research for two decades, whether it has involved the palatial administrations of Knossos and Pylos in the 2nd millennium B.C., or Venetian and Ottoman colonial administrations in early modern times. His two case studies here, the Peloponnese and Kythera, are in a sense mirror images, in that the former represents an instance in which Ottoman territory was lost to Venice and then regained at a later date, whereas the latter was Venetian territory lost for a brief period to the Ottomans.

One Colony, Two Mother Cities: Cretan Agriculture under Venetian and Ottoman Rule

by Allaire B. Stallsmith

In the late medieval and modern periods, Crete was ruled by two polities that hardly could have been more different in their political and economic organization: the Venetian Republic (1211–1669) and the Ottoman Empire (1669–1898).[1] For 450 years the island was controlled by the Venetian Republic, a maritime commercial empire whose territorial holdings were widely scattered but whose economic system was highly centralized. Under the direction of its merchant oligarchy, the Senate, Venice was able to plan and administer a system of state capitalism in its possessions. This system was intended to benefit the citizens of the mother city before all others.

Venice's crucial support for the Fourth Crusade in 1204 was an indication of the republic's ascendancy to world power. Originally a humble vassal of the Byzantine emperor, eager for the protection of the Byzantine navy and for the honor bestowed on its doge by an imperial title, Venice was now the dominant maritime power of the eastern Mediterranean and able to demand a significant reward for its transport of Crusader troops. In addition to gaining various ports and trading concessions, the city also was offered the opportunity to purchase the still unconquered island of Crete for 5,000 gold ducats.

Earlier, Venice had possessed coastal watering stations and ports around the Adriatic and Mediterranean; now it had its first colony of significant size, 38,000 km^2 of coastal, arable, and mountainous land. By 1211, the Serene Republic controlled Crete, Euboia, Corfu, a number of Aegean islands such as Cerigo, and the vital Peloponnesian ports of Coron and Modon. *L'isola e regno di Candia* (the island and kingdom of Candia) became Venice's prized possession,[2] valued not only as a center of trade and a bastion against Saracens and pirates, but also as a producer of essential commodities such as grain.

The acquisition of Crete required the Venetian Senate to work out a plan for its settlement and agricultural exploitation. The government of the island was tightly controlled; every detail of export, import, taxes, prices, military conscription, and forced labor was micromanaged by Venice's many boards and officials. The system was also flexible, however, as the frequent visits of various officials and their detailed reports enabled the Senate to evaluate the situation and institute new policies.[3]

1. I thank the Department of Classics of the University of Cincinnati and Siriol Davies and Jack Davis, the convenors of the workshop "Between Venice and Istanbul," for inviting me to present the paper on which this chapter is based, and for making my stay in Cincinnati so pleasant. I also thank the workshop participants for helpful discussion.

2. Isepo Civran, *provveditore generale* in 1639, called Crete "the most beautiful crown ever to adorn the head of the most Serene Republic" (Spanakis 1969a, p. 429). The capital city (Iraklion), as well as the island, was called Candia (Turkish Kandiye).

3. On Venetian Crete, see Detorakis 1994; Greene 2000; Maltezou 1990; Margaritis 1978; McKee 2000; and Spanakis 1940, 1950b, 1958a, 1958b, 1969c, 1969d, 1991.

Crete, conquered between 1645 and 1669, was the last significant territorial addition to the Ottoman Empire, whose westward expansion was halted in 1687 by defeat at the Second Battle of Mohács in Hungary.

For Istanbul, the conquest of Crete did not represent, as it had for Venice, a significant increase in territory and a sign of the growth of its power. The acquisition of Crete was almost an afterthought: at one stroke, to deprive Venice of its "crown" and to complete Ottoman control of the eastern Mediterranean. Nor apparently, did the Ottoman conquerors share the Venetian capitalist mentality; their exploitation of Crete's agricultural resources was intended to support the island's Ottoman administrative and military personnel.[4]

It was not feasible for the Sublime Porte to monitor conditions on Crete closely, in the manner of the Venetian Senate. This was the result of changes in Ottoman administrative structure during the 17th century, in which greater authority, especially in financial matters, was delegated to provincial rulers from the imperial center in Istanbul. Decentralization and corruption at all levels meant that the sultan's decrees could easily be evaded. A gift to the right person expedited the export of grain or olive oil from the island; payments to the appropriate janissaries enabled the wine houses of Kandiye (Iraklion) to stay in business.[5]

It is apparent from this brief summary that the origins of the Venetian and Ottoman regimes on the island were very different, as were their administrative purposes. Venice had a master plan for its mercantile colony: The settlement of Venetians on the island would provide military control and estates for landless citizens; taxation from the rich agricultural produce of the island would support the Serene Republic; commodities such as grain and wood, in shorter and shorter supply on terra firma,[6] could be exported by mandate to the mother city; and production of exports, particularly the sweet malmsey wine, would benefit the Venetian state, whose galleys monopolized the trade. Situated between North Africa, the Levant, and Constantinople, Crete served as a center for Venice's lucrative eastern trade as well as a stop on the pilgrimage route to the Holy Land.[7]

The Ottoman state's classical conception of its mission was the enlargement of the *dar al-İslam* (the realm of Islam) at the expense of the infidel realm *(dar al-harb);* hence the conquest of Crete was, in itself, a noble and holy endeavor. Although Istanbul expected the treasury to profit from Cretan agriculture and trade, mercantile concerns were not paramount as they had been for Venice. Unlike the Venetians, the Ottomans never reserved commercial privileges for their own elites, nor did they assert a monopoly for Ottoman bottoms.[8] In the early years the dominant Ottoman concerns were military security and the prevention of Venetian reconquest.[9] The Porte had no interest in micromanaging the economy of the island from afar, but ceded considerable independence to local Cretan authorities.

Different as their motives and methods were, the two imperial powers employed remarkably similar systems to exploit and control the peasant population, called *villani* (villeins) in Venetian documents, and *reaya* (the flock) in Ottoman decrees. Whether the farm was called a *feudum* or a *timar,* the impact of the system on the peasant was much the same. The Venetians may have called the landholders *feudatarii,* but, strictly speaking,

4. On Ottoman Crete, see Detorakis 1994; Triandafyllidou-Baladié 1988; and Greene 1996, 2000.

5. Greene 2000, pp. 89, 124.

6. McNeill 1974, pp. 144–146.

7. Greene 2000, p. 111; Maltezou 1990, pp. 63–67. Venice was the most common embarkation point for Western European pilgrims to the Holy Land; for their testimonia, see Hemmerdinger-Iliadou 1967, 1973.

8. Greene 2000, p. 10.

9. Venice gave up its ambition to reconquer Crete only in 1715; until then, Venetian raids were constant. See Greene 2000, p. 70.

their regime on Crete was not feudal, as the Venetian state did not delegate judicial and financial authority to the feudatories.[10] Likewise, even though the classical Ottoman system in theory regarded all land as the possession of the sultan, who granted its use to his *sipahi*s, these cavalrymen were not feudal lords, nor were their dependents serfs.[11]

Crete's agricultural regime, although ultimately dependent on the ecological limits of the Mediterranean soil and climate, has changed drastically over the millennia. From a pastoral Minoan landscape dotted with sheep and goats,[12] to a sea of grapevines in the Venetian period, to a forest of olive trees in the Ottoman era, the landscape has undergone radical alteration in tune with the political or economic policies of the ruling elite, who exercised powerful, even if sometimes unintended, effects on the people and the landscape.[13]

The Venetians implemented a commercial master plan to benefit the distant mother city, whereas the Ottomans supported a military settlement on the island. Both aimed to control the production of staples through tax and trade policies, and to deny them to hostile states. The focus of this chapter is the changes in the Cretan system of agricultural exploitation and the ways in which the policies of Venice and Istanbul affected the crops and agricultural techniques favored by its cultivators.

SOURCES FOR AN AGRARIAN HISTORY OF VENETIAN AND OTTOMAN CRETE

The archives of Venetian Crete reside today in the State Archives in Venice, under the terms of the Venetian treaty of surrender.[14] These archives contain Venetian senatorial decrees relating to Crete as well as the reports of visiting inspectors. Legal documents in Latin, Greek, and Italian provide examples of property relations, dowry agreements, and wills.[15]

Anecdotal accounts of conditions on the island can also illuminate the workings of the local administration. The observations of travelers, pilgrims, officials, and learned topographers can be useful. Their bias appears when they venture political or religious opinions. They are more reliable regarding the mundane details of life in city or countryside.

The most accessible sources for the Ottoman period are the Turkish archives in Iraklion, which were retained by the government of Crete after independence. These texts, beginning before the fall of Iraklion in 1669, contain information on the Ottoman land tenure system, marriage,

10. McKee 2000, p. 33.

11. In the case of Crete, however, settlement was not carried out in the classical Ottoman manner; see Greene 1996, 2000.

12. Halstead 1981.

13. Rackham and Moody 1996; Rackham, Grove, and Moody 1990; Grove 1990.

14. Detorakis 1994, p. 243; McKee 2000, p. viii.

15. Between 1940 and 1969, Steryios Spanakis edited and translated (into Greek) many 16th- and 17th-century reports to the Venetian Senate in his six-volume *Μνημεία της Κρητικής Ιστορίας* (Spanakis 1940, 1950b, 1958a, 1958b, 1969c, 1969d), and in numerous articles in the journal *Κρητικά Χρονικά* (Spanakis 1949, 1950a, 1955, 1957, 1958c, 1969a, 1969b). Venetian documents in Latin, Greek, and Italian have also been published: see Gasparis 1999; Manousakas 1949, 1961; Mavromatis 1994; McKee 1998; Mertzios 1965; Noiret 1892; Santschi 1976; Stahl 2000; Theotokis 1933, 1936–1937; Thiriet 1978. See McKee 2000, pp. vii–xiii, for a discussion of Venetian sources.

inheritance, taxes, conversion, crime, censuses, sales of land, prices, export permits, and imperial decrees.[16] Archival sources in Ankara and Istanbul are more informative regarding the settlement of Crete; they are, however, unpublished.[17]

Travelers' accounts from the 18th and 19th centuries are especially useful for their precise economic and agricultural observations. These reporters, primarily Western Europeans, had commercial or scientific interests. Their bias tends to be cultural rather than religious, as they generally regard the "slothful Turk" as backward and lazy.[18]

One final source of information is the remains of villages and agricultural settlements, the ruins of the premodern agricultural infrastructure, such as abandoned olive oil mills, cobbled paths, winepress vats, shepherds' huts and pens, vineyards, grain mills, threshing floors, and terraces. Such data, as recovered by archaeological surface survey, are more plentiful for the Ottoman period than for the Venetian period, although information of this sort is spotty for all periods. The decay and reuse of village buildings erase useful remains. Resurgence of dense maquis in fields and hamlets alike obscures the remains of terraces, buildings, and open-air processing sites.

The identification of these remains can be difficult. The simple machines that once crushed and pressed olives can be mistaken for others such as winepresses and dyeing vats. Once the machines are taken apart and their elements reused, the loose millstones or press weights are essentially undatable.[19] Remains of ἀλετρουβειδιά,[20] one-stone olive mills, are found only in villages that have not experienced growth and rebuilding. Large water mills or windmills for grinding grain, built in the later Venetian period, can be found in appropriate spots: in ravines, near water sources, or on hilltops. Smaller hand mills or donkey mills are not as easily identified, however. Despite these caveats, archaeological survey provides datable material evidence that often can be linked to local family and village histories, and can help to reconstruct the patterns of agricultural life in the recent past.[21]

VENETIAN SETTLEMENT AND ADMINISTRATION OF THE ISLAND

After 1211, Venice's efforts to take possession of its prize were disputed by large Cretan landowners, the *archontoromaioi* or *archontopouloi;* according to legend, these archons had been settled in Crete by the Byzantine emperor Alexius Comnenus (1081–1118). Eager to retain their privileged status, these local warlords instigated numerous rebellions during the 13th and 14th centuries.[22]

16. Texts from 1657 to 1765 were published by Nikolaos Stavrinidis (1975, 1976, 1978, 1984, 1985). The original documents, of which Stavrinidis translated only a part, are in Ottoman Turkish dialect and Arabic script, and readable only by specialists.

17. Greene 1996, pp. 68–69, n. 32.

18. An example of "orientalism"? There is a significant difference in tone between earlier Venetian and later French attitudes. Modern nationalism contrasts with the fluid identity shifts possible in the earlier era; see Greene 2000, p. 205.

19. On the reuse of agricultural machinery, see Forbes and Foxhall 1978.

20. In eastern Crete dialect for ἐλαιοτριβείο.

21. For examples of such a reconstruction, see Brumfield 2000; Hayden et al. 2004.

22. Detorakis 1994, pp. 135–136.

The rebellion of 1283, led by Alexios Kalleryis, came to a head in a legendary conference on Easter Sunday 1293 at the monastery of the Panayia Phaneromeni, near Ierapetra. Summoned by the abbot to resolve their differences, the various Greek rebel factions ended up brawling instead. The rebellion ended in failure, but it did result in the Kalleryides being given the status of *nobili veneti;* they were the only Cretan archontic family to achieve such status.[23]

Under the terms of the Charter of 1211, the island was settled by Venetian colonists, who were given land in return for protecting the island from internal as well as external threat.[24] Originally, the land available for distribution was divided into *feuda,* most of which were allotted to noble Venetian *feudatarii,* with small numbers held by the Latin Church, the Cretan archons, and the *Comune,* the government of the island. These *feuda* consisted of estates, houses, mills, and entire villages, along with their peasant cultivators. The income from these lands would theoretically enable the feudatories to furnish men-at-arms for local defense.

Although the hierarchy of the Cretan church was replaced by Latin bishops, Orthodox churches and monasteries retained their lands and peasants, paying a portion of their income to the Catholic bishop as they had before to the Orthodox.[25] All priests, Greek or Latin, were *privilegiati,* exempt from taxes and forced labor.[26]

The Cretan peasants, called *villani* or *contadini,* were bought and sold with their villages and lands, even though such sales were not legally permitted. They were assigned a particular plot on the *feudum* and lived where the feudatory designated. Even though they built their own houses, they still paid rent to the feudatory. The amount of land cultivated by the peasant depended on the number of oxen he owned. If he had no oxen, he cultivated one-fourth of a ζευγάρι; if he had one ox, it was half of a ζευγάρι; if he had a pair of oxen, it was an entire ζευγάρι.[27] Fields were measured in ζευγαρά or βουδέα.[28] Land was also measured in terms of the amount of seed needed to sow it, for example, χωράφη μουζουριῶ τριῶ, a field requiring three μουζούρια (Italian *mesure,* Turkish *muzur*).[29] Orchard and vineyard land was measured by the number of workers required per day.

The peasant gave the feudatory one-third of everything he grew (the *terzaria* or τρίτος),[30] whether cereals, must (unfermented grape juice), oil, or fruit. The peasant also owed the feudatory a fixed number of days of ἀγγαρεία, or forced labor. In addition, the *Comune* could require the peasant to work on fortifications and serve galley duty. Buying himself out of this latter obligation might require him to sell all he owned.[31]

As early as the 13th century there was a class of free peasants (*habitatores* or *choriti franchi*) that had the resources to rent land from the state, a monastery, or a feudatory. These small entrepreneurs could employ *villani* to work their properties, and paid their rent in kind, commonly in grain and must. The free peasants seem to have achieved this status as a result of services rendered to the *Comune* in time of rebellion. Their number was never large, but there may have been more free peasants in the first two centuries of Venetian rule, when insurrections were more frequent. Although they were *privilegiati,* they were still liable to forced labor.[32]

23. Psilakis 1909, pp. 73–88; D. L. Papadakis 1977.

24. McKee 1998, pp. x–xi; 2000, pp. 35–39.

25. Thiriet 1966, p. 211.

26. Yiannopoulos 1978, pp. 49–53; Spanakis 1969b.

27. Yiannopoulos 1978, p. 51. A ζευγάρι was the surface area that could be cultivated by a pair of oxen annually. The Turkish *çift* and the Greek ζευγάρι both can be translated as "yoke of oxen."

28. E. M. Papadakis 1977, p. 14. A βουδέα was 30–35 μουζούρια of land, ca. 146 ha (360 acres); see Triandafyllidou-Baladié 1990, p. 49.

29. E. M. Papadakis 1977, p. 13. A μουζούρι equals 19 kg of wheat or 15 kg of barley; Chourmouzis 1842, p. 34.

30. Yiannopoulos 1978, p. 52.

31. Yiannopoulos 1978, pp. 49–50, 55, 59.

32. Thiriet 1967, pp. 39–41; Yiannopoulos 1978, pp. 63–65.

Another category of peasants were the *gonicari* (from Greek γονικοί, inheritors), who could will or sell their property. *Goniko* land was separate from that of the other *villani* and was usually in better condition. Peasants became *gonicari* as a result of their long residence and payment of rent. The status of *gonicarus* also seems to have been awarded to encourage the cultivation of abandoned land. *Gonicari* were not freehold owners. Like the *villani,* they owed the feudatory one-third of all their crops. They owed forced labor and served in the galleys. Still, they had a kind of security unknown to other *villani,* as they could not be dispossessed or moved to other properties.[33]

Early in the Venetian period, intermarriage between Cretan archontic families and Venetian nobles, as well as irregular unions between Venetians and lower-status Cretans, fostered a Veneto-Cretan culture. That Venetian colonial nobles joined native Cretans in the 1363 revolt of St. Titus indicates how early this cultural synthesis had begun.[34]

By the 16th century, Venice had to assume the defense of the island, as the feudatories were clearly unable to muster a local militia, one of their original duties.[35] Many *feuda* had passed into the hands of Cretans. The feudatories themselves had "gone native"; they spoke Greek, married Greek Orthodox women, attended the Orthodox church, and no longer identified their interests with those of the Venetian Republic.[36] Indeed, Venice no longer trusted its colonists and regarded them as essentially Greek.[37]

Venetian sources report that by the 16th century the situation of the peasant had not improved, but rather had become even more desperate. According to Mocenigo in 1589, "the *villani* are still treated completely as slaves by the feudatories. The feudatories do not think of themselves as owning only the land, but the people as well."[38]

In this period, the feudatories began to engage in trade. Even high officials, although forbidden to engage in commerce, were exporting goods and using their position to avoid taxes.[39] Consequently, officials sent out from Venice to report on the situation in Crete found themselves championing the destitute peasantry against their oppressors, the feudatories.[40]

Meanwhile, the Ottoman threat grew ever more pressing. The last century of Venetian rule, from the fall of Cyprus in 1573, was a period of military preparation, marked by constant examinations of the able-bodied population, of the fortifications and harbors, and of the agricultural resources of the island.[41] Despite all this effort, however, by the mid-17th century even the considerable bureaucratic and military resources of the Venetian state would prove inadequate to repel the sultan's armada.

33. Yiannopoulos 1978, p. 63; E. M. Papadakis 1976, pp. 30–32; 1977, p. 11.
34. McKee 2000, pp. 135, 165.
35. McKee 2000, pp. 37–38; Greene 2000, p. 32.
36. Tafur 1926, pp. 50–51; Spitael 1981, p. 23.
37. Greene 2000, pp. 43–44, 61; Yiannopoulos 1978, p. 41.
38. Yiannopoulos 1978, p. 49.
39. Yiannopoulos 1978, pp. 57–58.
40. Greene 2000, p. 13.
41. Yiannopoulos 1978, pp. 87–100.

AGRICULTURAL PRODUCTION IN VENETIAN CRETE

Since the Bronze Age, grapes, olives, and grain, the "Mediterranean triad," have been the primary crops of Crete.[42] Grain has ever been the essential food of the peasant, so much so that "bread" is synonymous with "food" in ancient and modern Greek.[43] As in most of the Mediterranean, wine has been an important source of calories, and the fat content of olive oil made it a significant source of energy. In the preindustrial period, olive oil was not only a food; it was also the major lubricant, soap, and lamp fuel.[44]

Crete alone among Venice's territories exported wheat.[45] The fertility of the island was famous and the quality of its bread was praised by travelers and merchants.[46] Venice controlled the wheat trade and exacted one-fourth of the wheat harvest from the feudatories as tax. Producers were forbidden to export wheat without the permission of the Venetian Senate and had to sell it to the state at a fixed price.[47] The grain yield, however, was never predictable. In 1414, a bumper crop led the Senate to allow Cretan producers to export grain; only seven years later, the grain supply was so low that grain importation had to be authorized.[48] Frequent senatorial decrees regulating imports and exports fine-tuned the wheat supply of the mother city and the fleet.

The other major Cretan export in the Venetian period was wine. Already in the 14th century, Cretan *malvoisie* (malmsey) was in great demand in northern Europe, where it cost twice as much as other "brands."[49] The great appeal of this wine was that it kept much longer than the dry wines of Italy and France. Crete's central position in the wine trade was assured by the protectionist policy of Venice, which held the monopoly on Cretan malmseys and muscatels from the early 14th century to the last of the annual Flanders galleys in 1535.[50]

Olive trees, so numerous today in the Cretan countryside, were far less visible in the early Venetian period. Indeed, in 1415, the traveling priest Buondelmonti reported that he learned from a local notary why there were so few olives: Cretans are lazy![51] Far from being a result of the laziness of the *villani,* the lack of olive groves was a result of Venetian economic policy, which did not encourage olive oil production. The Venetian olive oil ministry, the Ternaria, enforced stringent policies regarding oil production, prices, and trade throughout the Venetian dominions. Incentives were not offered for the export to Venice of Cretan olive oil, as they were for grain.

Perhaps fearing shortages on Crete, Venice did not permit the feudatories to trade in olive oil, either within or outside the island. The price of Cretan oil was relatively high, in part because of its limited supply. This situation resulted from Venice's policy of managing its subjects' mercantile activities for the benefit of the ruling oligarchy and the mother city, and the policy was frequently contrary to the interests of its Cretan colonists.[52]

Viticulture and the wine trade continued to expand. In 1512, half of Crete's wine production of 100,000 metric tons was exported.[53] The feudatories, influenced by Venetian mercantile policy and responding to demand from abroad, concentrated on wine to the near exclusion of all

42. How early the term "triad" came into use is debated among prehistorians; see Rackham 1990; Blitzer 1993; Sarpaki 1992.

43. Liddell and Scott 1968, s.v. σίτος, gives the translation "food" as well as "bread"; modern Greek uses ψωμί (bread) for "food."

44. Unwin 1991, p. 149; Mattingly 1996, pp. 222–223; Allbaugh 1953, p. 106.

45. Thiriet 1959, pp. 317–318.

46. Tafur 1926, pp. 50–51; Hemmerdinger-Iliadou 1967, p. 557; Dandini 1698, p. 6; Villamont 1627, p. 67; Newett 1907, p. 316; Falkener 1854, p. 266.

47. Yiannopoulos 1978, p. 55; Maltezou 1990, pp. 64–65.

48. Thiriet 1959, p. 414.

49. Thiriet 1959, p. 320. Cretan wine was also imported by the Muslim emirates of Anatolia; see Zachariadou 1983, p. 171.

50. Francis 1973, pp. 31, 39.

51. Spitael 1981, p. 152: *rusticorum inertia.*

52. Gasparis 1996, pp. 156–157.

53. Hemmerdinger-Iliadou 1967, p. 564.

other agricultural products, managing the winemaking process and the profit.[54] By the mid-16th century, despite other Venetian policies designed to ensure the supply of grain for the island population, cereal production in Crete had ceased to meet local demand and grain had to be imported, largely from Anatolia.[55]

The wealth that could be gained in the wine trade was an incentive to peasant and feudatory alike. The lucrative character of the trade in grape must is evident from the fact that a peasant who cultivated grapevines instead of cereals on the land assigned him by the feudatory was still obliged to pay the *terzaria* in wheat, in addition to one-third of his must. That peasants nevertheless did grow grapes shows that it was worth their while; they made a better profit selling must than grain.[56]

Thus, despite Venetian policies intended to ensure cereal cultivation, the peasants and feudatories followed their own economic interests by producing must to sell to winemakers in the cities, rather than wheat to be sold to the state at a controlled price.[57]

The Fourth Veneto-Ottoman War of 1569–1573 resulted in a rise in piracy and a deterioration in trade relations between the Ottomans and Venice. The grain shortage became particularly noticeable after 1575, when the export of cereals from Ottoman lands was forbidden.[58]

Other reasons may be adduced for Crete's 16th-century grain shortage. Cooler conditions and crop failures in temperate Europe and Anatolia beginning in the late 16th century are attributed to the climatic period known as the Little Ice Age, ca. 1500–1700, which was characterized by lower temperatures, the growth of Alpine glaciers, and major anomalies in precipitation.[59]

On Crete, the period of 1548 to 1648 was marked by severe winters, deluges causing massive erosion of soil into valleys, mountain snow cover lasting longer than normal, and early winter droughts that prevented the sowing of cereals. Spring droughts were caused by a burning south wind from the Sahara, which could destroy an entire year's wheat crop in three days.[60]

Reports to the Venetian Senate in 1577 and 1602 noted a decline in cereal production, particularly in view of the fleet's great need for "biscuit" (*biscotti*, παξιμάδι). The solution offered was the uprooting of Cretan vineyards to plant grain.[61]

The Venetian Senate had been issuing decrees intended to promote Cretan grain cultivation since the 15th century.[62] In 1584, landowners in the Candia area were ordered to replace vineyards with cereals.[63] Venetian inspectors throughout the 16th century urged the replacement of vines with wheat—which did not happen.[64]

A number of factors contributed to the new Venetian policy toward Cretan viticulture. The trade in sweet wines declined in the 16th century, due to economic crisis in Western Europe.[65] Already in 1532 the Venetian trading galleys had made their last official visit to England, and Venice lost its monopoly on the sweet wine trade to northern European ports. Cretan wine exports up the Dniester River to Poland came to an end in 1592, when foreign traders were excluded from the Ottoman Black Sea ports.[66]

In the first half of the 17th century, malmsey went out of fashion in England. Sweet wine now came from Spain, where the muscat grape had

54. Triandafyllidou-Baladié 1990, p. 48.

55. Triandafyllidou-Baladié 1988, p. 168.

56. Yiannopoulos 1978, pp. 52, 54.

57. Thiriet 1959, pp. 317–318.

58. Triandafyllidou-Baladié 1988, p. 168.

59. Fagan 2000, p. 100. Braudel (1972, pp. 179–187), writing before the development of the concept of the Little Ice Age, makes frequent reference to the harsh weather conditions of the 16th-century Mediterranean.

60. Grove 1990; Grove and Grove 1992; Grove and Conterio 1995, pp. 233, 239; Rackham and Moody 1996, pp. 81–82.

61. Spanakis 1958b, p. 158.

62. Noiret 1892, entry for March 21, 1465.

63. Triandafyllidou-Baladié 1988, p. 169.

64. Yiannopoulos 1978, pp. 74–75.

65. Triandafyllidou-Baladié 1988, p. 168.

66. İnalcık 1973, p. 132.

been planted.[67] By 1700, the French traveler Tournefort reported that he could find no malmsey in Crete.[68]

The drop in Cretan grain production, which was increasingly evident during the 16th century, was certainly not the result of a strategic plan, but rather the unintended consequence of Venetian trade and tax policies as applied to the agricultural producers of Crete. As badly as Venice needed Cretan grain for consumption and trade, and as much as its war galleys needed biscuit, especially after the escalation of the Ottoman threat, the trade in sweet wine had become central to the Cretan economy. The Venetian Senate, though instrumental in instituting this trade, was not able to reverse the trend, even by ordering the uprooting of vines and the planting of wheat, the price of which was controlled. Having invested in the specialized and labor-intensive viticultural enterprise in order to participate in the lucrative market in sweet wines, the agricultural population understandably resisted the order. The economic interests of the Cretan feudatories thus conflicted with the strategic needs of the Venetian state.[69]

At the end of the 17th century the European market for Cretan wine slackened, while trade routes were threatened or lost.[70] Many skilled vintners departed with the Venetians and many vineyards were destroyed during the lengthy siege of Candia (1647–1669).[71] Despite the Prophet Muhammad's prohibition of alcohol, wine continued to be domestically produced, especially by Orthodox monasteries, which bought up the vineyards abandoned by fleeing Venetian landowners.[72] Both Muslim and Christian merchants were involved in the wine trade, as is evident in documents from the Muslim court of Kandiye.[73]

An additional factor that ensured the demise of the Cretan wine trade was the invention in France of the cork and glass bottle at the end of the 17th century. The sweet wine of Crete had dominated the markets because of its ability to keep for long sea voyages, unlike dry wines, which could turn to vinegar within a year. Once wine could be tightly sealed and fermentation stopped, vintage wine could be produced, and even dry wines could be stored for years.[74]

As we have seen, Venetian policy focused on the export of wine and wheat. Cretan olive oil was strictly regulated and reserved for local consumption, not for export. Olive oil production methods had remained primitive on Crete and had changed little since antiquity. The rotary olive mill, with its single immense vertical millstone, was the most advanced machine available for crushing olives into paste until the 19th century. It was paired with the beam-press, which used the principle of the lever to squeeze the oil out of the paste. Such crude and laborious methods hampered production of a surplus and limited the amount available for export.[75]

Such primitive methods were sufficient in the earlier period, when Venice was not promoting olive oil production and export.[76] By the 17th century, however, large olive plantations and oil production facilities were being developed in Venetian territories such as Corfu.[77] Venice began to promote the Cretan olive oil trade as well, in an effort to stem the economic decline resulting from the failure of the wine trade and the shortfall in grain production.[78] By the time this new policy began to bear fruit, however, Venice had lost possession of its "most beautiful crown."

67. Francis 1973, p. 52.

68. Tournefort 1741, p. 38.

69. Triandafyllidou-Baladié 1988, pp. 168–169.

70. Spanakis 1969a, pp. 422–425.

71. Of major crops, vines are easily the most vulnerable in war (especially compared to olives). They represent an investment of at least eight years' labor, yet uprooting or burning them is quickly done; see Hanson 1998, pp. 68–71.

72. Triandafyllidou-Baladié 1988, pp. 186–187.

73. Stavrinidis 1984, p. 143; Greene 2000, p. 124.

74. Unwin 1991, p. 261; Triandafyllidou-Baladié 1990, p. 49.

75. On the history of olive oil technology in Crete, see Brumfield 2000, pp. 64–69.

76. Processing olive oil "by hand" continued on a small scale even into the 20th century; see Brumfield 2000, p. 69.

77. Sordinas 1971, p. 14; Thiriet 1959, p. 415.

78. Triandafyllidou-Baladié 1988, p. 136.

THE OTTOMAN CONQUEST AND SETTLEMENT OF THE ISLAND

The Ottoman conquest of Crete was completed in 1669, when the fortress of Candia fell to the Ottoman commander, Grand Vizier Köprülüzade Fazıl Ahmet Pasha. Most of the island had already yielded to the Ottoman armies by 1647, and had been subject to a fairly routine Ottoman administration for some years.[79] The Orthodox Cretans expected the Ottoman system to be more tolerant than the rule of Catholic Venice had been, in accordance with the saying, "Better the Turkish turban than the Latin miter."[80]

The loss of Crete marked the end of Venetian dominance of the eastern Mediterranean. Crete, however, would prove to be the last significant territorial addition to the Ottoman Empire. The absorption of this new province was not carried out by the Ottoman administrative system in its classical form, as it had existed in the time of Süleyman I (1520–1566). According to one Ottoman historian, "The incorporation of Crete was peculiar for several reasons. It came a century after the age of Ottoman expansion had come to an end and at a time when the classical institutions of conquest had fallen into disuse."[81]

During the 17th century the structure of the Ottoman government was changing, as was the administration of its vast territorial empire, stretching from Egypt to Hungary. The central government in Istanbul was losing the ability to maintain close surveillance and control over the provinces. This was so for a number of reasons. Changes in the manner of succession to the sultanate after Süleyman the Magnificent, and the consequent rise of the harem, have often been seen as contributing to a decline in the sultan's capability; succession by primogeniture undermined the centralizing power and effectiveness of the Porte.[82] Decentralization of imperial administration, coupled with the rise in power of janissaries and provincial tax-farmers, meant a loss of authority for the military and the imperial administration. This loss of authority is reflected in the slow abandonment of the *timar* (land-grant) system.[83] The institution of the tax-farming system *(malikane)* decentralized economic life throughout the empire.[84]

At this point in our narrative, the "Ottoman decline thesis" raises its ugly head. This theory, no longer accepted by Ottoman historians, posits that the Ottoman Empire began a slow dissolution in the late 16th century, a lengthy senescence that ended only with the First World War and the rise of Atatürk.[85]

We cannot engage here the issue of change versus decline in the Ottoman Empire as a whole. The evidence from Crete, however, clearly indicates that the Ottoman administration of the island was less systematic than the Venetian had been. In the 17th century the Cretan economy became decentralized and more regional; the Ottomans employed "more archaic forms of business organization" than had the Venetians.[86]

The length of the siege of Candia (1647–1669) is as good an indication as any of the decline of the Ottoman military; it was no longer the juggernaut it had been a century earlier.[87] The insanity of Sultan İbrahim IV (1640–1648) and the indecisiveness of Mehmed IV (1648–1687) made Ottoman policy erratic. Only with the rise of Grand Vizier Fazıl Ahmet,

79. The Turkish archives in Iraklion begin documenting the Ottoman administration in Rethymnon in 1657; see Stavrinidis 1975 and Greene 2000, p. 18.

80. Credit for this bon mot is usually given to the Grand Duke Notaras of Constantinople, on the occasion of the last-minute union of the Orthodox and Catholic churches in 1452 (Franzius 1967, p. 421).

81. Greene 2000, pp. 7, 18–19.

82. Goffman 2002, pp. 112, 121.

83. Sugar 1977, p. 208; Goffman 2002, p. 199.

84. On the later Ottoman economy, see İnalcık 1994; Keyder and Tabak 1991; Goffman 2002, pp. 112–121. On the *malikane* in Crete, see Greene 2000, pp. 20–21.

85. Faroqhi et al. 1994, pp. 468–469, 545–575; Greene 2000, p. 20; Goffman 2002, pp. 123–126.

86. Greene 2000, pp. 169, 173.

87. Sugar 1977, p. 197.

beginning in 1661, did Ottoman policy regain coherence. Fazıl Ahmet reenergized the siege of the fortress of Candia and brought about the Venetian capitulation in 1669.[88]

As the successful conqueror of the island, Fazıl Ahmet undertook the organization of the administration of Crete and the repopulation of the deserted capital of Kandiye. The treaty signed by Morosini permitted the evacuation of the entire urban population, military and civilian, along with their movable property. When the conquerors entered the city, they found only two Greek priests and three Jews.[89]

The depopulation of the capital city was only one of the ways in which the settlement of Crete differed from the incorporation of any previously conquered Ottoman province. Another was the nonmilitary nature of the 17th-century Ottoman administrative system. Few *timar*s were distributed on Crete, an indication that the local janissary corps (mostly converts to Islam), not the *sipahi*s, were expected to police and defend the island.[90] Few Ottoman Muslims actually settled on Crete; the majority of janissaries, *bey*s (commanders), and *ağa*s (officials) were in fact converted Cretan peasants, who embraced Islam not only to escape the head tax but also to join the *askeri* (military) class and rise in the Ottoman hierarchy.[91]

Also distinctive to Crete was the massive conversion of the population to Islam, which took place on a scale much greater than in any other conquered Christian province. Crete's high rate of conversion is the reason many of the Muslim landowners mentioned in the Turkish archives in Iraklion were in fact Cretan converts who acquired the properties of those who fled the island.[92] Conversion to Islam by entire villages began in the 1650s, when the Ottoman army controlled the countryside, but before the Venetian surrender of Candia.[93]

The ethnic terminology used by contemporary observers and later historians has served only to confuse the issue. Greek historians and, later, Greek government documents, refer to all Muslims as Τούρκοι, even when they are Albanians or Cretan converts. On the other hand, the official category "Christian" can include Armenians, Venetians, and French as well as Cretan Greeks. This usage has much obscured the reality, which is that the "beastly" janissaries described by popular Greek histories were, in fact, converted Cretans. European travelers noted that the Turks of Crete were rarely of Turkish origin, but were Greek-speaking converts, referred to as "renegades" or "Turcocretans."[94]

The classical Ottoman ideology of conquest characterized non-Muslim lands (*dar al-harb*) as available for conquest and incorporation into the Islamic state (*dar al-İslam*). The *Gazi*s, the warriors of Islam, were rewarded for their fighting skills with spear-won land. In the classical Ottoman system of land ownership, land was either *mîrî,* belonging to the sultan, or *mülk,* privately owned. The *timar* was *mîrî;* it was granted by the sultan to a *sipahi* (cavalryman) in return for military service. The *sipahi* was given the use of the land and the care of the non-Muslim *reaya* (flock), which paid the *cizye* (head tax) in return for protected status. The land grant or *timar* was not hereditary, as it was not private property and never could be. Land could become private only if it was made *vakıf,* property dedicated to the support of a charitable institution, such as a Muslim or Christian shrine.[95]

88. Goffman 2002, pp. 215–222.
89. Greene 2000, pp. 55, 79–82.
90. Greene 2000, pp. 25, 87–88.
91. Goffman 2002, pp. 215–216; Greene 2000, pp. 7, 40–44.
92. Stavrinidis 1975, pp. 11–13.
93. Stavrinidis 1975, pp. 23–24.
94. Tournefort 1741, p. 79; Greene 2000, pp. 38–39.
95. İnalcık 1973, p. 46; Imber 2002, pp. 193–194.

Crete was divided into four *sancak*s (provinces), each ruled by a pasha (military governor).[96] Legally, the settlement of Crete differed drastically from those of earlier conquests, especially in the definition of property. One reason for this was a legal reform movement in late-17th-century Istanbul to restore the importance of *shari*ʿ*a* (Holy Law) at the expense of Ottoman custom; another was the practical necessity of keeping the land cultivated and preventing the peasantry from fleeing.[97]

The *kanunname* (legal code) promulgated for Crete after the final surrender in 1669 declared the land to be *haraçı* (tribute); it was to remain in the possession of its Christian owners as long as they acknowledged Ottoman authority and paid the *haraç* (land tax). Venetians who resisted the Ottomans or fled the island forfeited their land, which was then sold at auction to Ottoman military officials, tax collectors, peasants, and newly enrolled janissaries.[98]

An imperial *fermân* (edict) from 1671 *(kanunname i-cedid)* documents the unique nature of the Ottoman settlement of Crete:

> It is necessary to impose on the inhabitants of this conquered island who agree to the tribute, the land tax on taxable land and the head tax on its inhabitants.
>
> The taxable land is the complete freehold of its owners. They are allowed to sell it and buy it and dispose of it as they wish. After death their land may be inherited just like all other property, among their heirs, on the basis of inheritance law as provided by Holy Law *(shari*ʿ*a)*.[99]

The anomalous nature of landholding in Ottoman Crete has been noted.[100] This document makes it clear, however, that fields, houses, and all immovable properties, instead of being *mîrî,* property of the sultan, were *mülk,* freehold property that could be bought, sold, and inherited;[101] this was similar to the Venetian category of *goniko,* inheritable property. Ottoman policy goals were to keep land under cultivation and to ensure the loyalty of the peasantry by making abandoned Venetian agricultural land available to them.[102] Cretan monasteries, as *vakıf* institutions, retained their lands and villages; their peasants were exempt from certain taxes and from forced labor.[103]

Those landowners who had initially fled the Ottoman invasion could regain their lands by submission to Ottoman rule and payment of the head tax, as the Miliotis brothers did in 1658.[104] In one instance Christian villagers who had resisted the Ottoman army forfeited their property to an *ağa* (official), who rented out the collection of the village taxes to the Orthodox Metropolitan of Crete.[105] In cases where Christian villagers converted to Islam in order to avoid certain agricultural taxes, they were instructed that new Muslims and Christians were to pay the land tax at the same rates, based on the extent of their property.[106] Muslims, of course, did not pay the *cizye.*

Tax assessment and collection were of great importance to the Ottoman rulers of Crete. On the one hand, income was needed for the support of the military establishment; on the other, rapacious tax collection might

96. Stavrinidis 1976, pp. 134–135.

97. Greene 1996, pp. 60–63.

98. Greene 2000, p. 85.

99. Stavrinidis 1975, pp. 307–311; cf. Barkan 1943; Greene 1996.

100. Veinstein 1991; Veinstein and Triandafyllidou-Baladié 1980; Barkan 1983, p. 22; Greene (1996, 2000) discusses the implications of this new policy.

101. Veinstein 1991, pp. 40–41.

102. Greene 1996, pp. 74–77.

103. Detorakis 1994, p. 388.

104. Stavrinidis 1975, pp. 52–54; Greene 2000, pp. 29, 194–197.

105. Stavrinidis 1975, p. 12.

106. Stavrinidis 1975, pp. 21–22, 123–124. This equalization of tax rates originated in the 16th-century legal reforms of Ebuʾs Suʿud; see Greene 2000, p. 24, n. 43. On the question of whether converts must pay the *çift* (land) tax, see Greene 2000, p. 100, n. 40.

drive the *reaya* into the hills, leaving land uncultivated.[107] In the Turkish archives in Iraklion, legal authorities frequently address the question of equitable taxation according to *shariʿa.*[108]

The difficulties that faced the new rulers in the early years are apparent from an Ottoman archival document that explains a tax shortfall in 1691, the result of a poor harvest as well as attacks by "our warlike enemies from Spinalonga [the Venetians], the attacks made by pirate frigates, and the actions of Cretan outlaws and thieves."[109]

Travelers to Crete report a severe drop in the Christian population after 1669, which is ascribed to the length of the siege and the departure of the Veneto-Cretans.[110] Travelers' reports may not be reliable, but Ottoman census figures and agricultural yield figures do show that population dropped in certain parts of the island. In 1671 there were 26,674 Christian heads of household liable for the payment of the head tax or *cizye.* This number declined to 18,246 in 1693.[111]

The last Venetian census, in 1644, recorded a Cretan population of 257,066.[112] In 1671, according to the first Ottoman census, the total Christian population was 133,370; by 1693 it had dropped to 91,230.[113] Is this drop in Christian population the result of war and the departure of the Venetians, or is it the effect of Christian conversion to Islam? One traveler estimated that, within a few years of the conquest, 60% of the Cretan population had converted to Islam.[114] Another gave the population in 1679 as 80,000: 50,000 Christians and 30,000 Muslims.[115] Reliable statistics for Christians and Muslims become available only in the 19th century.

Classical Ottoman administration had been known as relatively efficient and equitable, but during the 17th century this began to change. Taxes previously collected in kind were collected in cash; temporary taxes became permanent. After 1720 the right to collect taxes in a certain area could be purchased for life, and could even be hereditary.[116] The *malikane* system came to replace the *timar* system as a way for the imperial government to collect land taxes, particularly on Crete.[117]

Yet, well into the 18th century, the documents held in the Turkish archives in Iraklion continued to employ the traditional terminology, describing landowners as *sipahi*s or *timar*-holders, which masks the reality that the *timar* system was no longer significant for imperial defense or finance.[118] Tax-farmers (in Crete mostly janissaries), not *sipahi*s, were the agents of the imperial fisc.[119]

Another new development in Ottoman agricultural organization in the 17th century was the *çiftlik* system. The *çiftlik* developed out of the basic farming unit of the *çift,* the amount of land needed to sustain one peasant family and a yoke of oxen, roughly 56–140 *stremmata,* ca. 5.7–14 ha (14–35 acres); on it taxes were calculated.[120]

*Çiftlik*s were large estates, often fraudulently converted into private property, that were typically worked by tenant farmers, who received one-half of the crop. The *çiftlik* system encouraged the commercialization of agriculture and the cultivation of specialized crops for export.[121] On Crete the favored export turned out to be olive oil, despite an imperial prohibition on the export of agricultural goods and strategic minerals.[122]

107. Peasant flight was a problem in the 17th-century Ottoman Empire; see Faroqhi et al. 1994, pp. 433–452.

108. Stavrinidis 1975, pp. 21, 23, 47.

109. Stavrinidis 1978, pp. 107–109; Triandafyllidou-Baladié 1988, p. 47.

110. Randolph 1687, pp. 93–94; Detorakis 1994, p. 71; and see the reference to Pouqueville in Raulin 1869, p. 48.

111. Greene 2000, pp. 52–54, 69, n. 92. Such surveys list only male Christian heads of household; Muslims are not counted.

112. Spitael 1981, p. 34.

113. Using a multiplier of five per male head of household as an estimate of family size.

114. Raulin (1869, p. 48) credits Pouqueville for this information.

115. Randolph 1687, p. 93.

116. Detorakis 1994, p. 253; Greene 2000, pp. 20–21.

117. Faroqhi et al. 1994, pp. 531–547; Greene 2000, pp. 19–21.

118. Stavrinidis 1975, 1976, 1978, 1984, 1985.

119. Greene 2000, pp. 33–36.

120. Sugar 1977, p. 98; İnalcık 1994, p. xlvi.

121. On the *çiftlik,* see Faroqhi et al. 1994, pp. 447–452; İnalcık 1991; Veinstein 1991.

122. Sugar 1977, pp. 213–218.

THE OTTOMAN AGRICULTURAL EXPLOITATION OF CRETE

Major changes in the agriculture of the island accompanied the Ottoman conquest of Crete, in part because of changing international markets and in part because of the unintended consequences of government policies. Generally, the Porte did not micromanage Crete's economy to the extent that Venice had tried to. Ottoman agricultural planning focused on keeping taxable land in cultivation and ensuring a supply of staples for the military administration and the city population.

The Ottomans did actually manage to increase Crete's grain production, so that at the end of the 17th century there was a surplus for the first time in decades. This increase in grain production was accompanied by an expansion of olive cultivation and a decline in vineyards. Venetian rule was the era of the wine trade; the cash crop and export of Ottoman times was olive oil.[123]

As viticulture declined, the cultivation of the olive greatly increased, for a number of reasons. Venetian efforts to de-emphasize viticulture did not actually come to fruition on Crete until after 1669, although other areas under Venetian control began to develop olive plantations and large, factory-style pressing operations.[124] In the 16th and 17th centuries Venice was losing its monopoly on eastern Mediterranean trade.[125] French merchants began to play a greater role on Crete, and the commodity that interested them most was olive oil for the soap factories of Marseilles.

Driving the increased European demand for olive oil was the repeated failure of the French olive harvest in the 17th century, perhaps a result of climatic change. The period after 1690 saw some of the harshest decades of the Little Ice Age in northwestern Europe. Weather manifested in wildly erratic shifts from drought to deluge, from freezing cold to parched harvests.[126]

What would have been the effect on Crete? Such a climatic pattern could have negatively affected grain cultivation. Yet olive orchards, we may speculate, would have benefited from increased rainfall and would not have been destroyed by even the most determined deluge. The burning south wind might have destroyed the grain, but in early spring the olive trees would not have been sufficiently in fruit to suffer damage.[127] Could this unevenly destructive weather pattern be a partial reason for the increase in olive cultivation?

After the departure of the Venetians, French merchants were able to negotiate more favorable trade terms with the Ottoman rulers, and as a result became the main carriers of Cretan olive oil to Western Europe in the 18th century. Unlike the Venetians, the Ottomans did not reserve long-distance trade privileges for their own nationals, but granted trading rights to other nations, especially the French and the Venetians.[128] The traditional view of Crete's trade as dominated by the French is contested by Greene, who points out the size and longevity of the Muslim merchant population of Kandiye.[129] The economy of the eastern Mediterranean between 1645 and 1720 was diverse, rather than being based on only one export crop, wine. The excellent record-keeping systems of Venice and

123. Triandafyllidou-Baladié 1988, pp. 133–136.

124. Sordinas 1971, p. 14.

125. Greene 2000, pp. 142–147.

126. Fagan 2000; see above, p. 158.

127. Grove 1990; Grove and Grove 1992; Grove and Conterio 1995, pp. 233, 239.

128. Triandafyllidou-Baladié 1988, pp. 14–15, 137.

129. Greene 2000, pp. 155–158.

Marseilles tend to make Ottoman Crete's economic activity, by contrast, relatively invisible. Crete's regional trading network was geared to accommodate local consumption.[130] After 1720, olive oil became the primary export of Crete, carried by French, Russian, Greek, Ottoman, Jewish, and Venetian merchants.[131]

Demographic change that favored olive cultivation over grapes was another reason for the increase in Crete's olive production after the Ottoman conquest. The Ottomans who took over Venetian estates tended to live in the cities, leaving dependent laborers to till their *çiftlik*s.[132] The long siege of Candia had caused great destruction; vineyards (unlike olive groves) are easily destroyed, and quickly die when untended. Olive trees, to the contrary, do not require the constant and specialized care that vines need, but can be tended seasonally by unskilled women and children.[133] Also, olive trees can easily share the same field with wheat or barley. Polycropping in vineyards is less benign, especially if vintage wine grapes are the desired product.[134]

Venetian viticulture produced fine-quality wines for export, using 16th-century "state of the art" methods. Ottoman oil production aimed only at producing oil in quantity, with little regard for its quality, since most of it was destined not for eating but for the soap factories of Marseilles and Kandiye. For all these reasons, Crete converted from an intensive form of cultivation, viticulture, to a more extensive system of oleoculture.[135]

Ottoman methods for directing agricultural production and assessing taxes were similar to those of their Venetian predecessors. Just as Venetian feudatories had controlled the building of wine vats so that they could exact the *terzaria,* Ottoman landowners in each community owned the olive mills.[136]

The military authorities in Kandiye scrutinized the movement of goods to ensure that no support was being given to the enemies of Islam. Exporters of oil from Crete, whether Muslim or European, had to give guarantees that they were not trafficking in enemy-controlled areas.[137] As early as 1659, and on many subsequent occasions, the Porte forbade the export of olive oil from Crete. This enabled local governors to extract payments from merchants for allowing its export.[138]

French merchants were the primary purchasers of Cretan olive oil, accounting for at least one-third of exports. When the Provençal crop failed in 1669, the French bought two-thirds of the Cretan olive oil crop.[139] During the course of the 18th century Cretan olive oil production tripled. This was perhaps due to a population increase in that century, but also to a rise in demand and hence in price.[140] Beginning in 1723, Cretan soap makers became major purchasers of olive oil; by the end of the century, soap was second on the list of Cretan exports, after olive oil.[141]

Olive oil became Crete's most important export after the mid-18th century, even though, as the French commercial attaché at Chania commented, "the oil of Crete is nauseating and almost uneatable. . . . It is only good for making soap."[142] Picking and pressing the olives in a timely manner to minimize rancidity and separating the first pressing from the coarser product required skilled labor and capital investment on a scale unavailable on Crete in this period.

130. Greene 2000, pp. 9, 132.
131. Stavrinidis 1976, p. 275; 1978, pp. 143–146, 316, 331–332, 429, 430, 433–444.
132. For a detailed description of a mid-19th-century Cretan *çiftlik,* see Hitier 1881, pp. 589–591.
133. Hitier 1881, pp. 589–610; Triandafyllidou-Baladié 1988, p. 186.
134. Fieldwork with Loeta Tyree has contributed greatly to my understanding of Cretan viticulture and oleoculture.
135. Triandafyllidou-Baladié 1988, pp. 133–136.
136. Stavrinidis 1975, pp. 13–14.
137. Stavrinidis 1978, pp. 143–144.
138. Stavrinidis 1975, p. 103; 1978, pp. 146, 429–430.
139. Tournefort 1741, p. 23.
140. Triandafyllidou-Baladié 1988, pp. 137–144.
141. Olivier 1801, p. 365.
142. Hitier 1881, p. 602.

The Ottoman policy forbidding the export of grain was the reverse of the Venetian one, since the Porte's main concern was an adequate grain supply for the island's administration in the cities of Crete. As early as 1671, an imperial *fermân* directed the storage of grain sufficient to supply the city population of "peaceful *reaya*" and the Ottoman troops stationed in the fortress of Kandiye.[143] For these and other reasons, toward the end of the 17th century the grain supply of Crete seems to have improved, despite fluctuating harvests.[144]

The erratic nature of the grain supply meant that the situation had to be monitored constantly. A bad harvest could mean famine, a crisis to which the local authorities might respond by importing grain. Why did grain production and supply, as reflected in available statistics and changing government policies, vary so widely? Even though the productive capacity of the arable land is not a static quantity, the question must be asked: How could the famine of 1693, which caused deaths from hunger in the city of Chania, have been followed so quickly, in 1699, by massive surpluses making possible the export of 500 metric tons of wheat?[145] In part these fluctuations in the grain yield may have been the result of the erratic weather characteristic of the Little Ice Age, mentioned earlier.[146]

The authorities attempted to ensure a regular supply of grain for administrative and military units stationed in the cities, and for the city population of useful Christians and converted Muslims. This was a reasonable goal, given the fertility of Crete. That they had such great difficulty doing so is the result of two often underestimated factors that apply particularly to Crete: the natural irregularities of agricultural yield, and the scarcity, before the 20th century, of adequate overland transportation for agricultural goods.[147]

As population rose in the 18th century, grain shortages became more common, and grain had to be imported into Crete. Undoubtedly the great growth in olive orchards also accounts for an underproduction of wheat. Like the Venetians before them, the Ottomans controlled the price and distribution of bread and grain, but this only encouraged hoarding among the peasants and made grain production less attractive to the agricultural entrepreneur.[148]

Travelers to Crete in the 18th century noted that the island was no longer self-sufficient in grain, as it had been in the earlier, now idealized Venetian period. Grain was now imported; under the Venetians, it had been exported. Under Ottoman rule, large areas of land went uncultivated. These conditions were ascribed to the laziness and poor management of the Ottomans; to their confiscatory tax system, which discouraged enterprise among Christians; and to a supposed Ottoman lack of interest in commerce. These charges especially came from the French, who were competing for the olive oil trade and felt they could manage the entire business much better than the Ottomans did.[149]

This negative picture requires comment. The criticisms of Ottoman Cretan agricultural technology are just; improvements coming into use in the West by the 18th century, such as the four-field crop rotation system, advances in animal breeding and manuring, metal plows, screw presses, and

143. Stavrinidis 1975, pp. 319–320.

144. Triandafyllidou-Baladié 1988, p. 171.

145. Triandafyllidou-Baladié 1988, pp. 169–170.

146. Fagan 2000; Grove and Conterio 1995, pp. 233, 239.

147. These two factors had even greater impact in antiquity; see Garnsey 1988, pp. 3–16.

148. As far as can be determined, the peasantry lived on barley; the authorities were concerned with wheat bread for the urban population.

149. Savary 1781, pp. 415–417; Olivier 1801, pp. 365–366; Sonnini 1801, p. 405.

other machines did not spread to Crete until much later, undoubtedly as a result of the lack of capital and entrepreneurial spirit. The Venetian system of taxation certainly did not fall more lightly on the rural population than did the Ottoman, however, nor was Venetian direction of the agricultural system any more designed to benefit the peasantry.

Throughout both periods, tax-collection methods and amounts varied constantly. If the general observations of historians and vistors can be trusted, it appears that the landowners became more rapacious toward the end of each period of rule over the island, as each imperial power felt itself in a military pinch with regard to the rest of its domains and its relations with other states. In the 16th and 17th centuries, Venice felt Ottoman military pressure most severely, and this is also the time when we have the clearest evidence from Venetian officials that the peasantry was in a desperate state. In the 18th and 19th centuries, the Ottoman Empire experienced nationalist rebellions in the Balkans as on Crete, and this was also when taxes were being multiplied to support the military.

A MODERN EXAMPLE

A recent example of how political and economic factors influence land use comes from a small group of fields located in a village in eastern Crete, where a history of land use has been obtained.[150] Terraces on these upper slopes, built in the Late Ottoman period, if not earlier, were sown with grain before the Second World War. After the war, grapevines were planted. By the late 20th century, these terraces were all planted with olive trees, the oil from which is exported to Europe and America.

Why did these changes occur? Before the war, the top priority for the population (at its peak in 1940) was sufficient grain. The immediate postwar era saw a boom in raisins produced from Sultanina grapes, exported to Athens and to northern Europe, where they were a popular condiment. Raisin production is labor-intensive, however, and as the rural population emigrated to the cities in the 1960s and 1970s, and as the raisin market's "bubble" burst, orchards of μουρέλα (olive slips), less demanding in terms of labor, took the place of the vineyards.[151]

The preceding shows a population making its own decisions about what crops to cultivate, unlike the downtrodden *villani* of the 13th century, who operated under the direction of the feudatories. Nevertheless, the policies of the central authority, and market forces, whether directed by that authority or uncontrolled, obviously play the most important role in what crops are emphasized.

150. Hayden et al. 2004, pp. 312–318.

151. Today, for the first time in history, self-sufficiency in grain production is not the primary concern of the Cretan peasant. The "green revolution," and rapid development in markets and transportation, mean that peasants can export the exotic fruits of Cretan hothouses, and import grain, while receiving a cash subsidy from the European Union for every liter of olive oil they produce.

CONCLUSION

The Venetian and Ottoman landholding systems were similar, but the management techniques used to control the economy were vastly different. Venetian mercantilism involved centralized planning and a conscious attempt to counteract the greed and corruption of the individual economic actor. Ottoman economic administration seems to have been simpler and more laissez-faire. Both empires needed the agricultural riches of the island to support a military force. The Venetian emphasis was on the mother city and its trade; the Ottomans emphasized the support of the "warriors of Islam."

The cultivated crops changed between the two periods for a number of reasons. International trade movements were influential, but a loss of population, especially of skilled farmers and vintners, meant that an intensive farming system had to be replaced by an extensive one.

The Quran's prohibition against wine for the believer does not seem to have been an important factor in the demise of the Cretan malmsey trade. Rather, a number of unrelated events—the invention of the cork and bottle, the transplantation of the muscat grape to Spain, the wartime destruction of the Cretan vineyards, and the loss of a skilled agricultural population—all contributed to the switch from grapes to olives and the concomitant increase in grain production.

Venice and Istanbul each in turn, for their particular purposes, attempted to manage the Cretan grain supply. Poor land transportation, administrative inefficiency, and corruption impeded their efforts as much as crop failure. Both powers attempted to ensure the wheat supply by controlling its price and distribution; these actions appear often to have brought about shortages instead.

The systems of taxation employed by the two imperial powers were similar. Both exacted taxes in kind, from the produce of the land *(haraç),* although the Ottoman head tax *(cizye)* was paid in coin. The amounts of the tax burdens of each may differ, but it is difficult to ascertain which was heavier. If anything, one could argue that the Cretan peasant paid lower taxes under the Ottoman system. The Venetians required one-third of the crop, whereas the Ottoman landlord required only one-fifth. Under the Ottoman system, however, there was also the head tax. Under both systems we have anecdotal evidence of abuses: the Venetian feudatory exacting more than his share, the Ottoman *ağa* expropriating the property of the *reaya.*

The conclusions to be drawn from this brief survey of Cretan agricultural history under Venetian and Ottoman dominion were anticipated in the first paragraphs of this chapter. The potential of the Cretan landscape—the crops that can be grown there and the carrying capacity of its arable land, although restricted to some extent by the ecological parameters imposed by the landscape and climate—is not determined only by these physical factors. Equally important are the policy goals of the elite managers of the economy, whether resident on the island or directing matters from a distant capital. Whether the effects of their policies are planned or are an unintended side effect, it is the tax policies, import-export controls, and military-political goals of these elites that determine what crops are grown and in what proportions.

REFERENCES

Allbaugh, L. G. 1953. *Crete: A Case Study of an Underdeveloped Area,* Princeton.

Barkan, Ö. L. 1943. *Asırlarda Osmanlı İmparatorluğunda Zirai Ekonominin Hukuki ve mali Esasları,* Istanbul.

———. 1983. "Caractère réligieux et caractère séculier des institutions ottomanes," in *Contributions à l'histoire économique et sociale de l'empire ottoman,* ed. J.-L. Bacque-Grammont and P. Dumont, Louvain, pp. 11–58.

Blitzer, H. 1993. "Olive Cultivation and Oil Production in Minoan Crete," in *La production du vin et de l'huile en Méditerranée* (*BCH* Suppl. 26), ed. M.-C. Amouretti and J.-P. Brun, Paris, pp. 163–176.

Braudel, F. 1972. *The Mediterranean and the Mediterranean World in the Age of Philip II,* trans. S. Reynolds, New York.

Brumfield, A. 2000. "Agriculture and Rural Settlement in Ottoman Crete, 1669–1898: A Modern Site Survey," in *A Historical Archaeology of the Ottoman Empire: Breaking New Ground,* ed. U. Baram and L. Carroll, New York, pp. 37–78.

Chourmouzis, M. 1842. *Κρητικά: Συνταχθέντα καὶ ἐκδοθέντα,* Athens.

Dandini, J. 1698. *A Voyage to Mt. Libanus, wherein Is an Account of the Customs, Manners, etc. of the Turks: Also a Description of Candia, Nicosia, Tripoli, Alexandretta, etc. Written Originally in Italian by the Rev. Fr. Jerome Dandini,* London.

Detorakis, T. 1994. *History of Crete,* trans. J. C. Davis, Iraklion.

Fagan, B. 2000. *The Little Ice Age: How Climate Made History, 1300–1850,* New York.

Falkener, E. 1854. *Description of Some Important Theatres and Other Remains in Crete; from a Ms. History of Candia by Onorio Belli in 1586,* London.

Faroqhi, S., B. McGowan, D. Quataert, and Ş. Pamuk, 1994. *An Economic and Social History of the Ottoman Empire* 2: *1600–1914,* New York.

Forbes, H. A., and L. Foxhall 1978. "The Queen of All Trees," *Expedition* 21, pp. 37–47.

Francis, A. D. 1973. *The Wine Trade,* London.

Franzius, E. 1967. *History of the Byzantine Empire,* New York.

Garnsey, P. 1988. *Famine and Food Supply in the Greco-Roman World,* Cambridge.

Gasparis, C. 1996. "Η ελιά και το λάδι: Παραγωγή και εμπόριο στη μεσαιωνική Κρήτη, 13ος–14ος αιώνας," in *Ελιά και λάδι,* ed. S. Papadopoulos, Athens, pp. 151–158.

———. 1999. *Franciscus de Cruce: Notarios ston Chandaka = notaio in Candia: 1338–1339,* Venice.

Goffman, D. 2002. *The Ottoman Empire and Early Modern Europe,* Cambridge.

Greene, M. 1996. "An Islamic Experiment? Ottoman Land Policy on Crete," *Mediterranean Historical Review* 2, pp. 60–78.

———. 2000. *A Shared World: Christians and Muslims in the Early Modern Mediterranean,* Princeton.

Grove, J. M. 1990. "Climatic Reconstruction in the Eastern Mediterranean with Particular Reference to Crete," in Rackham, Grove, and Moody 1990, pp. 16–20.

Grove J. M., and A. Conterio. 1995. "The Climate of Crete in the Sixteenth and Seventeenth Centuries," *Climatic Change* 30, pp. 223–247.

Grove, J. M., and A. T. Grove. 1992. "Little Ice Age Climates in the Eastern Mediterranean," in *European Climate Reconstructed from Documentary Data: Methods and Results,* ed. B. Frenzel, C. Pfister, and B. Gläser, Stuttgart, pp. 45–50.

Halstead, P. 1981. "Counting Sheep in Neolithic and Bronze Age Crete," in *Patterns of the Past,* ed. I. Hodder, G. Isaac, and N. Hammond, Cambridge, pp. 307–329.

Hanson, V. D. 1998. *Warfare and Agriculture in Classical Greece,* Berkeley.

Hayden, B. J., H. Dierckz, G. W. M. Harrison, J. Moody, G. Postma, O. Rackham, and A. B. Stallsmith. 2004. *Reports on the Vrokastro Area, Eastern Crete* 2: *The Settlement History of the Vrokastro Area and Related Studies,* Philadelphia.

Hemmerdinger-Iliadou, D. 1967. "La Crète sous la domination vénitienne et lors de la conquête turque, 1322–1684: Renseignements nouveaux ou peu connus d'après les pèlerins et les voyageurs," *Studi Veneziani* 9, pp. 535–623.
———. 1973. "La Crète sous la domination vénitienne et lors de la conquête turque, 1322–1684: Renseignements nouveaux ou peu connus d'après les pèlerins et les voyageurs," *Studi Veneziani* 15, pp. 451–584.
Hitier, M. 1881. "Appendice sur l'état de l'agriculture et le production de l'île de Crète," in *Les îles de la Grèce,* ed. L. Lacroix, Paris, pp. 588–612.
Imber, C. 2002. *The Ottoman Empire, 1300–1650,* New York.
İnalcık, H. 1973. *The Ottoman Empire: The Classical Age, 1300–1600,* London.
———. 1991. "The Emergence of Big Farms, *Çiftliks:* State, Landlords, and Tenants," in Keyder and Tabak 1991, pp. 17–34.
———. 1994. *An Economic and Social History of the Ottoman Empire* 1: *1300–1600,* New York.
Keyder, Ç., and F. Tabak, eds. 1991. *Landholding and Commercial Agriculture in the Middle East,* Albany.
Liddell, H. G., and R. Scott, eds. 1968. *A Greek-English Lexicon,* Oxford.
Maltezou, C. A. 1990. *Η Κρήτη στη διάρκεια της περιόδου της Βενετοκρατίας (1211–1669),* Iraklion.
Manousakas, M. I. 1949. "Ἡ παρὰ Τρίβαν ἀπογραφὴ τῆς Κρήτης (1644) καὶ ὁ δῆθεν κατάλογος τῶν κρητικῶν οἴκων Κερκύρας," *CretCron* 3, pp. 35–59.
———. 1961. "Βενετικὰ ἔγγραφα ἀναφερόμενα εἰς τὴν ἐκκλησιαστικὴν ἱστορίαν τῆς Κρήτης τοῦ 14ου –16ου αἰῶνος: Πρωτοπαπάδες καὶ Πρωτοψάλται Χάνδακος," *Δελτίον Ιστορικής και Εθνολογικής Εταιρείας της Ελλάδος* 15, pp. 144–233.
Margaritis, S. 1978. *Crete and Ionian Islands under the Venetians,* Athens.
Mattingly, D. J. 1996. "The Olive in the Roman World," in *Human Landscapes in Classical Antiquity: Environment and Culture* (Leicester-Nottingham Studies in Ancient Society 6), ed. G. Shipley and J. Salmon, London, pp. 213–253.
Mavromatis, Y. K. 1994. *Ιωάννης Ολόκαλος, νοτάριος Ιεράπετρας: κατάστιχο (1496–1543),* Venice.
McKee, S., ed. 1998. *Wills from Late Medieval Venetian Crete, 1312–1420,* 3 vols., Washington, D.C.
———. 2000. *Uncommon Dominion: Venetian Crete and the Myth of Ethnic Purity,* Philadelphia.
McNeill, W. H. 1974. *Venice: The Hinge of Europe, 1081–1797,* Chicago.
Mertzios, K. D. 1965. "Κρητικὰ συμβόλαια τῶν χρόνων τῆς Ἑνετοκρατίας," *CretCron* 19, pp. 111–145.
Newett, M. M., trans. 1907. *Canon Pietro Casola's Pilgrimage to Jerusalem in the Year 1494,* Manchester.
Noiret, H. 1892. *Documents inédits pour servir à l'histoire de la domination vénitienne en Crète de 1380 à 1485, tirés des archives de Venise,* Paris.
Olivier, G. A. 1801. *Voyage dans l'Empire Othoman, l'Egypte et le Perse* 2, Paris.
Papadakis, D. L. 1977. "Ἡ συνέλευσις στὴ μονὴ Φανερομένης Ἱεράπετρας," *Αγία Φωτεινή η Ισαπόστολος* 7, pp. 66–69, 85–89.
Papadakis, E. M. 1976. "Μορφαὶ τοῦ λαϊκοῦ πολιτισμοῦ τῆς Κρήτης τοῦ 15ος καὶ 16ος αἰῶνος κατὰ τὰς γραμματειακὰς πηγὰς" (diss. Univ. of Athens).
———. 1977. "Συμβολὴ στὴ μελέτη τῆς γεωργίας καὶ τῆς ἀμπελουργίας τῆς Κρήτης στὸν 15ος καὶ 16ος αἰῶνας," *Kretologia* 4, pp. 5–25.
Pouqueville, F. C. H. L. 1826–1827. *Voyage dans la Grèce: Deuxième édition revue, corrigée et augmentée,* 6 vols., Paris.
Psilakis, B. 1909. *Ἱστορία τῆς Κρήτης* 2, Chania.
Rackham, O. 1990. "Vegetation History of Crete," in Rackham, Grove, and Moody 1990, pp. 29–39.
Rackham, O., A. T. Grove, and J. A. Moody, eds. 1990. *Petromaroula* I: *Stability and Change in the Cretan Landscape,* Cambridge.
Rackham, O., and J. A. Moody. 1996. *The Making of the Cretan Landscape,* Manchester.

Randolph, B. 1687. *The Present State of the Islands in the Archipelago, Sea of Constantinople, and Gulph of Smyrna, with the Islands of Candia, and Rhodes,* Oxford.

Raulin, V. 1869. *Description physique de l'île de Crète,* 2 vols., Paris.

Santschi, E., ed. 1976. *Régestes des arrêts civils et des mémoriaux (1363–1399) des archives du Duc de Crète,* Venice.

Sarpaki, A. 1992. "The Paleoethnobotanical Approach: The Mediterranean Triad or Is It a Quartet?" in *Agriculture in Ancient Greece (7th International Conference of the Swedish Institute at Athens),* ed. B. Wells, Stockholm, pp. 61–75.

Savary, C. 1781. *Lettres sur la Grèce,* Paris.

Sonnini, C. S. 1801. *Voyage en Grèce et en Turquie, fait par l'ordre de Louis XVI et avec autorisation de la cour ottomane* 1, Paris.

Sordinas, A. 1971. *Old Olive Oil Mills and Presses on the Island of Corfu, Greece: An Essay on the Industrial Archaeology and the Ethnography of Agricultural Implements* (Memphis State University Anthropology Research Center Occasional Papers 5), Memphis.

Spanakis, S. G. 1940. *Μνημεία της Κρητικής Ιστορίας* 1: *Zuanne Mocenigo 1589,* Iraklion.

———. 1949. "Zuane Sagredo, Relatione (1604)," *CretChron* 3, pp. 519–533.

———. 1950a. "Ἡ ἔκθεση τοῦ δοῦκα τῆς Κρήτης Ντολφὶν Βενιὲρ (1610), Relatione di Duca di Creta Dolfin Venier," *CretChron* 4, pp. 312–352.

———. 1950b. *Μνημεία της Κρητικής Ιστορίας* 2: *Relatione di Candia del general Moresini, 1629,* Iraklion.

———. 1955. "Ἡ διαθήκη τοῦ Ἀντρέα Κορνάρου (1611)," *CretChron* 9, pp. 379–478.

———. 1957. "Ἀνέκδοτος κατάλογος τῶν 100 πόλεων τῆς Κρήτης," *CretChron* 11, pp. 277–301.

———. 1958a. *Μνημεία της Κρητικής Ιστορίας* 3: *Filippo Pasqualigo, Relatione, 1594,* Iraklion.

———. 1958b. *Μνημεία της Κρητικής Ιστορίας* 4: *Benetto Moro, Relatione, 1602,* Iraklion.

———. 1958c. "Στατιστικὲς εἰδήσεις περὶ Κρήτης τοῦ τέλους τοῦ 16ου αἰῶνα," *CretChron* 12, pp. 321–334.

———. 1969a. "Ἡ ἔκθεση τοῦ γενικοῦ Προβλεπτὴ Κρήτης Isepo Civran τοῦ 1639," *CretChron* 21, pp. 365–462.

———. 1969b. "Ἡ θρησκευτικό-εκκλησιαστικὴ κατάσταση στὴν Κρήτη τοῦ XVI αἰῶνα," *CretChron* 21, pp. 134–152.

———. 1969c. *Μνημεία της Κρητικής Ιστορίας* 5: *Francesco Basilicata, Relatione di tutto il regno di Candia, 1630,* Iraklion.

———. 1969d. *Μνημεία της Κρητικής Ιστορίας* 6: *A. Priuli and Barbero, 1667,* Iraklion.

———. 1991. *Πόλεις και χωριά της Κρήτης στο πέρασμα των αιώνων,* ed. T. Detorakis, Iraklion.

Spitael, M.-A. van, ed. 1981. *Buondelmonti, Cristoforo, descriptio insule Crete et liber insularum, cap. XI: Creta, edition critique,* Iraklion.

Stahl, A., ed. 2000. *The Documents of Angelo di Cartura and Donato Fontanella, Venetian Notaries in 14th-Century Crete,* Washington, D.C.

Stavrinidis, N. S. 1975. *Μεταφράσεις τουρκικῶν ἱστορικῶν ἐγγράφων ἀφορόντων εἰς τὴν ἱστορίαν τῆς Κρήτης* 1: *1657–1672,* Iraklion.

———. 1976. *Μεταφράσεις τουρκικῶν ἱστορικῶν ἐγγράφων ἀφορόντων εἰς τὴν ἱστορίαν τῆς Κρήτης* 2: *1672–1694,* Iraklion.

———. 1978. *Μεταφράσεις τουρκικῶν ἱστορικῶν ἐγγράφων ἀφορόντων εἰς τὴν ἱστορίαν τῆς Κρήτης* 3: *1694–1715,* Iraklion.

———. 1984. *Μεταφράσεις τουρκικών ιστορικών εγγράφων αφορόντων εις την ιστορίαν της Κρήτης* 4: *1715–1752,* Iraklion.

———. 1985. *Μεταφράσεις τουρκικών ιστορικών εγγράφων αφορόντων εις την ιστορίαν της Κρήτης* 5: *1752–1765,* Iraklion.

Sugar, P. F. 1977. *Southeastern Europe under Ottoman Rule,* Seattle.

Tafur, P. 1926. *Travels and Adventures, 1435–1439,* trans. M. Letts, London.

Theotokis, S. M., ed. 1933. *Ἱστορικὰ κρητικὰ ἔγγραφα ἐκδιδόμενα ἐκ τοῦ Ἀρχείου τῆς Βενετίας: Ἀποφάσεις Μείζονος Συμβουλίου Βενετίας, 1255–1669,* Athens.

———. 1936–1937. *Ἱστορικὰ κρητικὰ ἔγγραφα ἐκδιδόμενα ἐκ τοῦ Ἀρχείου τῆς Βενετίας: Θεσπίσματα τῆς Βενετικῆς Γερουσίας, 1281–1385,* 2 vols., Athens.

Thiriet, F. 1959. *La Romanie vénitienne au Moyen Âge: Le développement et l'exploitation du domaine colonial vénitien, XIIe–XVe siècles,* Paris.

———. 1966: "La situation réligieuse en Crète au début du XVe siècle," *Byzantion* 36, pp. 201–212.

———. 1967. "La condition paysanne et les problèmes de l'exploitation rurale en Romanie greco-vénitienne," *Studi Veneziani* 9, pp. 35–69.

———. 1978. *Duca di Candia: Ducali e lettere ricevute (1358–1360, 1401–1405),* Venice.

Tournefort, J. Pitton de. 1741. *A Voyage into the Levant* 1, trans. J. Ozell, London.

Triandafyllidou-Baladié, Y. 1988. *Το εμπόριο και η οικονομία της Κρήτης (1669–1795),* Iraklion.

———. 1990. "The Cretan Rural Landscape and Its Changes in Late Medieval and Modern Times," in Rackham, Grove, and Moody 1990, pp. 47–51.

Unwin, T. 1991. *Wine and the Vine: An Historical Geography of Viticulture and the Wine Trade,* London.

Veinstein, G. 1991. "On the *Çiftlik* Debate," in Keyder and Tabak 1991, pp. 35–53.

Veinstein, G., and Y. Triandafyllidou-Baladié. 1980. "Les inventaires après décès Ottomans de Crète," in *Probate Inventories: A New Source for the Historical Study of Wealth, Material Culture, and Agricultural Development,* ed. A. van der Woude and A. Schuurman, Utrecht, pp. 191–204.

Villamont, L. S. D. 1627. *Les voyages de la Terre Saincte et autres lieux remarquables et signalez d'icelle; ensemble de l'Italie, Sclavonie, Grèce, Turquie, Morée, Cephalonie, Candie, Cypre, . . . etc.,* Paris.

Yiannopoulos, I. G. 1978. "Ἡ Κρήτη κατὰ τὸν τέταρτο Βενετοτουρκικὸ Πόλεμο (1570–71)" (diss. Univ. of Athens).

Zachariadou, E. 1983. *Trade and Crusade: Venetian Crete and the Emirates of Menteshe and Aydin (1300–1415),* Venice.

Contrasting Impressions of Land Use in Early Modern Greece: The Eastern Corinthia and Kythera

by Timothy E. Gregory

From the beginning, the Eastern Korinthia Archaeological Survey (EKAS) and the Australian Paliochora-Kythera Archaeological Survey (APKAS) have been especially interested in the post-medieval periods, the Ottoman/Venetian as well as the modern.[1] Since 1999, EKAS has been investigating the area east of the Xeropotamos River and south of the Corinth Canal, encompassing the eastern Corinthian plain, the Oneion mountain chain, and the Saronic coast (Fig. 9.1). EKAS has focused most of its attention on the Examilia and Isthmia basins, as defined by geomorphological criteria, an area of about 65 km^2. APKAS also has been working since 1999. It has devoted most of its attention to an area of the northern part of Kythera, almost identical in size to the EKAS region currently under investigation (Fig. 9.2).

The history of these two regions was, of course, very different during the 15th–18th centuries. The Corinthia fell under Ottoman control in the 1450s and, although there were brief periods of Venetian ascendancy in the 1460s and again from 1686 to 1715, the Ottoman imperial system dominated the area.[2] Kythera, by contrast, was almost continuously under Venetian control

1. EKAS is a project of Florida State University and The Ohio State University, and operates under the authority of the American School of Classical Studies at Athens. APKAS is a project of the University of Sydney and the Australian Archaeological Institute in Athens. For the Corinthia I thank, first, the officials of the 4th (now 37th) Ephorate of Prehistoric and Classical Antiquities, especially Panayiota Kasimi, and those of the 6th (now 25th) Ephorate of Byzantine and Post-Byzantine Antiquities, especially Konstantina Skarmoutzou. In addition, thanks are due my codirector of EKAS, Daniel Pullen; the field director, Thomas Tartaron; as well as William Caraher and David Pettegrew, who helped enormously with the analysis and the Geographical Information System (GIS). For Kythera and APKAS I thank officials of the 2nd (now 26th) Ephorate of Prehistoric and Classical Antiquities, especially Aris Tsaravopoulos, and the 1st Ephorate of Byzantine and Post-Byzantine Antiquities, especially Eleni Tsophopoulou, Marina Papakonstantinou, and Nicholas Vardas. Special thanks are extended to Alexander Cambitoglou, director of the Australian Archaeological Institute in Athens, who was warmly supportive of this project from the beginning. Thanks are also due to successive directors of the project, Ian Johnson and Stavros Paspalas, to Lita Diacopoulos, and to the people of Karavas. William Caraher prepared several of the figures and much of the information on the travelers for the Corinthia.

2. On the Peloponnese (and more specifically the Corinthia) in the Ottoman period, see Sathas [1869] 1962; Sakellariou 1939; Kremmydas 1972, 1980; Christopoulos 1971–1972; Topping 1976. For Ottoman Greece more broadly, see Alexander 1985 (pp. 178–197, 354–374 on the Morea); Balta 1989, 1992. For Venetian Greece, see Dokos 1971–1972, 1975; Dokos and Panagopoulos 1993; Liata 2002. On EKAS, see Tartaron et al. 2006.

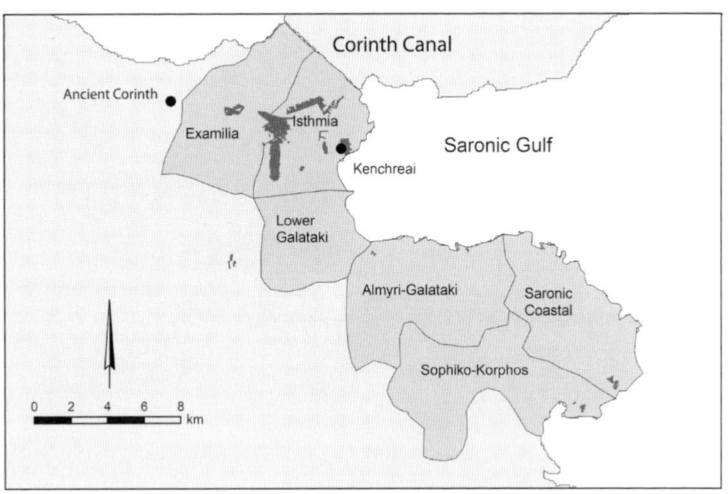

Figure 9.1. Eastern Korinthia Archaeological Survey, study area (darker shade). Courtesy EKAS

during this period.[3] It is true that Venetian power was not uninterrupted; it was broken by a three-year Ottoman occupation from 1715 to 1718 (which probably had more effect than previous scholars have assumed), while the Venier family and those who rented lands from it continued to exercise considerable independence. In addition, the northern part of the island maintained close connections with the Ottoman-controlled mainland. Nonetheless, Kythera as a whole was "Venetian territory" for most of the period under consideration.[4] Furthermore, in the early modern period, as more generally throughout history, the Corinthia has been at the center of political and economic activity in Greece, whereas Kythera has always been marginal, dominated by greater powers. Both areas, however, were economic and military crossroads, important for their strategic value.

For purposes of the present study, it should be emphasized that I am not attempting to characterize either the whole of the Corinthia or the whole of Kythera. On the contrary, one of the presuppositions of this work is that there probably will have been considerable differences, across time, in the way in which subregions reacted to, and were influenced by, the broader forces of history and historical change. Thus, the comments I make are restricted, in the first instance, to the eastern part of the Corinthia (the area between the ancient city and the coast of the Saronic Gulf), and, in the second instance, to the northern part of Kythera, an area far from the primary Venetian interests in Chora, indeed more closely bound to the Peloponnese than to the southern part of the island.

The basic but not exclusive tool of both projects discussed here is archaeological surface survey.[5] Aside from the obvious goals of studying these two regions on their own terms, EKAS and APKAS were organized

3. Leontsinis 1987; Maltezou 1991. For APKAS, see Coroneos et al. 2002.

4. For the medieval period, see Herrin 1972; Ince, Koukoulis, and Smyth 1987; Koukoulis et al. 1989; Koukoulis 1992.

5. As several chapters in this collection illustrate, it has now become common for archaeological surveys in Greece to pay considerable attention not only to the medieval period, but also to the post-medieval period; see Davis 1991; Mee and Forbes 1997; Stedman 1996; Sutton 2000; Bennet, Davis, and Zarinebaf-Shahr 2000.

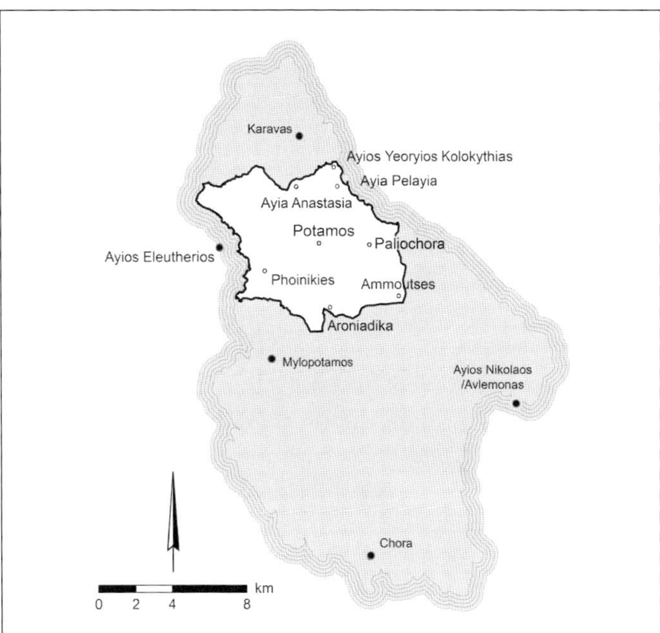

Figure 9.2. Australian Paliochora-Kythera Archaeological Survey, study area (unshaded). Courtesy APKAS

from the beginning to encourage comparison between the two areas, both because these two regions had very different historical trajectories, and because those differences could, it was hoped, be exploited in order to understand individual periods in a wider historical context and also to provide reflexive data for the development of archaeological methods and analysis. Thus, the two projects used field methods and tools that were either identical or closely similar.

A key element in these methods is what I have elsewhere called a "low-impact" approach to archaeological survey.[6] For ethical as well as practical reasons, this approach seeks to remove as little as possible of the archaeological material from the surface, while insisting on a tightly organized taxonomy for artifacts, a tool developed as part of the Sydney Cyprus Survey Project (SCSP).[7] The name of this taxonomy, the chronotype system, is derived from the concept of the "fossil-type" used originally in geology and subsequently in archaeology. The prefix "chrono-" was added to create a neologism and to emphasize the concept that individual identifications had to carry with them, first and foremost, some chronological definition (however broad), since chronology is the first and most important consideration in survey (or any) archaeology.

The chronotype system is nothing more than a regularization of naming practices used by ceramic (and other) specialists. Its hierarchical arrangement, however, is designed to maximize the amount of information that can be derived from the notoriously problematic material observed in survey work (as discussed later). The taxonometric aspect of the chronotype system is also conceived explicitly to facilitate comparison of data across projects as well as to encourage standardization and data rigor within a given project. The analysis of the archaeological data from EKAS and APKAS will be based, at least in part, on the chronotype system, and it will be important to keep this in mind in the discussion that follows.

6. Gregory 2004.

7. Given and Knapp 2003, pp. 14–16. See also Chap. 7 in this volume.

THE EASTERN CORINTHIA IN OTTOMAN TIMES

The Written Sources

Before we look at the evidence from this recent archaeological work, let us first summarize what is known about settlement and land use in the eastern Corinthia in the Ottoman period. In this regard the excavations at Isthmia, the origination point for the EKAS project, revealed evidence of significant activity in the 15th–18th centuries.[8] The same can be said for the castles of Ayios Vasilios and Ayionori on the borders of the Corinthia,[9] as well as Corinth itself, which remained an important center throughout the Ottoman/Venetian period.[10] Indeed, the attempts to refortify the Hexamilion during the second Venetian period left considerable evidence at Isthmia.[11] Of the 634 coins discovered in the University of California/ Ohio State University excavations, 66 (more than 10%) are of Venetian date. Significant quantities of ceramics dating to the post-Byzantine era also have been found. Architectural evidence from Isthmia also confirms that a settlement survived at least into the 16th century, if not beyond. Furthermore, travelers report that there was a recently abandoned "city" at the site of the Panhellenic sanctuary of Poseidon (which they identified with what we now know was the Byzantine Fortress), although it was much in decay by the time they saw it. The travelers, of course, may simply have been mistaken, taking the remains within the fortress as evidence of a city, but the consistent reference to churches in and around the fortress seems to confirm the archaeological indications of a significant settlement in the area in Byzantine and at least early Ottoman times.[12]

Nonetheless, the documentary sources provide us with little evidence of settlement in the eastern Corinthia in the Ottoman and Venetian periods.[13] Two settlements in the broader EKAS area were in the mountainous region of the southeast: Sophiko and Ryto.[14] Although we remain interested in the area of Sophiko and have conducted systematic survey on one highland plain east of the village (at a place called Lakka Skoutara, which is being published separately),[15] most of this region has not yet been subject to systematic examination. The terms of the permit from the Ministry of Culture that authorized our fieldwork did not allow us to carry out extensive survey in this area. As a result, my comments will be confined to the two northernmost drainage basins of the eastern Corinthia: the Examilia and the Isthmia (Figs. 9.1, 9.3).

8. *Isthmia* V, p. 150.

9. Kordosis 1981, pp. 141–176.

10. Beldiceanu and Beldiceanu-Steinherr 1986; Robinson 1985, esp. pp. 158–160; Robinson 1976, esp. pp. 223–224.

11. On this attempt, see Maltezou 1978.

12. Gregory and Kardulias 1990.

13. Beldiceanu and Beldiceanu-Steinherr 1980, 1986 (for the Ottoman register of 1461); Panayiotopoulos 1985 (for the Grimani census of 1700).

14. Sophiko: Grimani census (Panayiotopoulos 1985, p. 247, no. 18, and p. 294, no. 18). Ryto: Grimani census (Panayiotopoulos 1985, p. 242, no. 87, and p. 292, no. 87); it is uncertain whether this was the village between Athikia and Ayios Ioannis (Kordosis 1981, p. 327) that has a church with a building inscription of 1611, or the one on the pass between Galataki and Sophiko (Kordosis 1981, p. 328), that was apparently known by that name in antiquity (see Thucydides 4.42.2; Beldiceanu and Beldiceanu-Steinherr 1980, 1986). The Grimani census also mentions the villages of Angelokastron and Ayios Ioannis, outside the EKAS area, but not far removed from it. On the population of the Corinthia in general, see Alexopoulos 1971.

15. Preliminary comments are in Diacopoulos 2004, pp. 194–198.

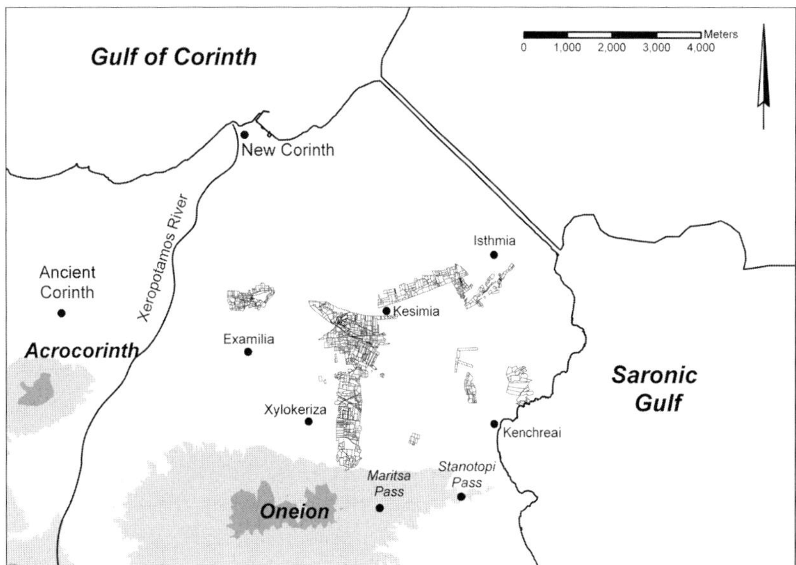

Figure 9.3. The Eastern Corinthia: The Examilia and Isthmia basins. Courtesy EKAS

The majority of people who live on the Corinthian plain today are Arvanites (i.e., the descendants of speakers of Albanian), whose ancestors moved into the mountainous areas of the Corinthia in the 14th–17th centuries, especially to places such as Ayionori/Limnes, Ayios Ioannis, Angelokastron, and Sophiko.[16] Many of these families then moved north from the mountains in the 19th century, especially in the tumultuous years after the end of the Greek War of Independence, but it is not entirely certain how many villages were occupied before this time.[17]

The Ottoman tax register *Tapu Tahrir* (TT) 10 (dated 1461) provides especially rich information about the Morea shortly after the Ottoman conquest.[18] Fragments of the original document are preserved in Paris and Istanbul and a summary of the document was published in 1980. The register contains data, region by region, concerning population; ownership of animals, mills, oil presses, and other sources of wealth; and basic agricultural produce and trade. The city of Corinth (Qoritos) and its territory (*nahiye* of Qoritos) are included in the register and one therefore can assess the relative position of the Corinthia vis-à-vis other parts of the Morea in the second half of the 15th century.[19] This is not the place to discuss this information in detail, in part because the document has not been published in full and because it is currently impossible to distinguish information from the eastern Corinthia from that from other parts of the region. It is clear, however, that the wealth of the Corinthia in this period was of a moderate level, based primarily on the cultivation of wheat and barley and the production of wine, although the Corinthia was the only place in the Morea where customs dues were collected. In addition, the Corinthia is recorded as possessing half of the oil presses in the Morea (probably an error in the recension).[20]

Another document, preserved in the National Library of Cyril and Methodius in Sofia, is apparently a part of TT10. It provides remarkable detail about the city of Corinth and 20 villages that were given by the sultan to the *sancakbey* (governor of a provincial subdivision) of the Morea.[21] As far as we can tell, no villages in this document were found in the EKAS

16. Biris 1960; Kordosis 1981, pp. 137–138; Topping 1980; Panayiotopoulos 1985, pp. 68–100; Beldiceanu and Beldiceanu-Steinherr 1980, 1986; according to the latter (p. 41), Albanians composed 38.4% of the rural population of the Corinthia in the register of 1461; the more complete document *Tapu Tahrir* 10 shows that Albanians made up 18.65% of the population of the entire territory of Corinth (163 out of 874 families); see Beldiceanu and Beldiceanu-Steinherr 1980, p. 38.

17. Wright et al. 1990, pp. 594–603, 616–617, 642–643; cf. Leake 1830, pp. 263, 357; Pouqueville 1826–1827, p. 430.

18. Beldiceanu and Beldiceanu-Steinherr 1980.

19. Beldiceanu and Beldiceanu-Steinherr 1980, p. 20: Qoritos is represented on pp. 161–166 of the register, and the Corinthia on pp. 167–176.

20. Beldiceanu and Beldiceanu-Steinherr 1980, p. 27, tables 2, 3.

21. Beldiceanu and Beldiceanu-Steinherr 1986, p. 37.

area. Most of those that can be identified are located in the western (e.g., Vasiliqa = Vasilika = ancient Sikyon) or, more commonly, in the southern part of the Corinthia in the vicinity of ancient Tenea and Kleonai (Ayo Vasil = Ayios Vasilios, Qondostavlo = Kondostavlos, Qotala = Koutala).[22] Nonetheless, this text provides important information about land use and the different agricultural pursuits of the Greek and the Albanian communities of the region.

First, on the basis of the document, Beldiceanu and Beldiceanu-Steinherr concluded that the economy of the city of Corinth was based overwhelmingly on agricultural production and that trade and industry were minor contributors to the city's vitality.[23] Second, silk production, which apparently had been an important source of wealth in the Middle Ages, was negligible in the 15th century, with a tiny amount of production carried out by the Albanian population of the area.[24] The villages recorded in the document were listed according to the ethnicity of their inhabitants, four being Greek and 16 Albanian. Both the Albanian and the Greek villages were engaged in a mixed agriculture, including production of wheat, barley, and wine, although the Greeks produced significantly larger percentages of each of these. The Albanians, however, did not engage in the production of cotton (a minor crop at this point) or raisins.

In the central corridor, between (Ancient) Corinth and Isthmia, one known settlement was Examilia (or Hexamilia),[25] whose relationship with the Hexamilion and the settlement at Isthmia is not yet fully clear.[26] Examilia is already attested by Spon in 1676, who says that it was "un mêchant village d'Albanois."[27] Wheler, who was Spon's companion, says that they spent the night in Examilia, presumably at an inn.[28] Today there is a strong tradition in Examilia that the ancestors of the current residents had arrived considerably earlier than the Albanian ancestors of the people of Ancient Corinth and Xylokeriza, with whom they are not always on good terms. If we accept the testimony of Spon and Wheler, we must assume that the Albanians of Examilia had already arrived by the latter part of the 17th century. Perhaps the source of differences between them and their neighbors is that they had, in fact, settled in the area at an earlier time.[29]

As Siriol Davies has pointed out, in 1700 (during the second Venetian period) some villagers from Perachora (opposite Corinth, on the Ottoman side of the isthmus) wished to settle and build houses in "Xamili," so that they could sow grain (on land extending as far as Kenchreai), plant vines, and keep animals there, while having permission to leave for two months every year to attend to their interests back on the Ottoman side of the border.[30]

In addition to Examilia, other settlements existed on the coast of the Saronic Gulf in the eastern Corinthia, at Schoinous, near the mouth of the present-day canal, and at the ancient harbor at Kenchreai (Cenchreae, Kenchries, which Kordosis argues was fortified in 1687).[31] Neither of these villages, however, is apparently listed in the Grimani census of 1700.[32] Indeed, although many settlements on the Grimani list have not yet been identified, there is no clear evidence that any place in the eastern Corinthia is included; most of the settlements were in the mountainous southwest and, to a lesser degree, on the northwestern plain (at Vocha and in other places).[33]

22. Cf. Kordosis 1981, pp. 173–174, 196–203.

23. Beldiceanu and Beldiceanu-Steinherr 1986, p. 39.

24. Beldiceanu and Beldiceanu-Steinherr 1986, p. 40, table.

25. Pacifico 1704, pp. 117–120.

26. Indeed, there is a real question of whether the Ottoman-period location of "Examilia" (attested in written sources, see below) is the same as that of the modern village of Examilia, which in modern times has been divided into at least two separate settlements; cf. the evidence of Pouqueville discussed below.

27. Spon 1678, p. 292.

28. Wheler 1682, p. 446.

29. Topping (1980, p. 261) writes briefly of the passage of Albanians across the Isthmus of Corinth into the Peloponnese in the late 14th century (cf. p. 269, n. 4).

30. Davies 2002, p. 244.

31. Kordosis 1981, p. 219, and p. 219, n. 326, based presumably on Pouqueville's (1826–1827, pp. 492–493) citation of Desmouceaux.

32. Panayiotopoulos 1985, pp. 231–311, esp. pp. 240–243, 291–292.

33. See Panayiotopoulos 1985, pp. 291–292, for an attempt to correlate the names in the census with specific places; Angelokastron and Sophiko, of course, were included in the Venetian territory of Porto Porro (pp. 247, 294).

The evidence of the travelers has not yet been fully assembled for the Corinthia, although it is clear that much of what they say is derivative, based either on Pausanias or on authoritative accounts such as those of Spon, Wheler, and Leake. Nonetheless, the evidence provided by the travelers suggests that the eastern Corinthia was indeed sparsely inhabited in the period of Ottoman domination. As expected, most travelers mention the settlement of Examilia, which one may reasonably identify with the modern village of the same name.[34] The accounts supply little actual information about the place since most were interested mainly in the name, but they do show that in the 19th and early 20th centuries it had a *han* (guest house) and a *dimarchos* (mayor), suggesting that it was a village of some importance. Most of the sources mention no other settlement between (Ancient) Corinth and the Saronic Gulf. The information provided by the travelers shows that the port of Kenchreai was used but in poor condition, although there was (just prior to the War of Independence) an Ottoman customs official who could be bribed easily.[35] Dodwell and Gell mention Galataki and possibly Ryto.[36]

Pouqueville, who visited the area in the decade before the Revolution, is the only traveler who provides significant information about the settlements in the interior of the eastern Corinthia.[37] He tells us that his party set out from Corinth and traversed the suburb of Kraneion before coming to the "beautiful village" of Examilia. There, he says, he encountered a group of Albanian women sitting beside a large fountain (perhaps the one that was just west of the church of Ayios Dimitrios until it was covered over some time ago), and that they offered his party refreshments. They then visited the grand country house of the Corinthian magnate Kamil Bey, which was to the southeast, apparently at a place called Epano Examili (in the area today called Chaloupi?). Three-quarters of an hour to the northwest (from Examilia itself?) was the village of Kato Examili. Pouqueville also mentions the village of Messano, or Xylo-Djara, which is presumably modern Xylokeriza (Fig. 9.3).[38] Altogether, Pouqueville notes that this complex of settlements had a population of 67 Christian families. He concludes his account by observing that the Albanian villages were better built than those of the Greeks, and provides a description of how the picturesque rows of pyramidal white ovens placed before the houses contrasted beautifully with the green of the orange and other trees behind.[39]

34. But see the caveat in n. 26 above.

35. Williams 1820, p. 390.

36. Dodwell (1819, pp. 196–197) had passed from Kenchreai and was on his way to (Ancient) Corinth on "a bad and circuitous route," apparently along the south side of Mt. Oneion, when he came to the village of Gallatachi (modern Galataki); a half-hour more brought him "to a miserable village called Mertese," where he found ancient pottery in a house and persuaded the inhabitants to take him to the tombs from which the pottery had been taken. This was "about a quarter of a mile from the village toward Corinth." Although Mertese could have been modern Athikia, it is perhaps more likely to have been Ryto. Gell (1810, p. 141–142) writes, "In the whole journey [from Epidauros to Corinth via Angelokastron and Ayios Ioannis], there is little worthy of remark, in point of antiquities. There were the towns of Rhetum [presumably Ryto], Solygia [Galataki?], and Contoporia in the way, and the two ports of Bucephalium and Piraeus."

37. Pouqueville 1826–1827, pp. 489–495.

38. Pouqueville 1826–1827, p. 491. Kordosis (1981, p. 321, n. 1000) accepts this identification and cites other modern authorities on it.

39. Pouqueville 1826–1827, pp. 491–492.

The Expédition scientifique, shortly after the end of the War of Independence, reported that Examilia had a population of 14, Ryto 53, and Sophiko 291; Loutraki (at the eastern end of the Gulf of Corinth), Kenchreai, and Kalamaki (at the eastern end of the isthmus on the Saronic Gulf) are mentioned but no figures are given. Interestingly, the Expédition scientifique states that the American establishment, known to have been somewhere in the vicinity of Examilia, had a population of about 100.[40]

The travelers also provide more general information about the emptiness of the eastern Corinthian landscape at this time. Spon and Wheler both mention the abandonment of the countryside as a result of pirate raids.[41] Dodwell has more specific information from just before the Revolution: "The great part of the Isthmus is uncultivated, and in a perfect state of nature, composed of undulating elevations covered with short stunted shrubs and a few small firs. Near the town, however [Ancient Corinth], some fine arable land is seen, and the soil is black and rich although Strabo asserts that it was not fertile."[42] Later he notes that the local *bey* (ruler) of Corinth controlled 163 villages (most of which were probably located in the west). He goes on to say that the "chief produce of the territory is corn, cotton, tobacco, and oil, and better wine than that of Athens, which the Turks quaff freely in spite of their prophet, in order to counteract the bad effects of the air, which in summer is almost pestilential."[43] William Turner wrote that the ground between Examilia and the Saronic Gulf was "in many places very hilly, and uneven."[44] Later he crossed the whole of the isthmus on foot, noting that he "frequently walked over ploughed fields, and through furze [gorse, a spiny green shrub]." In 1858, Sir Thomas Wyse traveled from Corinth to Isthmia: "At present all is barrenness and waste, no trees except a few scattered pines, being visible in the neighborhood. For some distance the road follows the line to Cenchreae, until the village of Hexamili is reached, when it divides into two branches, one leading down to the old harbour and the other continuing in a northerly direction to the Poseidonium and Kalamaki. Pine-trees of small growth are scattered over all this tract."[45]

EKAS: The Archaeological Information

The evidence from both the documentary and the literary sources suggests a low level of habitation in the eastern Corinthia in the Ottoman period, with only a single settlement except for those on the coast. The archaeological data seem to confirm this impression. To be sure, the archaeological survey has only sampled the area, and "sites" can be missed. On the other hand, we followed up, as best we could, stories from local inhabitants about the location of "palaces" of various Ottoman landlords (Nuri Bey, Kemil Bey,[46] Kasim Bey), all of them legendary figures from the area or folk-etymological explanations for local toponyms. Further, we had in mind the generally accepted maxim that in southern Greece the large commercial *çiftlik* (plantation) was rare and "the small family farm, attached to a hamlet and producing mostly for subsistence, remained the dominant pattern" during the Tourkokratia (the period of Ottoman rule).[47] Yet, we were also aware of the large landholdings of the Notaras family (perhaps mainly in the Vocha area)[48] and the extensive farms of Albanians located

40. *Expédition scientifique,* pp. 67–68. The settlement at Examilia named Washingtonia was established by the American philanthropist and educator Samuel Gridley Howe in 1829, and was made up of some 26 destitute families. No trace of Washingtonia apparently exists today.

41. Spon 1678, p. 295; Wheler (1682, p. 437), describing the isthmus, writes that it has as much cultivable ground as the Plain of Megara, "but it is utterly neglected and uninhabited for fear of the Corsairs."

42. Dodwell 1819, p. 185.

43. Dodwell 1819, p. 192.

44. Turner 1820, p. 292.

45. Wyse 1865, p. 332; Taylor (1859, p. 30) says much the same thing: "The country is a wilderness, overgrown with mastic, sage, wild olive, and pale green Isthmian pine."

46. On Kemil Bey's relations with peasants living on his land, see Richards 1906, p. 353; Christopoulos 1971–1972, pp. 464–465.

47. McGrew 1985, p. 30; cf. Veinstein 1991.

48. McGrew 1985, p. 221; Koutivas 1968.

on the Isthmus of Corinth. We therefore sought evidence that might shed light on the question of whether the Corinthia was dominated by large or small holdings in the Late Ottoman period, an issue that must be viewed in light of the continuing debate over the larger issue of the alleged "retreat" of settlement into the mountains during the Tourkokratia.[49]

Our archaeological work included a carefully delimited sampling program. But at the same time, we sought to take advantage of local information and "memory" of the Tourkokratia.[50] In this regard, one interesting case study concerns traditions about the area between Examilia and Kyras Vrysi known locally as Kesimia (Fig. 9.3). There were several explanations given for this name by local inhabitants, but the most common one was that these were the fields (or the "palace" area) of someone called Kesim Bey; the locals say that he was a tax collector or rent collector in the region. The Turkish term *kesim* (Greek κεσίμι) refers (among other things) to an agreed price or rent, and a *kesimci* is a contractor who manages the revenue from these rents.[51] Therefore, *kesim* may have been the payment made to powerful Ottoman *bey*s in a situation where an independent village (or villages) sought to avoid incorporation into a *çiftlik*.[52] Presumably this local toponym arose as a result of a historical situation involving *kesim* in some way, and the toponym might have referred either to the fields that were farmed as a result of the payment of *kesim* or, alternatively, to the site of the residence of the *kesimci*. Naturally, we thought that intensive survey in this area might reveal traces of such a village, or even the reputed "palace" of the *bey* that the locals insisted had been there, but virtually nothing datable to the Tourkokratia was found. It is not impossible, of course, that the village to which these fields belonged was Examilia, which is a short distance to the west of the area, but our expectations in general were disappointed in this regard.

Intensive survey in the EKAS area was generally based on a sampling scheme that sought to investigate reasonably large contiguous areas while at the same time including the different geographical and geomorphological regions (areas surveyed are shown in Fig. 9.1).[53] As mentioned earlier, both EKAS and APKAS made use of the so-called chronotype system for standardizing the recording and collection of information. A major goal of this scheme is to allow us to carry out preliminary analysis at different levels of resolution. As is generally known, by far the majority of ceramic information encountered in survey is essentially "undiagnostic," and the chronological components of sites are determined commonly by analysis of only a very small percentage of the artifacts actually on the ground (both because most are not identified and because the vast majority of artifacts are neither observed nor described, even in very intensive surveys).[54]

For this preliminary analysis, we look at the chronological data at two (or more) levels of detail: "broad period" information and "narrow-period" information, something that the chronotype system easily accommodates because it is built on hierarchical relationships. (In fact, there is yet another, coarser level of analysis that is based on the broadest periods: "ceramic age," normally described in other surveys as "unknown date," and other periods nearly as broad, such as "ancient–medieval," "medieval," or even "post-prehistoric"—pottery from ca. 1000 B.C. onward.) The reason for this is

49. Frangakis and Wagstaff 1987; Frangakis-Syrett and Wagstaff 1992; Forbes 2000; Bennet, Davis, and Zarinebaf-Shahr 2000.

50. Cf. Forbes 2000.

51. İz, Hony, and Alderson 1992, p. 287; Redhouse 1987, p. 643.

52. McGrew 1985, p. 39.

53. Tartaron et al. 2006.

54. Given and Knapp 2003, pp. 14–16 and passim.

TABLE 9.1. EKAS OBJECTS DATABLE TO BROAD PERIODS (REPRESENTING 30% OF ENTIRE COLLECTION)

Period	*Start Date*	*Stop Date*	*Quantity*	*Percentage*
Bronze Age	3100 B.C.	1050 B.C.	1,538	13.1
Protogeometric–Hellenistic	1050 B.C.	31 B.C.	4,183	35.7
Roman	31 B.C.	A.D. 700	4,538	38.7
Byzantine/Frankish	A.D. 700	A.D. 1453	65	0.6
Post-Byzantine	A.D. 1453	A.D. 2004	1,398	11.9

simply that many artifacts from survey can be dated only broadly, and it is unreasonable to lose the information from the artifacts just because they cannot be dated precisely. ("Precisely" in terms of survey data commonly means within a century or two.) Table 9.1 shows the breakdown of artifacts identified in the eastern Corinthia by one set of "broad periods"—others could just as easily have been used. The percentages given in Table 9.1 are not of the total number of artifacts but of the 30% of the total number that could be assigned to these broad periods. Those that were identified with even broader periods, sometimes overlapping with those examined here, were ignored.

One should note the predominance of material from antiquity (ca. 88% of the objects identified) and the minuscule percentage assigned to the Byzantine period (less than 1%). The post-Byzantine material is significant in amount, representing more than 10% of the total. It is important to remember, however, that this latter category contains 20th-century as well as Ottoman/Venetian-period artifacts.

For this reason, one must almost always proceed to the examination of narrow periods (Table 9.2) that are, essentially, breakdowns of the broader periods set out in Table 9.1. This point may seem obvious, but we shall return to the "broad-period" data shortly.[55] The dominance of material from Late Antiquity is striking, and there is, as we have seen, some evidence of Byzantine-period activity. What is most interesting is that there is so little evidence of material from the Ottoman/Venetian period in the survey area. Nearly all the post-Byzantine artifacts were assigned to the modern periods, from 1830 onward. Thus we have, for the entire Ottoman/Venetian period, a secure identification for only 19 items.

TABLE 9.2. EKAS OBJECTS DATABLE TO NARROW PERIODS

Period	*Start Date*	*Stop Date*	*Quantity*	*Percentage*
Early Roman	31 B.C.	A.D. 250	272	8.3
Late Roman	A.D. 250	A.D. 700	2,416	73.3
Early Byzantine	A.D. 700	A.D. 1200	17	0.5
Late Byzantine/Frankish	A.D. 1200	A.D. 1453	48	1.5
Ottoman/Venetian	A.D. 1453	A.D. 1830	19	0.6
Early Modern	A.D. 1830	A.D. 1960	116	3.5
Contemporary Modern	A.D. 1960	A.D. 2004	406	12.3

55. For convenience in the present discussion, Table 9.2 eliminates all material earlier than Roman, so the information in Table 9.1 cannot be compared with that in Table 9.2.

As is generally known, one of the most significant problems in studying the early modern landscape of Greece is the poor state of knowledge of ceramics of this period. Although recent work has begun to rectify this,[56] it is likely that our failure to identify all the Ottoman/Venetian ceramic material encountered is one of the reasons for our inability to see clearly the archaeological landscape of this period in the eastern Corinthia. The chronology of coarse wares remains particularly elusive, especially since many were produced locally and followed traditions that arose in the Middle Ages. The difficulty of recognizing Ottoman ceramics in the landscape does not, of course, demonstrate their absence, and as our knowledge of Ottoman ceramics increases over time, we should be able to extract more information from our data.

One of the criticisms raised about methods used in the EKAS and APKAS projects is that not "enough" material has been collected to allow period specialists to go back and reexamine the pottery in detail.[57] In this regard, it is worth emphasizing that EKAS has collected some 4,000 objects, representative of each of the individual chronotypes encountered in the survey, and these are all available for examination (and indeed, many have already been studied by period specialists from both inside and outside the project). In addition, the long-term nature of our projects means that we, or our successors, will be able to go back into the field to check and refine our observations, since most of the material remains where it was found.[58]

Some refinement of our observations, however, is possible, even now, by a restudy of the objects collected and those images in the project's database of photographed and drawn artifacts.[59] Survey projects, of course, examine enormous numbers of objects and features in the landscape. EKAS described in detail some 58,674 artifacts, and the prospect of reexamining this archive for a possibly "missing" Ottoman component, although possible, must wait for specialist interest and the time for this to be accomplished. At this point, however, what we seek is to identify areas where material of Ottoman date is likely to have been overlooked. We also suggest, cautiously, some interpretation based on extrapolation of the data. The method for this is rather simple.

The periodization scheme developed with the chronotype system, as we have seen, assigns broad categories to artifacts that cannot be placed within a more narrow time span. In general, these time periods serve to group similar kinds of ceramics that do not resemble material from narrower known periods. Consequently, when artifacts are assigned to one of these broad periods, they receive a kind of negative identification, being marked not only as artifacts that are perceived to be difficult to identify, but also as material that is unlikely to fall *outside* a given time range.

Table 9.3 identifies several chronological periods that "include" or "cross over" the Ottoman/Venetian and therefore might mask hitherto unidentified pottery from that period. The table lists the broad periods according to the percentage of a given broad time period that overlaps with the relatively narrow Ottoman/Venetian period. This percentage can give us a very rough (and perhaps only heuristic) idea of the likelihood that a particular artifact assigned to a broad time period may in fact be better associated with the Ottoman/Venetian period.

56. See esp. Vroom 2003; also Chap. 4 in this volume.

57. See Newhard 2005 (a review of Given and Knapp 2003), which discusses briefly the chronotype system and the attempts of SCSP to deal with the problem of the collection and study of survey pottery. Preliminary presentation of Gregory 2004 at the 2001 meeting of the Society for American Archaeology generated some criticism from the audience about the methods used in SCSP, APKAS, and EKAS. This criticism, essentially, was that proper results could not be achieved without a 100% collection of artifacts, something we believe is both impossible and unnecessary.

58. The criticism that the artifacts on which our work is based are not available for later study seems rather disingenuous, inasmuch as the reexamination by outside specialists of finds from other projects has almost never taken place.

59. Caraher, Nakassis, and Pettegrew 2006, pp. 26–34.

TABLE 9.3. EKAS MATERIAL FROM PERIODS OVERLAPPING THE OTTOMAN PERIOD

Period	*Start Date*	*Stop Date*	*Span of Years*	*Percentage of Overlap*	*Number of Survey Units*	*Number of Artifacts*
Medieval, Ottoman/Venetian	A.D. 1453	A.D. 1830	377	100	17	19
Medieval	A.D. 700	A.D. 1800	1,100	34	27	34
Medieval–Modern	A.D. 700	A.D. 2000	1,300	29	32	39
Roman–Medieval	31 B.C.	A.D. 1800	1,831	21	39	92
Roman–Modern	31 B.C.	A.D. 2000	2,031	19	5	6

This percentage of overlap can then be divided by the number of artifacts from all overlapping periods in a survey unit, and an average total of overlap can be calculated. Units with a higher average of total overlap warrant further investigation in the search for information concerning activity in the Ottoman/Venetian period. This kind of analysis, of course, does not produce any binding, substantial figures upon which firm conclusions can be based, but can serve to indicate areas where additional attention to the ceramics present might produce more refined results.

This approach to the artifacts produces more substantive results when combined with the spatial data. There are several areas in the Corinthia where easily recognizable Ottoman glazed tablewares appear in conjunction with ceramics of one or more of these broad chronological categories. I will focus on three areas that seem to offer the best prospects for small-scale Ottoman/Venetian occupation (Fig. 9.4).

The first area is a half-kilometer east of the village of Xylokeriza, in the fertile fields that stretch between the north slope of Mt. Oneion and the gentle south slope of Perdikaria (Figs. 9.4, 9.5). This area is sometimes called Marougka. In four units (34, 52, 74, 554), Ottoman/Venetian fine wares were found in an area of about 100 × 400 m, bounded by units of generally lower visibility and density. Medieval glazed ware that could not be assigned to any definite date was found nearby in units 38, 42, 46, and 72. Unlike the units on the ridge above Kyras Vrysi (see below), these units did not produce the large quantity of utility wares that were considered candidates for an Ottoman/Venetian date. Instead we found quantities of medium coarse and kitchen wares assignable only to the "Ceramic Age," the broadest period to which we assign pottery.

The second area stretches along a ridge overlooking the modern village of Kyras Vrysi and the sanctuary of Poseidon at Isthmia (Figs. 9.4, 9.6). Three contiguous units (2122, 2123, 2125) and two others (2561, 3051) had Ottoman/Venetian sgraffito fine ware as well as less diagnostic medium coarse wares from broad periods. Although a considerable amount of Late Roman pottery was also found in this area, the majority of pottery from these units was not diagnostic of any particular period.

The final area encompasses both the north and south base of the hill of Gonia in the western part of the survey area where Blegen excavated prehistoric material long ago (Figs. 9.4, 9.7).[60] Two units (1760, 1772) had clearly identified Ottoman fine ware, and two additional units (1774, 1776) had glazed medium coarse wares datable to the medieval period. The

60. Blegen 1930.

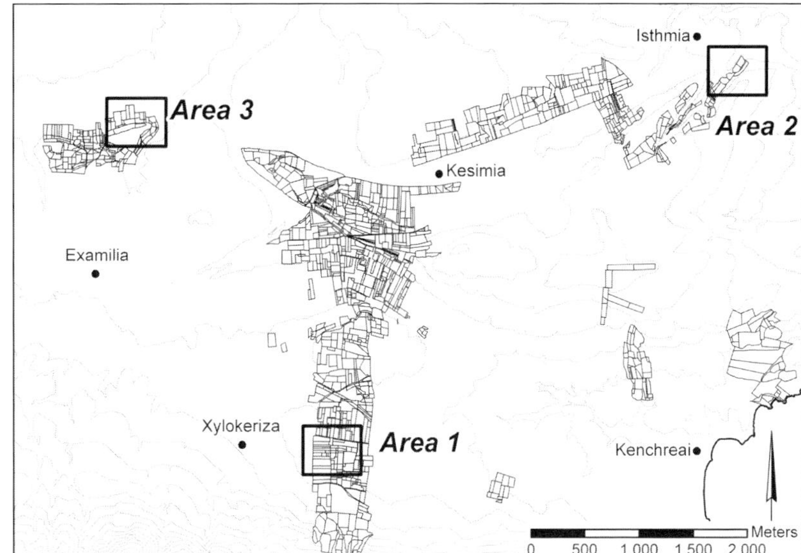

Figure 9.4. Areas with possible Ottoman-period material in the Eastern Corinthia: Marougka (1), the ridge above Kyras Vrisi (2), and Gonia (3). Courtesy EKAS

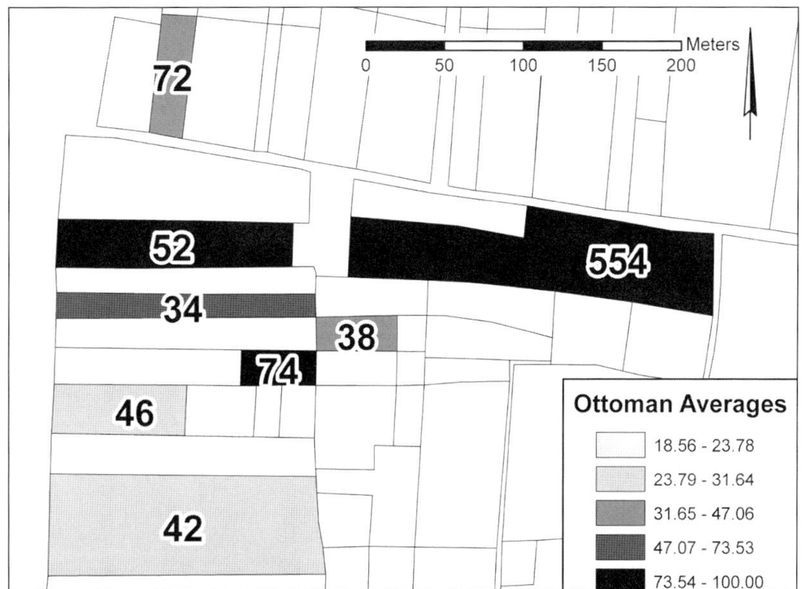

Figure 9.5. The Eastern Corinthia: Marougka, area 1 of possible Ottoman/Venetian activity. Units of various shades of gray to black are those where pottery from either the Ottoman/Venetian period or any periods that overlap with the Ottoman/Venetian period has been located. The darker the shade, the higher the average percentage of chronological overlap of all the pottery in the unit. Given that the overall number of Ottoman or potential Ottoman sherds remains relatively low, any unit with the darkest shades of gray or black must have some Ottoman-period pottery in it. Courtesy EKAS

concentration of artifacts appears to have been limited to the eastern part of the hill. Field work, including intensive grid-based collections (LOCA 9009, 9010), did not recover any pottery of likely Ottoman date from the western part of the hill or the valley between the hill of Gonia and the neighboring hill of Yiriza.

Informal Analysis

One can draw several conclusions from this distribution of pottery. First, for at least two of the places identified as possessing Ottoman pottery, arguments can be advanced for the suitability of these locations for settlement. The bluff that often runs along the north side of upturned marine terraces, such as that at Gonia, provides access to water running just below

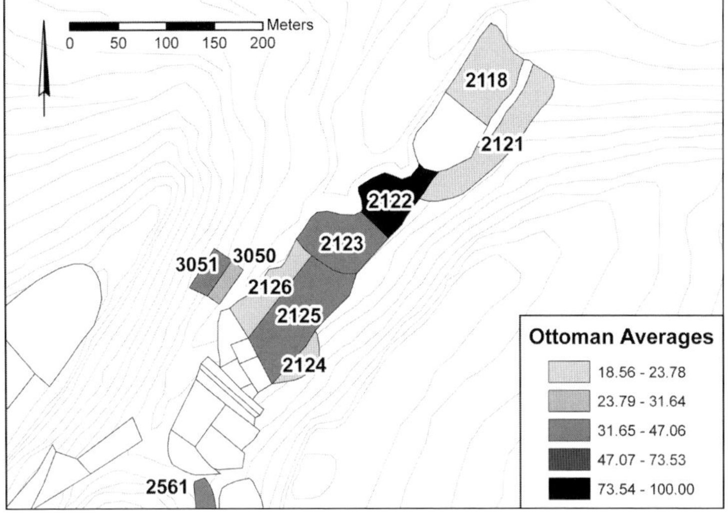

Figure 9.6. The Eastern Corinthia: Ridge above Kyras Vrysi, area 2 of possible Ottoman/Venetian activity. See the explanation of the shading in the caption of Fig. 9.5. Courtesy EKAS

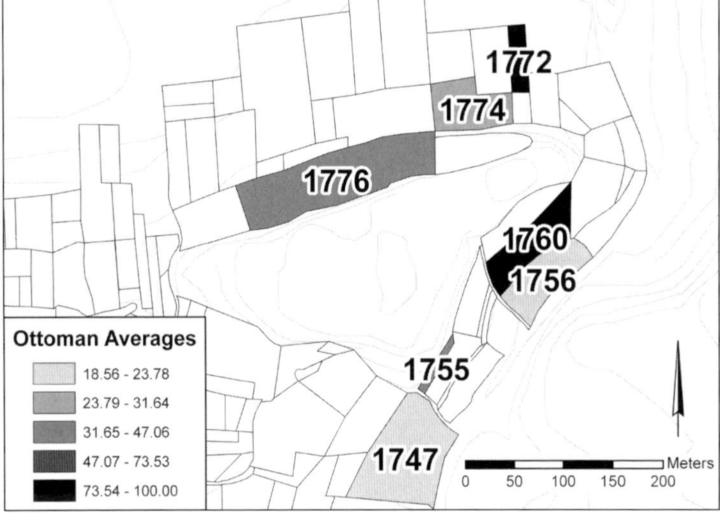

Figure 9.7. The Eastern Corinthia: Gonia, area 3 of possible Ottoman/ Venetian activity. See the explanation of the shading in the caption of Fig. 9.5. Courtesy EKAS

the limestone cap. Consequently, the base of the bluff is well suited for habitation, agriculture, or manufacturing activities that are dependent on water. In fact, within the survey area at Gonia we identified at least one manufacturing facility along this bluff line. Blegen, in addition, described the market gardens maintained in this area, presumably with water available at the base of the bluff. The proximity of the units below Gonia to the (probably) 16th-century church of Ayios Athanasios also suggests that a small medieval–Ottoman settlement once rested in the shadows of these hills.

The ridge overlooking Kyras Vrysi is another predictable place for settlement, although it is worth noting that none of the travelers to the area described an Ottoman village or settlement on the heights above the Isthmian sanctuary. As we have seen, several of the earliest travelers—Wheler in particular—claim that a village with several churches stood within the ruins of the Byzantine fortress there. It is possible that there were small settlements in the vicinity of Xylokeriza and Kyras Vrysi that were not noticed by travelers more concerned with antiquities than with contemporary settlement patterns. Interestingly, Fowler mentions the "ruins of a small Frankish castle" to the southwest of the Hellenistic stadium,[61] which would be in the general area we have been discussing. Perhaps the fortification, of which no trace now survives, was Venetian.

Nonetheless, even if we accept this extrapolated data to indicate the possibility of small settlements in the EKAS area during the Ottoman/Venetian period, the archaeological evidence does not suggest that we can add more large settlements to the few that are known from the written sources. Further research on the archaeological material will certainly add to our knowledge of this area in early modern times, and we cannot argue that this was a totally empty landscape. But we must admit that the major population centers of the period apparently were located outside the Examilia and Isthmia basins where survey was conducted.

NORTHERN KYTHERA IN VENETIAN TIMES

The Written Sources

Even though the Corinthia has always been a more important region than the relatively poor island of Kythera, we know much more about the latter than we do about the former in the 16th–18th centuries, in part because of the relatively rich archival sources, both in Venice and on Kythera itself. These have, in turn, encouraged scholarship and given rise to the publication of collections of documents[62] and to ever more sophisticated synthetic works on the history and the society of the island.[63] Much of this work has focused on the capital, Chora (Fig. 9.2), and the southern part of the island, as the evidence for that area is much more plentiful. Although most of the archival information has not yet been incorporated into synthetic studies, the 18th-century census data[64] and the notarial and other archival information[65] certainly will allow much greater understanding of the northern part of the island in the years to come. Even a preliminary examination of the census records provides us with information about demographic changes and the centers of population, including the many villages in the area of interest to the Australian survey.[66] They show that the following modern villages in the survey area were inhabited in the 18th century: Aroniadika, Christophorianika, Phrilingianika, Kastrisianika, Katsoulianika (Gouria), Kominianika, Kousounari, Logothetianika, Melitianika, Perlengianika, Pitsinades, Potamos, and Triphylianika, along with the Monastery of Osios Theodoros, which had parish status and apparently served as the church for Zanglanikianika (see Fig. 9.8 for some of these places).[67]

The dominant historical event, the one that lay behind the organization of APKAS, is the destruction of Ayios Dimitrios (modern Paliochora) in 1537 by the Ottoman admiral Hayreddin Barbarossa.[68] According to a Venetian report of 1563, some 7,000 people were taken prisoner in the raid, although most modern scholars do not accept that number.[69] Partly as a result of the Veneto-Ottoman wars, the population of the island plummeted, and the first information we have after the sack records the population as only 1,850.[70] Further, the report of 1563 states that 16 years after Barbarossa's attack, the former inhabitants of Ayios Dimitrios were

61. *Corinth* I.1, p. 60.
62. Maltezou 1997; Drakakis 1999, 2003; Kalliyeros 2002.
63. Leontsinis 1987; Maltezou 1980a, 1980b, 1989, 1991; Tsitsilias 1993–1994 remains very useful, although it is not well documented.
64. Maltezou 1997.
65. Drakakis 1999, 2003; Kalliyeros 2002; Papadaki 2001.
66. Gregory 2003.
67. Maltezou 1997.
68. See Chap. 2 in this volume, p. 38.
69. Maltezou 1980a, pp. 154–155; Tsitsilias 1993–1994, vol. 1, p. 246, n. 58; Lamansky 1884, p. 274.
70. Maltezou 1980a, p. 157, table 1.

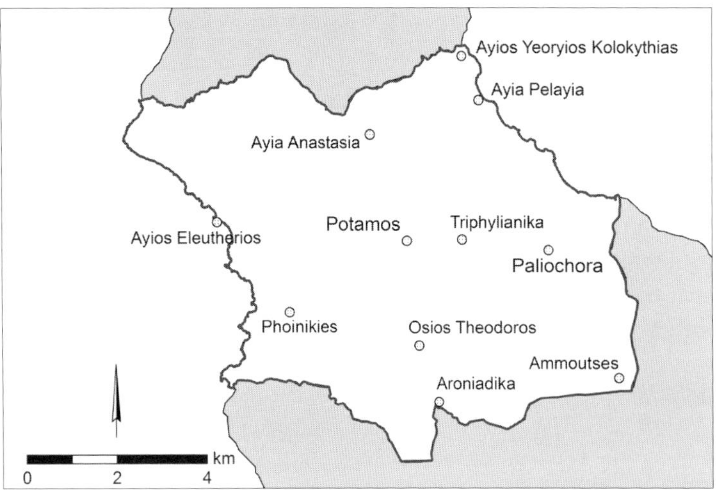

Figure 9.8. Kythera: Locations in the APKAS study area. Courtesy APKAS

still living in the forests during the summer, afraid that the pirates would return to enslave them.[71] Meanwhile, the administration of the island had been transferred to the south. Thus the northern area lost its former prominence, the villages presumably sinking into relative obscurity. The powerful Venier family, which at one time had been essentially independent of Venetian power, still retained holdings in the north, but these were in large part rented out. The evidence is slim, but one has the impression that the northern part of the island (including the APKAS survey area) slipped largely out of the control of the noble families. Probably because of this relative independence, Potamos, the largest settlement on the island, slowly began to develop as a commercial center, with connections that went far beyond the island and even the Greek-speaking world.

The Archaeology of Northern Kythera

Although some archaeological research had previously been done on Kythera,[72] the past 15 years have witnessed a veritable explosion of interest in the material culture of the island, encouraged in part by the excavation of a Minoan peak-sanctuary at Ayios Yeoryios tou Vounou.[73] One of the most important of these new initiatives is the Kythera Island Project, directed by Cyprian Broodbank and Evangelia Kiriatzi. This major interdisciplinary project operates in the east-central area of the island and shares a common border with APKAS along the latter's southern side.[74]

Let us turn to the data generated by APKAS from the northern part of Kythera. With regard to the evidence from the broad periods (Table 9.4), the results seem quite similar to those for the Corinthia, except that the amount of Roman material is dramatically smaller and the amount of Byzantine and post-Byzantine evidence is significantly larger.

Examination of the narrow-period data (Table 9.5), however, brings out significant differences. The medieval material is roughly similar to that in the Corinthia in its proportional representation within the assemblage as a whole, but the modern, especially the early modern, data is quite strikingly plentiful, suggesting (provisionally) considerable activity in the 19th and early 20th centuries. Just as important, the Venetian-period material represents 4% of the artifacts identified in the survey area. To be sure, one

71. Lamansky 1884, p. 274.
72. Waterhouse and Hope Simpson 1961; Coldstream and Huxley 1972.
73. Sakellarakis 1996.
74. Broodbank 1999.

TABLE 9.4. APKAS OBJECTS DATABLE TO BROAD PERIODS

Period	*Start Date*	*Stop Date*	*Percentage*
Bronze Age	3100 B.C.	1050 B.C.	14
Classical–Hellenistic	500 B.C.	31 B.C.	19
Roman	31 B.C.	A.D. 700	8
Byzantine/Frankish	A.D. 700	A.D. 1537	5
Post-Byzantine	A.D. 1537	A.D. 2000	54

has to be careful in claiming statistical significance for a difference based on small numbers, but what is suggestive is that much of this Venetian-period material seems (tentatively at least) to cluster in several places.

Thus, Figure 9.9 shows significant areas of concentration at, among other places, Phoinikies, Aroniadika, Ammoutses, Ayia Katerina, Vythoulas, and around Paliochora. One must remember, first, that survey was not conducted directly in the inhabited areas of the modern villages, most of which are known to have existed from the census records. Second, the Australian project has not worked within the urban area of Paliochora, so the heavy concentrations found are not from the city itself, but rather from areas surrounding it. It remains questionable to what extent habitation within Paliochora continued after 1537, but there seems to be sound evidence of significant activity around the city after its destruction.

This is just the beginning of our analysis of the material from the APKAS study area, but one can easily see the direction in which our observations are taking us: although there is little evidence of Ottoman-period settlement in the EKAS study area, the evidence from northern Kythera is very different from that in the Corinthia, suggesting substantial activity in the same period and the existence of an extensive network of settlements. Again, the textual evidence indicates that at least 15 villages existed in this area during the Venetian period, and the concentrations discovered in survey seem to represent other small settlements as well as isolated farmsteads. As noted earlier, the absence of substantial evidence from the Ottoman-period eastern Corinthia does not suggest an empty landscape. Rather, the archaeological as well as the written evidence leads us to conclude, tentatively at least, that settlement in the Ottoman eastern Corinthia was highly nucleated, whereas that in Venetian Kythera was highly dispersed.

TABLE 9.5. APKAS OBJECTS DATABLE TO NARROW PERIODS

Period	*Start Date*	*Stop Date*	*Percentage*
Bronze Age	3100 B.C.	1050 B.C.	15
Classical–Hellenistic	500 B.C.	31 B.C.	21
Roman	31 B.C.	A.D. 700	9
Early Medieval	A.D. 700	A.D. 1200	0
Late Byzantine/Frankish	A.D. 1200	A.D. 1537	6
Ottoman/Venetian	A.D. 1537	A.D. 1800	4
Early Modern	A.D. 1800	A.D. 1960	39
Present Modern	A.D. 1960	A.D. 2000	6

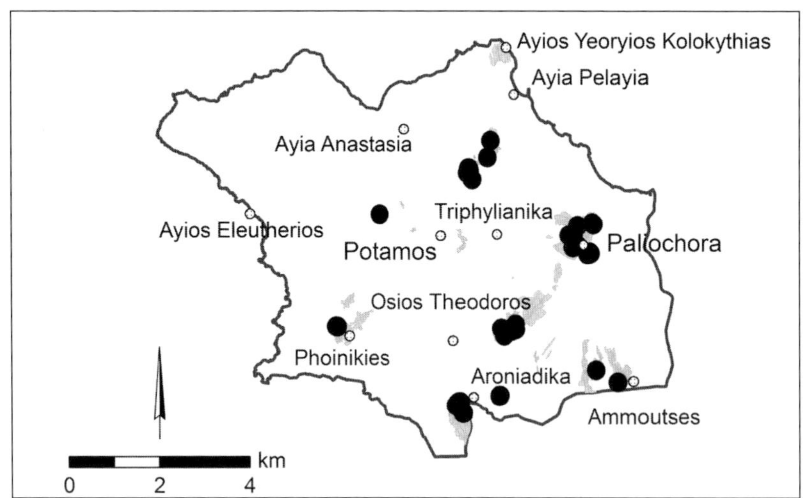

Figure 9.9. Kythera: Locations of Venetian-period artifacts in the APKAS study area. Courtesy APKAS

CHURCHES IN THE CORINTHIA AND ON KYTHERA

Another means of examining the question of the extent of land use, independent of the ceramic data, is to look at the chronology and location of churches in the survey areas.[75] This is not to suggest that all churches are "markers" of villages, since they may have been built or maintained as parts of monasteries or located on estates or in isolated locations. Kythera is known for its privately founded churches that may have been constructed for any number of personal, family, or social reasons.[76]

Nonetheless, the churches certainly were (and are) connected with land use in one way or another. For example, the construction and maintenance of churches undoubtedly was a significant investment that required economic surplus. Furthermore, churches (or, more properly, their owners) commonly owned or managed land for their upkeep. The buildings frequently were located near settlements or in areas in which individuals and families owned fields. Therefore, the location and characteristics of a church (date, style, decoration, maintenance, etc.) can provide significant information, especially when used with documentary sources and other kinds of archaeological data. This has the potential to help us better understand the regions under consideration and similarities and differences between them.[77]

In the eastern Corinthia the number of churches is remarkably small. In the region in which EKAS has conducted intensive survey, only 16 churches have been found. Perhaps even more significantly, of these all but four clearly were built in the 20th century and there is no evidence that an earlier church had existed on the site (Table 9.6).[78] The location of 20th-century churches is certainly important, but our failure to identify more than four churches in this region that may be older than 100 years supports our suggestion that there were few settlements in the study area during the Ottoman/Venetian period.

The situation is far different on Kythera, where, as we have indicated, the size of the study area is approximately the same as that of the Examilia and Isthmia basins in the eastern Corinthia. There, however, instead of 16 churches, we have documented more than 80.[79] Naturally these churches are of widely different ages and many of them are no longer in use,[80] but

75. Whitelaw 1991, p. 426, fig. 21.1; Koukoulis 1997; Forbes 2000, pp. 215–217.

76. Leontsinis 1982.

77. For Kythera, see Maltezou 1980a, 1989; for Methana, see Koukoulis 1997.

78. One should remember that this absence of churches contrasts notably with the situation in the mountainous south of the Corinthia. See, e.g., Orlandos 1935; Kordosis 1981.

79. Of course, the number of churches on Kythera is comparable to that on many other islands (witness the common claim that a given Greek island has 365—or some similar number—of churches). Yet, similarly high concentrations of churches can be found in many mainland areas, e.g., the Methana peninsula, the Mani, and the mountainous Corinthia. The phenomenon may perhaps be more closely linked either to "marginal" areas or (what may arguably be the same thing) to areas that did not experience development in the 19th and early 20th centuries.

80. Sotiriou 1923.

TABLE 9.6. CHURCHES IN THE EASTERN CORINTHIA (EXAMILIA AND ISTHMIA BASINS)

Village	*Church*	*Location*	*Estimated Date of Original Construction*
Examilia	Ayios Dimitrios	Center of village	19th century? (rebuilt 1966)
Examilia	Ayios Andreas*	Center of village	1979
Examilia	Ayios Theodoros	Cemetery east of village	second half of 20th century
Examilia	Ayios Phanourios	Southwest of village	second half of 20th century
Examilia	Analipsi	Southwest of village	1912 (rebuilt 1925)
Examilia	Ayia Triada†	Southwest of village	second half of 20th century
Gonia	Ayios Athanasios	Northeast of Examilia	16th century
Kenchreai	Metamorphosis Sotiros	Center of village	19th century
Kenchreai	Ayia Paraskevi	Between Kenchreai and Xylokeriza	Unknown, now destroyed
Kyras Vrysi	Ayios Ioannis Prodromos	Cemetery east of village	Probably Byzantine
Kyras Vrysi	Ayios Nikolaos	At eastern end of canal	second half of 20th century
Kyras Vrysi	Ayios Dimitrios	Summit of eponymous ridge southwest of village	second half of 20th century
Mt. Oneion	Profitis Elias	On top of mountain	1980–2000
Xylokeriza	Ayia Paraskevi	Center of village	1980–2000
Xylokeriza	Koimisis tis Panayias	Center of village	19th century
Xylokeriza	Ayios Ioannis Prodromos	Cemetery northeast of village	1979

*In the building inscription, this is called παρεκκλήσιον rather than the more common ιερός ναός.

†There are actually three churches within the monastery, but all are new.

their architecture is monotonously the same: all but three are small, simple (mainly one-aisled) vaulted structures.[81] Nonetheless, the architectural decoration, frescoed interiors, current condition, and—occasionally, at least—documentary evidence help in developing a chronology for these buildings. This is not the place to go into a detailed analysis of this information, but one may note several potentially overlapping chronological categories: churches with documented frescoes dating to the Byzantine period (i.e., prior to 1453, since that is the date used by the Greek Archaeological Service and Chatzidakis and Bitha, although it has little significance for the history of Kythera); those with post-Byzantine frescoes; and those listed as parishes in the eight Venetian censuses of the 18th century. This latter evidence is of extraordinary importance. We have been able to identify and place on the map the 25 churches in our survey area mentioned in the censuses. This, then, allows us to see in a spatial dimension how individual parishes grew or shrank over time (in the 18th century), and also to trace individuals through the century and make observations about family size and structure, and changes over time.[82]

Figure 9.10 shows the locations of churches in the survey area plotted on a three-dimensional representation (a digital elevation model, DEM) of the survey area. Figure 9.11 plots the locations of the churches we have dated to the Byzantine period, and Figure 9.12 does the same for the churches of all periods. In both of the latter plots, black polygons and dots, respectively, near each church show the theoretical areas that might reasonably be assigned to each if "everything else were equal," which, of course, does not occur in a real-world situation. We are using the location, date, and other information associated with the Kytherian churches as the starting place for a series of investigations into their role in the landscape and the ways in which they can be used to understand society on the island over time.

81. See discussion in Chatzidakis and Bitha 1997, pp. 22–30.

82. Cf. Maltezou 1980a, 1980b, 1989, 1991; Gregory 2003.

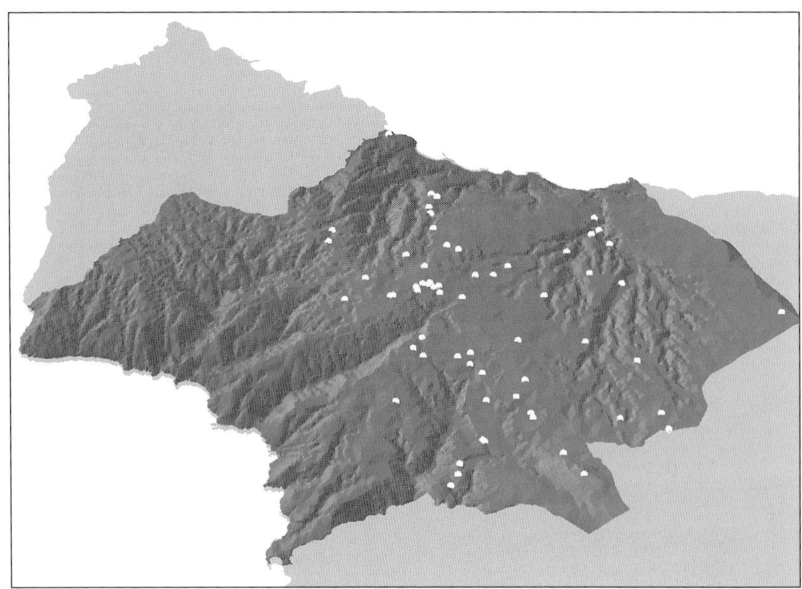

Figure 9.10. Kythera: Locations of churches of all periods shown on a DEM of the APKAS study area. Courtesy APKAS

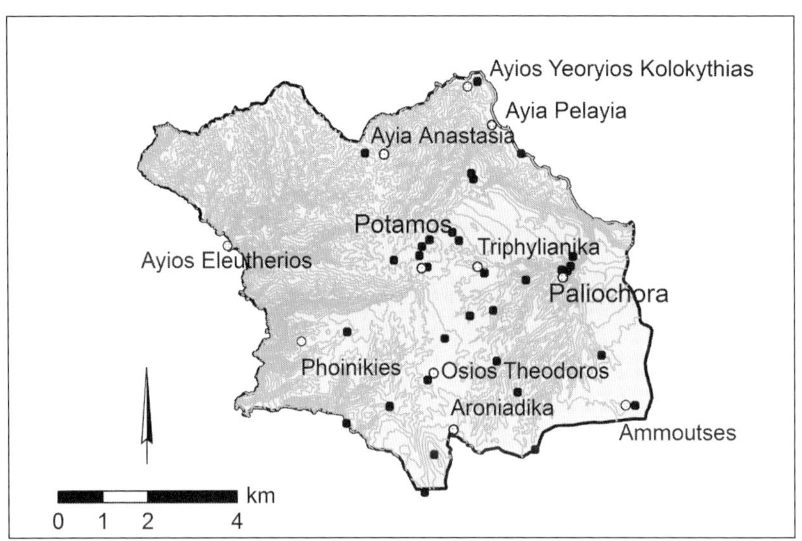

Figure 9.11. Kythera: Locations of churches in the APKAS study area dated to the Byzantine period. Courtesy APKAS

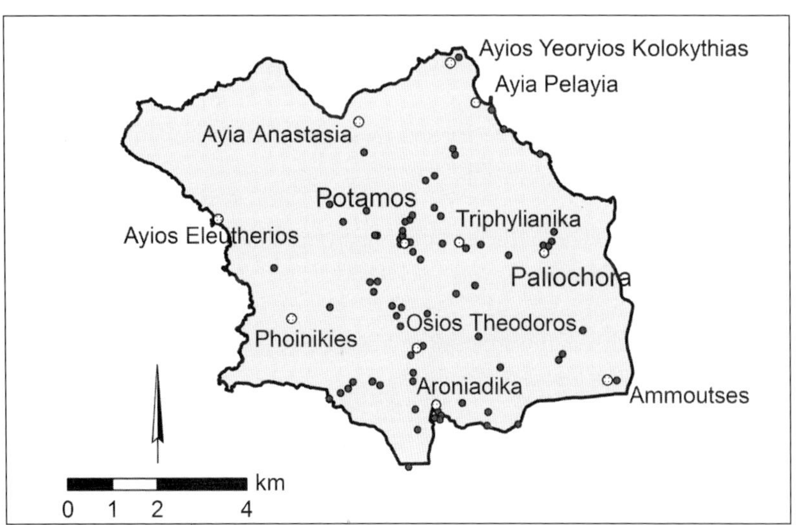

Figure 9.12. Kythera: Locations of churches in the APKAS study area dated to all periods. Courtesy APKAS

FORTIFICATIONS IN THE CORINTHIA AND ON KYTHERA

Certainly an important characteristic of the Ottoman/Venetian period is the construction of fortifications, especially those built by the Venetians in an attempt to defend the Morea in the period after 1687.[83] Much less is known about Ottoman fortifications. On Kythera the Ottoman "domination" lasted only three years, and in the Corinthia the Ottomans had little to fear. With the exception of repairs on Acrocorinth, the most interesting Ottoman fortifications are those on the tiny island of Evraionisos (Omvrios) in the Saronic Gulf, whose purpose long eluded us, but which I now believe were designed to protect the coast of the Corinthia (especially Kenchreai) from attack by western pirates.[84]

There is significantly more information about the Venetian fortifications of the Corinthia.[85] Not much in this connection need be said about the plans for reconstruction of the Hexamilion, which was, during the period 1687–1715, the northern the boundary of the Venetian Morea. As is generally known, this defensive work constructed across the Isthmus of Corinth had been severely damaged by Ottoman attacks in the 15th century, despite major rebuildings by the Emperor Manuel II and the despot (and later emperor) Constantine XI. During the second Venetian period several proposals were advanced for the reconstruction of the great barrier wall; the issue was debated by the Venetian Senate, but nothing came of the attempt.

Nonetheless, Venetian sources refer to projects to build other walls in the Corinthia.[86] We know, from earlier topographic studies, of the earthen forts and walls near Corinth.[87] These were designed both to block a hostile army from passing Corinth to the north and to strengthen the defenses along the Xeropotamos Valley. They were, of course, erected in case the Ottomans were able to get past the Hexamilion (see Figs. 9.1, 9.3).

The EKAS project has recently studied another series of defensive installations in the passes through Mt. Oneion (Fig. 9.13) that were designed to prevent the Ottomans from moving onto the plain of Galataki, and from there either ascending to Sophiko and Epidauros, or turning west and entering the Xeropotamos Valley from the east, again eluding the defenses of Acrocorinth. (Interestingly, these areas did figure significantly in the events following the Battle of Dervenakia in 1822, during the War of Independence.)[88]

These two Venetian fortresses (so dated on the basis of their masonry) are each located so as to block an army seeking to cross one of the passes through Mt. Oneion from north to south. The eastern of these is the Stanotopi Pass, not far from Kenchreai, and west of this is the Maritsa or Trypeio Lithari Pass, between Kenchreai and Xylokeriza.[89] Their exact forms are somewhat different, but the masonry and the basic designs are quite similar and suggest that they were built at the same time, probably either shortly after Morosini's capture of the Peloponnese or in the years before the Ottoman reconquest in 1715.

The major characteristics of each fortification were a barrier wall with fighting platform and terminations defended by rectangular towers (assumed for the west end of the one in the Stanotopi Pass, which has

83. Andrews 1953.
84. Gregory, Kardulias, and Sawmiller 1995.
85. Maltezou 1978.
86. Maltezou 1978.
87. *Corinth* I.1, fig. 46, p. 79.
88. Athousakis 1986, map on p. 189.
89. *Corinth* I.1, pp. 104–106; Stroud 1971; Peppas 1990, pp. 142–145, fig. 16. The foregoing refer to the fortifications in the Stanotopi Pass. As far as we know, that in the Maritsa Pass is not mentioned in any publication, but see now Caraher and Gregory 2006 for a fuller study of both of these Venetian fortifications.

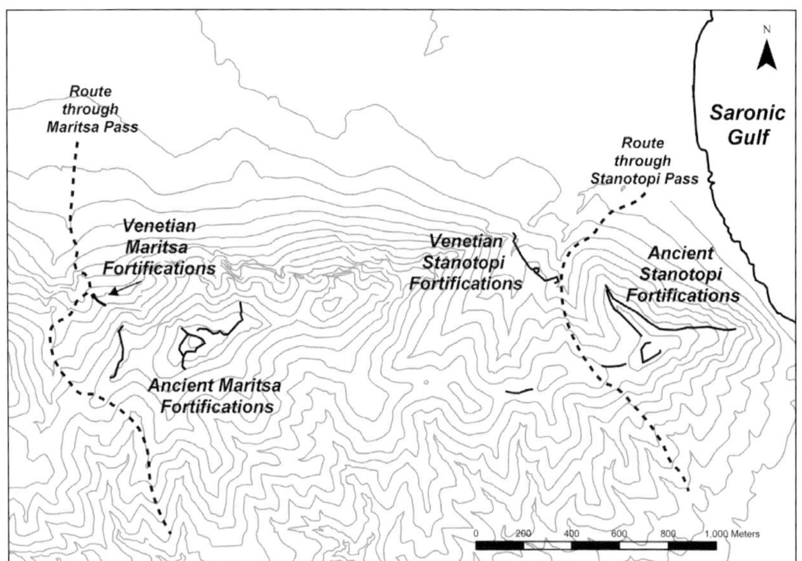

Figure 9.13. The north–south passes through Mt. Oneion in the Eastern Corinthia. Courtesy EKAS

been destroyed by quarrying over the past 30 years). In each case the wall crosses the road through the pass at a point about one-third of the distance to the top and where the road itself changed course and the natural lay of the land made evasion difficult; the tower was intended to block evasion downslope, while providing a base for enfilading gunfire back up across the road. The fortification in the Maritsa Pass continued up the mountain above the tower, in order to prevent an army from ascending the pass in this manner or from getting behind the fortification, where the defenders would have been unprotected.

The design of the fortification in the Stanotopi Pass was more complex, since the wall continued upward to two natural heights, each of which was fortified by nearly rectangular bastions, unprotected to the rear but presenting a formidable obstacle to any force that sought to ascend the pass by an alternative route. We have no idea whether these two fortifications were actually used to defend the Peloponnese at the time of the final Ottoman attack. Probably they were not, since their usefulness depended on the Venetians being able to hold the main lines of attack—at the Hexamilion, along the coastline near Kenchreai, and in the Xeropotamos Valley. The Venetians apparently offered no resistance at any of these points, so the defense of Oneion was probably moot.

On Kythera, the main fortifications after the raid of Hayreddin Barbarossa in 1537 were in areas outside the APKAS survey region: at Chora, Mylopotamos, and Ayios Nikolaos/Avlemonas (Fig. 9.2). Nonetheless, there is interesting documentary evidence, most of it published by Sathas in the 19th century, concerning the attempts to refortify the Byzantine settlement of Ayios Dimitrios/Paliochora, which had been the main center until 1537. Several Venetian governors reported on these attempts and the hope (indeed expectation) that the Venier family would contribute to the undertaking, since they had significant land in the vicinity. The so-called *L'antiche memorie dell'isola di Cerigo* confirms this observation and shows that some of the land under Venier control—even after the Cretan revolt of the nobles against Venetian rule (1363)—was located in the northern part of the island at Phoinikies, apparently within the APKAS survey area.[90]

90. Sathas 1880–1890, p. 304: "in iscambio della Finicchia posto in comune Hortolito," with the note, "Questo è loco petroso et arido, et di niuna utilità." The area of Ortholithos is just to the north of the APKAS area and it is interesting that the text speaks of a "comune" there, to which Phoinikies belonged. Could this be modern Prongi, Gerakari, or another now abandoned settlement identified by local people as Kaloyerous? This area is also close to Ochailais, a now abandoned area in the northwest of the island, mentioned in the notary records; see, e.g., Drakakis 1999, no. 1 (p. 79: Ωχαίλαις), and no. 155 (p. 244: Ωχαλαίς).

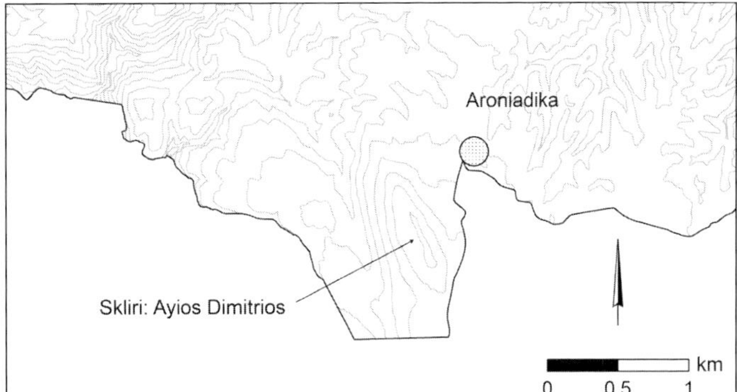

Figure 9.14. Kythera: Southern part of the APKAS study area, showing the location of Ayios Dimitrios west of Aroniadika. Courtesy APKAS

Nonetheless, the governors' reports make it clear that no serious attempt was made to refortify Ayios Dimitrios, in part because its location was vulnerable to attack from the "two mountains" that surrounded it, an obvious reference to the change that had taken place since the emergence of gunpowder as an important factor in Mediterranean warfare. Although the location of Ayios Dimitrios might have been viewed as impregnable in the period before 1450, after that time it could be taken easily by any force able to mount cannon on the heights above it.

Instead, one official suggested the fortification of another place in the general vicinity.[91] This report also mentions that the local inhabitants had fields that were some distance from Paliochora. This supports our hypothesis, based in part on the distribution of late medieval artifacts collected from intensive survey, that the dispersed settlement and land-use pattern of northern Kythera was not, as local legend has it, determined by the sack of Paliochora, but that it was a preexisting situation. Furthermore, the report provides information about the proposed new fortification, near these fields but in a location that could not be reached easily by raiders from the sea. Although certainty is not yet possible, we think that this site is the location of the church of Ayios Dimitrios (a suggestive name for a military establishment, since Dimitrios is one of the premier military saints!) on a height to the west of Aroniadika called Skliri (Fig. 9.14). Although there is substantial evidence for use of this site and remains of what we take to be rough fortifications, it is clear that the plans suggested by the Venetian official were never put into place and that proper, permanent fortifications were never built. Presumably the funds were not forthcoming from the Venetian Senate, and Venice, in any case, had little interest in the northern part of the island.

CONCLUSION

These brief remarks comparing the eastern Corinthia and Kythera are meant to be suggestive rather than definitive, but they imply that the situations in these two regions were very different, in part because of the nature of the two places, but also because of differences in the two systems of imperialism—Ottoman and Venetian. The Ottomans, although they left some regions alone, wished to capitalize on the rich produce of areas that could easily be manipulated.[92] The great plain of the eastern Corinthia had good soil. There cash crops could easily be grown on large estates. Thus,

91. Lamansky 1884, p. 274.

92. McGrew 1985, pp. 22–40; Davis 1991.

the area may have been dominated by large landowners and, in part to maximize output, agricultural work could have been provided by tenant farmers or day laborers. As a result, settlement would have been highly nucleated, thereby fitting the established paradigm for imperial regimes in other periods of Mediterranean history.[93]

On northern Kythera, by contrast, the land is marginal at best and not suited for the development of large estates. In addition, the Venetians were not primarily interested in the production of cash crops; rather, they insisted on the production of wheat as a means to feed their fleet and to make the island self-sufficient (and not dependent on Venetian support). As a result, although much of the land remained in the hands of the "renters," the rapacious families who made use of the land that was owned by the absent Venieri, production remained on a small scale and farmers lived near the land they worked, in villages, hamlets, and perhaps even on small farmsteads scattered across the landscape. This situation seems to be described in the report of 1563 concerning the fields far from Paliochora. Certainly, the appearance and the use of the landscape in these two places would have made a striking contrast.

93. See, e.g., Alcock's (1989, 1993) interpretation of the Roman-period settlement in Greece and large-scale commercial agriculture; also Davis 1991.

REFERENCES

Alcock, S. E. 1989. "Roman Imperialism in the Greek Landscape," *JRA* 2, pp. 5–34.

———. 1993. *Graeca Capta: The Landscapes of Roman Greece,* Cambridge.

Alexander, J. C. 1985. *Toward a History of Post-Byzantine Greece: The Ottoman* Kanunnames *for the Greek Lands, circa 1500–circa 1600,* Athens.

Alexopoulos, C. 1971. "Ὁ πληθυσμὸς τῆς Κορινθίας," *Αρχείον Κορινθιακών Μελετών* 1, pp. 346–386.

Andrews, K. 1953. *Castles of the Morea* (Gennadeion Monographs IV), Princeton.

Athousakis, A. 1986. "Η Μάχη Μύλου-Σκάλας Κεχριών (6 Αυγούστου 1822)," in *Πρακτικά Β΄ Τοπικού Συνεδρίου Κορινθιακών Ερευνών (Λουτράκι 25–27 Μαΐου 1994),* Athens, pp. 183–189.

Balta, E. 1989. *L'Eubée à la fin du XVe siècle: Économie et population, les registres de l'année 1474,* Athens.

———. 1992. "Rural and Urban Population in the *Sancak* of Euripos in the Early 16th Century," *Αρχείον Ευβοϊκών Μελετών* 29, Athens, pp. 55–185.

Beldiceanu, N., and I. Beldiceanu-Steinherr. 1980. "Recherches sur la Morée (1461–1512)," *Südost-Forschungen* 39, pp. 17–75.

———. 1986. "Corinthe et sa région d'après le registre TT 10," *Südost-Forschungen* 45, pp. 37–61.

Bennet, J., J. L. Davis, and F. Zarinebaf-Shahr. 2000. "Pylos Regional Archaeological Project, Part III: Sir William Gell's Itinerary in the Pylia and Regional Landscapes in the Morea in the Second Ottoman Period," *Hesperia* 69, pp. 343–380.

Biris, K. 1960. *Ἀρβανίτες: Οἱ Δωριεῖς τοῦ νεωτέρου ἑλληνισμοῦ,* Athens.

Blegen, C. W. 1930. "Gonia," *MMS* 3, pp. 55–86.

Broodbank, C. 1999. "Kythera Survey: Preliminary Report on the 1998 Season," *BSA* 94, pp. 191–214.

Caraher, W. R., and T. E. Gregory. 2006. "Fortifications of Mount Oneion, Corinthia," *Hesperia* 75, pp. 327–356.

Caraher, W. R., D. Nakassis, and D. K. Pettegrew. 2006. "Siteless Survey and Intensive Data Collection in an Artifact-Rich Environment: Case Studies from the Eastern Corinthia, Greece," *JMA* 19, pp. 7–43.

Chatzidakis, M., and I. Bitha. 1997. *Ευρετήριο βυζαντινών Τοιχογραφιών Ελλάδος* I: *Κύθηρα,* Athens.

Christopoulos, P. N. 1971–1972. "Ἡ περὶ τῶν Κορινθιακῶν περιοχὴ κατὰ τὰ τέλη τοῦ ΙΗ´ αἰῶνας," *Επετηρίς Εταιρείας Στερεοελλαδικών Μελετών* 3, pp. 439–471.

Coldstream, J. N., and G. L. Huxley. 1972. *Kythera: Excavations and Studies Conducted by the University of Pennsylvania Museum and the British School at Athens,* London.

Corinth I.1 = H. N. Fowler and R. Stillwell, *Corinth* I: *Introduction, Topography, Architecture,* Cambridge, Mass. 1932.

Coroneos, C., L. Diacopoulos, T. E. Gregory, I. Johnson, J. Noller, S. A. Paspalas, and A. Wilson. 2002. "The Australian Paliochora-Kythera Archaeological Survey: Field Seasons 1999–2000," *MeditArch* 15, pp. 126–143.

Davies, S. 2002. "Venetian Corinth in 1700: The Letters of Argiro Besagni," *Thesaurismata* 32, pp. 235–250.

Davis, J. L. 1991. "Contributions to a Mediterranean Rural Archaeology: Historical Case Studies from the Ottoman Cyclades," *JMA* 4, pp. 131–216.

Diacopoulos, L. 2004. "The Archaeology of Modern Greece," in *Mediterranean Archaeological Landscapes: Current Issues,* ed. E. F. Athanassopoulos and L. Wandsnider, Philadelphia, pp. 183–198.

Dodwell, E. 1819. *A Classical and Topographical Tour through Greece, during the Years 1801, 1805, and 1806* 2, London.

Dokos, K. 1971–1972. "Ἡ ἐν Πελοποννήσῳ ἐκκλησιαστικὴ περιουσία κατὰ τὴν περίοδον τῆς Β´ Ἑνετοκρατίας," *Byzantinisch-neugriechische Jahrbücher* 21, pp. 43–168.

———. 1975. *Ἡ Στερεὰ Ἑλλὰς κατὰ τὸν ἑνετοτουρκικὸν πόλεμον, 1684–1699, καὶ ὁ Σαλόνων Φιλόθεος,* Athens.

Dokos, K., and G. Panagopoulos. 1993. *Το βενετικό κτηματολόγιο της Βοστίτσας,* Athens.

Drakakis, E. G. 1999. *Εμμανουήλ Κασιμάτης, νοτάριος Κυθήρων (1560–1582),* Athens.

———. 2003. *Ληξιαρχικά βιβλία Κυθήρων: Ενορία Παναγίας Ιλαριωτίσσης Ποταμού, 1731–1856,* Athens.

Expédition scientifique = M. Bory de Saint-Vincent, *Expédition scientifique de Morée: Section des sciences physiques* 2. *Géographie et géologie,* Paris 1834.

Forbes, H. 2000. "Security and Settlement in the Medieval and Post-Medieval Peloponnesos, Greece: 'Hard' History versus Oral History," *JMA* 13, pp. 204–224.

Frangakis, E., and J. M. Wagstaff. 1987. "Settlement Pattern Change in the Morea (Peloponnisos), c. A.D. 1700–1830," *Byzantine and Modern Greek Studies* 11, pp. 163–192.

Frangakis-Syrett, E., and J. M. Wagstaff. 1992. "The Height Zonation of Population in the Morea, c. 1830," *BSA* 87, pp. 439–446.

Gell, W. 1810. *Argolis: The Itinerary of Greece: With a Commentary on Pausanias and Strabo and an Account of the Monuments of Antiquity at Present Existing in That Country in the Years 1801–6,* London.

Given, M., and A. B. Knapp. 2003. *The Sydney Cyprus Survey Project: Social Approaches to Regional Archaeological Survey* (Monumenta archaeologica 21), Los Angeles.

Gregory, T. E. 2003. "Churches, Landscape, and the Population of Northern Kythera in Byzantine and Early Modern Times," in *First International Congress of Kytherian Studies: Kythera, Myth and Reality* 1, Kythera, pp. 219–236.

———. 2004. "Less Is Better: The Quality of Ceramic Evidence from Archaeological Survey and Practical Proposals for Low-Impact Survey in a Mediterranean Context," in *Mediterranean Archaeological Landscapes: Current Issues,* ed. E. F. Athanassopoulos and L. Wandsnider, Philadelphia, pp. 15–36.

Gregory, T. E., and P. N. Kardulias. 1990. "Geophysical and Surface Surveys in the Byzantine Fortress at Isthmia," *Hesperia* 59, pp. 467–511.

Gregory, T. E., P. N. Kardulias, and J. Sawmiller. 1995. "Bronze Age and Late Antique Exploitation of an Islet in the Saronic Gulf, Greece," *JFA* 22, pp. 3–21.

Herrin, J. 1972. "Byzantine Kythera," in Coldstream and Huxley 1972, pp. 41–51.

Ince, G. E., T. Koukoulis, and D. Smyth. 1987. "Paliochora: Survey of a Byzantine City on the Island of Kythera. Preliminary Report," *BSA* 82, pp. 95–106.

Isthmia V = T. E. Gregory, *The Hexamilion and the Fortress* (*Isthmia* V), Princeton 1993.

İz, F., H. C. Hony, and A. D. Alderson. 1992. *The Oxford Turkish Dictionary,* 3rd ed., Oxford.

Kalliyeros, E. P. 2002. *Κυθηραϊκά επώνυμα: Ιστορική, γεωγραφική και γλωσσική προσέγγιση,* Athens.

Kordosis, M. S. 1981. *Συμβολὴ στὴν ἱστορία καὶ τοπογραφία τῆς περιοχῆς Κορίνθου στοὺς Μέσους Χρόνους,* Athens.

Koukoulis, T. 1992. "A Late Byzantine Windmill at Kythera," in *ΦΙΛΟΛΑΚΩΝ: Studies in Honour of Hector Catling,* ed. J. M. Sanders, London, pp. 155–163.

———. 1997. "Catalog of Churches," in Mee and Forbes 1997, pp. 92–100.

Koukoulis, T., G. E. Ince, A. N. Ballantyne, and D. Smyth. 1989. "Paliochora: Survey of a Byzantine City on the Island of Kythera, Second Report," *BSA* 84, pp. 407–416.

Koutivas, S. A. 1968. *Οἱ Νοταράδες στὴν ὑπηρεσία τοῦ ἔθνους καὶ τῆς ἐκκλησίας,* Athens.

Kremmydas, V. 1972. *Τὸ ἐμπόριο τῆς Πελοποννήσου στὸ 18ο αἰῶνα (1715–1792),* Athens.

———. 1980. *Συγκυρία καὶ ἐμπόριο στὴν προεπαναστατικὴ Πελοπόννησο 1793–1821,* Athens.

Lamansky, V. 1884. *Secrets d'état de Venise,* St. Petersburg.

Leake, W. M. 1830. *Travels in the Morea* 3, London.

Leontsinis, G. N. 1982. "The Rise and Fall of the Confraternity Churches of Kythera," *JÖBG* 32, no. 6, pp. 59–68.

———. 1987. *The Island of Kythera: A Social History (1700–1863),* Athens.

Liata, E. D. 2002. *Το Ναύπλιο και η ενδοχώρα του από τον 17ο στον 18ο αι.: Οικιστικά μεγέθη και κατανομή της γης,* Athens.

Maltezou, C. A. 1978. "Βενετσιανικὲς ἐκθέσεις γιὰ τὴν οχύρωση τοῦ Ἰσθμοῦ τῆς Κορίνθου στὰ τέλη τοῦ 17ου αἰῶνα," in *Πρακτικὰ τοῦ Α´ Διεθνοῦς Συνεδρίου Πελοποννησιακῶν Σπουδῶν, Σπάρτη, 7–14 Σεπτεμβρίου 1975* 3, Athens, pp. 269–276.

———. 1980a. "A Contribution to the Historical Geography of the Island of Kythira during the Venetian Occupation," in *Charanis Studies: Essays in Honour of Peter Charanis,* ed. A. E. Laiou-Thomadakis, New Brunswick, N.J., pp. 151–175.

———. 1980b. "Cythère: Société et économie pendant la période de la domination vénitienne," *BalkSt* 21, pp. 33–43.

———. 1989. "*Ειδήσεις για ναούς και μονές στα Κύθηρα από αρχειακές πηγές,*" in *Πρακτικά του Ε΄ Διεθνούς Πανιονίου Συνεδρίου, Αργοστόλι–Ληξούρι, 17–21 Μαΐου* 1986, ed. G. N. Moschopoulos, Argostoli, pp. 269–288.

———. 1991. *Venetian Influence on Kythera,* Athens.

———, ed. 1997. *Απογραφές πληθυσμού Κυθήρων (18ος αι.),* 3 vols., Athens.

McGrew, W. W. 1985. *Land and Revolution in Modern Greece, 1800–1881: The Transition in the Tenure and Exploitation of Land from Ottoman Rule to Independence,* Kent, Ohio.

Mee, C., and H. Forbes, eds. 1997. *A Rough and Rocky Place: The Landscape and Settlement History of the Methana Peninsula, Greece. Results of the Methana Survey Project,* Liverpool.

Newhard, J. M. L. 2005. Rev. of Given and Knapp 2003, in *BMCR* 2005.05.04, posted online at http://ccat.sas.upenn.edu/bmcr/2005/2005-05-04.html, accessed November 11, 2005.

Orlandos, A. K. 1935. "Βυζαντινοὶ ναοὶ τῆς ἀνατολικῆς Κορινθίας," *Ἀρχεῖον τῶν βυζαντινῶν μνημείων τῆς Ἑλλάδος* 1, pp. 53–90.

Pacifico, P. A. 1704. *Breve descrizzione corografica del Peloponneso o Morea,* 2nd ed., Venice.

Panayiotopoulos, V. 1985. *Πληθυσμός και οικισμοί της Πελοποννήσου: 13ος–18ος αιώνας,* Athens.

Papadaki, A. 2001. *Ληξιαρχικά βιβλία Κυθήρων: Ενορία Εσταυρωμένου Χώρας 1671–1812,* Athens.

Peppas, I. E. 1990. *Μεσαιωνικές σελίδες Αργολίδος, Αρκαδίας, Κορινθίας,* Athens.

Pouqueville, F. C. H. L. 1826–1827. *Voyage dans la Grèce: Deuxième édition revue, corrigée et augmentée* 4, Paris.

Redhouse, J. W. 1987. *Turkish and English Lexicon, New Edition,* Beirut.

Richards, L. E., ed. 1906. *Letters and Journals of Samuel Gridley Howe: The Greek Revolution,* London.

Robinson, H. S. 1976. "Excavations at Corinth: Temple Hill, 1968–1972," *Hesperia* 45, pp. 203–239.

Robinson, R. C. W. 1985. "Tobacco Pipes of Corinth and of the Athenian Agora," *Hesperia* 54, pp. 149–203.

Sakellarakis, I. 1996. "Minoan Religious Influence in the Aegean: The Case of Kythera," *BSA* 91, pp. 81–99.

Sakellariou, M. B. 1939. *Ἡ Πελοπόννησος κατὰ τὴν Δευτέραν Τουρκοκρατίαν (1715–1821)* (Texte und Forschungen zur byzantinisch-neugriechischen Philologie 33), Athens.

Sathas, K. [1869] 1962. *Τουρκοκρατούμενη Ἑλλάς, 1453–1821,* repr. Athens.

———. 1880–1890. *Documents inédits relatifs à l'histoire de la Grèce au Moyen Âge* 6, Athens.

Sotiriou, G. 1923. "Μεσαιωνικὰ μνημεῖα Κυθήρων," *Κυθηραϊκὴ Επιθεώρησις* 1, pp. 313–332.

Spon, J. 1678. *Voyage d'Italie, de Dalmatie, de Grèce, et du Levant,* 2 vols., Lyon.

Stedman, N. 1996. "Land Use and Settlement in Post-Medieval Central Greece: An Interim Discussion," in *The Archaeology of Medieval Greece,* ed. P. Lock and G. D. R. Sanders, Oxford, pp. 179–192.

Stroud, R. 1971. "An Ancient Fort on Mt. Oneion," *Hesperia* 40, pp. 127–145.

Sutton, S. B., ed. 2000. *Contingent Countryside: Settlement, Economy, and Land Use in the Southern Argolid since 1700,* Stanford.

Tartaron, T. A., T. E. Gregory, D. J. Pullen, J. S. Noller, R. M. Rothaus, J. L. Rife, L. Tzortzopoulou-Gregory, R. Schon, W. R. Caraher, D. K. Pettegrew, and D. Nakassis. 2006. "The Eastern Korinthia Archaeological Survey: Integrated Methods for a Dynamic Landscape," *Hesperia* 75, pp. 453–523.

Taylor, B. 1859. *Travels to Greece and Russia with an Excursion to Crete,* New York.

Topping, P. 1976. "The Population of the Morea (1685–1715)," *Πελοποννησιακά* 1, pp. 119–128.

———. 1980. "Albanian Settlements in Medieval Greece: Some Venetian Testimonies," in *Charanis Studies: Essays in Honour of Peter Charanis,* ed. A. E. Laiou-Thomadakis, New Brunswick, N.J., pp. 261–271.

Tsitsilias, P. 1993–1994. *Η ιστορία των Κυθήρων* (Εταιρεία Κυθηραϊκών Μελετών 2–3), 2 vols., Athens.

Turner, W. 1820. *Journal of a Tour in the Levant,* London.

Veinstein, G. 1991. "On the *Çiftlik* Debate," in *Landholding and Commercial Agriculture in the Middle East,* ed. Ç. Keyder and F. Tabak, Albany, pp. 35–53.

Vroom, J. 2003. *After Antiquity: Ceramics and Society in the Aegean from the 7th to 20th Century A.C. A Case Study from Boeotia, Central Greece* (Archaeological Studies, Leiden University 10), Leiden.

Waterhouse, H., and R. Hope Simpson. 1961. "Prehistoric Laconia: Part II," *BSA* 56, pp. 148–160.

Wheler, G. 1682. *A Journey into Greece by George Wheler, Esq., in Company of Dr. Spon of Lyons,* London.

Whitelaw, T. M. 1991. "The Ethnoarchaeology of Recent Rural Settlement and Land Use in Northwest Keos," in *Landscape Archaeology as Long-Term History: Northern Keos in the Cycladic Islands* (Monumenta archaeologica 16), ed. J. F. Cherry, J. L. Davis, and E. Mantzourani, Los Angeles, pp. 403–454.

Williams, H. W. 1820. *Travels in Italy, Greece, and the Ionian Islands in a Series of Letters, Descriptive of Manners, Scenery, and the Fine Arts* 2, Edinburgh.

Wright, J. C., J. F. Cherry, J. L. Davis, E. Mantzourani, S. B. Sutton, and R. F. Sutton, Jr. 1990. "The Nemea Valley Archaeological Project: A Preliminary Report," *Hesperia* 59, pp. 579–659.

Wyse, T. 1865. *An Excursion in the Peloponnesus in the Year 1858* 2, London.

Fragmentary "Geo-metry": Early Modern Landscapes of the Morea and Cerigo in Text, Image, and Archaeology

by John Bennet

BACKGROUND

My goal here is twofold.[1] First, I outline examples of how a combination of text, image, and archaeology has facilitated archaeological-historical research in the context of two regional studies projects in which I have been involved: the Pylos Regional Archaeological Project (henceforth PRAP) and—somewhat programmatically—the Kythera Island Project (henceforth KIP). Second, I suggest how the use by controlling groups of what might broadly be termed "geo-metrical"—that is, land-measuring—techniques might offer insights into the ways in which control over land was conceptualized and facilitated by those groups and by indigenous populations.

Although the link between the two areas may appear entirely contingent on my own experience, they are both interlinked in the shifting patterns of domination in the Aegean between Western (primarily Venetian) and Eastern (Ottoman) powers. In some ways their histories are inversions of each other. Messenia, Ottoman from before 1500 to 1829, experienced a 30-year period of Venetian control, ending in 1715, during which, as I discuss later, cartography was used as a controlling strategy. Kythera, on the other hand, was a Venetian possession almost continuously from the 13th century until 1797, experiencing Ottoman control for a three-year period (1715–1718) in the wake of the same reconquest that brought the Morea back into the Ottoman Empire. As I hope to demonstrate, the 30 years of Venetian control in the Morea was the exception rather than the rule with regard to systems of land measurement in the wider region.

My interest in early modern landscapes arises from a broader intellectual fascination with the integration of textual and material evidence, particularly in relation to spatial structures. I originally explored this topic in my doctoral research on Late Bronze Age Crete, but, after participating in fieldwork on the Kea survey with Jack Davis and John Cherry, I examined the data available to reconstruct changing settlement patterns on the island from the late Byzantine period to 1821.[2] The results of that particular project were published some time ago and I do not dwell on them here, but I want to highlight one aspect illustrated by Rosaccio's late-16th-century map of Kea (Fig. 10.1), which is not atypical of premodern representations of the island.

1. I thank Siriol Davies for inviting me to participate in the workshop "Between Venice and Istanbul," and her and Jack Davis, as editors of this volume, for their tolerance and assistance. I thank particularly Jack Davis, Fariba Zarinebaf, and Debi Harlan, all of whom contributed to the synergy of research in Messenia. Equally, research on Kythera, still ongoing, has been greatly facilitated by the project directors, Cyprian Broodbank and Vangelio Kiriatzi; by the director and staff of the Local Historical Archive (Τοπικό Ιστορικό Αρχείο); and by Andrew Bevan, Siriol Davies, and Debi Harlan. This chapter has benefited from information and comments from Andrew Bevan, Cyprian Broodbank, Stella Chrysochoou, Siriol Davies, Jack Davis, Debi Harlan, Machiel Kiel, Vangelio Kiriatzi, Mark Pearce, and Malcolm Wagstaff. It is offered in the spirit of crossing academic boundaries, and none of the above should be held responsible for any errors of fact or judgment that I may have introduced.

2. Bennet and Voutsaki 1991. The conclusions drawn there are relevant to Machiel Kiel's chapter in this volume (Chap. 2); see also the Introduction.

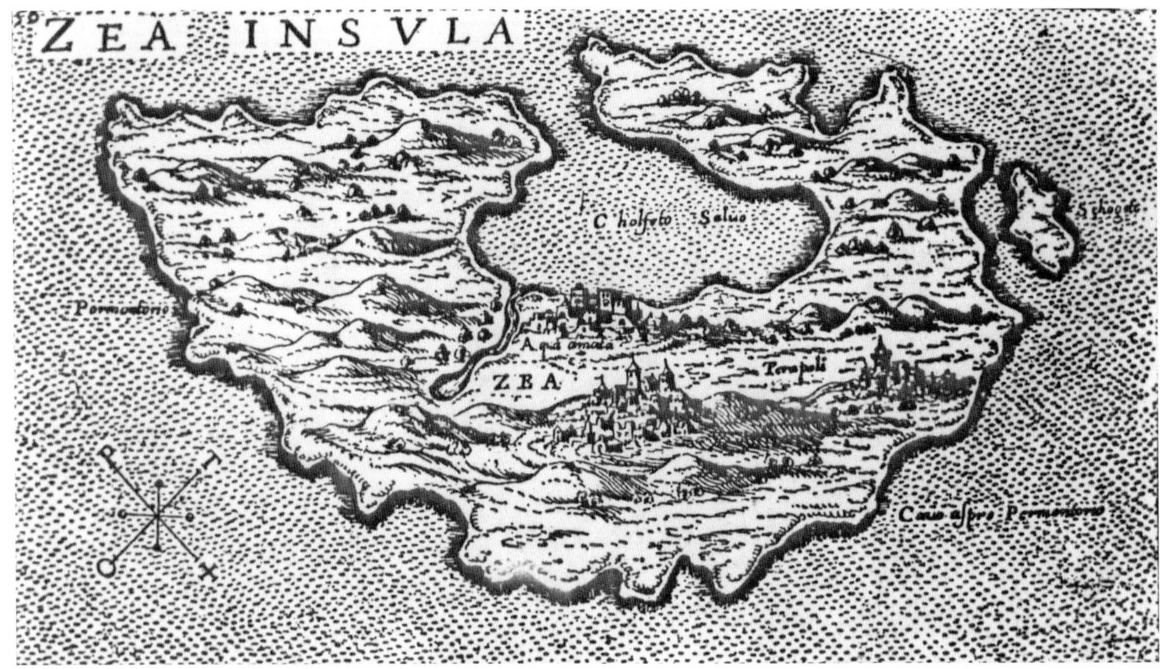

Figure 10.1. Map of the island of Kea (Zea). Rosaccio 1598, p. 62

Although we think of maps as offering unambiguous spatial information, they are constructions, not reflections, and demonstrate the way in which space is perceived, rather than the way it appears. So, in this case, the size of the Bay of Korisia is significantly exaggerated, reflecting its importance as a safe harbor, as the map itself proclaims.

Representations such as Rosaccio's map remained in the back of my mind as I became involved in PRAP's program of regional studies field research in southwestern Messenia from 1991 to 1995, and as I became interested in reconstructing the Late Bronze Age political geography of the area, for which we have no maps but only texts in the Linear B script.[3] Fortunately, these texts display two features common to mapping in many regions in different periods: the "itinerary," or list of places in fixed order, reflecting routes between them; and the "conceptual" map view, reflecting how the landscape is perceived by someone living within it. In this instance, it is the prominent ridge—the Aigaleon range—running northwest to southeast across the region, to the east of the so-called Palace of Nestor at Pylos, that shapes the "conceptual" map.

Both of these geographical concepts emphasize "practice": the experience of moving through a landscape along familiar, well-traveled paths, from which the landscape will offer certain characteristic views.

If we look at a different map of the island of Kea (Fig. 10.2), we can see a similar element of "practice" behind this map of the harbor, designed to aid the navigator by showing what lies on the skyline when approaching: the row of windmills on the ridge above Chora, with a solitary tower to the right.

This map also offers, however, what we take for granted in the kinds of maps with which we are utterly familiar: a plan view with a compass rose and water depths within the bay indicated by numerals. Much of the history of Western cartography deals with the evolution of entirely conventional means of representing the three-dimensional space of the real world in two

3. Bennet 1995, 1998, 1999.

Figure 10.2. The approach to Kea (Zea) harbor. Seller 1753, p. 65, by permission of the Syndics of Cambridge University Library

dimensions on a map sheet: the use of contour lines, symbols for different types of buildings, symbols for vegetation, and so on.[4] I characterize these three modes of geo-metrical representation as the "itinerary" mode, the "plan" mode, and the "conceptual" or, for reasons that will become clear later, "performative" mode. Bearing these categories in mind, I explore the two case studies mentioned earlier.

OTTOMAN MESSENIA

Given my experience on Kea and in Messenia, plus some "practical" experience of the local Messenian landscape gained through field walking in the region, I was excited about the possibility of collaborating on a project to examine parts of the PRAP survey area—formerly Navarino or Anavarin—through an Ottoman documentary source located, copied, and translated by Fariba Zarinebaf.[5]

The document is a section of a detailed tax-survey register, a *mufassal defter, Tapu Tahrir* (TT) 880, in the Başbakanlık Archives in Istanbul dealing with the district *(kaza)* of Anavarin. It contains information about 49 properties: two forts (*kale*s), four villages (*karye*s), 24 estates (*çiftlik*s), and 19 areas of uninhabited agricultural land (*mazraᶜa*s). Of significant interest is that it was compiled within months of the Ottoman reconquest of the Morea in 1715; it is dated 20 *Muharram* A.H. 1128, or January 15, 1716.

4. See, e.g., Harvey 1980.
5. Zarinebaf, Bennet, and Davis 2005.

The first entry in the Anavarin section of the document—the *çiftlik* of Ali Hoca—shows the basic layout of most entries (Fig. 10.3):

A heading, giving the type of property *(çiftlik)* and its status;
A description of real property (structures, orchards, etc.), with dimensions;
A list of the sharecroppers *(ortakçıyan),* with their property (sheep, pigs, houses);
A list of the yield *(hasil):* head tax *(ispence);* tithes *(uşr)* on wheat, barley, oats, and the like; plus taxes *(resm)* on sheep, presses, etc.

Unusually, in the case of Ali Hoca there is a section that gives an estimate of the productivity of crops grown in the area, expressed as the ratio of seed grain to yield and the expected value of the yield in Ottoman silver coin *(akçe).*

Lastly, written diagonally along the bottom of the entry are the boundaries of the property, in this case, "This *çiftlik* is bounded by Çurukdun, Klurun, Vidizmadun [Βυθίσματα], Mavriliçne [Μαύρη Λίμνη], and Evluyol."

Typically, a document like this would be compiled immediately following the incorporation of territory into the empire—as this one was—or on other occasions such as the accession of a new sultan. Where an earlier document was available, it would be used as the basis for compiling the new one. Such documents were, it seems, compiled "in the field" by Ottoman scribes, presumably with a translator, who gathered data from local inhabitants, as is clear in a number of instances in this document.[6]

In the course of our research on this document, my colleagues and I decided that we would attempt to locate as many as we could of the place-names mentioned in the document. In general, villages and estates were often identifiable with recent settlements, but some settlements in the region have been deliberately renamed. A prominent example of such renaming in the region is the application, in May 1915, of the ancient name "Koryphasion" to the settlement formerly known as Osman Ağa at least since the mid-17th century.[7] Other settlements have been abandoned and a few new ones established. Identification was a greater problem for the abandoned farms (*mazraᶜa*s), since many of these have remained uninhabited and are known solely as rural place-names, not as names of human habitations. There are more than 250 place-names in TT880. In addition to the 49 property headings, the remaining 200 or so are local place-names that appear among the lists of boundaries arranged obliquely at the end of each entry.

In order to achieve the goal of identifying all place-names with actual locations, we exploited various resources:

1. Local 1:5,000 and 1:50,000 maps;
2. Older maps, especially the one prepared by the Expédition scientifique de Morée,[8] together with unpublished earlier drafts at larger scale held in the National Historical Museum of Athens (see below, Figs. 10.5 and 10.6, respectively);[9]
3. An unpublished Venetian map, probably dating to ca. 1700, preserved in the Austrian State Archive (Fig. 10.4 below);[10]
4. An inventory of several thousand place-names in the region published in 1967 by Demetrius Georgacas and William A. McDonald;[11]
5. Local informants.

6. On the process, see Kiel 1997, p. 317; cf. İnalcık 1954, pp. 110–111; Zarinebaf, Bennet, and Davis 2005, pp. 116–117, 145–147.
7. Politis 1915, p. 281.
8. *Atlas* 1835, pl. III.5.
9. I thank Philippos Mazarakis-Ainian for permitting Jack Davis and me to consult these draft maps (item no. 1870) in the National Historical Museum. (It should be noted that in Zarinebaf, Bennet, and Davis 2005, p. 121, n. 35, these maps are erroneously referenced as accession no. 6334.)
10. Katsiardi-Hering 1993, p. 302. I thank the War Archive of the Austrian State Archive for supplying a reproduction of this map (cat. no. B.III.a.124.A), entitled "Doi territorii Modon et Navarino divisi dal color rosso," and shortly to be published, together with others for the Peloponnese, by Olga Katsiardi-Hering.
11. Georgacas and McDonald 1967, where each place-name is given a unique number.

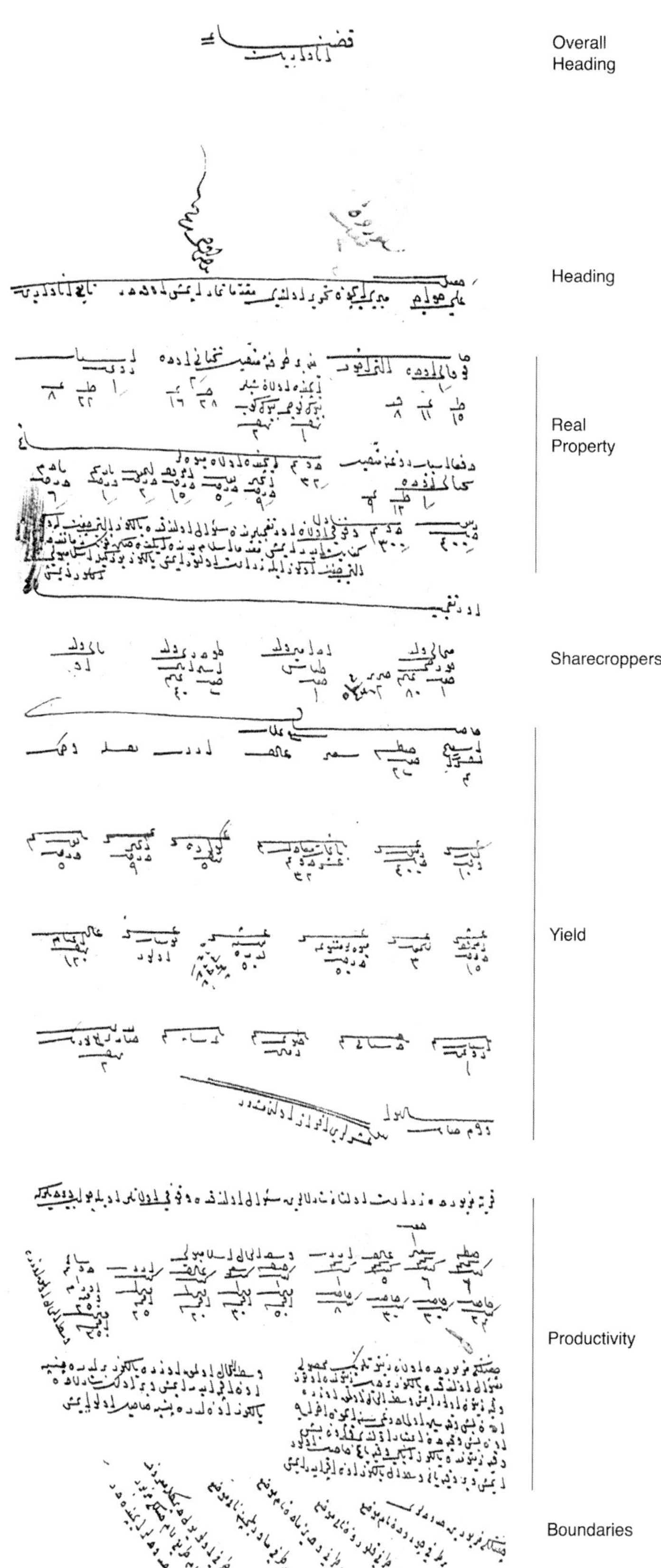

Figure 10.3. TT880: Entry no. 1, Ali Hoca. After Zarinebaf, Bennet, and Davis 2005, CD-ROM facsimile edition of *Tapu Tahrir* 880, p. 78; translation on pp. 56–58. Reproduced by permission of the Başbakanlık Archives, Istanbul

Figure 10.4. Excerpt from an unpublished Venetian map of the territory of Modon and Navarino, ca. 1700, showing the location of "Casanaga." War Archive of the Austrian State Archive, cat. no. B.III.a.124.A, by permission

Unfortunately, Venetian detailed cadasters *(catastici particolari)* of the type that were prepared for some other parts of the Morea, such as Vostizza (modern Aigion), are not preserved for this part of the Peloponnese.[12] These offer great detail, including verbal descriptions of boundaries and accompanying maps *(disegni).*

Two examples highlight the difficulties and possibilities in attempting to link textual information such as that offered by TT880 with specific locations on the ground.[13]

Hasan Ağa (TT880, entry no. 5) does not appear as a place-name on modern maps, but we were given the name by a local informant on the site.[14] The name also appears on the Expédition scientifique's *Atlas* map and is listed in Georgacas and McDonald, associated with the nearby modern villages of Lefki (formerly Mouzousta) and Tragana.[15] In TT880, the *çiftlik*'s boundaries are given as "the great valley with the river [presumably the Selas, which runs immediately below the site], Bey Konaki [the 'mansion of the Bey,' unfortunately unlocatable], Rustem Ağa *çiftlik*, and the sea." When viewed on a modern map, this represents an extensive territory, and obviously one that would be difficult, if not impossible, to define from archaeological remains alone.

The unpublished Venetian map mentioned earlier shows not only the location of Hasan Ağa (as "Casanaga"), but also its boundaries, which indeed do extend to the coast (Fig. 10.4). Moreover, it helps explain a textual

12. Dokos and Panagopoulos 1993; Katsiardi-Hering 1993, pp. 289–290.

13. For more detailed discussion of these and other place-names mentioned in TT880, see Zarinebaf, Bennet, and Davis 2005, esp. chap. 3.

14. Brief studies in Davis et al. 1997, pp. 481–482; Alcock 1998; Bennet, Davis, and Zarinebaf-Shahr 2000, pp. 365–366.

15. Georgacas and McDonald 1967, p. 280 (no. 8452).

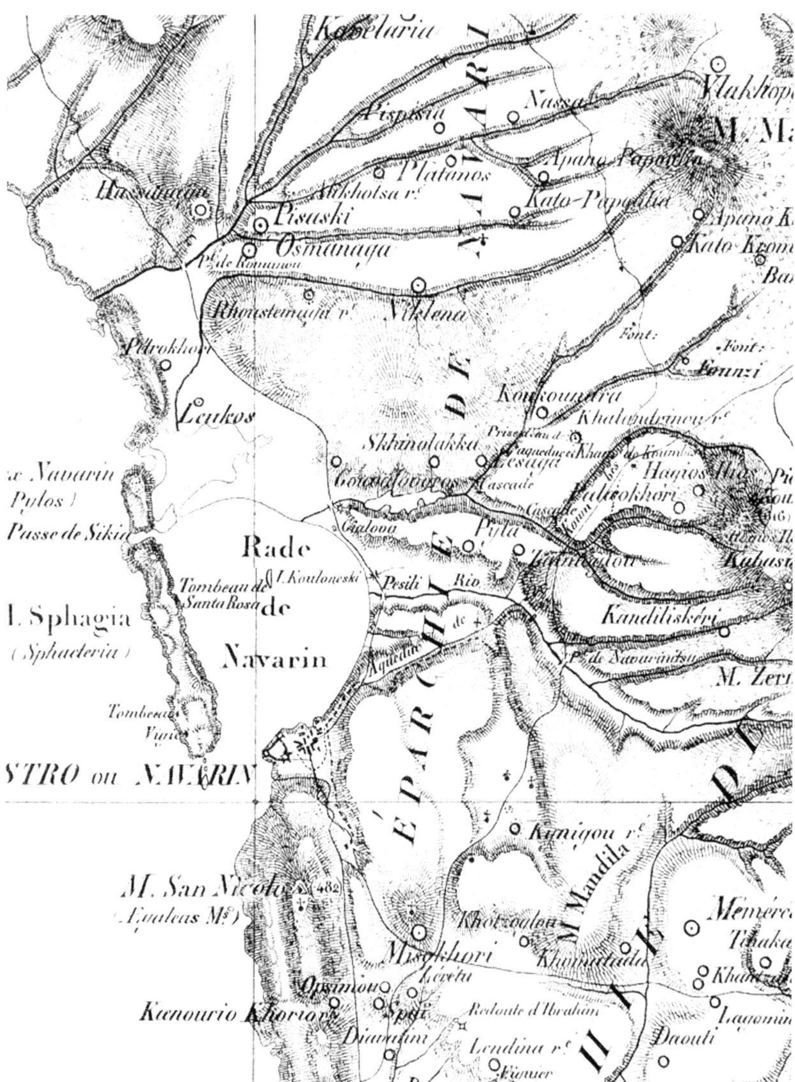

Figure 10.5. Excerpt from the *Atlas* prepared by the Expédition scientifique de Morée. *Atlas* 1835, pl. III.5

reference in TT880, where the next entry, the *çiftlik* of Rustem Ağa, is said to be "attached" to other *çiftlik*s: "Alafine, Hasan Ağa, and Rustem Ağa are attached and share the same taxes and *tarla*s [arable land, fields]."

The Venetian map shows a single boundary around Alafine, Hasan Ağa, and Rustem Ağa, as well as around the villages of Curu, Pisaschi piccolo, and Pisaschi grande (unlike in TT880). The Venetian map also solves a toponymic conundrum that puzzled us for some time, my second example. In the Expédition scientifique's *Atlas*, "Rhoustemaga" is not located in the same position as it is on the unpublished Venetian map (Fig. 10.5, straddling the easting north-northeast of Leukos). That this is a simple error on the *Atlas* map is demonstrated by an unpublished earlier draft of this region, where Rustem Ağa ("Roustamaga") appears in the correct location (Fig. 10.6, immediately below the northing, marked with a rectangle by me).[16]

No modern villages exist in either of these locations, but PRAP fieldwork at both defined archaeological sites with early modern material. They are designated here as PRAP POSIs (places of special interest) C4 (Hasan Ağa) and B6 (Rustem Ağa).[17]

16. Although it is interesting to note that, on this draft, nearby Hasan Ağa is incorrectly labeled "Lexaga." For a broader study of the process by which the *Atlas* was produced, see Saïtas 1999.

17. Davis et al. 1997, p. 393, fig. 2, pp. 481–482. For the term "POSI," see Davis et al. 1997, p. 401.

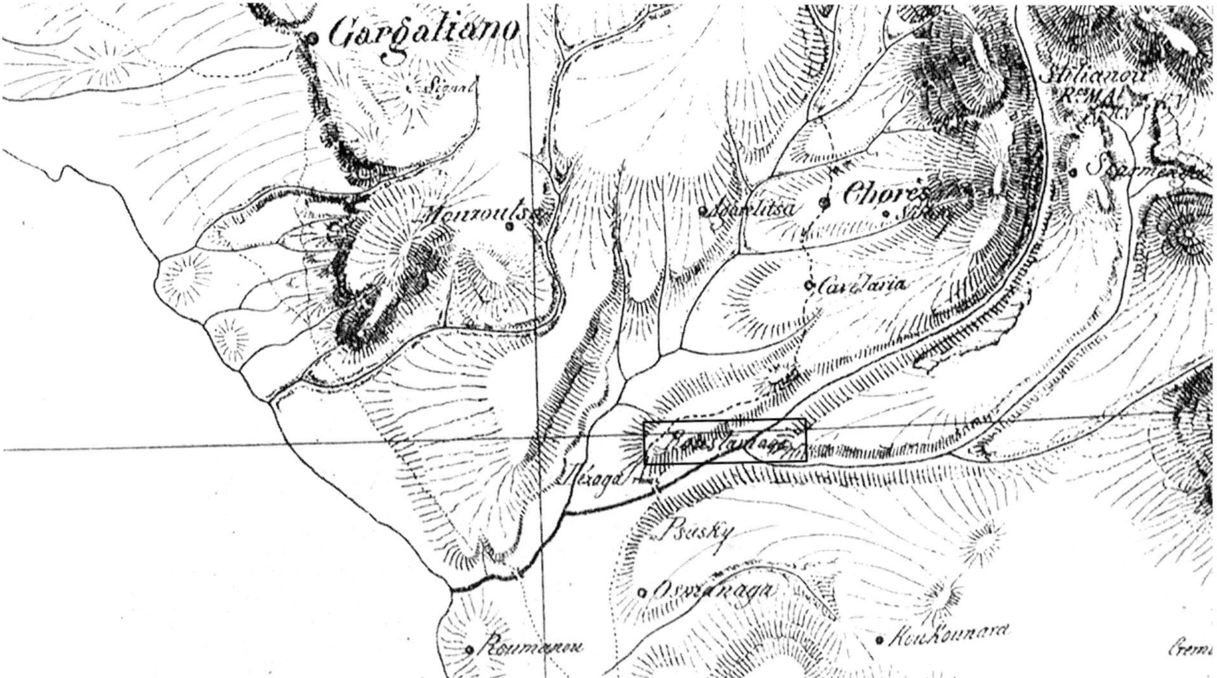

Figure 10.6. Detail of an Expédition scientifique de Morée draft map in the National Historical Museum, Athens (item no. 1870). Reproduced by permission of the Historical and Ethnological Society of Greece (rectangle added by author)

Why is this important? A minor point of interest is that the solution came initially from textual information in TT880—where the implied relative locations of Hasan Ağa and Rustem Ağa were inconsistent with the published Expédition *Atlas*—not from a map, although plan-view maps have been enormously useful to us in many other cases. More significant is the fact that detailed examination of the documentary resources should allow the identification of specific locations that might then be examined archaeologically. Without both PRAP's fieldwork and our study of TT880 and other documents, Rustem Ağa would not have been definitively located, and, equally, the status of our POSI B6 would have remained enigmatic: how would we have accounted for an apparently isolated settlement dated loosely to the early modern period? Documentary evidence refines this picture and suggests it was occupied before, during, and after the Venetian occupation right up until the early 19th century.

There is also a broader implication. Rustem Ağa is one of a small number of *çiftlik*s listed in TT880 that existed prior to the Venetian reconquest of the region in 1685 and are known only (or predominantly) by their Turkish names.[18] The majority of the *çiftlik*s and *mazraᶜa*s in TT880 either have local village names (Platne = "Platanos"; Pispitsa = "Pispis(i)a" [now modern Myrsinohori]), or have double names of the pattern "village name or *çiftlik* of [Turkish personal name]," such as "Papla [= "Papoulia"] or *çiftlik* of Mustafa Ağa." The location of these particular "Ottoman" *çiftlik*s (Hasan Ağa, TT880 no. 5; Rustem Ağa, no. 6; Kurd Bey, no. 36; Osman Ağa, no. 15; and Ali Hoca, no. 1) is significant: they dominate the lower reaches of the major valleys leading into the Bay of Navarino. This suggests a concerted effort already in the First Ottoman period by the Ottoman authorities to exploit these areas of extensive lowland agricultural land.

18. For further discussion, see Bennet, Davis, and Zarinebaf-Shahr 2000, pp. 374–376; Zarinebaf, Bennet, and Davis 2005, pp. 206–208. Balta (2004, pp. 57–59) sketches the situation in the 17th century.

The nature of the geographical information offered by TT880 itself does not depend on plan-view maps. There is an element of an "itinerary" in the document, in that the order in which properties appear displays some geographical coherence, perhaps reflecting the daily "stints" of the team of scribe and translator in gathering information.[19] The only way to locate oneself in the landscape using TT880, however, is by knowing the topographic references of the place-names. This fact was vividly brought home to us while carrying out research in the field to identify minor place-names. The modern maps we had with us were of little value, and in many instances we were simply taken to the place we were trying to locate—either on foot or in a pickup truck. I would suggest that this appreciation of the intimacies of a landscape through intensive "practice" is, in fact, a true legacy of agricultural regimes that go back to the Ottoman period (and probably much earlier). It is an example of the third mode of geographical representation I outlined earlier, and I would suggest the term "performative geography" for it.

I have one last observation in relation to the "geo-metry" implied by TT880. The inclusion of boundaries for almost all properties is, to my mind at least, strongly reminiscent of the practice of the Venetian land surveyors, whose textual entries in the *catastici* (cadasters) include very similar descriptions of property boundaries, as in this example from the Vostizza *catastico*, relating to the *zeugolatio* (equivalent to *çiftlik*) of Rizomylo:

> Confina questo Zeogolatio a Tramontana con li Zeogolatini Terrazza Pano, e Catto, principiando dal Mare, e ua a Metochiliali da doue alle case dello stesso Zeogolatio, e poi à Coraglio doue confinando per Ostro con Trano Zeogolatio, non hauendo per la figura confine per Ponente, ua ad' Alapochi confinando con le appartinenze del Monasterio di Gierusaleme ua alla Valle Luzza mediante la qualle confina con la Villa Bucuschia Catto Sino al fiume de Clapazuna mediante il qualle per leuante ua alla Mare confinando con la Villa Diacofto, poi confinando con lo steso Mare ritorna al punto la doue principiò a confinare per Tramontana con li Zeogolatini Terrazza Pano, e Catto.[20]

The difference between this and the entries in TT880 lies in the inclusion in the Venetian *catastico particolare* of a *disegno,* a plan, accompanying the verbal description. In this instance, the same boundary names are marked on the accompanying plan quite clearly.[21] In addition, Siriol Davies has suggested that the practice in TT880 of giving "fixed" measurements for arable land (*tarla*s) in *dönüm* (approx. 919.3 m^2) resembles the (often fraught) Venetian attempts to render land in various "fixed" measures such as *stremmata,* rather than in "variable" measures such as the Greek ζευγάρι, the Venetian *para di bo,* or the Ottoman *çift.*[22]

I would argue that this pattern implies "interference" between Venetian and Ottoman practice in the wake of the Ottoman reconquest. This may have been deliberate on the part of the Ottoman administrators, or it may simply have been a function of the "practice," established under Venetian control, among those providing information who continued to

19. For discussion, see Zarinebaf, Bennet, and Davis 2005, pp. 116–117, and fig. 3.2.

20. Dokos and Panagopoulos 1993, p. 384.

21. Dokos and Panagopoulos 1993, pl. 66.

22. Davies 2004, pp. 103–104, 112–116.

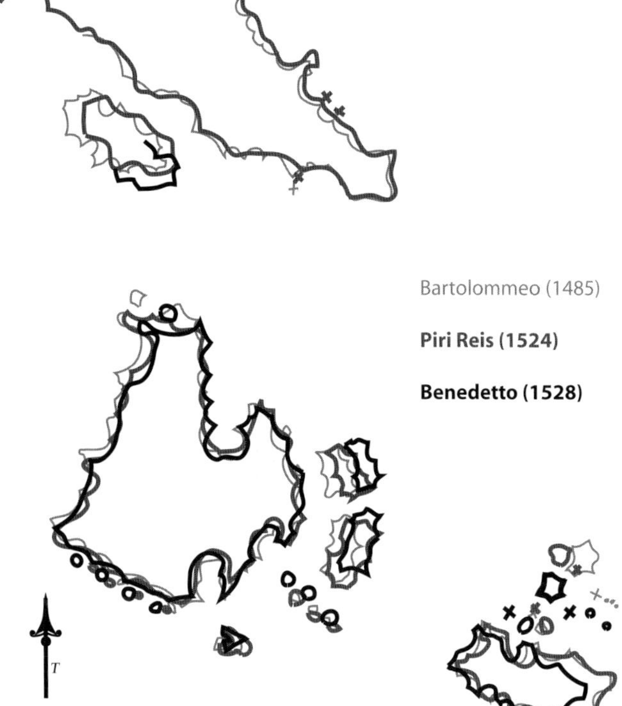

Figure 10.7. Outlines of Kythera (Cerigo) on 15th- and 16th-century maps by Bartolommeo da li Sonetti (1485), Piri Reis (1524), and Benedetto Bordone (1528). A. Bevan, after Bartolommeo da li Sonetti [1485] 1972, pl. 1; Piri Reis [1524] 1988, p. 632; Bordone [1528] 1966, p. xxxix verso

work the land. It is, I think, striking, and it reminds us of the intense cross-fertilization of terms in nautical vocabulary[23] and in the preparation of sea charts.[24] We can see this clearly, for example, in the similarity of outlines on Venetian and Ottoman 15th- and 16th-century maps of the island of Kythera (Fig. 10.7).[25]

17TH- AND 18TH-CENTURY KYTHERA

Turning to Kythera (Venetian Cerigo, Ottoman Çuha), I should like to make some brief observations about the island (Fig. 10.8).[26] In many ways Kythera presents a colonial landscape, as reflected, for example, in a number of prominent structures built during British rule between 1813 and 1863. Since prehistory, the landscape has been "torn" between Crete and the Peloponnese. It is an excellent example of an island whose "social landscape" has rarely

23. Kahane, Kahane, and Tietze 1958.

24. Soucek (1996, pp. 122–123, pl. 13) offers a colorful example of such "interference" in his comparison of the representations of the tiny island of Kaloyeros in Benedetto Bordone's *isolario* of 1528 with that in the Khalili portolan atlas, which is probably 17th century but based on that of Piri Reis, a contemporary of Bordone's.

25. For other examples, see Soucek 1992.

26. For further observations on Ottoman Kythera, see Chap. 2 in this volume.

Figure 10.8. Kythera: Locations of 18th-century parishes and districts, and other significant place-names mentioned in the text. A. Bevan

been coterminous with its physical boundaries.[27] This point is vividly brought home by the modern world of air travel, whereby the large island of Australia should be included in Kythera's "social landscape" because there has been so much migration to it from Kythera.[28] The island's major post-Byzantine settlement lay in the north (notably at Paliochora, more correctly Ayios Dimitrios),[29] whereas, with Venetian domination (principally from 1309 onward), the Kapsali region in the south was established as a major focal point, although not necessarily its main articulation point with the outside world. The harbor at Avlemonas (Ayios Nikolaos) was superior to that at Kapsali and this contributed to the increasing importance of the northern part of the island once again in the late 18th to early 19th century.[30]

27. E.g., Broodbank, Bennet, and Davis 2004.

28. This "social landscape" is now further facilitated by the ultimate in barrier-lowering technology, the Internet, with a site "for the worldwide Kytherian community": www.kythera-family.net/.

29. Ince, Koukoulis, and Smyth 1987; Ince et al. 1989; Chap. 9 in this volume.

30. Leontsinis [1987] 2000, pp. 203–211.

Unlike Messenia, Kythera has a rich data source on the island itself in the local archive (the Τοπικό Αρχείο Κυθήρων), which contains documents from the Venetian period (as early as the 16th century, but mainly from the 17th century onward) to the period of British rule.[31] Use of these documents, some of which are now published, makes it possible to triangulate between "human" data, preserved in registers of births, marriages, and deaths[32] or the series of 18th-century censuses;[33] "economic" data, such as the records of rents *(affitti)* that are organized by individuals, but locate their holdings through extensive toponymic references; and "geographical" data on their situation on the island itself. There are similar records of tithes: the *terzarie* and *decatie.* All of these data are mediated through "notarial" records, where individuals appear for varying reasons, both economic and social. Kythera has an outstanding collection of notarial books. The earliest dates to the period 1560–1582 and belonged to Emmanouil Kasimatis, who was based in Chora although he was also active elsewhere.[34] Later notaries appear in bases on the rest of the island through the 18th century and particularly in the 19th.

Surprisingly, however, there appear to be no cadastral maps like those that were produced for the Morea in the late 17th and early 18th centuries.[35] Why this might be so we return to later, but it creates practical difficulties for one of KIP's major goals, namely, linking the textual data to particular locations in the landscape in order to engage them with the material remains collected during the four seasons of field research. Kythera has suffered extensive out-migration, and therefore the possibilities of accessing "practical knowledge" of the landscape through "performative geography" are less plentiful. There is, however, considerable continuity of settlement. In practice it has proved relatively unproblematic to locate almost all settlements and the majority of their subdivisions into parishes (the basic unit by which censuses were compiled) back to the early 18th century, particularly through identifying churches (Fig. 10.8).

It seems clear from our work, however, that this apparent continuity potentially masks a shift in settlement. This is implied by the more limited distribution of pre–18th-century churches,[36] many of them at some distance from later settlement (Fig. 10.9).

In the absence of detailed maps, or even censuses like those of the 18th century, it is difficult to understand settlement in the 16th and 17th centuries. A question here is when the island's characteristic -anika/-adika

31. On the archive in general and its history, see Maltezou 1991, articles A, B, Γ.

32. Two such registers have been published to date: see Papadaki 2001 (the Estavromenos, in Chora) and Kalliyeros 2001 (Ayios Ioannis Strapodi).

33. Maltezou 1997.

34. This has been published in transcription with indexes (Drakakis 1999). For a full catalogue of the notarial archive, see Maltezou 1991, article Γ.

35. I thank Stella Chrysochoou for information on a map of Cerigo in a private collection, part of a series produced in 1837 on Corfu but probably based on a Venetian original (Chrysochoou-Stavridou 2000). Subsequent research revealed another copy of the same map in the National Archive, Kew (reference MFQ_1/673/6); I owe this discovery to Debi Harlan. This map covers the entire island, however, and so does not have the detail of the mainland *catastici.* Leonhard (1899, p. 4) refers to a "hand drawn" map in the Bibliotheca San Marco, Venice, dated 1765, although the citation is to a publication dated 1768 (*Anagrafi,* following p. 130). I am indebted to Siriol Davies, who located this map in Venice. It is clear that it is not the basis for the 1837 map, but rather resembles very closely that of Porcacchi (see Fig. 10.10 below): i.e., it depicts the whole island and does not show comtemporary settlements.

36. See Chatzidakis and Bitha 1997; Lazaridis 1965.

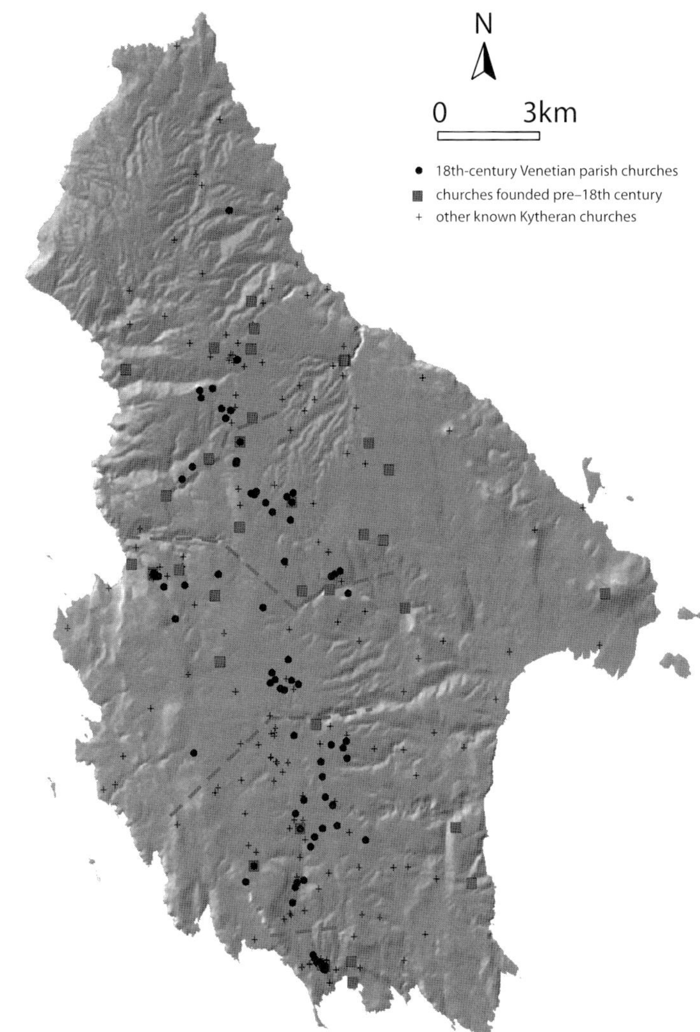

Figure 10.9. Kythera: Locations of pre–18th-century churches, 18th-century parish churches, and other known churches on the island.
A. Bevan

settlement names that reflect extended family groupings appear. We have one 16th-century census, the famous Kastrofylaka census of 1583 (Table 10.1).[37]

At first glance, the number of settlements listed here—14, other than the *fortezza* (fortress) and its "town" or *borgo*—seems tiny compared with the number in 18th-century records, where 50 or more villages are listed, subdivided into many more parishes. In addition, the actual names listed have severely taxed the ingenuity of scholars who have tried to match them to known settlement names. In Table 10.1, I show the names as they have been transcribed by Maltezou and interpreted by Tsitsilias in his *Η Ιστορία των Κυθήρων*, together with some of my own suggestions. It seems to me that we should be looking for place-names attested in 16th-century sources to compare with those in this document, not more recent names. An obvious source available to us would seem to be 16th-century maps of the island, but these are remarkably disappointing in this regard, showing no overlap in place-names.[38] We do, however, have extensive references to locations in the oeuvre of the notary Kasimatis, whose career includes the year of the census.[39] Table 10.2 lists the place-names that occur in his books.

37. E.g., Maltezou 1974; 1991, article Θ, p. 159; Lazari 2004, pp. 305–308.

38. E.g., Porcacchi 1572 (Fig. 10.10 below) and Rosaccio 1598 (Fig. 10.1 above), which span the year of the census. It is interesting, in light of the traditions of travel to and past Kythera, that Porcacchi does indicate "the temple where Helen was taken from Paris" (cf. Broodbank, Bennet, and Davis 2004, p. 232, on this trope).

39. Drakakis 1999.

TABLE 10.1. THE KASTROFYLAKA CENSUS OF KYTHERA, 1583

Place-Name Maltezou	*Place-Name Tsitsilias*	*Identification*		*Total Population*
[Fortezza]	Fortezza	Phortetsa		992
[Borgo]	Borgo	Chora		727
San Dimitri	Ayios Dimitrios	Paliochora		96
Mittata	Mitata	Mitata		82
Catto Chiperi	Kato Kiperi	Phrilingianika		43
Apano Chiperi	Apano Kiperi	Kastrisianika		46
Callamutades	Kalamos	Karvounades??	(J. Bennet)	56
Pizanades	Pitsinades	Pitsinades		72
Grisoti	Viarades	Viaradika??	(Tsitsilias)	113
Coniana	Koniana	?		75
Cusunari	Kouzoumani	Kousounari		24
Platano	Platanos	Potamos??	(J. Bennet)	146
Biotica	Protika	Phratsia??	(J. Bennet)	44
Allicangri	Alikarigni	Alexandrades??	(J. Bennet)	125
Arcario	Arkarion	?		60
Milopotamo	Mylopotamos	Mylopotamos		459
Total				3160

Sources: After Maltezou 1991, article Θ, p. 159; Tsitsilias 1994, pp. 238–239.

TABLE 10.2. PLACE-NAMES ON KYTHERA ATTESTED IN 16TH-CENTURY NOTARIAL ACTS OF KASIMATIS

Ayios Ilias	Koutsaka
Alexandrades	Livadi
Apanochori	Manitochori
Ayios Dimitrios	Mitata
Drymonas	Mylopotamos
Phratsia	Opiso Pigadi
Kalamos	Potamos
Kapsali	Pourko
Karvounades	Riza
Kasteli Kapsaliou	Samiadika
Kato Chorio	Strapodi
Keramoto	Tsikalaria
Kontoletous	Vourgos

Source: Drakakis 1999.

Notable in their almost complete absence are -anika/-adika names.[40] It is possible that some prominent later villages, such as Alexandrades, Karvounades, or Phratsia, present in the notarial records, might also lurk unidentified in the Kastrofylaka census, and I have made some very tentative suggestions along these lines in Table 10.1.[41]

The prominence of the place-name "Phratsia" is, I believe, reflected on some island-scale maps of the 16th and 17th centuries, for example that by Tommaso Porcacchi (Fig. 10.10). He situates a place-name "Prati Chiea" in approximately the correct location for Phratsia, as does Piacenza on a

40. A point also noted by Lazari (2004, p. 306) in relation to the Kastrofylaka census.

41. Another source for 16th-century place-names is a document in the Τοπικό Αρχείο Κυθήρων (Maltezou 1991, article I, p. 278, n. 37) relating to the 1583 census. In addition to names already attested in Kasimatis, this document includes "Calochiernes," "Furnus," and "Milapidhea." Lazari (2004, p. 307) also notes the potential value of this document in relation to the 1583 census.

Figure 10.10. Map of Kythera (Cerigo). Porcacchi 1572, p. 106

map published in 1688,[42] whereas Beauvau, on a map published in 1615, gives the name "Froaci Chea" in the same spot, at number 12 on his map.[43] By the 18th century, Phratsia has nine parishes, six of which are explicitly associated with -anika "neighborhoods."[44]

Given its early attestation and its later prominence, I wonder if the name itself might be significant. It certainly looks as if it ought to derive from an Italian form: "Franzia" or the like. One of the peculiarities of Kythera's history is that, although Venetian, the island originally was administered by the Venier family. Kythera was divided into 24 subdivisions, or *carati,* shared equally among the four sons of Marco Venier upon his death in 1311.[45] The Venieri participated in the Cretan rebellion of 1363 and were stripped of their lands on Kythera. In 1393, 13 *carati* were reinstated to the family, and the island came to be administered jointly with the Venetian state, which retained the other 11 *carati.* From this period, it seems,[46] the lands of the Venieri were known to the Venetian administration as "Gabrilianà," after the name of one of Marco Venier's sons, Gabriele.

42. Piacenza 1688, pp. 578, 585.

43. Beauvau 1615, p. 23. The map is very clearly based on that of Rosaccio (1598, p. 44). Somewhat similar is Dapper's map, on which the name appears as "Prat Chiea" (Dapper 1703, p. 376).

44. Maltezou 1997. In the 1715 Ottoman *defter* (see Chap. 2 in this volume), five of these districts appear: Phratsia, Ayo Pandi (Ayioi Pantes), Lendarakianika, Kendrotianika, and Raïsianika.

45. Hopf [1873] 1966, p. 526.

46. Maltezou 1991, article Θ, p. 159; article IA, p. 34.

After the Venieri recovered some of their land, it is striking that a single member of the family, known as "Frangia" (an abbreviation for Francesco), acquired significant portions from other family members, such that he held 11¼ *carati* by his death in 1424.[47] I wonder if this name lies behind the place-name "Phratsia," which might, therefore, signify "the lands of Frangia." If so, it would allow us to do something that is quite difficult for Kythera:[48] to suggest a specific location for some of the land-holdings of the Venier family. We know that their holdings were administratively distinct from those of the Venetian state in most cases, but whether they were spatially intermixed or separated is unknown, so far as I am aware. This is, of course, exactly the sort of issue that one might have expected to be illuminated by plan-view maps, but again, to the best of our knowledge, such do not exist for Kythera, despite its long Venetian rule.

CONCLUSION

From this discussion, I hope it is clear how a detailed understanding of early modern landscapes in Messenia and on Kythera can emerge through the exploitation of text, image, and archaeology. The development of such an understanding demands the use of diachronic series of texts and also, as admirably demonstrated by other contributors to this volume, of texts from different sources and contexts. Given the pressures within the modern academy to specialize, achieving an effective understanding requires collaborative research among scholars competent in different academic disciplines and in different linguistic and documentary traditions.

In closing, can we turn the evidence around and say something about "geo-metrical" practice in the two areas, Messenia and Kythera? It is, at first glance, paradoxical that for Kythera, an area that was under continuous Venetian control for five centuries, it appears that cadastral maps were not made, whereas for the Morea, during a 30-year period spanning the end of the 17th century and beginning of the 18th, such maps were made.[49] The absence of such maps of the Ottoman Morea both before and after the Venetian conquest, I had assumed, was attributable to the lack of a tradition of Ottoman large-scale mapping, as opposed to the vivid tradition of small-scale mapping—world maps, navigational charts, and so on, heavily influenced by Italian and Arab cartographies.[50]

I would like to suggest, however, that the crucial factor is how knowledge of the landscape was acquired and maintained in these different regions. In each case, I would imagine, such knowledge was held primarily by those who cultivated the land and whose families, by and large, remained there generation after generation. This knowledge was, therefore, based on "practice" and represents a "performative" geo-metry. Any strategy of exploitation—Venetian or Ottoman—would harness rather than attempt to bypass or subvert this knowledge. We know, for example, that the Ottomans were sensitive to local social structures and practices within the different regions conquered, which led to diverse modes of organization across the empire.[51]

47. Hopf [1873] 1966, p. 526.

48. See also p. 192 above, where Gregory also discusses Venier holdings in the north of the island.

49. On the history of the cadastral map, see Kain and Baigent 1992.

50. Karamustafa 1992; Soucek 1996.

51. See, e.g., İnalcık 1954; on the circumstances of the Kythera *defter,* see Chap. 2 in this volume.

In fact, such knowledge is prominent in the Ottoman and Venetian records, where place-names are used to signal locations and the articulation between rulers and ruled was achieved through personal relationships. Kythera offers a good example in the *affitti* records, which are organized by individual but contain place-name information. Notarial records are essentially similar, in more varied contexts. Disputes over land presumably would have been solved on the spot (in "performance"), not by reference to a plan-view representation. Equally, it is clear to me that when TT880 was compiled, it was compiled on the spot, making use of local knowledge, not only geo-metrical, but also of local agricultural productivity and so on.[52]

What emerges from this study is that, in fact, the Venetian program of plan-view mapping is the anomaly and is largely epiphenomenal, presumably deployed as a strategy of conquest and driven by contemporary trends in mapping land. Although the *disegni* seem to represent an entirely new mode of geo-metry, fundamentally they merely enshrined verbal data describing the boundaries of various properties. In this respect our Ottoman *defter* and the Venetian *catastici* are very similar: they both use a technology largely unknown to the local cultivators—writing—to record practical knowledge of geo-metry. A similar process had taken place in 16th-century colonial Central America, where local informants were used to create maps of the newly colonized territory for the Spanish.[53]

This point reminds us that we should not ignore historical particularities. On Kythera, Venetian domination was almost continuous, whereas it was interrupted in the Morea, and reinstated only for a 30-year period. On Kythera the system grew organically, creating a "hybrid" culture, one arguably materialized in the famous icon preserved in the church of the Panayia Myrtidiotissa on the *kastro* (citadel; fortress; castle) in Chora that commemorates the end of a late-17th-century outbreak of plague. It shows San Rocco, a Latin saint, and Ayios Theodoros, an Orthodox saint, together with a representation of the island's *kastro*.[54] The detailed mapping of the Morea, on the other hand, belongs to a period of reconquest, at a time when quite large areas of land lay abandoned either by the owners or because the land had belonged to the Ottoman state.[55] The mapping of this land formed part of a larger process of measurement, or geo-metry, carried out by a newly installed external authority in order to quantify the land's potential productivity. Equally important, however, was the symbolic goal of measuring, quantifying, and representing the land with an alien technology. Here again, the situation is similar to that which followed: the Ottoman remeasurement to determine its yield from the Morea, embodied in TT880 and, we might add, in the *defter* compiled for Kythera, Çuha, during the three years the Ottomans ruled it.

52. Zarinebaf, Bennet, and Davis 2005, chaps. 2–4, esp. pp. 194–195 on local productivity figures.

53. Mundy 1996.

54. Gkini-Tsophopoulou 1989–1991. One could argue that a similar situation applied on Crete, a Venetian province from the early 13th century until the Ottoman takeover completed in 1669, for which cadastral maps are, to the best of my knowledge, unknown and whose hybrid "renaissance" culture is well known (see, e.g., Holton 1991).

55. See, in general, Davies 2004.

REFERENCES

Alcock, S. E. 1998. "Hasanaga: A Glimpse into the Ottoman Countryside," in *Sandy Pylos: An Archaeological History from Nestor to Navarino,* ed. J. L. Davis, Austin, pp. 262–266.

Anagrafi = *Anagrafi di tutto lo stato della Serenissima Republica di Venezia* 1, Venice 1768.

Atlas 1835 = *Expédition scientifique de Morée: Section des sciences physiques* 5: *Atlas,* Paris.

Balta, E. 2004. "Settlements and Population in the Morea in 1645," *Osmanlı araştırmaları* 24, pp. 53–63.

Bartolommeo da li Sonetti. [1485] 1972. *Isolario,* repr. Amsterdam.

Beauvau, H. baron de. 1615. *Relation journalière du voyage du Levant faict et descrit par haut et puissant seigneur Henry de Beauvau,* Nancy.

Bennet, J. 1995. "Space through Time: Diachronic Perspectives on the Spatial Organization of the Pylian State," in *Politeia: Society and State in the Aegean Bronze Age,* ed. W.-D. Neimeier and R. Laffineur (*Aegaeum* 13), Liège/Austin, pp. 587–602.

———. 1998. "The Linear B Archives and the Organization of the Kingdom of Nestor," in *Sandy Pylos: An Archaeological History from Nestor to Navarino,* ed. J. L. Davis, Austin, pp. 111–133.

———. 1999. "The Mycenaean Conceptualization of Space or Pylian Geography . . . Yet Again," in *Floreant Studia Mycenaea: Akten des X. internationalen mykenologischen Colloquiums in Salzburg vom 1.–5. Mai 1995,* ed. S. Deger-Jalkotzy, S. Hiller, and O. Panagl, Vienna, pp. 131–157.

Bennet, J., J. L. Davis, and F. Zarinebaf-Shahr. 2000. "Pylos Regional Archaeological Project, Part III: Sir William Gell's Itinerary in the Pylia and Regional Landscapes in the Morea in the Second Ottoman Period," *Hesperia* 69, pp. 343–380.

Bennet, J., and S. Voutsaki. 1991. "A Synopsis and Analysis of Travelers' Accounts of Keos (to 1821)," in *Landscape Archaeology as Long-Term History: Northern Keos in the Cycladic Islands from Earliest Settlement until Modern Times* (Monumenta archaeologica 16), ed. J. F. Cherry, J. L. Davis, and E. Mantzourani, Los Angeles, pp. 365–382.

Bordone, B. [1528] 1966. *Libro . . . de tutte l'isole del mondo,* repr. Amsterdam.

Broodbank, C., J. Bennet, and J. L. Davis. 2004. "Aphrodite Observed: Insularity and Antiquities on Kythera through Outsiders' Eyes," in *Explaining Social Change: Studies in Honour of Colin Renfrew,* ed. J. Cherry, C. Scarre, and S. Shennan, Cambridge, pp. 227–239.

Chatzidakis, M., and I. Bitha. 1997. *Ευρετήριο βυζαντινών τοιχογραφιών Ελλάδος: Κύθηρα,* Athens.

Chrysochoou-Stavridou, S. 2000. "Κτηματογραφικοί χάρτες των Επτανήσων: Η περίπτωση της Ζακύνθου," in *Proceedings of the 6th International Panionian Congress* 1, Thessaloniki, pp. 421–433.

Dapper, O. 1703. *Description exacte des isles de l'Archipel,* Amsterdam.

Davies, S. 2004. "Pylos Regional Archaeological Project, Part VI: Administration and Settlement in Venetian Navarino," *Hesperia* 73, pp. 59–120.

Davis, J. L., S. E. Alcock, J. Bennet, Y. G. Lolos, and C. W. Shelmerdine. 1997. "The Pylos Regional Archaeological Project, Part I: Overview and the Archaeological Survey," *Hesperia* 66, pp. 391–494.

Dokos, K., and G. Panagopoulos. 1993. *Το βενετικό κτηματολόγιο της Βοστίτσας,* Athens.

Drakakis, E. G. 1999. *Εμμανουήλ Κασιμάτης, νοτάριος Κυθήρων (1560–1582),* Athens.

Georgacas, D. J., and W. A. McDonald. 1967. *Place Names of Southwest Peloponnesus,* Athens.

Gkini-Tsophopoulou, E. 1989–1991. "Σχόλια σε εικόνα από ναό του κάστρου της Χώρας Κυθήρων," *ArchDelt* 44–46, pp. 179–190.

Harvey, P. D. A. 1980. *The History of Topographical Maps: Symbols, Pictures and Surveys,* New York.

Holton, D., ed. 1991. *Literature and Society in Renaissance Crete,* Cambridge.

Hopf, C. [1873] 1966. *Chroniques gréco-romanes inédites ou peu connues publiées avec notes et tables généalogiques,* repr. Paris.

İnalcık, H. 1954. "Ottoman Methods of Conquest," *Studia islamica* 2, pp. 103–129.

Ince, G. E., T. Koukoulis, A. N. Ballantyne, and D. Smyth. 1989. "Paliochora: Survey of a Byzantine City on the Island of Kythera, Second Report," *BSA* 84, pp. 407–416.

Ince, G. E., T. Koukoulis, and D. Smyth. 1987. "Paliochora: Survey of a Byzantine City on the Island of Kythera, Preliminary Report," *BSA* 82, pp. 95–106.

Kahane, H., R. Kahane, and A. Tietze. 1958. *The Lingua Franca in the Levant: Turkish Nautical Terms of Italian and Greek Origin,* Urbana, Ill.

Kain, R. J. P., and E. Baigent. 1992. *The Cadastral Map in the Service of the State: A History of Property Mapping,* Chicago.

Kalliyeros, E. P. 2001. *Ληξιαρχικά βιβλία Κυθήρων: Ενορία Αγίου Ιωάννου Στραποδίου 1687–1850,* Athens.

Karamustafa, A. T. 1992. "Military, Administrative, and Scholarly Maps and Plans," in *The History of Cartography* 2.1: *Cartography in the Traditional Islamic and South Asian Societies,* ed. J. B. Harley and D. Woodward, Chicago, pp. 209–227.

Katsiardi-Hering, O. 1993. "Venezianische Karten als Grundlage der historischen Geographie des griechischen Siedlungsraumes (Ende 17. und 18. Jh.)," *Mitteilungen des Österreichischen Staatsarchivs* 43, pp. 281–316.

Kiel, M. 1997. "The Rise and Decline of Turkish Boeotia, 15th–19th Century (Remarks on the Settlement Pattern, Demography, and Agricultural Production According to Unpublished Ottoman-Turkish Census and Taxation Records)," in *Recent Developments in the History and Archaeology of Central Greece. Proceedings of the 6th International Boeotian Conference* (*BAR-IS* 666), ed. J. L. Bintliff, Oxford, pp. 315–358.

Lazari, S. 2004. "Η συγκρότηση του επτανησιακού πληθυσμού: η απογραφή του Πέτρου Καστροφύλακα (1583) και του Fr. Grimani (1760)," in *Πρακτικά του Ζ΄ Πανιονίου Συνεδρίου, Λευκάδα, 26–30 Μαΐου 2002* 2, Athens, pp. 301–347.

Lazaridis, P. 1965. "Τα μεσαιωνικά μνημεία των Κυθήρων," *ArchDelt* 20, Β΄1, pp. 183–199.

Leonhard, R. 1899. *Die Insel Kythera: Eine geographische Monographie,* Gotha.

Leontsinis, G. N. [1987] 2000. *The Island of Kythera: A Social History (1700–1863),* repr. Athens.

Maltezou, C. A. 1974. "Νεο άγνωστο χειρόγραφο της 'Περιγραφής της Κρήτης' του Πέτρου Καστροφύλακα (1583) και το πρόβλημα της κριτικής εκδόσεως της," in *Proceedings of the 3rd Cretological Congress* 2, Athens, pp. 176–183.

———. 1991. *Βενετική παρουσία στα Κύθηρα: Αρχειακές μαρτυρίες,* Athens.

———. 1997. *Απογραφές πληθυσμού Κυθήρων (18ος αι.),* 3 vols., Athens.

Mundy, B. 1996. *The Mapping of New Spain: Indigenous Cartography and the Maps of the* Relaciones Geográficas, Chicago.

Papadaki, A. 2001. *Ληξιαρχικά βιβλία Κυθήρων: Ενορία Εσταυρωμένου Χώρας 1671–1812,* Athens.

Piacenza, F. 1688. *L'Egeo redivivo, o' sia chorographia dell' arcipelago,* Modona.

Piri Reis. [1524] 1988. *Kitab-ı Bahriye,* ed. E. Z. Ökte, 4 vols., repr. Istanbul.

Politis, N. G. 1915. "Τοπωνυμικά," *Λαογραφία* 5, pp. 249–308, 522–552.

Porcacchi, T. 1572. *L'isole piu famose del mondo . . . intagliate da Girolamo Porro . . . ,* Venice.

Rosaccio, G. 1598. *Viaggio de Venetia a Costantinopoli,* Venice.

Saïtas, Y. 1999. "La documentation cartographique des trois péninsules méridionales du Péloponnèse élaborée par l'armée française (1829–1832)," in *Enquêtes en Méditerranée: Les expéditions françaises d'Égypte, de Morée et d'Algérie,* ed. M.-N. Bourguet, D. Nordman, V. Panayiotopoulos, and M. Sinarellis, Athens, pp. 105–129.

Seller, J. 1753. *The English Pilot* 3, London.

Soucek, S. 1992. "Islamic Charting in the Mediterranean," in *The History of Cartography* 2.1: *Cartography in the Traditional Islamic and South Asian Societies,* ed. J. B. Harley and D. Woodward, Chicago, pp. 263–292.

———. 1996. *Piri Reis and Turkish Mapmaking after Columbus: The Khalili Portolan Atlas* (Studies in the Khalili Collection 2), 2nd ed., London.

Tsitsilias, P. 1994. *Η ιστορία των Κυθήρων* 2, Athens.

Zarinebaf, F., J. Bennet, and J. L. Davis. 2005. *A Historical and Economic Geography of Ottoman Greece: The Southwestern Morea in the 18th Century* (*Hesperia* Suppl. 34), Princeton.

PART IV: TOWARD AN INTEGRATED HISTORY AND ARCHAEOLOGY OF EARLY MODERN GREECE

In the final section of this book, four distinguished archaeologists contribute their perspectives. The appearance of these particular authors in our volume may seem surprising to some readers and certainly requires explanation.

John Bintliff, Björn Forsén, Priscilla Murray, and Curtis Runnels all have participated in the organization and execution of regional studies projects in Greece for many years and, in that capacity, became aware, as did one of the editors of this volume (Davis), of the enormous gaps in historical knowledge concerning rural settlement and population levels, and local agricultural practices in Venetian and Ottoman Greece. A lack of detailed information about post-Byzantine pottery, particularly plain and coarse wares, also severely hampered efforts to reconstruct patterns of land use from the finds retrieved through intensive surface survey.

As a result, the organizers of regional studies projects were in a predicament: the professed aim of integrating evidence from material culture with that extracted from texts was being frustrated. Later chapters in their final publications frequently were based solely on generalized historical sources. These writings often were presented entirely from a Greek perspective because of a lack of access to Ottoman documents.

Bintliff was one of the first archaeologists to try to cut this Gordian knot by forming a partnership with an Ottomanist, Machiel Kiel. In his contribution here, Bintliff describes the enormous progress that has been made in the archaeology of early modern Greece in the past two decades, often with reference to his own work in Boiotia, and outlines a sensible course of action for the future.

Runnels, a prehistorian, Murray, an ethnoarchaeologist, and Forsén, a Roman historian, were invited to compose short commentaries on the chapters in this volume. Each contribution, while properly celebrating successes, recognizes that the reconstruction of early modern patterns of settlement and land use is not a simple matter, even when ample textual evidence is available.

Considerations for Creating an Ottoman Archaeology in Greece

by John L. Bintliff

A popular view of the Ottoman era in Greece, after the Ottoman conquest of Constantinople in 1453, is of an unrelieved period of wicked Turkish oppression lasting until 1830 or later. This view, still shared by some academics, holds that among the supposed characteristics of the period are: first, a population count that falls dramatically and stays low throughout the period; second, an immediate flight by the Greek population to the hills to plan its commercial rise in the 18th and 19th centuries and then the Revolution; third, little cultural achievement in Greece by the Ottomans, a barbarous people who stifled the creativity of the gifted Greeks by banning the construction of churches and converting most of the existing ones into mosques; and finally, no notable changes over time in how the Ottomans ruled except owing to the initiatives of their subjects.

The Ottomans' perception of themselves was, however, one of a cultivated society; even the briefest trip to Old Istanbul is enough to convince anyone of their impressive artistic and architectural talents (see, e.g., the Süleymaniye complex).[1] Actually, both the traditional Greek and Western European views of the Ottoman Empire stem from the final era of its decline, when there was widespread arbitrary violence and corruption, and a lack of economic, technological, and political progress compared with the West. In the 16th and 17th centuries, however, Westerners had a very different and frequently admiring view of the Ottoman world. The popularity of products of that world (e.g., rich carpets and tapestries, like the one shown in the painting *The Ambassadors* by Hans Holbein the Younger)[2] matches the healthy respect shown to Ottoman military prowess abroad.

This very different and nuanced history is absolutely consistent with the now considerable information available from the Ottoman imperial archives[3] and the gradually increasing, but still rare, archaeological data from rural and urban studies conducted within the bounds of the former empire. Here we might note that our ability in Greece to recognize Ottoman-era ceramics has leapt forward over the past two decades. In the 1980s, most field projects did not systematically collect post-medieval finds and, if they did, they had to be content with classifying them as Ottoman/Venetian to modern (or even just medieval to modern!). Now most pottery sherds,

1. For an authoritative overview of the splendors of Ottoman architecture, see Goodwin 1971.
2. Jardine 1996, p. 429.
3. See, e.g., Chap. 2 in this volume.

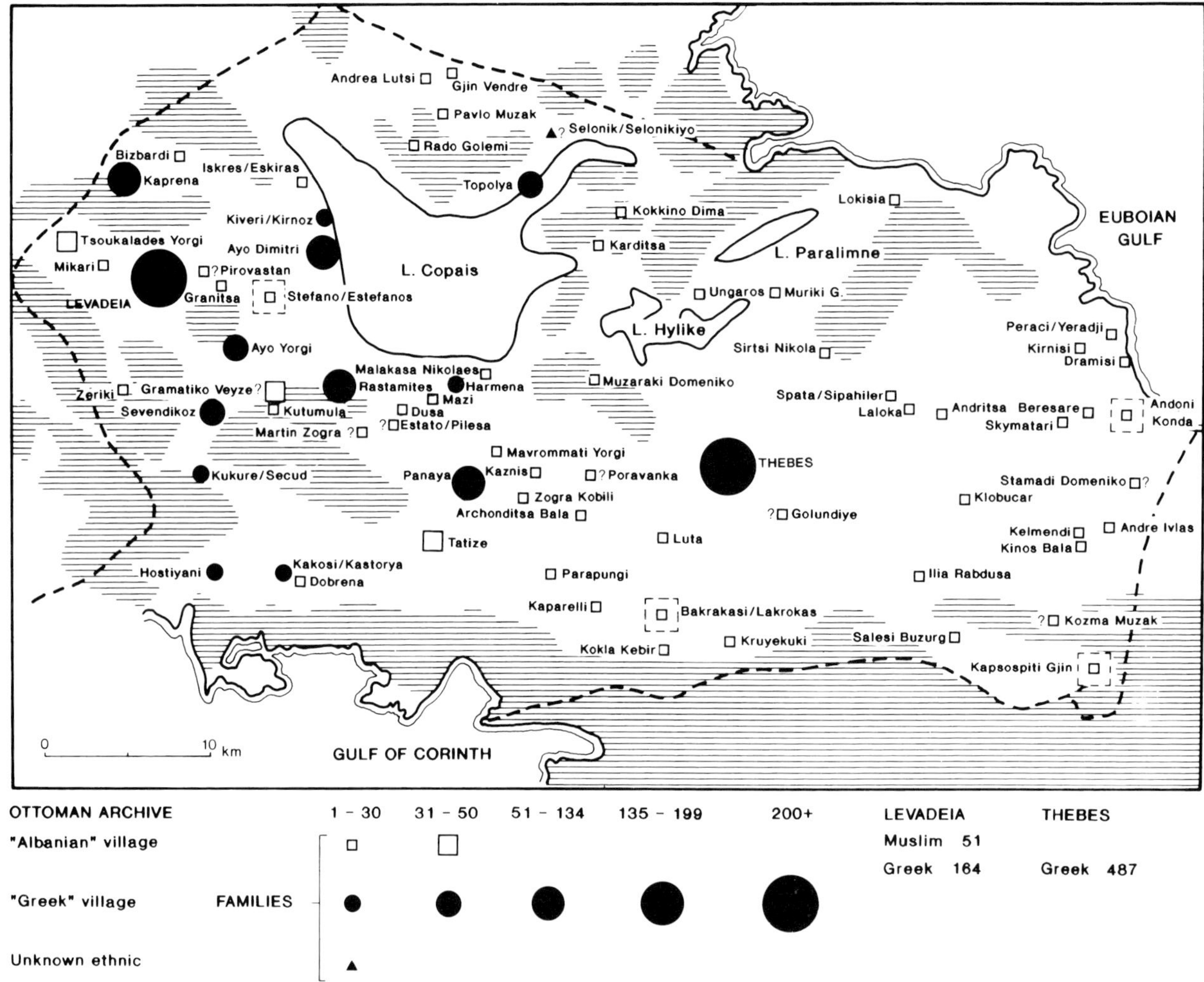

Figure 11.1. The towns and villages of Boiotia in 1466, according to Ottoman tax records. Elevations above 400 m are shaded and hatched. Courtesy the Boiotia Project; archival research by M. Kiel, geographical research by J. L. Bintliff

even those in the damaged condition of surface finds discovered during regional surveys—whether coarse, domestic, or fine ware—can be phased not merely into broad chronological divisions such as Byzantine, Frankish, Ottoman, and early modern, but also, through assemblage reconstruction, into subdivisions such as Early, Middle, or Late Ottoman.[4] John Hayes has been the pioneer in this development. More recently, the addition of fabric study collections to our analytical tools has increased our ability to attribute pottery to narrower time periods. This now permits a further stage of assemblage study, in which we can raise questions about an Ottoman farm or village regarding the relative wealth, economic behavior, and mentality of its inhabitants. Nonetheless, it is regrettable that one still observes current and planned field projects in Greece in which no specialist collection and study have been proposed for post-medieval ceramics.

In the following discussion I present relevant results from my own field project in Boiotia, in which the following periods are discussed: the High Medieval Crusader or Frankish occupation phase, from 1204 to 1453; the Early Ottoman occupation, from 1453 to ca. 1600; and the Late Ottoman, from ca. 1600 to 1827.

4. See, e.g., the recent analyses by Vionis of the deserted village assemblages recovered by the Tanagra Project (Vionis 2006); also Chap. 4 in this volume.

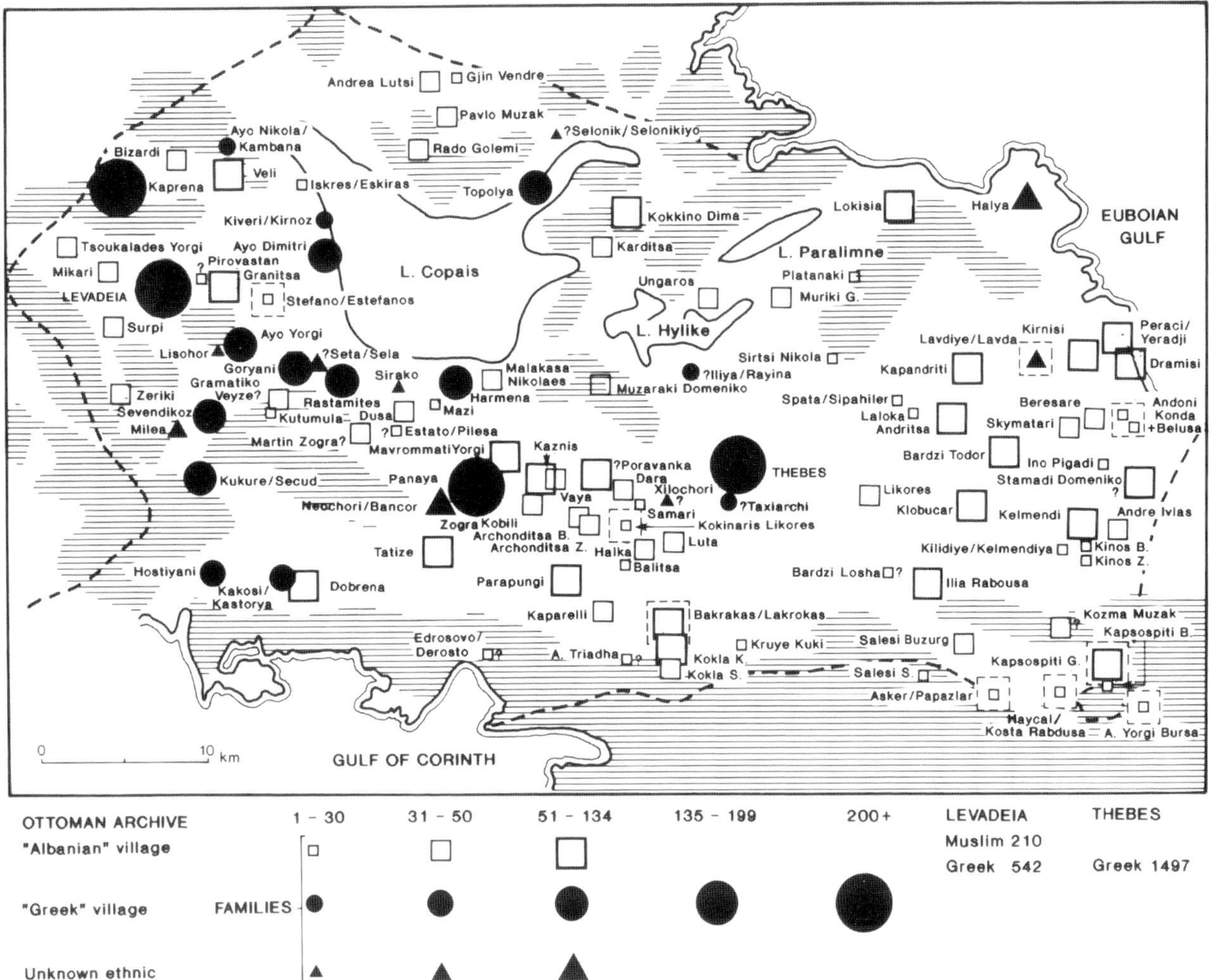

Figure 11.2. The towns and villages of Boiotia in 1570, according to Ottoman tax records. Elevations above 400 m are shaded and hatched. Courtesy the Boiotia Project; archival research by M. Kiel, geographical research by J. L. Bintliff

For our project in Boiotia, central Greece, we have been fortunate to have had, since the 1980s, the expertise of John Hayes for fine-dating our post-Roman surface survey finds, and Machiel Kiel for providing detailed breakdowns of the Ottoman imperial tax archives for the 15th–18th centuries. In particular, the collaboration between Kiel and myself in locating and surveying deserted villages has provided a detailed illustration of the historical changes at work in a regional landscape in the long period from early Frankish rule to the post-Ottoman period.[5] Even if, as Kiel has suggested, the first preserved *defter* (tax register) of 1466 reflects, in the restricted spread of Greek villages (Fig. 11.1), the devastating collapse of Greco-Slav populations resulting from 14th-century warfare and Black Death outbreaks, it also points to planned recovery, with the arranged colonization under Frankish and Ottoman administration, of the abandoned countryside by invited Albanian communities.

The first 150 years or so of the *Pax Othomanica* results in a population and economic boom for both Greek and Albanian settlements and towns, as the 1570 *defter* makes clear (Fig. 11.2). Intensive archaeological survey at villages such as Panaya in the Valley of the Muses[6] (a large Greek village

5. Bintliff 1995; Kiel 1997. See also the settlement analysis for 15th- and 16th-century Aitolia carried out by the Dutch Aetolia Project, which combines Ottoman archival research with historical geography (Doorn 1989); although he was the source of the relevant translated village archives, Machiel Kiel was inadvertently omitted as an author from that article.

6. Bintliff 1996a, 1996b.

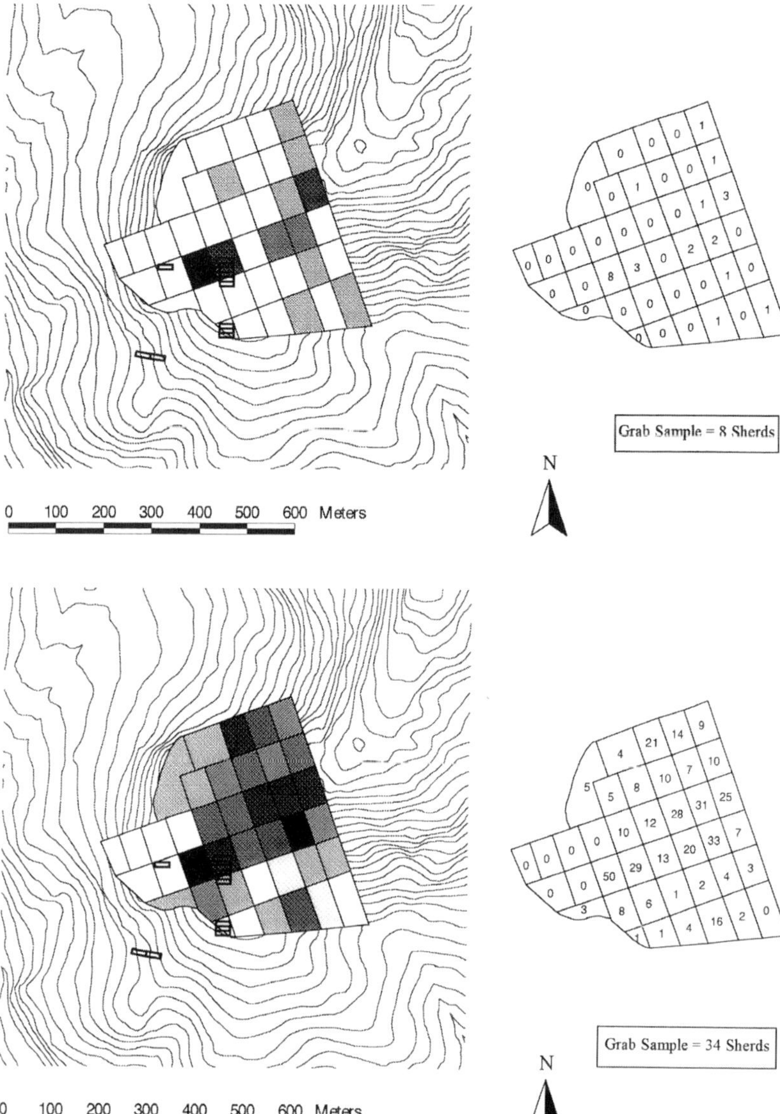

Figure 11.3. The deserted village site of Panaya (VM4) in the Valley of the Muses, Boiotia. Distribution of diagnostic pottery of the Frankish period (13th–early 14th centuries) based on a gridded surface ceramic collection. The term "grab sample" refers to other sherds of the same phase that were found in addition to those of the gridded collection. Courtesy the Boiotia Project; ceramic dating by J. W. Hayes

Figure 11.4. The deserted village site of Panaya (VM4) in the Valley of the Muses, Boiotia. Distribution of diagnostic pottery of the Final Frankish and Early Ottoman periods (late 14th–16th centuries) based on a gridded surface ceramic collection. The term "grab sample" refers to other sherds of the same phase that were found in addition to those of the gridded collection. Courtesy the Boiotia Project; ceramic dating by J. W. Hayes

slightly left and below center in Fig. 11.1) gives more detailed confirmation of the tax records when we observe the dramatic expansion of the site between its modest scale in the Frankish 13th–14th centuries and its heyday of some 1,100 inhabitants in the Early Ottoman 16th century, based on the dispersal of dated surface ceramics across the gridded site area (Figs. 11.3, 11.4). Moreover, further details enrich this impression of prosperity: imports of fine tableware from both Italy and Anatolia at Panaya and other contemporary Early Ottoman villages[7] match the results of our archaeological mapping of several of the 10 water mills listed in the village's tax records, as well as our work at the two monasteries in the valley founded by the village itself at this time. We are very much reminded of Hugo Blake's model of tracing rural prosperity and poverty through the quality of tablewares reaching country dwellers,[8] with the Greek Ottoman zenith beginning only a little later than that of Renaissance Italy (16th rather than 15th century). Both, periods, however, are marked among other

7. Vroom 1999.
8. Blake 1980.

Figure 11.5. Sketch of a traditional mainland Greek longhouse, believed to be of 18th-century construction.
Stedman 1996, p. 189, fig. 2, by permission

indicators by tin-glazed dishes and jugs, or majolica, and it is notable that Greece produced its local versions of these Italian wares. Likewise, in Italy the remarkable Anatolian Ottoman glazed tableware and tile made chiefly at İznik[9] was both a status tableware and imitated locally.

A similar revision of standard history and archaeology has begun for other parts of Greece. Sadly, though, the seriously inaccurate portrayal of Ottoman Athens, which can still be bought in that city today,[10] is far better known than Kiel's pioneer study of the town and its countryside as portrayed in the Ottoman archives.[11] Exactly as in Boiotia, after serious depopulation in final Frankish times, the number and size of settlements in the Attic countryside both grow in the Early Ottoman period to 1570, with Athens and its 14,000 occupants being one of the major towns of the Early Ottoman Balkans.

From archival research, also primarily by Kiel,[12] we can discern that every town in Greece during this period would have seen the construction of major architectural works: mosques, seminaries, covered markets, bathhouses, as well as water installations and bridges. These seem to have been almost entirely destroyed or, if surviving, are rarely protected and conserved. The current Greek Antiquities Law, with its 100-year threshold to monument status, offers hope that such remains can be preserved, but only if an active policy of registering post-Byzantine monuments is pursued throughout the entire country. We can also be sure that every town would have included elaborate private mansions of the wealthier classes; these generally have been rebuilt in post-Ottoman styles or have been destroyed.[13] Many more Ottoman-era peasant houses can now be recognized as still standing (occupied or ruined), from which longer stylistic stability can be argued, alongside the renewal that follows traditional lines of houses built in Ottoman times. The most prominent mainland form is the single-story or one-and-a-half-story longhouse (Fig. 11.5 is a sketch of a surviving structure).[14] Such a longhouse, which sheltered both the family and some domestic animals, survives widely (notably on the Skourta Plain) and is a type that, as we have been able to demonstrate, dates back to deserted Boiotian villages of the 16th–17th centuries, if not earlier (as, most recently, on the acropolis of ancient Tanagra.)[15]

During the 17th century the Ottoman world suffered a series of crises,[16] although some of the same problems beset Christian Europe, too. Our

9. Atasoy and Raby 1994.
10. Mackenzie 1992.
11. Kiel 1987.
12. Kiel 1990, 1992, 1996.
13. Sigalos 2004.
14. See also Sigalos 2004, chap. 5 and figs. 81, 82.
15. Stedman 1996; Bintliff et al. 2001; Bintliff et al., in press.
16. The classic study is İnalcık 1972.

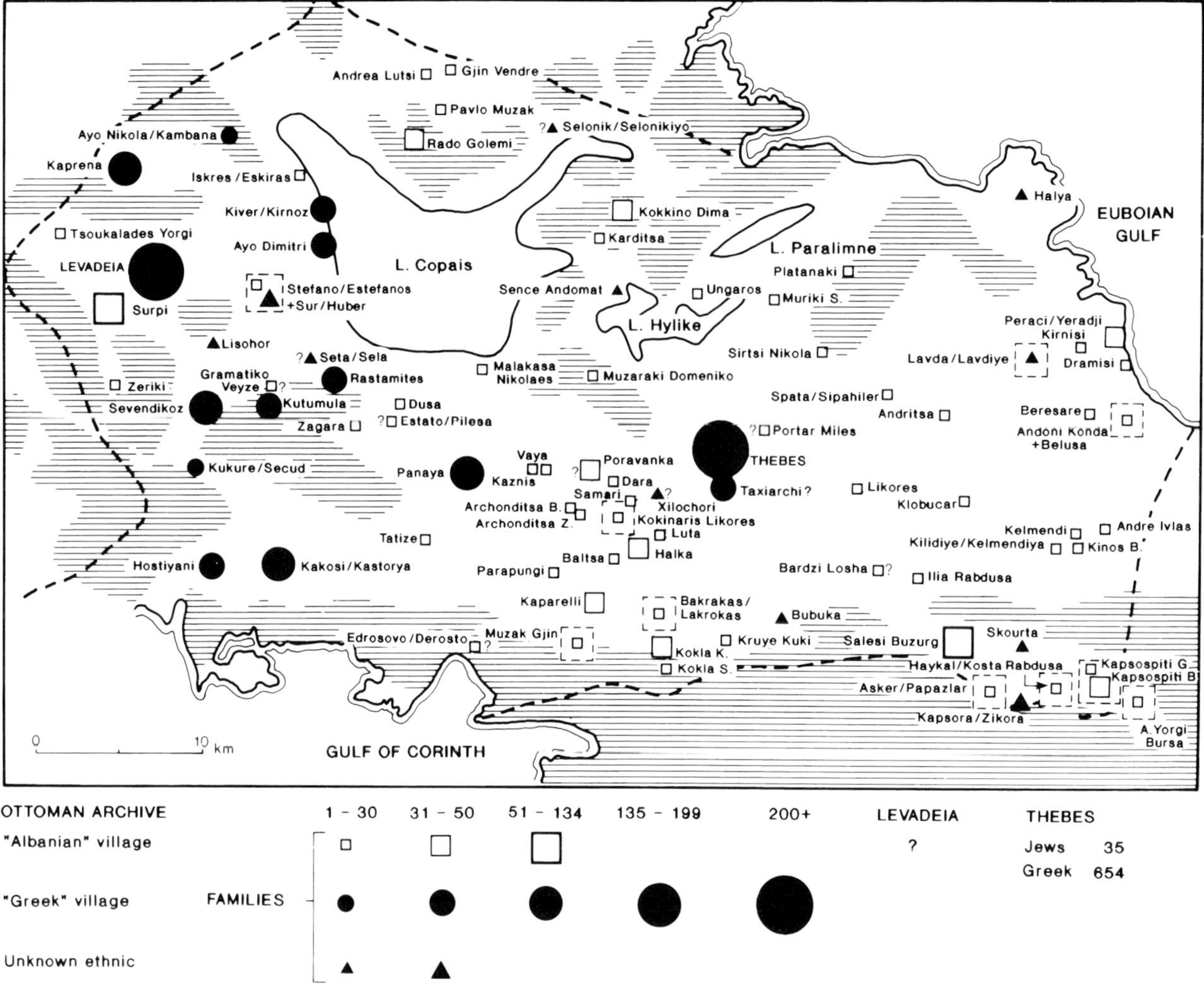

Figure 11.6. The towns and villages of Boiotia in 1687/8, according to Ottoman tax records. Elevations above 400 m are shaded and hatched. Courtesy the Boiotia Project; archival research by M. Kiel, geographical research by J. L. Bintliff

collaboration with Kiel has allowed us to relate the archaeological study of deserted villages to the tax registers of this age of crisis and of the previous phase of florescence. Thus the 1687/8 records for Ottoman Boiotia (Fig. 11.6) clearly show a severe decline in the number of villages and in the size of those that survive. This pattern is well documented by examples such as the village of Panaya, where we can observe a reduction of population to one-third of its 16th-century size, at the same time that its previous settlement form as a prosperous centralized community is broken up into a dozen *çiftlik*s, or "serf-estates." Indeed, archaeological surface ceramic evidence testifies unambigously to a virtual abandonment of this village and the start of occupation at the modern village site (Fig. 11.7).

Current discussion focuses on the increased development of *çiftlik*s during this troubled century, stimulated by the thoroughly negative judgment of them by 18th- and 19th-century Western travelers and, more recently, by their role in arguments regarding core-periphery, world system, and secondary feudalism models for some of the economic and social changes observed in the later Ottoman period.[17] Some Ottoman historians suggest that the impact of Western commercialism and capitalism, as well as industrial incursion, was significant in Ottoman society from the 17th

17. Study of this topic was pioneered by Immanuel Wallerstein (1979); for more recent discussions, see Berktay and Faroqhi 1991.

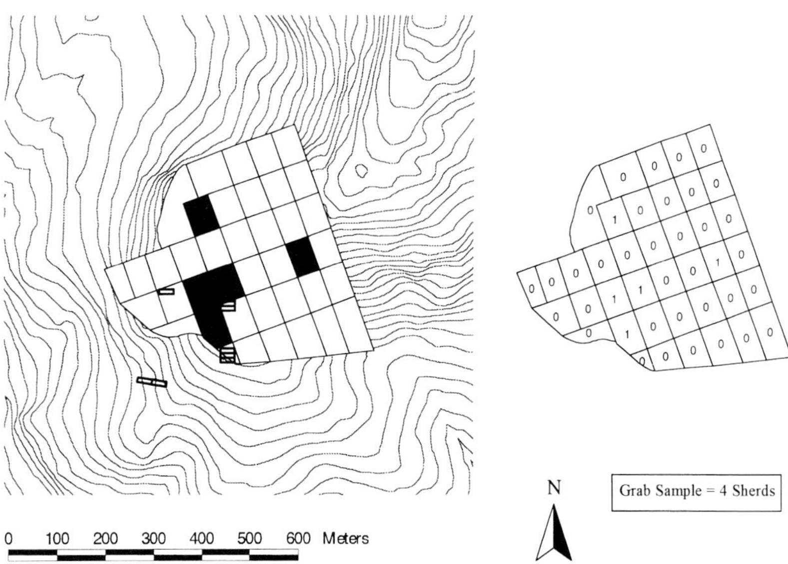

Figure 11.7. The deserted village site of Panaya (VM4) in the Valley of the Muses, Boiotia. Distribution of diagnostic pottery of the later Ottoman period (17th–18th centuries) based on a gridded surface ceramic collection. The term "grab sample" refers to other sherds of the same phase that were found in addition to those of the gridded collection.
Courtesy the Boiotia Project; ceramic dating by J. W. Hayes

century on, but was not terminally crippling until the end of the 18th century and during the 19th.[18]

In any case, we are fortunate to have for archaeological study one clear example of a deserted *çiftlik* at the abandoned Boiotian settlement site of Harmena, and a smaller example—what we now believe to be four longhouses, arranged end to end—within the ancient city of Tanagra.[19] The ceramics from both sites are surprisingly plentiful and include a large component of glazed wares. We intend to take this opportunity to look at the nature of domestic assemblages and their social significance in this era, as at neither site is there evidence of significant earlier Ottoman occupation. Moreover, very much in tune with classic illustrations of the class distinction between the manager/owner class and the peasant workers, as shown, for example, in Cvijić's classic work on the human geography of the Balkans,[20] we found at Harmena a finely built multistory structure at the summit of the site and a traditional dispersed longhouse village below (Fig. 11.8 shows part of a comparable deserted village). There dwelt the 300 or so peasants itemized in a tax record of the early 18th century.[21]

As both Ottoman history and the beginnings of a regional Ottoman archaeology benefit from the growing amount of data and an increased level of sophistication, we can see significant local variation underlying the general portrayal of the empire as a whole. In the Near East, some areas enjoyed only a limited Early Ottoman florescence,[22] whereas in Thessaly, by contrast, Kiel has shown that in the 17th–18th centuries the towns and some village areas remained prosperous and populous.[23] In his Ph.D. research on the Cycladic islands in Frankish and Ottoman times—focusing on settlement history, vernacular architecture, and material culture—Athanasios Vionis also has argued that there was an equally flourishing period for most of the islands in the 17th–18th centuries.[24] Even in Boiotia, where the stereotypical 17th-century decline does appear to be the rule, there were still major achievements, as symbolized by the joint discovery by Kiel and me of a lost great mosque in Thebes that is now dated to the 1660s by Kiel (and the subject of a fascinating and exhaustive paper by him).[25]

18. See, e.g., Çizakça 1985.
19. For Harmena, see Bintliff 1997a, 2000; Kiel 1997. For Tanagra, see Bintliff et al. 2001; Bintliff et al., in press.
20. Cvijić 1918.
21. Kiel 1997.
22. Faroqhi 1990; Hütteroth 1975; Singer 1990.
23. Kiel 1996.
24. Vionis 2003, 2005.
25. Kiel 1999.

Figure 11.8. Ruined longhouse in the deserted village of Dusia in Boiotia, from northwest, 2004 season.
Courtesy Leiden Ancient Cities of Boiotia Project

In the 18th century there are signs in the Ottoman world of a modest recovery of population and economy, together with evidence of some new directions. For central Greece, those documents so far released from, or discovered in, the imperial archives for this period remain extremely rare. Once again, however, the general trend is shared with the rest of Europe, and indeed some of the economic developments are a response to Western stimuli. A famous mainland Greek example of regional prosperity is presented by the textile villages of the Thessalian hill and mountain periphery,[26] although, to avoid the general temptation to attribute this to inherent ethnic talent, we can note that similar foci of productivity are also active in Anatolia and other Ottoman provinces at the same time. These are symptoms of wider growth and investment.

The surviving traces of such prosperity are the wonderful multistoried, finely decorated houses of Mt. Pelion.[27] As Kiel points out, the tendency to package the Thessalian protoindustrial flourishing as the product of entrepreneurial Greeks prospering in the uplands, far from the despotic, antiprogressive hand of the lowland Ottoman authorities, conveniently ignores—probably from ignorance as well as bias—the fact that those upland industries were part of a program to stimulate economic growth by those very authorities and, in particular, the regional Ottoman dynasty of the Turahanids.[28] The most famous modern tourist village of the villages on Mt. Pelion, Ambelakia, was founded by the local Ottoman administration for such purposes. Moreover, as Petmezas shows, the decline and collapse of the Thessalian textile centers and other foci elsewhere in the empire were due largely to the growing effectiveness of Western European competition, and to the lack of technological development within these industries themselves in the late 18th and early 19th centuries, rather than to the dead hand of Ottoman control. For other regions, however, it has been argued that Ottoman trade and industry could adapt, with positive long-term effects, to encroaching globalization through modifications to their existing practices, as in the case of Syria.[29]

26. Petmezas 1990.
27. Kizis 1994.
28. Kiel 1996.
29. Rafeq 1991.

In passing, we might note that a similar and effective response to Western stimuli can be seen in the absorption and adaptation of Western models and styles of public architecture to Oriental tastes and traditions—the Baroque and Rococo mosques, kiosks, and other buildings in the great cities of the Ottoman Empire are increasingly being seen as a selective merging of East and West rather than the slavish following of art styles of dominant political and financial centers in Western Europe.[30]

It should not be surprising, therefore, that during the 18th and 19th centuries, the indigenous elites of the Ottoman provinces such as the Balkans looked upon Ottoman house styles, furnishings, and even domestic arrangements for gender, as bearing the cachet of class. As Vionis shows, this applies equally well to regions such as the Cyclades, where there was very little Ottoman presence.[31] For those of us interested in documenting the development of vernacular architecture in Ottoman Greece, however, the survival pattern of buildings occupied by different social groups is variable in time and space. This has been shown clearly in Eleutherios Sigalos's research, in which he has analyzed most of the published domestic structures in medieval and post-medieval Greece.[32] His maps and charts of the frequency of recorded and published houses by period and geographical region show that there is a low survival rate of Ottoman-style houses in southern Greece compared with the north; this is largely a result of heavy destruction in the south during the War of Independence, and subsequent (post-1830) replacement of these (or their external transformation) in favor of newer styles (notably Neoclassicism).[33] In the north, by contrast, a higher survival rate reflects the delay of incorporation into the Greek state and a different attitude toward architectural reorientation (with the exception of Thessaloniki).

In our own region of Boiotia, most of the town of Livadia suffered major destruction in the War of Independence, and since then progressive updating of the houses of the middle and upper classes has left just one prominent Ottoman-era and Ottoman-style house, ironically preserved as a monument because it belonged to a prominent Greek archontic family (Logothetis).[34] Elsewhere in the town, protected historic houses are exclusively Neoclassical townhouse facades of the post-1830 era; a small but fine mosque survives, by sheer accident, as a shell for a modern shop along the former main street of the Old Town, Odos Stratigou Ioannou (Fig. 11.9).

If, indeed, it is during the 18th and early 19th centuries that Ottoman rule deserves most criticism for abuse of power, corruption, and inefficiency, it still remains for modern archaeological and archival scholarship to clarify the realities of rural life. Kiel's lengthy and fascinating presentation of the detailed archival evidence for Thessaly[35] reveals no support for the idea that the lowlands were largely abandoned by Greek peasants fleeing oppression; rather, he suggests a trend among Greek upland inhabitants to migrate to the lowlands, where Muslim villages had low birth rates compared to those of neighboring Christian villages. New archival and topographical research in Messenia is also beginning to document the rural realities behind the rather black-and-white picture offered by Western travelers, offering already significant corrections to the scenario.[36] In Boiotia, after the significant population decline and relocation phase of the 17th century,

30. I owe this insight to my participation in the Fourth Congress of Ottoman Archaeology, held in Zaghouan, Tunisia, in March of 2000; one of the themes of the congress was Western architectural influences on Ottoman architecture.

31. Vionis 2003, 2005.

32. Sigalos 2004.

33. Sigalos 2004, chap. 5 and figs. 79, 82.

34. Bintliff et al. 1999.

35. Kiel 1996.

36. Bennet, Davis, and Zarinebaf-Shahr 2000; Chap. 10 in this volume.

Figure 11.9. A small Ottoman mosque on Stratigou Ioannou Street in the Old Town of Livadia, Boiotia. Courtesy Leiden Ancient Cities of Boiotia Project

surviving villages remain stable until the next phase of disruption caused by the War of Independence. But it appears that a more important change occurred in the later 19th century, when rural insecurity in the early Greek state brought about the nucleation of many villages and a final phase of abandonment.[37]

I have argued elsewhere that for south-central mainland Greece we can now identify at least two major transitions in rural village dynamics.[38] The first is the great decline and recolonization documented for Late Frankish and Early Ottoman times (14th–15th centuries) that leads into a flourishing period of numerous and populous rural settlements during the 16th-century *Pax Othomanica.* The second is a more protracted process in which village numbers and size generally decline over the 17th to later 19th centuries, the result of military and socioeconomic (and probably also climatic) problems. This results in a thinner distribution of villages that then blossom to substantial size in the last third of the 19th century and the first half of the 20th century. We do know that other regions of Greece, and indeed of the wider Ottoman Empire, vary considerably in the timing of their cycles of growth, stagnation, or decline, and that although many do follow this broad pattern, many clearly have cycles out of phase with this scheme. Such variability offers material essential for clarifying the historical processes at work in regional trajectories, as I have suggested for regional diversity in the Greco-Roman Aegean.[39] Comparisons and contrasts with parts of the Aegean under Venetian rule, especially those passing from Ottoman to Venetian and vice versa, given the often fine detail offered by Venetian archival sources, are already revealing fascinating insights, as other chapters in this volume illustrate.

An area of focus for the Boiotia Project and also for my Ph.D. students working in other parts of Greece is the wider transformation of material culture, which seems in many ways to parallel the rise of Ottoman styles of

37. Bintliff 1995, 1997a, 2000; Slaughter and Kasimis 1986.
38. Bintliff 1995.
39. Bintliff 1997c.

domestic houses and interior furnishings among the middle classes in the 17th–early 19th centuries. In the Frankish period and still in the "Golden Age" of the Early Ottoman 16th century, table manners and table vessels reveal a common culture shared by Western and Eastern Europe that is enhanced by the actual import and export of some wares between the Italian cities and the Ottoman provinces. At some stage in the Middle to Late Ottoman period, most of Greece seems to have shifted toward more Near Eastern forms of tableware and table customs, with the general abandonment of chairs or benches, high tables, and a proliferation of dishes shared by several people. These customs were replaced by low tables, very low stools or floor seating, and single large dishes shared by many diners. Such changes are discussed in detail by Vionis and by Joanita Vroom.[40] In contrast, the rise of individualism, associated with the retention of high tables and chairs and the introduction of personal place settings, is traceable from the late 15th century in Italy in the context of emergent capitalist society in the north and center of that country. We can observe imitation of these table manners and equipment in the Italianized Ionian islands during the 18th century and in the Cyclades, where Vionis finds a fascinating opportunistic eclecticism of fashions among the leading families (of Italian and Greek origin) regarding table manners and also dress codes.[41] These significant symbols of identity are an active area of research in our ongoing study of ceramics from Ottoman-era villages.

As is well known, the 19th to early 20th centuries witnessed the final subversion of the Ottoman Empire by Western military, political, economic, and social pressure.[42] The empire's dismemberment is associated with its replacement by many nationalisms, as strong in Greece as in the survival capsule created by Atatürk in the form of a created rather than rediscovered Turkish nationalism. For Atatürk this meant, almost literally, turning the state's back on the old cosmopolitan, multinational Istanbul and starting again in Ankara, a small, dusty, provincial town of a mere 20,000 people at the time.[43] In southern mainland Greece, as we have seen, rejection of the Ottoman past meant rebuilding middle-class homes in Neoclassical style, and erecting new public buildings in the same style. Rural life, however, was far less radically transformed, except by prolonged decay and stagnation. In many parts of the countryside, severe economic problems lasting until the last quarter of the 19th century held back the remodeling of peasant life—whether we look at houses, portable material culture, or lifestyles in general. Travelers of the period were frequently struck by the poverty and stagnation, but even though their accounts are often colored by class and nationalistic prejudice, their impression of very simple lifestyles seems confirmed by the evidence of material culture.

Yet as Aschenbrenner shows in his fine contribution to the 1972 Minnesota Expedition volume on Messenia, the last three decades of the 19th century began to bring dramatic changes in the Greek countryside, with improved transportation and the rise of national and international trade (both aiding rural areas).[44] By the end of the 19th century, the rural population in many landscapes returned at last to the level of the late-16th-century Ottoman climax, but most of southern Greece, it seems, remained well below the rural population levels of classical Greek times.[45]

40. Vionis 2003, 2004; Vroom 2003.

41. For relevant icons of this period in Zakynthos, see Mylona 1998, e.g., fig. 22; for the Cyclades, see Vionis 2003.

42. Insights into these processes can be found in two excellent studies (Çelik 1986 and Mansel 1995) of their impact at the imperial capital of Istanbul.

43. For a study, which archaeologists will find stimulating, of how this was made manifest in Ankara through architectural ideology, see Kezer 1996.

44. Aschenbrenner 1972.

45. Bintliff 1997b, 1997c, 2005.

Ceramic assemblages from villages can be studied in this light, too, as Joanita Vroom shows in her publication of our Boiotia Project finds from modern Mavrommati, where the modern flourishing of that village required us to collect surface finds from garden zones between the houses and in the peripheral sectors of traditional rubbish disposal.[46] Despite the technical challenge, we were able to illustrate the participation of such an inland agricultural community in new networks of ceramic exchange including distant Greek centers of production as well as Italian and Western European factories. Significantly, these new orientations include the arrival of cheap industrial tablewares for individual consumption.

CONCLUSION

The prospects for revaluation and presentation of Ottoman-era material culture in Greece still remain poor, although to be fair, serious study of the period is a recent phenomenon.[47] Among topics where work is possible or in progress one might mention the following.

1. The ubiquitous and barely researched water-management systems. Canal systems linked to river valley fields and 16th-century water mills are a regular discovery on the Boiotia survey project.[48]
2. Khans, or travelers' hostels, recorded by travelers and recently mapped by the Dutch Aetolia Project. Structural and functional study of this class of monument could link the sparse surviving traces of these building complexes to their frequent depictions in 19th-century travelers' books.[49]
3. Regional programs for mapping vernacular architecture. Our own work in Boiotia and in other regions of Greece[50] can be compared with the ongoing work of the University of Minnesota in the Peloponnese[51] and other projects that are essentially emanating from the foreign schools of archaeology in Greece.[52] There are also many Greek architectural recording schemes (most notably represented by studies published by Melissa Publishing in Athens in its series *Ελληνική Παραδοσιακή Αρχιτεκτονική*), although they generally lack any study of chronology and archival context.[53] The model must be the long-running program of the British School in Jerusalem for recording medieval and Ottoman buildings in Palestine.
4. Mosque recording and contextual study in terms of the social, political, and economic framework of the community for which the mosque was built. Kiel's recent articles on the great mosque at Thebes (mentioned earlier) and a similar mosque in Athens, both constructed in the 1660s, offer fine examples to follow,[54] while his previous work exposes the extraordinary potential for similar case studies in other parts of Greece.[55]
5. Military architecture. Many castles and towers and, in some cases, urban walls of Byzantine-Frankish-Venetian foundation

46. Vroom 1998.

47. The first attempt, to my knowledge, to promote Ottoman archaeology on an international scale is the edited volume by Baram and Carroll (2000). It presents many good ideas and concepts but is rather short on data, perhaps as is to be expected in an early publication of a nascent subdiscipline.

48. Bintliff 1996a.

49. Bommeljé and Doorn 1996; see Lee, Raso, and Hillenbrand 1992 for archaeological documentation of khans in Palestine.

50. Stedman 1996; Bintliff et al. 1999; Sigalos 2004; Vionis 2001.

51. Brenningmeyer, Cooper, and Downey 1998; Cooper 2002.

52. E.g., Sanders 1996; Lee 2001.

53. Kizis 1994 is a fine exception in this respect.

54. For Thebes, see Kiel 1999, a discovery based on my recognizing the mosque in the background of an Orthodox icon; for Athens, see Kiel 2002.

55. See Kiel 1990. For a fine example of a surviving rural mosque providing rich insights into later Ottoman provincial developments, see Edwards, Livingstone, and Petersen 1993.

continued in use and were modified during Ottoman times. Ottoman archives are full of details pertaining to the maintenance of such installations. Much valuable work could be done on the Ottoman constructional evidence at Greek fortifications, although one has to admit that little has been published to modern monument-recording standards for the building-sequence phases of these monuments. Standard books and articles on Greek castles remain remarkably vague on questions of phasing.[56] Our colleagues in the Levant are well ahead of us in this respect, as evidenced by the magnificent volume on Belmont Castle by Harper and Pringle, and Petersen's study of an Ottoman fortress.[57] Promising developments should, one can hope, follow the recent detailed tower and castle recording of Frankish fortifications in Greece.[58] A new page indeed has been opened through the recent collaboration of Machiel Kiel and members of the Pylos Regional Archaeological Project in the study of texts and physical monuments at the Ottoman fortress of Anavarin-i cedid (Navarino).[59]

6. For the ideal combination of archival evidence, narrative historical information, historical geography, and the study of standing buildings, pride of place goes to the magnificent study by Karydis and Kiel of Ottoman Lesbos.[60]

It is worth noting that Kiel has estimated that only 1% of the named major Ottoman buildings mentioned in sources in the city of Larissa survive today.[61] What are left are often fragments that are not protected or conserved, and these are frequently misinterpreted. Only a few modern Greek towns (such as Chalcis) have an active policy of protecting and displaying Ottoman-era monuments. Kiel also has introduced us to an even more unimagined world that has become lost to Greek consciousness—the flourishing of Ottoman literature, scholarship, and art that once characterized the major and minor towns of Greece. He has given hints of this in his discussions of the vanished city of Yiannitsa in western Macedonia, and also of Larissa.[62]

Indeed, we have made a start in studying deserted villages, in mining the archives, and in documenting changing material culture and artistic representations, but we might hope that eventually the almost 500 years of Ottoman rule in Greece will be depicted in a more balanced and respectful way in the story of the country. As archaeologists, we have abundant data awaiting us from this period, and the prospects for a nuanced reconstruction of everyday life, settlement systems, demography, and economic developments are excellent. Indeed, the meeting in Cincinnati that gave rise to this volume, following the Corfu conference on medieval and post-medieval Greece, shows a growing awareness of the exciting potential for Ottoman archaeology in modern Greece.[63]

56. E.g., Andrews 1953; Harrison 1993.
57. Harper and Pringle 2000; Petersen 1998.
58. Lock 1986; Kardulias 1997.
59. See appendixes III and IV in Zarinebaf, Bennet, and Davis 2005.
60. Karydis and Kiel 2002.
61. Kiel 1996.
62. Kiel 1990, chap. 4; Kiel 1996.
63. The Corfu conference was sponsored by the British School of Archaeology at Athens and the Ionian University, and was jointly convened in May 1998 by Dimitris Tsoungarakis, Eleni Angelomatis-Tsoungaraki, and me. The publication of the proceedings is in preparation.

REFERENCES

Aalen, F., J. L. Bintliff, P. Spoerry, and E. Sigalos. 1997. "Η παραδοσιακή, τοπική αρχιτεκτονική της Λιβαδειάς," in *Συμπόσιο: Η Λιβαδειά χθες, σήμερα, Αύριο,* Livideia, pp. 85–103.

Andrews, K. 1953. *Castles of the Morea* (Gennadeion Monographs IV), Princeton.

Aschenbrenner, S. 1972. "A Contemporary Community," in *The Minnesota Messenia Expedition: Reconstructing a Bronze Age Regional Environment,* ed. W. A. McDonald and G. R. Rapp, Jr., Minneapolis, pp. 47–63.

Atasoy, N., and J. Raby. 1994. *İznik: The Pottery of Ottoman Turkey,* ed. Y. Petsopoulos, London.

Baram, U., and L. Carroll, eds. 2000. *A Historical Archaeology of the Ottoman Empire: Breaking New Ground,* New York.

Bennet, J., J. L. Davis, and F. Zarinc baf-Shahr. 2000. "Pylos Regional Archaeological Project, Part III: Sir William Gell's Itinerary in the Pylia and Regional Landscapes in the Morea in the Second Ottoman Period," *Hesperia* 69, pp. 343–380.

Berktay, H., and S. Faroqhi, eds. 1991. *New Approaches to State and Peasant in Ottoman History* (*PastPres,* Special Issue, 18, nos. 3–4).

Bintliff, J. L. 1995. "The Two Transitions: Current Research on the Origins of the Traditional Village in Central Greece," in *Europe between Late Antiquity and the Middle Ages: Recent Archaeological and Historical Research in Western and Southern Europe* (*BAR-IS* 617), ed. J. L. Bintliff and H. Hamerow, Oxford, pp. 111–130.

———. 1996a. "The Archaeological Survey of the Valley of the Muses and Its Significance for Boeotian History," in *La montagne des muses,* ed. A. Hurst and A. Schachter, Geneva, pp. 193–224.

———. 1996b. "The Frankish Countryside in Central Greece: The Evidence from Archaeological Field Survey," in Lock and Sanders 1996, pp. 1–18.

———. 1997a. "The Archaeological Investigation of Deserted Medieval and Post-Medieval Villages in Greece" in *Rural Settlements in Medieval Europe. Papers of the "Medieval Europe Brugge 1997" Conference* 6, ed. G. De Boe and F. Verhaeghe, Zellik, pp. 21–34.

———. 1997b. "Further Considerations on the Population of Ancient Boeotia," in *Recent Developments in the History and Archaeology of Central Greece. Proceedings of the 6th International Boeotian Conference* (*BAR-IS* 666), ed. J. L. Bintliff, Oxford, pp. 231–252.

———. 1997c. "Regional Survey, Demography, and the Rise of Complex Societies in the Ancient Aegean: Core-Periphery, Neo-Malthusian, and other Interpretive Models," *JFA* 24, pp. 1–38.

———. 2000. "Reconstructing the Byzantine Countryside: New Approaches from Landscape Archaeology," in *Byzanz als Raum,* ed. K. Belke, F. Hild, J. Koder, and P. Soustal, Vienna, pp. 37–63.

———. 2005. "Explorations in Boeotia Population History," *The Ancient Word* 36, pp. 5–17.

Bintliff, J. L., A. Ceulemans, K. de Craen, E. Farinetti, D. Kramberger, B. Music, J. Poblome, K. Sarri, K. Sbonias, B. Slapsak, V. Stissi, A. Vionis. In press. "The Tanagra Project: Investigations at an Ancient Boeotian City and in Its Countryside (2000–2002)," *BCH* 128–129 (2004–2005).

Bintliff, J. L., N. Evelpidou, E. Farinetti, B. Music, I. Riznar, K. Sbonias, L. Sigalos, B. Slapsak, V. Stissi, and A. Vassilopoulos. 2001. "The Leiden Ancient Cities of Boeotia Project: Preliminary Report on the 2001 Season," *Pharos: Journal of the Netherlands Institute in Athens* 9, pp. 33–74.

Blake, H. 1980. "Technology, Supply or Demand?" *Medieval Ceramics* 4, pp. 3–12.

Bommeljé, Y., and P. Doorn. 1996. "The Long and Winding Road: Land Routes in Aetolia (Greece) since Byzantine Times," in *Interfacing the Past,* ed. H. Kamermans and K. Fennema, Leiden, pp. 343–351.

Brenningmeyer, T., F. Cooper, and C. Downey. 1998. "Satellites, Silicon, and Stone," *Geo Info Systems* 8.1, pp. 20–28.

Çelik, Z. 1986. *The Remaking of Istanbul: Portrait of an Ottoman City in the Nineteenth Century,* Seattle.

Çizakça, M. 1985. "Incorporation of the Middle East into the European World Economy," *Review* 8, pp. 353–377.

Cooper, F. 2002. *Houses of the Morea: Vernacular Architecture of the Northwest Peloponnesos (1205–1955),* Athens.

Cvijić, J. 1918. *La peninsule balkanique,* Paris.

Doorn, P. K. 1989. "Population and Settlements in Central Greece: Computer Analysis of Ottoman Registers of the Fifteenth and Sixteenth Centuries," in *History and Computing* II, ed. P. Denley, S. Fogelvik, and C. Harvey, Manchester, pp. 193–208.

Edwards, C., K. Livingstone, and A. Petersen. 1993. "Dayr Hanna: An Eighteenth-Century Fortified Village in Galilee," *Levant* 25, pp. 63–92.

Faroqhi, S. 1990. "Towns, Agriculture, and the State in Sixteenth-Century Ottoman Anatolia," *JESHO* 33, pp. 125–156.

Goodwin, G. 1971. *A History of Ottoman Architecture,* Baltimore.

Harper, R. P., and D. Pringle, eds. 2000. *Belmont Castle: The Excavation of a Crusader Stronghold in the Kingdom of Jerusalem* (British Academy Monographs in Archaeology 10), Oxford.

Harrison, P. 1993. "Castles and Fortresses of the Peloponnese," *Fortress* (May 17), pp. 2–20.

Hütteroth, W. 1975. "The Pattern of Settlement in Palestine in the Sixteenth Century," in *Studies on Palestine during the Ottoman Period,* ed. M. Maoz, Jerusalem, pp. 3–10.

İnalcık, H. 1972. "The Ottoman Decline and Its Effect upon the *Reaya,*" in *Aspects of the Balkans: Continuity and Change,* ed. H. Birnbaum and S. Vryonis, The Hague, pp. 338–354.

Jardine, L. 1996. *Worldly Goods: A New History of the Renaissance,* London.

Kardulias, P. N. 1997. "Reconstructing Medieval Site Locations in the Corinthia, Greece," in *Aegean Strategies,* ed. P. N. Kardulias and M. T. Shutes, Lanham, pp. 107–122.

Karydis, D. N., and M. Kiel. 2002. *Μυτιλήνης αστυγραφία και Λέσβου χωρογραφία (15ος–19ος αι.),* Athens.

Kezer, Z. 1996. "The Making of a Nationalist Capital: Socio-Spatial Practices in Early Republican Ankara," *Built Environment* 22, pp. 124–137.

Kiel, M. 1987. "Population Growth and Food Production in 16th-Century Athens and Attica according to the Ottoman *Tahrir Defters*," in *Proceedings of the VIth Cambridge CIEPO Symposium,* ed. J. L. Bacque-Grammont and E. van Donzel, Istanbul, pp. 115–133.

———. 1990. *Studies on the Ottoman Architecture of the Balkans,* Aldershot.

———. 1992. "Remarks on Some Ottoman-Turkish Aqueducts and Water Supply Systems in the Balkans: Kavalla, Chalkis, Aleksinac, Levkas, and Ferai/Ferecik," *Utrecht Turcological Series* 3, pp. 105–139.

———. 1996. "Das türkische Thessalien: Etabliertes Geschichtsbild versus osmanische Quellen. Ein Beitrag zur Entmythologisierung der Geschichte Griechenlands," in *Die Kultur Griechenlands in Mittelalter und Neuzeit. Bericht über das Kolloquium der Südosteuropa-Kommission 28.–31. Oktober 1992* (*AbhGött,* Philologisch-Historische Klasse, 3rd ser., no. 212), ed. R. Lauer and P. Schreiner, Göttingen, pp. 109–196.

———. 1997. "The Rise and Decline of Turkish Boeotia, 15th–19th Century (Remarks on the Settlement Pattern, Demography, and Agricultural Production According to Unpublished Ottoman-Turkish Census and Taxation Records)," in *Recent Developments in the History and Archaeology of Central Greece. Proceedings of the 6th International Boeotian Conference* (*BAR-IS* 666), ed. J. L. Bintliff, Oxford, pp. 315–358.

———. 1999. "The Icon and the Mosque: Orthodox Christian Art as a Source to Retrieve the Lost Monuments of Ottoman Architecture of Southern Greece: The Case of İstife/Thebes," in *Aptullah Kuran için yazılar/Essays in Honor of Aptullah Kuran,* eds. Ç. Kafecioğlu and L. Thys-Senocak, Istanbul, pp. 223–232.

———. 2002. "The Quatrefoil Plan in Ottoman Architecture Reconsidered in Light of the 'Fethiye Mosque' in Athens," *Muqarnas: An Annual on the Visual Culture of the Islamic World* 19, pp. 109–122.

Kizis, G. 1994. *Πηλιορείτικη οικοδομία,* Athens.

Lee, M., C. Raso, and R. Hillenbrand. 1992. "Mamluk Caravanserais in Galilee," *Levant* 24, pp. 55–94.

Lee, W. E. 2001. "Pylos Regional Archaeological Project, Part IV: Change and the Human Landscape in a Modern Greek Village in Messenia," *Hesperia* 70, pp. 49–98.

Lock, P. 1986. "The Frankish Towers of Central Greece," *BSA* 81, pp. 101–123.

Lock, P., and G. D. R. Sanders, eds. 1996. *The Archaeology of Medieval Greece,* Oxford.

Mackenzie, M. 1992. *Turkish Athens,* Reading.

Mansel, P. 1995. *Constantinople: City of the World's Desire, 1453–1924,* London.

Mylona, Z. A. 1998. *Μουσείο Ζακύνθου,* Athens.

Petersen, A. 1998. "Qal at Ras al-Ayn: A Sixteenth-Century Ottoman Fortress," *Levant* 30, pp. 97–112.

Petmezas, S. D. 1990. "Patterns of Protoindustrialization in the Ottoman Empire: The Case of Eastern Thessaly, ca. 1750–1860," *Journal of European Economic History* 19, pp. 575–603.

Rafeq, A.-K. 1991. "Craft Organization, Work Ethics, and the Strains of Change in Ottoman Syria," *JAOS* 111.3, pp. 495–511.

Sanders, G. D. R. 1996. "Two Kastra on Melos and Their Relations in the Archipelago," in Lock and Sanders 1996, pp. 147–177.
Sigalos, E. 2004. *Housing in Medieval and Post-Medieval Greece,* Oxford.
Singer, A. 1990. "The Countryside of Ramle in the Sixteenth Century: A Study of Villages with Computer Assistance," *JESHO* 33, pp. 51–79.
Slaughter, C., and C. Kasimis. 1986. "Some Social-Anthropological Aspects of Boeotian Rural Society," *Byzantine and Modern Greek Studies* 10, pp. 103–159.
Stedman, N. 1996. "Land Use and Settlement in Post-Medieval Central Greece: An Interim Discussion," in Lock and Sanders 1996, pp. 179–192.
Vionis, A. K. 2001. "The Meaning of Domestic Cubic Forms: Interpreting Cycladic Housing and Settlements of the Period of Foreign Domination (ca. 1207–1821 A.D.)," *Pharos: Journal of the Netherlands Institute in Athens* 9, pp. 111–131.
———. 2003. "Much Ado about . . . a Red Cap and a Cap of Velvet: In Search of Social and Cultural Identity in Medieval and Post-Medieval Insular Greece," in *Constructions of Greek Past: Identity and Historical Consciousness from Antiquity to the Present,* ed. H. Hokwerda, Groningen, pp. 193–216.
———. 2004. "Post-Roman Pottery Unearthed: Medieval Ceramics and Pottery Research in Greece," *Medieval Ceramics* 25 (2001), pp. 84–98.
———. 2005. "'Crusader' and 'Ottoman' Material Life: The Archaeology of Built Environment and Domestic Material Culture in the Medieval and Post-Medieval Cyclades, Greece (c. 13th–20th A.D.)" (diss. Leiden Univ.).
———. 2006. "The Archaeology of Ottoman Villages in Central Greece: Ceramics, Housing, and Everyday Life in Post-Medieval Rural Boeotia," in *Studies in Honor of Hayat Erkanal: Cultural Reflections (Hayat Erkanal'a Armağan: Kültürlerin Yansıması),* ed. A. Erkanal et al., Ankara, pp. 784–800.
Vroom, J. 1998. "Early Modern Archaeology in Central Greece: The Contrast of Artefact-Rich and Sherdless Sites," *JMA* 11, pp. 131–164.
———. 1999. "Medieval and Post-Medieval Pottery from a Site in Boeotia: A Case-Study Example of Post-Classical Archaeology in Greece," *BSA* 92, pp. 513–546.
———. 2003. *After Antiquity: Ceramics and Society in the Aegean from the Seventh to the Twentieth Century A.C. A Case Study from Boeotia, Central Greece* (Archaeological Studies, Leiden University 10), Leiden.
Wallerstein, I. 1979. "The Ottoman Empire and the Capitalist World Economy: Some Questions for Research," *Review* 2, pp. 389–398.
Zarinebaf, F., J. Bennet, and J. L. Davis. 2005. *A Historical and Economic Geography of Ottoman Greece: The Southwestern Morea in the Early 18th Century* (*Hesperia* Suppl. 34), Princeton.

Regionalism and Mobility in Early Modern Greece: A Commentary

by Björn Forsén

Several aspects of the early modern period in Greece and the Aegean have until recently received far too little attention. There are many reasons for this. In Greek national historiography the post-Byzantine period is one of transition between the grand Byzantine culture and the birth of the Greek national state, and as such is of little interest. At the same time, Greece is consigned to a marginal place in the general development of the eastern Mediterranean. Most of present-day Greece was after 1453 either a distant colony of Venice or an outlying province of the Ottoman Empire. As suggested by the title of this book, Greece was thus indeed, and not only in geographical terms, located between Venice and Istanbul.

The approach of this book is interdisciplinary, the contributors seeking to combine and compare the findings of written and nontextual sources. Furthermore, the contributors strive to free themselves from preconceived ideas by impartially using both Venetian and Ottoman written sources. This is laudable and definitely shows the direction in which research will move in the future.

The Venetian and Ottoman empires in many ways represented two different worlds and, at first glance, seemingly opposing cultures, yet there was constant interaction between the two. During the period 1481–1645, the two states were at war for only nine years. The rest of the time they coexisted and even to some extent collaborated. Access to markets was more essential for Venetian commerce than actual dominion. And during the long periods of peace, the Ottoman Empire accepted the fact that Venetian merchants lived and traded in Ottoman ports and their hinterlands. A remarkable acculturation of individuals also took place. Doge Andrea Gritti, for instance, had one son with his wife in Venice and another four with his Ottoman concubine in Istanbul. The Istanbul offspring became fully assimilated into the Ottoman world.[1]

The constant interaction between the seemingly different and contrasting empires makes it easier to understand the surprising degree of similarity between them, such as in their systems of controlling the peasant population[2] or in their practices of surveying land.[3] Such similarities also explain why the transition from Venetian to Ottoman rule, or vice versa, often resulted in no significant difference for the majority of the Orthodox population.

1. Goffman 2002, p. 139. For a similar picture of a "shared world," see Greene 2000 and Faroqhi 2004.
2. See, e.g., Chap. 8 in this volume.
3. See, e.g., Chap. 10 in this volume.

When reading the chapters of this book, one is struck by two subjects that are mentioned repeatedly: regionalism and mobility. These two concepts will also recur throughout this commentary. The surprising degree of mobility of people enables sudden changes in regional populations and economies. Early modern Greece was far from a static unit, but rather a society that adapted surprisingly easily to external influences. In order to increase our knowledge, we need to study single regions and compare them with one another. This can best be done through regional survey projects that include both written and nontextual sources.

Field survey projects generally aim at reconstructing the diachronic development of settlement patterns, the way the people made use of their environment as well as regional demographic trajectories. For most periods, survey projects have to base their conclusions exclusively on archaeological data. The early modern period is actually the only premodern period for which we have sufficiently comprehensive archival sources. This makes it possible to weigh the validity of conclusions by comparing the archaeological sources with the written sources. The results are not only of interest for the study of the early modern period itself, but also of methodological interest with regard to the interpretation of archaeological material from other historical periods.

On the basis of recent studies we know that most of Greece experienced a strong population increase in the late 15th and 16th centuries, which often pushed the regional population to levels it would not reach again until in the mid-19th century.[4] For instance, this population increase in Boiotia clearly is paralleled by an increase in datable pottery.[5] At the same time, however, we have great difficulty in identifying pottery from these centuries in the Peloponnese and on the islands.[6] Therefore, Timothy Gregory is not to be blamed for having identified only small percentages of early modern pottery from surveys in the Corinthia and on Kythera.[7] Several other regional surveys in the Peloponnese, such as the Laconia Survey,[8] the Berbati-Limnes Survey,[9] and the Asea Valley Survey,[10] yielded even fewer finds from these centuries. In the case of the Laconia and Berbati-Limnes surveys, no use was made of Ottoman written sources; consequently, the Early Ottoman period was interpreted as a period of decline. The danger of relying exclusively on the evidence of datable surface pottery is clearly exemplified by the Asea Valley Survey, where only the inclusion of Ottoman sources in the analysis revealed that the area actually had experienced a population peak during this time.

As a parallel to the Peloponnese, Joanita Vroom mentions the Aitolian mountains, where virtually no Ottoman pottery could be identified. According to her, the lack of pottery could be explained by the phenomenon of the so-called sherdless site, which implies that people in certain parts of the Mediterranean at certain stages in history preferred to use vessels made of wood, stone, basketry, and so on, instead of pottery.[11] Another possibility is that we cannot identify Early Ottoman pottery in the Peloponnese either because the glazed pottery is of regional character or because only coarse pottery was used. The period would then be a "low-visibility phase."[12] In order to increase our knowledge of the pottery used in the Peloponnese

4. E.g., Kiel and Sauerwein 1994; Kiel 1997; Forsén and Forsén 2003.

5. See Chap. 11 in this volume.

6. See Chap. 4 in this volume.

7. Chap. 9 in this volume.

8. Cavanagh, Crouwel, Catling, and Shipley 1996, 2002.

9. Wells 1996.

10. Forsén and Forsén 2003.

11. See Chap. 4 in this volume.

12. For the invention of this term, see Rutter 1983.

during these centuries, we need to put more emphasis on studying sites that we know were inhabited at that time, based on historical sources. Anyway, the difficulty of identifying pottery from the Early Ottoman period should make field surveyors cautious in interpreting the existence of large amounts of glazed pottery as a necessary sign of great population pressure.

The strong population increase in Greece in the 15th and 16th centuries follows the general demographic development of the rest of Europe. On average, the European population seems to have doubled between 1450–1460 and 1550–1560,[13] a rate of increase that is similar to the one suggested, for instance, for Eastern (Opuntian) Locris and Arcadia.[14] According to Machiel Kiel, however, the population of Boiotia during the same century would have quadrupled, having an annual population growth that in some cases reached 1.36%.[15] A similar annual rate of growth (1.46%) likewise has been calculated for Eastern Locris during the shorter time span between 1466 and 1506. Similar or even higher rates of growth during the 16th century have been recorded in Attica, Euboia, and some other parts of central Greece.[16] For instance, in the Zagoria villages of Epirus, the annual population increase reached 3% between 1564 and 1579.[17] Such rates are not compatible with the demographic reality of early modern Europe,[18] and can be explained only by regional migration.

The existence of high peasant mobility within the Ottoman empire is today a well-established fact,[19] one that field surveyors in Greece should acknowledge. The reason for the migration varies by region. On 16th-century Euboia, where the immigrants are explicitly recorded in the *defter*s (tax registers) according to their place of origin, most of the immigrants originate from settlements nearby that had a low production of cereals.[20] The peasants who moved to the Zagoria villages between 1564 and 1579 probably came from the general area of Ioannina and Arta, where the population declined during the same years. Melek Delilbaşı, who has studied the *defter*s pertaining to Epirus, explains the movement as a response to changes in the Ottoman tax system after the Battle of Lepanto and the conquest of Cyprus in 1571.[21] The Macedonian *vakıf*s (i.e., property whose revenues supported religious or charitable purposes), as well as the Aegean coasts and the islands in general, enjoyed certain tax exemptions and thereby attracted peasants.[22]

Regional variations are also clearly discernible during the 17th century, which is characterized by an economic crisis and deteriorating climatic conditions during the Little Ice Age. In several regions, the population starts declining already during the late 16th century. For instance, the

13. Braudel 1972, p. 410.

14. Kiel and Sauerwein 1994, p. 44; Forsén and Forsén 2003, p. 328.

15. Kiel 1997, pp. 325–326.

16. For a summary, see Balta 1992, pp. 92–93.

17. Delilbaşı 1996.

18. For the general characteristics of Europe's demographic "old regime," see, e.g., Livi Bacci 1999.

19. See Adanır 1998, pp. 287–291.

20. Balta 1992, pp. 97–98. Thanks to the fact that the immigrants in this case are recorded, we can calculate how large a proportion of the villagers were immigrants: from ca. 2% to ca. 25%.

21. Delilbaşı 1996. Many thanks to Melek Delilbaşı for drawing my attention to her article and for discussing her results with me.

22. Adanır 1998, p. 290. Another reason for the rapid population increase in villages whose status was changed from *timar* to *vakıf* was that Ottoman dignitaries settled prisoners of war and freed slaves on the *vakıf*s (Balta 1995, pp. 61–62).

population of 16 Boiotian villages studied by Kiel declined by 46% from 1570 to 1642.[23] The pace of decline seems to be roughly similar in Eastern Locris and Arcadia,[24] but there are several exceptions. In the Megarid, where we now have a detailed study of the demographic development, the population continued growing well into the 17th century, with the decline not appearing until later, possibly even as late as during the Cretan War, 1645–1669.[25] The demographic trajectory of the Megarid thus resembles those of Kythera and Crete.[26] In the same way, the Cycladic islands and parts of Thessaly remained prosperous and populous throughout the 17th and 18th centuries.[27] In these cases, the cotton industry in Thessaly and the economic possibilities created by trade along the coast and on the islands may have attracted peasants from the mountainous parts of Greece.

As already noted, the Venetian and Ottoman worlds were not isolated from each other; to the contrary, there was constant interaction over the borders. Considerable numbers of people could cross the borders. Between 1689 and 1700, for instance, some 20,000 to 30,000 people moved from Ottoman-administered lands to the Venetian-controlled Peloponnese. After 1700, many of these refugees, dissatisfied with Venetian rule, chose to return to their native villages.[28] Further, in these instances economic factors seem to have played a more important role than political and religious ones. The peasants were primarily looking for better living conditions, which is clearly exemplified by the nearly 70,000 peasants who, in the mid-16th century, left the Hapsburg territories for Ottoman Bosnia, where the Ottomans had declared their peasants free.[29] Political and religious considerations seem to have been more important for the landowning families, who often collaborated with the Ottoman or Venetian authorities and thus felt themselves forced to leave when there was a change of power.[30]

Two methodological comments need to be made regarding the study of the high mobility of populations in early modern Greece. First, regional field surveys seem unable to detect or define this mobility in archaeological terms. If we did not have historical sources, we probably would not be aware of such mobility at all. This is something that field surveyors should keep in mind when drawing conclusions regarding other historical periods for which we lack similarly detailed historical sources.

23. Kiel 1997, p. 349, table VII.

24. Kiel and Sauerwein 1994, p. 100, table 2 (a decline of 47.8% from 1570 to 1642); Forsén and Forsén 2003, p. 328, fig. 187 (a decline of 41% from 1583 to 1642).

25. Balta 2002, pp. 111–113.

26. For Kythera, see Chap. 2 in this volume; for Crete, see Greene 2000, pp. 50–52; Rackham and Moody 1996, pp. 98–100, with fig. 8.3.

27. For the Cycladic islands, see Chap. 11 in this volume, with a reference to Vionis's dissertation of 2005 *(non vidi);* for Thessaly, see Kiel 1996.

28. See Chap. 5 in this volume; Malliaris writes of "thousands of refugees and immigrants." Panayiotopoulos (1987, pp. 125, 141–142, 146) has estimated the number of people moving as between 20,000 and 30,000. Topping's outdated figure of more than 100,000 people moving is totally improbable.

29. Adanır 1998, p. 287, with further references.

30. As an example, one could cite the large portion of the ca. 30,000 Muslims (Panayiotopoulos 1987, p. 125) who fled after the Venetian occupation of the Peloponnese only to return in 1716 to reclaim their property (e.g., Parveva 2003). In the same way, several of the landowning Greek families left the Peloponnese in 1715 (see Chap. 5 in this volume) or Crete in the mid-17th century (Greene 2000, p. 81; some 4,000 alone left the town of Candia before it was surrendered to the Ottomans). People also moved directly to Italy, as for instance the famous soldiers from the Peloponnese, the *stratioti.* According to Wright (1999, pp. 54–55), the number of *stratioti* fighting for Venice in Italy at one time in the 16th century reached 5,000.

Second, we need to keep in mind that the demographic trajectories and migrational movements reconstructed on the basis of Ottoman and Venetian archival documents are only approximations. As pointed out several times in this volume, the Ottoman *defter*s are tax documents and not genuine censuses. All inhabitants were not necessarily included and regional differences may well exist as to how many managed to avoid being registered.[31] The same is true of the so-called Venetian censuses, which should not be considered reliable. Although the Venetian census-takers themselves were aware of the inexactness in their reports, modern scholars often forget it. Thus, Panayiotopoulos takes the 176,844 inhabitants recorded for the Peloponnese by the Grimani census of 1700 at face value, although Grimani himself states that it was difficult to force all to take part in the census and that the real population of the peninsula very well could have reached 200,000.[32] Hardly surprisingly, it seems that the pastoral economy often was underrepresented in Venetian and Ottoman tax documents,[33] apparently because it was easier to avoid being registered in the mountains.

Now that I have emphasized mobility and regionalism, two concepts that I think are crucial for understanding early modern Greece, what else in this volume needs comment? One of the more important new conclusions that has emerged as a result of the interdisciplinary approach toward the study of this period is a new concept of the development of rural settlement patterns. We must abandon the old picture of a rather static settlement pattern dominated by the predecessors of today's villages. The reality is much more complicated, and several different phases can be discerned in the settlement pattern as we move from the medieval period through early modern into modern times.

The plethora of sites consisting of farmsteads, villages, and hamlets as well as *kastro*s that gradually fill the landscape in the 12th to 13th centuries is followed by a decline in the troublesome and war-torn 14th and 15th centuries. The remaining settlements are nucleated and often fortified, or at least show a tendency to withdraw higher up in the mountains. Then in the 16th century, the importance of fortifications once again diminished owing to the *Pax Othomanica;* the century instead is characterized by numerous and populous rural settlements of differing size. In the 17th to 19th centuries once again there is a tendency toward nucleation, which leads to modern Greek rural landscapes totally dominated by villages.[34]

31. Kiel (1997, p. 320) calculates that 20%–30% of the people did not appear in the Ottoman poll taxes in Boiotia, but the situation may have been different elsewhere. In general, on the use of Ottoman *defter*s as a basis of demographic calculations, see Faroqhi 1999, pp. 89–91.

32. Still, Panayiotopoulos (1987, p. 154) quotes Grimani, according to whom, "benchè la superstitione incredibile di queql'habitanti possa forse haver diminuita la vera quantità che per tal riguardo conviene credere piuttosto maggiore. Anzi è l'unico se in passato se ne raccolse il numero dalla voce, e dal concetto universale, che pur tuttavia corre siano duecentomille l'Anime di Morea." See also the discussion in Forsén and Forsén 2003, pp. 328–329.

33. See Chap. 7 in this volume. See also the discussion of the villages of the Asea Valley in Arcadia (Forsén and Forsén 2003, p. 328), where it appears that nearly every second household managed to avoid being registered in the Grimani census in 1700, although it later was included by the Ottomans in the *defter* of 1715. This should be compared with the region around Pylos, where the population recorded by Grimani in 1700 does not deviate largely in number from the one recorded by the Ottomans in 1715 (Bennet, Davis, and Zarinebaf-Shahr 2000, pp. 370–375).

34. See Chap. 11 in this volume; also Athanassopoulos 1997; Mee and Forbes 1997, p. 99; Forsén and Forsén 2003, pp. 320–321.

Yet there are—hardly surprisingly, one might add—regional differences in the settlement patterns. Kea, for instance, is dominated by a single nucleated village at the center of the island throughout the 15th to early 19th centuries.[35] The Kea pattern may very well be characteristic of the Aegean islands that so often were threatened by pirate attacks.[36]

This book certainly stresses the potential of combining written and nontextual sources. The interdisciplinary work presented here has already sketched the rough outlines of the colonial landscapes in early modern Greece. Future work along the same interdisciplinary lines, we hope, will fill in these outlines with paint. The palette emerging in front of us consists of vivid and varying colors—far from the gloomy, static picture previously conceived. But there is still much work to be done. John Bintliff defines some aspects of the material culture in which the prospects of future research are good. These include water-management systems, khans or travelers' hostels, and vernacular, sacral (mostly mosque), and military architecture.[37] I would add *kalderimia,* cobblestone roads, the majority of which seem to date to the early modern period.[38]

Furthermore, we should look beyond the Venetian and Ottoman cadastral documents into other classes of written sources, such as notarial and other legal documents.[39] There is much more information concerning the social and economic organization and management of the colonial landscapes to be gained from such sources. So, let us begin to write a fuller, more detailed, and more colorful history of early modern Greece.

35. See the Introduction.

36. Kythera, or at least its northern parts, seems in this respect to have constituted something of an exception; see Chap. 9 in this volume.

37. See Chap. 11 in this volume.

38. Once the settlement pattern of a region is clarified we also will be able to date the *kalderimia* that lead to villages now deserted, the floruit of which can be defined chronologically by studying tax documents and surface pottery. See, for instance, Forsén and Forsén 2003, pp. 71–74. In some cases we even have written sources stating that the Ottoman central authorities upgraded main *kalderimia* (e.g., see Pikoulas 1999, p. 252, with further references).

39. See, for instance, Chap. 3 in this volume. There is, however, no chapter in this volume that makes use of the rich Ottoman *kadı* (local magistrate and judge) archives. For the potential information to be found in them, see Faroqhi 1999, pp. 55–57.

REFERENCES

Adanır, F. 1998. "The Ottoman Peasantries, c. 1360–1860," in *The Peasantries of Europe from the Fourteenth to the Eighteenth Centuries,* ed. T. Scott, London, pp. 269–310.

Athanassopoulos, E. F. 1997. "Landscape Archaeology of Medieval and Pre-modern Greece: The Case of Nemea," in *Aegean Strategies: Studies of Culture and Environment on the European Fringe,* ed. P. N. Kardulias and M. T. Shutes, New York, pp. 79–105.

Balta, E. 1992. "Rural and Urban Population in the *Sancak* of Euripos in the Early 16th Century," *Αρχείον Ευβοϊκών Μελετών* 29, Athens, pp. 55–185.

———. 1995. *Les vakıfs de Serrès et de sa région (XVe et XVIe s.)* (Centre de Recherches Néo-Helléniques 53), Athens.

———. 2002. "Η Μεγαρίδα στα οθωμανικά αρχεία και η αμπελοοινική της ιστορία," in *Οἶνον ιστορῶ* II: *Μεγαρίς, η αμπελοοινική της ιστορία,* ed. Y. A. Pikoulas, Athens, pp. 103–144.

Bennet, J., J. L. Davis, and F. Zarinebaf-Shahr. 2000. "Pylos Regional Archaeological Project, Part III: Sir William Gell's Itinerary in the Pylia and Regional Landscapes in the Morea in the Second Ottoman Period," *Hesperia* 69, pp. 343–380.

Braudel, F. 1972. *The Mediterranean and the Mediterranean World in the Age of Philip II,* trans. S. Reynolds, London.

Cavanagh, W., J. Crouwel, R. W. V. Catling, and G. Shipley. 1996. *Continuity and Change in a Greek Rural Landscape: The Laconia Survey* 2 (*BSA* Suppl. 27), London.

———. 2002. *Continuity and Change in a Greek Rural Landscape: The Laconia Survey* 1 (*BSA* Suppl. 26), London.

Delilbaşı, M. 1996. "1564 Tarihli Mufassal Yanya Lirası Tahrir Defterine Göre Yanya Kenti ve Köyleri (26 sayfa belge, 1 harita ile birlikte)," *Belzeler: Türk Tarih Belgeleri Dergisi* 17, pp. 1–40.

Faroqhi, S. 1999. *Approaching Ottoman History: An Introduction to the Sources,* Cambridge.

———. 2004. *The Ottoman Empire and the World around It,* London.

Forsén, J., and B. Forsén. 2003. *The Asea Valley Survey: An Arcadian Mountain Valley from the Palaeolithic Period until Modern Times* (Acta Instituti Atheniensis Regni Sueciae 4°, 51), Stockholm.

Goffman, D. 2002. *The Ottoman Empire and Early Modern Europe,* Cambridge.

Greene, M. 2000. *A Shared World: Christians and Muslims in the Early Modern Mediterranean,* Princeton.

Kiel, M. 1996. "Das türkische Thessalien: Etabliertes Geschichtsbild versus osmanische Quellen. Ein Beitrag zur Entmythologisierung der Geschichte Griechenlands," in *Die Kultur Griechenlands in Mittelalter und Neuzeit. Bericht über das Kolloquium der Südosteuropa-Kommission 28.–31. Oktober 1992* (*AbhGött,* Philologisch-Historische Klasse, 3rd ser., no. 212), ed. R. Lauer and P. Schreiner, Göttingen, pp. 109–196.

———. 1997. "The Rise and Decline of Turkish Boeotia, 15th–19th Century (Remarks on the Settlement Pattern, Demography, and Agricultural Production According to Unpublished Ottoman-Turkish Census and Taxation Records)," in *Recent Developments in the History and Archaeology of Central Greece. Proceedings of the 6th International Boeotian Conference* (*BAR-IS* 666), ed. J. L. Bintliff, Oxford, pp. 315–358.

Kiel, M., and F. Sauerwein. 1994. *Ost-Lokris in türkischer und neugriechischer Zeit (1460–1981)* (Passauer Mittelmeerstudien 6), Passau.

Livi Bacci, M. 1999. *The Population of Europe: A History,* Oxford.

Mee, C., and H. Forbes, eds. 1997. *A Rough and Rocky Place: The Landscape and Settlement History of the Methana Peninsula, Greece.*

Results of the Methana Survey Project, Liverpool.

Panayiotopoulos, V. 1987. *Πληθυσμός και οικισμοί της Πελοποννήσου: 13ος–18ος αιώνας*, Athens.

Parveva, S. 2003. "Agrarian Land and Harvest in South-West Peloponnese in the Early 18th Century," *ÉtBalk* 38, pp. 83–123.

Pikoulas, Y. A. 1999. "Από την άμαξα στο υποζύγιο και από την οδό στο καλντερίμι (Δρόμοι και μεταφορές στο Βυζάντιο και την Τουρκοκρατία)," *Horos* 13, pp. 245–258.

Rackham, O., and J. Moody. 1996. *The Making of the Cretan Landscape*, Manchester.

Rutter, J. 1983. "Some Thoughts on the Analysis of Ceramic Data Generated by Site Surveys," in *Archaeological Survey in the Mediterranean Area* (*BAR-IS* 155), ed. D. R. Keller and D. W. Rupp, Jr., Oxford, pp. 137–142.

Wells, B., ed. 1996. *The Berbati-Limnes Archaeological Survey 1988–1990* (Acta Instituti Atheniensis Regni Sueciae 4°, 44), Stockholm.

Wright, D. G. 1999. "Bartolomeo Minio: Venetian Administration in 15th-Century Nauplion" (diss. Catholic Univ. of America); also in *Electronic Journal of Oriental Studies* 3, no. 5, posted online at www.let.uu.nl/oosters/EJOS/pdf2/w00.pdf.

CHAPTER 13

Between Venice and Istanbul: An Epilogue

by Curtis Runnels and Priscilla Murray

The Ottoman and Venetian periods in Greece and the Balkans are unpopular topics for archaeologists. An all too widely shared attitude toward the Ottoman Empire is expressed by the travel writer Robert Kaplan, who describes 500 years of Ottoman history in the Balkans "as the living death of Ottoman Turkish rule . . . with its physical cruelty, economic exploitation, and barren intellectual life."[1] This uninformed and indefensible opinion is not confined to the writers of popular books, and is, we fear, representative of the attitude of many field archaeologists working in the former dominions of the Ottoman Empire. And are the Venetians spared the obloquy of such facile judgments? Unfortunately, archaeologists who dismiss Ottoman culture as Kaplan does tend to sympathize with the comment attributed to the Byzantine grand duke Loukas Notaras, who, it is said, remarked that he would prefer the sultan's turban in the city to the Latin miter.[2] This hostility toward European "civilization" was not unusual in the 15th century, even if Notaras was exaggerating his views for political effect, and can still be seen today in many Orthodox countries. It is perhaps not surprising then that a latent hostility toward Ottoman and Latin culture can be detected among archaeologists and historians from the time of Edward Gibbon to the present day.

The purpose of the conference that gave rise to this volume was to counter these prejudices and to encourage a dialogue between historians and field archaeologists. The goal of the organizers is clearly the development of an interdisciplinary and multidisciplinary research design that brings together the analysis and interpretation of texts with archaeological excavation and survey in order to reconstruct and explain the Ottoman and Venetian periods in Greece. This is a lofty goal; the road leading to it is long and steep and, one suspects, strewn with many obstacles.

How well have they succeeded? To answer that question is to ask another: Until recently, who would have thought this dialogue was even possible? For decades we have conducted archaeological explorations of Greek landscapes marked by architecture, artifacts, and monuments from diverse historical episodes as part of regional surveys in the Argolid, Thessaly, Epirus, and elsewhere. Although archaeological remains from the Ottoman and Venetian periods made up a great deal of the archaeological

1. Kaplan 1994, p. 38.
2. Nicol 1992, p. 60.

record we were investigating, there were few archaeologists in the early days of survey who could say much about them.

The pottery, for example, created major difficulties. Although the diverse glazed wares were distinguishable from the earlier Greco-Roman and prehistoric ceramics, archaeologists trained in prehistoric archaeology and classical archaeology had little experience in properly and reliably attributing them to specific cultural contexts. Usually the best we could do was to assign them to overly broad units of time that were sometimes centuries in length. Tighter chronological control of potsherds and other classes of material cultural such as coins, glass, metal, and architectural remains was practical only when they could be examined by experts in Venetian and Ottoman material culture. A lack of such experts from the 1970s through the early 1990s, however, severely limited our ability to make effective use of these materials. In those simple times we were hard pressed to distinguish Venetian from Ottoman coarse ware sherds, or to discriminate between the sherds from the first and second periods of Venetian occupation of the Peloponnese.

If such simple tasks were generally beyond the capability of most practicing field archaeologists until the early 1990s, when experts in Ottoman and Venetian material culture and historians began to be routinely incorporated into regional survey projects (such as those in Boiotia and Messenia), it is not surprising that progress was slow. In the early days of survey, archaeologists made little substantive use of archival evidence. The greatest obstacle to making use of these archives, in our opinion, was the shortage of qualified historians who were available to work closely with archaeologists in the field to put textual information to use in conjunction with the material culture they were finding.

The contributions to this volume show how much progress has been made during the past 25 years in bridging the gulf between the archival texts and archaeological material culture. Thanks in part to the efforts of pioneers such as Peter Topping[3] in the study of Frankish records and in the Venetian archives, and Halil İnalcık[4] in the Ottoman archives, rich repositories of texts are now widely known and accessible to archaeologists and historians. The interdisciplinary spirit of field archaeologists involved in regional surveys in the 1970s to the 1990s has, pari passu, influenced historians and taken advantage of the flow of information from the archives. Drinking equally from the wellspring of the New Archaeology of the 1960s and 1970s and the approach to cultural ecology in anthropology pioneered by Robert Netting, a generation of field archaeologists turned away from the traditional approach of classical and historical archaeology in the Mediterranean. Classical archaeologists often were oriented toward the excavation of a single major site, preferably one that was well documented by ancient sources. Although this approach was clearly multidisciplinary in the way that texts and material culture were integrated, the methods developed in classical archaeology did not serve as a model for the work in the later Venetian and Ottoman periods. We believe that the reason for this was the near-exclusive focus of classical archaeology on one site belonging to a narrowly defined period of antiquity. If there was little interest in the study of the Byzantine period, there was almost no interest at all in

3. E.g., Topping 1949, 2000.
4. E.g., İnalcık 1973, 1994.

the Venetian and Ottoman periods. It was the archaeologists in the 1970s who were involved principally, but by no means exclusively, in regional surveys. (Here, in all fairness, one must not forget the long-term study of Frankish remains in the excavations at Corinth by the American School of Classical Studies at Athens.) It was these archaeologists three decades ago who developed the multidisciplinary study of archival texts and integrated textual data with settlement patterns and material culture. It is notable that several of the contributors to the present volume were participants in the early development of interdisciplinary survey design.

The collaboration of historians, anthropologists, and archaeologists has emerged after decades of tentative discussion and efforts to explain the results of field surveys. This collaboration is now leading to contacts among scholars in the different disciplines, often scattered widely among university departments in distant countries. The conference on which the present volume is based was among the first of its kind. It brought together scholars and specialists, instructing them to contribute more than vague programmatic suggestions for future work. The conference specifically sought meaningful contributions to the dialogue among the disciplines that began in the late 20th century. The contributions to the conference, now published in this volume, are on a wide range of subjects, admittedly not always clearly connected, but nevertheless illustrating the fruitful ways in which the results of archaeological surveys on a regional scale can be used by the historian and archival scholar. These contributions also demonstrate how archaeologists can use and evaluate the documents from the archives. Even a casual reading of the contents of this volume will supply numerous examples of how the contents of the imperial Venetian and Ottoman archives supply more than the names of villages or individual people (interesting as they are). There is so much more: an unfolding panorama of kinship, society, religion, government, law, taxation, trade, industry, economy, and agriculture, all in a detail that would be beyond the reach of the field archaeologist sorting sherds or bits of glass and brick in the laboratory. The need for a sure-footed guide to the use of the information available in the archives is demonstrated clearly.

Archaeologists, however, have their own contribution to make. Archaeological surveys in particular have uncovered and are producing a wealth of data on large regional scales, permitting scholars to expand their knowledge of the past beyond the limits of any archival documents. Just as the archives were designed to serve bureaucratic functions and are of little use to archaeologists without guidance and interpretation from historians, so archaeologists must guide historians in the use of the material culture from the field. The survey archaeologist can add much to the pictures of the imperial provinces arising from the documents. General examples might include the archaeological study of regional settlement patterns and the distribution of field boundaries and rural structures to flesh out the effects of tax laws, land tenure, and economic policies documented in the archives. Military policies discussed in the documents find concrete expression in fortifications, barracks, armories, harbors, roads, and bridges. Religious foundations, whether the Ottoman *vakıf* or the Venetian church, required numerous documents and in archaeological terms can be traced in the construction and distribution of mosques, *tekke*s (dervish lodges), churches, monasteries, baths, and fountains. Political actions find expression in archival documents of great variety and in archaeological remains such as palatial residences of officials, khans, markets, roads, bridges, and the inscriptions associated with these monuments.

The study of documents and monuments in the field can together lead to an understanding of economic, military, religious, political, and social patterns that would not be as well understood if only one class of evidence was examined. In other words, the distribution of rural settlements, coins, or dedications on fountains by local donors may be used in conjunction with archival texts to understand the decisions made in the palace or chancery. Documents and monuments require expert study and analysis, and a dialogue between historians and archaeologists is essential to integrate the data from the two fields. To work together effectively, the experts must strive for mutual understanding and comprehension of the strengths and weaknesses of the two fields. The archaeologist must become familiar with the limits and problems that the interpretation of archival documents poses for the historian, and the historian must be conversant in the special problems facing the archaeologist who attempts to work from an incomplete archaeological record.

We believe that as the collaboration between historians and archaeologists continues, the contributions of specialists from different disciplines will add up to more than the sum of the parts. In many ways the research reported in this volume represents in our view a new form of historical archaeology, based equally on the methods and theory of the field archaeologist and those of the historian working with texts. In this merging of history and archaeology, the contributions to this volume resemble the historical archaeology that emerged in the United States in the 20th century. American historical archaeology differed from classical archaeology as it was practiced traditionally, arising at the same time, and perhaps for the same reasons, as the New Archaeology, and eventually encompassing topics ranging from industrial archaeology and nautical archaeology to post-medieval archaeology (as it was called in the United Kingdom). It is perhaps premature, or presumptuous, to speak of a new form of historical archaeology, but we are convinced that the publication of this volume represents an important watershed in the historical and archaeological study of the Ottoman and Venetian periods in Greece.

REFERENCES

İnalcık, H. 1973. *The Ottoman Empire: The Classical Age, 1300–1600,* London.

———. 1994. *An Economic and Social History of the Ottoman Empire* 1: *1300–1600,* Cambridge.

Kaplan, R. D. 1994. *Balkan Ghosts: A Journey through History,* New York.

Nicol, D. 1992. *The Immortal Emperor: The Life and Legend of Constantine Palaiologos, Last Emperor of the Romans,* Cambridge.

Topping, P. W. 1949. *Feudal Institutions as Revealed in the Assizes of Romania, the Law-Code of Frankish Greece,* Philadelphia.

———. 2000. "The Southern Argolid from Byzantine to Ottoman Times," in *Contingent Countryside: Settlement, Economy, and Land Use in the Southern Argolid since 1700,* ed. S. B. Sutton, Stanford, pp. 25–40.

INDEX